"VERY ENGROSSING . . . IN THE FINEST YOU-CAN'T-PUT-IT-DOWN TRADITION"

—*The Hartford Courant*

"In a two-year period, seven young women were murdered in Michigan's Washtenaw County, some in so brutal a fashion as to make the Boston Strangler look like a mercy killer. . . .

"A series of lucky breaks—interspersed with some bungled police work that almost costs the arrest of the killer—brings an alleged 'All-American Boy' to the bar of justice."

—*The New Haven Register*

"This factual account of each murder, through the conviction of the killer, has all the excitement of a first-rate work of fiction, and it is told straight, without the usual sociological jargon. Keyes collaborated with Robin Moore on *The French Connection; The Michigan Murders* is his first solo effort, and it is a good one."

—*The Miami Herald*

THE MICHIGAN MURDERS

EDWARD KEYES

A KANGAROO BOOK
PUBLISHED BY POCKET BOOKS NEW YORK

POCKET BOOKS, a Simon & Schuster division of
GULF & WESTERN CORPORATION
1230 Avenue of the Americas, New York, N.Y. 10020

To DELLA AGNES MURRAY WALSH,
a grand lady who gave me my beloved Eileen;
who in turn honored me with Steve and Dara and
Ed and Terry and Kenan and Jeanine and Lisa and
Tom . . .
all of whom have put up with me for so long,
hoping for the best . . .

FOREWORD

WHAT FOLLOWS is true.

A few years ago, a normally peaceful mid-American community was wracked by a succession of inexplicable murders. The victims—seven young females—ranged in age from thirteen to twenty-three; each killed with unspeakable savagery.

The primary locale was Washtenaw County, Michigan, not far west of Detroit, seat of the University of Michigan at Ann Arbor and Eastern Michigan University in adjoining Ypsilanti. All the murders occurred within this twenty-five-square-mile area. The time span was from July of 1967 through July of 1969. Those two years became a period of maddening frustration and humiliation for policemen tormented by the case. It was also an unendurable crisis for those who looked to them for protection. As an inquisitive reporter and writer, I could not help but wonder how so "average" a community had dealt with so prolonged a period of anxiety and fear: how individuals were affected, by what misplacement of circumstances they'd become involved, where these tragedies had left them. And, of course, who had killed. And why.

It turned into a three-year project. I strove to re-create the situations, the scenes, the moods as they were when they were happening, as authentically as it was possible to do after the fact. What follows, then, is factual to the very best of my ability. But it does not, cannot, represent *all* the truth. For no matter how hard one may try, however deep the most enterprising reporter may dig, it is rarely possible to find out *everything* one wants to know . . . and, by the same token, one often turns up facts that in the end prove extraneous and must be discarded as irrelevant to the central theme. But everything here described did happen, and the account is limited only by my own powers of description and interpretation.

There *is* one element of "fiction" knowingly presented, nonetheless, and it is important for the reader to know of it. True names are used only of public officials and certain private individuals drawn unofficially into these events, and of police officers involved (with three exceptions, so as to safeguard decent reputations). Identifications of all other principals have been disguised—of the victims, their families and friends; of bystanders, witnesses, suspects; even of the one finally accused and tried. All these persons, not least the family of the convicted murderer, now that the horror is over (although for some the trauma may never be), have their own lives to lead, their own circles of peaceful association to protect and cherish. I have seen no need to expose any of them further to needless aggravation or harassment from either the unthinking or the malicious. To those who do *not* know them, their true names will not be significant to the drama in any case.

I will burden you here with practically none of the usual formal acknowledgments. Having spent an aggregate of six full months in Michigan, having interviewed and talked with many hundreds of helpful individuals, having been permitted access to countless volumes of records both public and confidential, I see hardly any way to begin, or end, such a list of all to whom I owe gratitude.

There are two warranting special mention nonetheless. One is the Michigan State Police as an organization—tough, uncompromising, one of the proudest and most capable law-enforcement agencies I have encountered anywhere—without whose thoughtful forbearance and subtle approval my efforts might have run into many a dead end.

The other is an erudite, interested, enthusiastic gentleman who had himself closely followed and noted many of these events before I'd ever entered upon the scene, and in whose perceptive insights I found much value. To Professor Paul McGlynn of Eastern Michigan University, my thanks and warm respects.

All others—many of whom deserve no less recognition—will find themselves in the narrative (appropriately, I trust), even if many will have to accommodate to their new identities. Each has contributed to what I hope all will find to be an accurate and sensitive representation of how it was in the time of *The Michigan Murders*.

Edward Keyes
New York   1976

CHAPTER 1

YPSILANTI, MICHIGAN. JULY 10, 1967. Hot, quiet, stagnant.

Marilyn Pindar's younger sister Sheila received the call. It was Nanette Langois, Marilyn's roommate. Had the Pindars heard from Marilyn? She had not come back to the apartment on Sunday night and had not shown up for work yet on Monday morning. Probably nothing to worry about, but . . .

Sheila Pindar, an alert, vivacious eighteen-year-old, was alarmed. She and a couple of friends had dropped by the apartment a little after 7:30 the previous evening, to find her sister out, and after waiting for a few minutes, had left, asking to have Marilyn call home when she got in. Now she learned that Marilyn had returned to the apartment ten or fifteen minutes later, puttered about for a few minutes, and then gone out to get some air. Nanette had not seen or heard from her since. Neither, it now began to appear, had anyone else who might have been expected to.

Sheila pondered this, then decided to tell her

mother. Margaret Pindar got into her car at once and
sped the seven miles north to her daughter's apartment
building at 413 Washtenaw Avenue, a tree-lined street
in the heart of Ypsilanti, only a few blocks from the
campus of Eastern Michigan University, where
Marilyn and her roommate were students.

As Mrs. Pindar drove into the tarmac parking area
in front, she noticed that her daughter's Comet was
not in its usual reserved space, but at the opposite side
of the lot. Using her spare key—she liked to be able
to drop in every so often when the girls were out, to
straighten up or bring things they might need—she
went through the apartment with a mother's practiced
eye and noted that her daughter's belongings seemed
in order. Then she picked up the phone and called
Nanette at the university's Field Services Office, where
she and Marilyn worked part-time. Marilyn still had
not reported in. Mrs. Pindar asked what she was
wearing when she went out last on Sunday evening.
Nanette said it was the orange tent dress with white
polka dots and her leather-and-straw sandals. Mrs.
Pindar checked Marilyn's closet. The dress and sandals were not there. Also, there was no sign anywhere
of either her apartment keys or her car keys. Yet she
had not taken her purse containing her driver's license.

Margaret Pindar next telephoned her husband at
the bronze plant in Flat Rock, where he was director
of engineering.

Charles Pindar listened quietly. He suggested that
Margaret telephone the police first, then go to Ypsilanti headquarters personally. He would leave the
plant at once and join her there.

At police headquarters the Pindars' concern turned
to frustration. Marilyn Pindar had been missing less
than twenty-four hours. Police are not aroused to quick
anxiety over a young person dropping out of sight for
a day or two—particularly in a town like Ypsilanti.

Ypsilanti and Ann Arbor, Michigan, are university
towns. Ypsilanti harbors Eastern Michigan Univer-

sity, which in 1967 had an enrollment of some 13,000 students. Just to the west, comprising a significant part of the city of Ann Arbor, is the University of Michigan, with almost three times as many students as E.M.U. Thus together, within a range of barely ten miles, the two communities swarmed ten months of the year with close to 50,000 young people, mostly transient, plus additional thousands of high-school age and younger.

In such environments, the typical missing persons case usually turns out to be some restless student taking off on a lark or to shack up somewhere for a couple of days. The local police had become so used to this that often they were hard put not to spell it out in plain language to distraught parents or guardians who descended to hound them about a son or daughter who had not been heard from in a day or so.

The desk officer and his sergeant, after dutifully asking routine questions of the Pindars and jotting a few notes, finally moved to cut the session short by suggesting with weary candor that, after all, there really might be less to the situation than met their eyes.

Mr. and Mrs. Pindar caught the inference and protested: Their daughter was definitely not the type of girl to just go off. Besides, she had left the car her father had just given her—a blue '63 Comet she prized. If she were off on a lark, wouldn't she have taken it? And then there was the matter of her belongings, which were still at the apartment. Except for the car keys and her apartment key, Marilyn had left everything behind except the clothes she'd been wearing. It was unlike Marilyn to take off with just the clothes on her back, even for a night—and particularly without her handbag.

The officers listened to all this without comment. They had heard stories like this from distraught parents a hundred times—and the kid usually showed up the next day. There was little that Margaret and Charles Pindar could do but return home and wait—

and hope for a call that would dispel their foreboding.

The Pindars were a close-knit, deeply religious family
of Polish-German stock. They lived in a spacious two-
story house of pale yellow brick in Willis, just south
of Ypsilanti. It is an area of manicured rolling farm-
land broken by dense wooded groves, with straight
paved roads lined with tall, symmetrical shade trees
and unpretentious but prosperous-looking houses.

There were seven children, the eldest a twenty-
one-year-old son. Marilyn was next at nineteen, then
Sheila, two younger girls and two boys. Much as Mr.
Pindar would try, he never was quite able to disguise
that Marilyn, his first-born daughter, was something
of a princess to him. There had always been a bond
between them that was just a little special, probably
stemming from Marilyn's frailty as an infant. But it
was honest and endearing enough so that none of the
other children seemed resentful.

Marilyn was, perhaps, the most studious and homey
of the children. She had won a four-year scholarship
to E.M.U., where she had just completed her sophomore year and was working part-time to earn extra
money. Self-assured but reserved, she applied herself with vigor both to her studies and to outside
activities that especially interested her. She possessed
unusual musical gifts and was proficient on the organ,
piano, violin, and guitar. The guitar had become her
favorite, and she could lose herself equally by enter-
taining family and friends with old favorites or by
curling up alone in her room strumming rhythmic
chords.

She was petite, scarcely five-two and 104 pounds,
and her figure was neatly proportioned for her frame.
Her face was pleasant, especially when smiling, which
distracted from the plain rimless eyeglasses that tended
to give her a bookish look. Still, while on the whole
not unattractive, she was not generally regarded as
pretty, much less sexually provocative.

All things considered, then, Marilyn Pindar did not

seem the type of young woman who should remain long unaccounted for.

Following her disappearance, however, the Pindars showed themselves to be people of extraordinary self-possession. Except for their determined dogging of the police, they remained on the surface unruffled. The father returned to his job, the mother to her normal household routine. Following their parents' lead, Marilyn's brothers and sisters likewise went about their daily activities without skipping too many beats. No one would have guessed from the family's outward calm that under the surface gnawed an agonizing premonition of disaster.

But Charles Pindar felt it the first night, after the younger children had gone to their rooms and the older ones out. He and Margaret were sitting opposite each other in the comfortable living room, its end tables and fireplace wall crowded with framed photographs and portraits of each of the children, and the two of them were silent, each lost in private thoughts.

It did not come upon him with any sudden sense of chilling clarity. He just acknowledged that it was there, inside him, as though it belonged there. Marilyn was dead. His Marilyn. They would never see her alive again. He glanced over at his wife. She had been watching him and now looked away again. They'd been married a long time. Did she know what he was thinking? Was she thinking it herself? Neither said anything.

By Wednesday, after two days of the Pindars' insistent contention that their daughter must be in some kind of trouble, the police, too, were at last sufficiently concerned to clack out a missing persons advisory:

WCT BC 30268   YPSILANTI PD TT 737   7/12/67

MISSING GIRL

MARILYN PINDAR 413 WASHTENAW AVENUE YPSILANTI W/F 19 YRS DB 12/4/47 HEIGHT FIVE-

FEET-TWO 104 POUNDS. DK BRN SHORT HAIR GREEN
EYES WEARS GLASSES. WAS WEARING ORANGE COL-
ORED POLKA DOT SUN DRESS WHEN LAST SEEN.
MISSING SINCE 7/9/67 AFTER SHE LEFT APT TO
GO FOR A WALK

DDD YPSILANTI

The Marilyn Pindar missing persons case was
picked up the next day by Detective Lieutenant Vern
Howard. A commanding six-foot-four two hundred
pounder, the fifty-three-year-old Howard was marking
his twenty-fifth anniversary as a cop with the Ypsilanti
Police Department, the last seventeen years as a detective. After a quarter of a century of such work
there can be few surprises left and few excitements.
Least of all, missing girl cases.

But Vern Howard, for all his impenetrable veteran-
cop exterior, was as compassionate as the next man.
He had a twenty-year-old daughter himself, so he could
sympathize with people like the Pindars. He started
by interviewing the family, then Marilyn's roommate,
a few of her friends, some of her coworkers at the
university who had seen her most recently, and finally residents of the immediate neighborhood in
which Marilyn lived in Ypsilanti. Soon he was able to
piece together a fabric of the missing girl's last known
movements on Sunday, July 9, the day she disappeared.

She arose that morning about 6:30, showered and
dressed in the loose orange tent dress and sandals and
went out. She walked two blocks north to Cross Street
and entered St. John's Church just after the start of
the seven o'clock mass. After mass, she walked west
up Cross Street to the university, stopping on the way
for a cup of coffee, and arriving at the Field Services
Office just at eight.

Field Services was an arm of the school administration that organized and coordinated extracurricular
activities, both for E.M.U. students and in consortium
with other schools elsewhere. This day, there was to
be registration for a week-long course in cheerleading.

Registration was heavy and continuous, and the processing of schedules and living accommodations piled up. At midday Marilyn scarcely had time to break for a quick snack. Later her sister Sheila telephoned to say that she and a cousin of theirs, Joanie, and a boy Marilyn used to date, Larry Busch, were going up to Silver Lake and would meet her there later if she could get away. Marilyn said she'd like to. She couldn't go swimming because she was having her period, but it would be nice to get away anyway.

The traffic was heavy on Sunday afternoon, and Marilyn didn't arrive at Silver Lake until after 5:00 P.M. There were no parking spaces left, and the state trooper guarding the entrance waved her away.

Marilyn drove on to Half Moon Lake, another five miles or so west. Though smaller, Half Moon usually wasn't as crowded as Silver Lake. If Sheila and the others hadn't been able to get into Silver Lake either, they might have tried this beach.

Half Moon was open. Her guitar slung across her back, Marilyn wandered through the park, from the wooded slopes with their picnic tables scattered beneath tall pines down to the rich open lawns that reached to the lake's edge, to the modern pavilion, and across the narrow curve of beach to the white metal lifeguard stand where Leo Glover, a boy she knew, was on duty. She asked about Sheila and her friends, but he said he hadn't seen them. Then she strolled down to the water's edge. After wading about aimlessly a bit, she made her way back to shore, took up her guitar, and went over to the lifeboat beached a short distance from Leo's stand. She sat down on the aft seat and began fingering low-key, melancholy tunes. Soon children were gathering around, and she picked up the tempo.

The impromptu concert lasted a half hour, until about 6:30. Then her young audience started to break up. By a quarter to seven, she sat alone in the lifeboat. Nobody remained in the water. Leo left his stand and busied himself gathering equipment for stowing back at the pavilion. The last he saw of Marilyn, she was walking slowly across the beach toward the parking field.

It could not be determined whether Marilyn Pindar had stopped anywhere between Half Moon Lake and her apartment in Ypsilanti. It was known only that she arrived back at 413 Washtenaw Avenue a little past eight, having just missed her sister Sheila, their cousin Joanie, and Larry Busch.

The three had in fact been at Silver Lake all afternoon and were unaware that the park had been closed to new arrivals from about three o'clock on. Figuring that Marilyn just had not been able to get away, they'd stopped by her apartment on their way home to Willis to say hello and pick up a book that Marilyn had been saving for Joanie.

But only Nanette Langois and her boyfriend, Mark Tanzi, were there. Sheila and the others sat around waiting for about ten minutes, trying to manufacture conversation, then murmured excuses and left. Sheila was relieved to be gone. Nanette was all right, but she did not much care for Tanzi, a swarthy, rawboned young man with a brooding manner, who seemed almost always to be there and sometimes acted as if he owned the place. Sheila knew that her sister was unhappy with the situation, and that, though she'd not said anything yet to Nanette, Marilyn was thinking of moving out, perhaps back home.

Marilyn returned about fifteen minutes after the others had gone, to find Nanette's boyfriend making himself at home in the small apartment. She poked about by herself in the small kitchen, flipped without interest through a magazine, then, about twenty past eight, said she was going out for some air. Nanette and her boyfriend scarcely paid any attention.

At first it appeared to Lieutenant Howard that Marilyn's roommate and her boyfriend were the last people to have seen the girl. But after a few more days of checking, he learned that at least three others had seen her approximately a half hour to forty-five minutes after she had left her apartment.

At about 8:45 P.M. an E.M.U. campus policeman, patrolling the Cross Street perimeter of the university, had seen her on the opposite side of the street, alone, strolling toward Hamilton. He'd recognized her not only as a student who worked somewhere in the university, but also because he had helped her start her car once when it had stalled on a campus driveway.

Five or ten minutes after that, a man relaxing on the darkened porch of his house on Hamilton Street, between Emmet and Washtenaw, had noticed her walking alone toward Washtenaw. He worked in Ypsilanti with an uncle of Marilyn's, and he and the girl had occasionally exchanged hellos and chatted since she'd moved nearby.

He watched her go past, apparently on her way to her apartment on the next corner. But then he witnessed something peculiar. Just as Marilyn passed his house, a car cruised up on Hamilton and slowed abreast of her. The driver, who appeared to be a young man, leaned toward her and said something through the open passenger-side window. Marilyn paused, shook her head, and kept walking. The car accelerated and wheeled around the corner at Washtenaw. Moments later, the man was surprised to see the same car race past his house again. It caught up with the girl farther up the block, where with a sharp turn it pulled across the sidewalk just in front of her and stopped halfway into a private driveway, blocking her path. The driver seemed to be trying to talk her into getting in. By the uncertain light of a street lamp, the car appeared to be a bluish gray, a fairly late model, possibly a Chevy. Again Marilyn shook him off, detoured around behind the vehicle, and continued walking. The car backed out of the driveway, then with an angry screech accelerated south on Hamilton and roared out of sight.

The man on the porch watched anxiously as Marilyn reached the corner of Washtenaw, but by the time

she'd crossed toward her building on the far corner
and was lost to his view, the car had not, so far as he
could tell, come back.

As a result of this painstaking legwork, Lieutenant
Howard could verify through two separate accounts
that, at some time before nine o'clock on Sunday
night, July 9, Marilyn Pindar was still alive, presumably
well, and in close proximity to her place of residence.
As to the third person who could place her at that
time and location—the driver of the blue-gray automobile—he was all but uncheckable, since the description of the car was too hazy and the witness had
been unable to distinguish plate numbers. The lieutenant could only wonder whether the driver might have
been the last to have seen her.

By the time Marilyn had been gone a week, Margaret
and Charles Pindar both accepted that they would not
see her alive again. Knowing their daughter, in the
given circumstances she could only be dead. They accepted this not with despair but, such was their wealth
of faith, with humble resignation. It was God's will.

Outwardly, at least, the six remaining children also
continued to reflect their parents' strength. At home,
around the dinner table or gathered in the living room
evenings, all discussed the situation openly and without noticeable tears. They prayed now, each of them,
not so much that Marilyn be found alive—miraculously
—but just that she be found. Their one wish was that
she would not have suffered too much.

The days continued to pass without much progress
by the police. Marilyn's car remained where it had
been found in front of 413 Washtenaw. As far as Mr.
and Mrs. Pindar could tell—one or another checked
back at the apartment almost every day—it had not
been touched by the police. The Pindars did not know
that Lieutenant Howard had had the Comet thoroughly examined by police technicians. He had also
removed several of Marilyn's possessions, both from
the apartment and from her office at the university,

and sent them on to the State Police crime lab at East Lansing to test for possible alien fingerprints or any other clues. But having drawn blanks, he decided to leave the car just as it was outside the apartment building, on the off chance that somebody—maybe even Marilyn herself—might feel secure enough after a time to come back to it.

Howard thus found himself confined to the laborious task of digging farther back, into the girl's recent history, behavior, and associations, in order to find some link to her trail since July 9. He learned that she had recently taken a trip to Canada, and while he didn't have much hope it would turn up anything, it was all he had to go on at the moment, so he turned his scrutiny to that.

A month earlier Marilyn and her sister Sheila and two girl friends had driven to Montreal to spend a few days at Expo '67, and on their way back they stopped off at Toronto. There, Sheila told the detective, Marilyn met an attentive young man named Barry Pearson, a waiter in the hotel restaurant where they were staying. He was twentyish, good-looking, outgoing, casually mod, with an easy bantering manner that disarmed all the girls, but especially Marilyn. They exchanged addresses and promised to write, but that was all there was to it.

Lieutenant Howard communicated with the police in Toronto, who looked up Barry Pearson. The young waiter remembered the American girls well enough and conceded that maybe he'd played up a bit to Marilyn. To his knowledge, nobody had accosted the girls while they were there, and nothing threatening had happened. When they'd left for home, all seemed in good spirits.

The Toronto police thoroughly checked out Pearson. His record was clean, and he had a good reputation. According to his employer, his family and acquaintances, he'd not been away from Toronto at any time since the Michigan girls' stay. There was just nothing to tie him to Marilyn Pindar.

Three weeks passed without another trace of Marilyn or, despite the inevitable false "leads," without the barest workable clue. Tips forwarded by interested citizens, meager enough, all proved fruitless.

On the second of August, Charles Pindar and his eldest son came to Ypsilanti and took Marilyn's Comet, which had sat unmoved in front of 413 Washtenaw, home to Willis.

And so it stood, nearly a month after Marilyn Pindar had seemingly vanished. For Howard, the case had become the most frustrating vacuum he'd ever got locked into. The hard-shelled professional, who'd embarked on it so coolly, now found himself bedeviled by it: Damn it, it was almost impossible for *anyone*, much less a green nineteen-year-old coed, to lose herself without a single trace . . . to just *vanish!* He'd come to fear, as the girl's family had long since accepted, that there could be only one answer. In his off-duty hours, he had taken to walking the banks of the murky Huron River where it crawled through Ypsilanti near his home . . . almost without being conscious of it, his eyes straining to glimpse the outlines of a girl's body in the silt.

CHAPTER 2

TWO TEEN-AGE BOYS found it the afternoon of Monday, August 7. They weren't sure what it was, except that it was something that once had lived.

Gerald Carmody, Jr., sixteen, and John Matthews, fifteen, were tinkering with a balky tractor in a corn field owned by Gerald's father in rural Superior Township, a couple of miles north of Ypsilanti. The Carmody family had lived on the adjoining property before moving to a larger farm in Saline; but they kept up this stand of corn, as well as a fruit orchard on the far side of the farm. The shabby gray shell of the old farmhouse still stood between the two fields, but the overgrowth of weeds and brush had almost succeeded in screening it off from Geddes Road out front. Now the place had become a somewhat shabby lovers' retreat.

One of the boys was gassing the tractor and the other testing the spark plugs when they heard a car door slam from the direction of the old homestead. The two boys looked at each other with knowing grins, and

13

Gerald Carmody said: "Let's sneak over and see what we can see."

They crept from the corn field into the thick brush and waited for a moment, listening. There was a sudden rustle of movement beyond their view, then they heard the car door slam again and an engine spinning over. In the several minutes it took them to reach the clearing, the car was gone. They thought they heard an acceleration of power out on Geddes Road, but the road was blocked from their sight.

The boys made their way around to the other side of the dilapidated building. At the curve near the top of the elliptical drive, they discovered a set of fresh tire tracks angling diagonally off deep into two-foot-high underbrush. Their curiosity aroused, the boys followed the tracks through the tangled growth for perhaps twenty feet, before Gerald brought them up short. "Do you smell something?" he asked, his features pinched up.

John inhaled and let out a breath of distaste. "Phew! Sure do. Smells like . . . shit."

Gerald sniffed again. "I don't know. It could be some kind of dead animal."

"Have to be dead a long time to smell that bad."

"Let's go see. We could bury it."

A small clearing lay a few yards farther on. Approaching it, Gerald stopped abruptly, and John, behind, heard an odd strangling sound escape from his friend's throat.

"What's the matter?" he asked, coming abreast.

Gerald stood frozen, staring across the littered clearing. Ten feet away, amidst a litter of trash, lay a black, misshapen bulk. Flies and insects by the hundreds, thousands maybe, flitted about it, crawled over it and into it. The stench was suffocating. It had to have been some living creature, but what? The thing appeared to have a head, but it was featureless, shapeless, only a rotten mass at the end of an unrecognizable torso. There were four limbs, or what was left of them,

but only stumps where paws or hoofs—or God!
hands and feet—should have been. John lurched into
a bush and retched uncontrollably.

As they stumbled back through the brush, Gerald
kept glancing behind him toward the awful scene.
When at last they reemerged into the warm, fresh or-
derliness of the corn field, Gerald paused again and
took his friend by the arm.

"Johnny, I think we ought to report that."

"To who? The police? For an old animal carcass?
They don't want to hear about that!"

Gerald breathed deeply. "Suppose it's not an animal?"

The Michigan State Police post in Ypsilanti was a
venerable, narrow two-story white frame building that
looked out of place, almost quaint, amidst the neoned
auto dealerships and shopping plazas clustered along
Michigan Avenue, just east of the city's commercial
hub. The cramped quarters seemed to belie the post's
strategic importance to the well-organized State Police
apparatus; it was the second largest in the state and
perennially one of the busiest.

A uniformed trooper, Corporal Harold Rowe, was
at the desk in the front cage when the two agitated
youngsters stumbled through the door around 2:30
Monday afternoon. In a stammering mixture of excitement and timidity they told of having come upon a
dead body—of some kind—on an abandoned farm.

The corporal eyed them warily for a possible prank,
made some notes, then rang upstairs to the Detective
Bureau.

Half of the post's four detectives were on duty in
the two small second-floor offices, Detective Sergeants
Ken Taylor and Ken Kraus. The senior of the two,
Taylor, took the call. After listening a few seconds he
groaned, "Oh, Christ." Then he sighed and said,
"Okay, somebody'll be down."

Taylor turned to Kraus at the desk opposite. "Ken,

two kids just came in with some story about a body out in a field somewhere. Want to go down and see what it's all about?"

Taylor was exercising the privilege that went with his unofficial ranking over Kraus. Taylor, aged forty, had seventeen years in the department, seven as a detective. Kraus, though technically of equal rank, was eight years younger, with only eleven years' service, and had been a detective less than a year. It was understood that the junior officer would submit himself, as required, to the less promising cases.

When Kraus came back upstairs after about fifteen minutes, however, he looked concerned. "I don't know," he said to Taylor, "there may be something in this. I think we ought to go over there and check it out."

"Well, what is it, male, female, what?"

"That's the problem. They couldn't tell for sure. Apparently it's been there for some time—it's all decomposed." Kraus quickly summarized the boys' account.

"I'll lay odds it's a dead deer." Taylor glanced at his schedule log. "Well, okay, it's a slow day anyway. And Schoonmaker ought to be back soon"—he rose and put on his suit jacket—"so let's take us a ride in the country."

The repulsive sight was sobering, and keeping the wide-eyed boys at a distance, the two detectives bent to the task of examining the remains.

Taylor knew at once that it was a human corpse, but it was in such a state of deterioration that there was no immediate way to determine its sex. What was left of its flesh had turned a dark, blackish brown, like stiff leather—it must have lain baking for weeks under the hot summer sun. There were no distinguishing features whatever. A number of punctures in the torso could have been stab wounds. The corpse had no feet, but it was impossible to tell whether they had been cut off or eaten away by animals. One of the hands also was missing, and the fingers of the other were barely stumps. No articles of clothing were evident in the vicinity.

The detectives, sweating, breathless from the stench, stood up and walked a few feet away, distastefully wiping off their hands with their handkerchiefs. "Not a hell of a lot to work with, is there?" Taylor grimaced.

"What a mess," Kraus agreed. "Want me to call it in?"

"Yeah. Have them run down all the 'missings' the past month or so. And you'd better have the county prosecutor's office alerted."

Within twenty minutes, other police cars began arriving, responding to the State Police bulletin that, as was customary, had been monitored by other law enforcement agencies throughout the area. Among the first newcomers to reach the location in an unmarked Ypsi P.D. car was a grim Lieutenant Vern Howard.

As soon as Howard had learned of the discovery, he'd felt a stab of premonition that the corpse had to be Marilyn Pindar. When he viewed the unidentifiable thing that lay there, he wanted to be wrong. He was a cop and had seen much of the ugliness that can afflict mankind, and he'd hardened himself as well as any cop must against personal reaction to it; but now all he could think of was the Pindar family and how they'd prayed for their daughter's recovery at least unviolated, alive or dead, and how this would destroy them.

Instinctively, Howard peered about, and then began to prowl the immediate area, searching for some sign of the victim's clothing. The one article that he was particularly alert for was an orange dress with white polka dots.

Soon there were a dozen official cars at the scene, lined up along Geddes Road outside the abandoned farm. Uniformed state troopers kept traffic, which was light, moving steadily past, not permitting the curious even to slow. There were several deputies from the Sheriff's Department and Sergeants Herb Smith and Don Howell of the Ypsi P.D., as well as Chief John Hayes and Lieutenant Mel Fuller of the E.M.U. campus police, who were deputized to assist local civil authorities in any investigation that might involve students or faculty members. Assistant Prosecutor Booker T. Williams arrived, a slight, soft-spoken, light-skinned black who directed the Ypsilanti office of Washtenaw County Prosecutor William F. Delhey, whose own headquarters was in the county seat, Ann Arbor.

Finally the county medical examiner, Dr. H. A. Scovill of Ypsilanti, came and, after a rapid examination of the cadaver, ordered a postmortem to be performed at the University of Michigan Medical Center in Ann Arbor. Dr. Scovill was peppered with questions:

"How long is it dead?"

"I'd say several weeks at least. Maybe a month."

"Is it male or female?"

"Appears to be female."

"Age?"

"No way to tell at this time."

"Color?"

"Can't say yet."

"Cause of death?"

"The autopsy should tell us that—I hope."

The doctor deferred all other inquiries to the findings of the autopsy, which would be performed first thing the next morning.

After the remains had been removed, the police reconstructed what few facts they had. The body of the presumed female had been found on the deserted Carmody farm at a point 192 feet north of Geddes Road and three-tenths of a mile west of LaForge Road. The odds seemed strongly against accidental or natural death in such a remote location. She could have been killed there, or anywhere and dumped there. The absence so far of any of her clothes might support the latter probability.

The consensus was that in any event, from indications on the ground and in the trash in which it lay, the corpse had been moved a number of times during the month or so that it probably had been there—five of six feet each time, in several different directions. This could be attributed to the tugging of voracious animals, or it could be that the killer had returned periodically to inspect his (or her) victim, perhaps to ascertain whether the body had been discovered, perhaps out of sheer perverseness. The investigators could not discount the two boys' story of having heard a car in the vicinity just prior to their stumbling upon the cadaver. If only they'd got a glimpse of that car. Nonetheless, this line of theory suggested that the killer might live or work in the area, close enough at any rate to be drawn back to the death site more than once.

About 4:30, one of the troopers who, with the detectives, had fanned out over the area to thrash laboriously through the wild growth let out a cry. Among thick weeds near the innermost curve of the driveway, some fifty yards from where the body had lain, he'd found a female's sandal. It was of leather with a kind of straw weave and, when cleaned off, looked relatively new. Its string laces were still tied in a bow. The instep was labeled "Qualicraft Casual—6½ B." It was for a right foot. There was no mate.

As the detectives considered this find, Vern Howard's heart sank. After examining the sandal, he said to Ken Taylor: "You know the 'missing' case I've been on—the E.M.U. coed?"

"Yes." Taylor eyed the older man. "You think this might be something?"

Howard studied the sandal again. "She was wearing something like this." He reflected a moment, then said: "I think the girl's family better be given a look." It sounded as though that was the last thing he wanted to do.

"You want me to go with you?"

"Would you?" Howard said, his eyes grateful. "It's the first thing that's turned up in a month. . . ." His gruff voice trailed off.

Charles and Margaret Pindar were seated silently on lawn chairs under a tree at the rear of their house in Willis, relaxing before dinner. A chill swept through them when they recognized Lieutenant Howard pulling into their driveway. Howard introduced Detective Sergeant Taylor of the State Police. Howard appeared ill at ease, as if unsure what to say. He seemed to be hoping that Sergeant Taylor would do the talking.

"Mr. and Mrs. Pindar," Taylor said, clearing his throat, "I'm sorry to have to tell you this, but we've found—a body. A woman, we think. She's been dead about a month, and we found something near the body. . . ."

Taylor turned to Howard, who produced the lone sandal. Mrs. Pindar turned it over and over in fluttering hands, then clutched it lovingly and stared at her husband. He put his arm around her shoulders.

"It's . . . Marilyn's," she said at last in a small voice.

There was an awkward silence.

"Tell us what you can, sergeant," Mr. Pindar asked, still holding his wife.

Taylor related how, where, and when the body had been discovered, leaving out only the more sordid details of its appearance and condition. Mr. Pindar listened without expression, nodding every so often in a manner suggesting he was already resigned that it was indeed his daughter. "But that's all we know so far," Taylor concluded. "It could be anybody. . . ."

"Could we see her, sergeant?" Mr. Pindar said quietly, as though not having heard.

Taylor shot a glance at Howard. "Well, not until we get an ID." He paused, then said: "She's—well, if it *is* your daughter, I'm sure you'd rather remember her the way she was." He clamped his lips shut, embar-

rassed at having failed to spare them additional heart-
ache as he'd intended. Now he looked to Howard for
support.

"We'd like to ask you folks to just sit tight a while
longer," the lieutenant said. "We'll let you know the
minute we find out anything positive . . . one way or
another."

The Pindars nodded numbly, and the two detectives
turned to leave. Then Howard turned back. "I
wonder," he asked, "if you'd be good enough to give
me the name and address of Marilyn's dentist?"

Howard and Taylor drove to the State Police post
in Ypsi, neither saying much. The post was busy. Local newspaper and radio reporters had assembled, and
after a private briefing with the other officers, Taylor
and senior detective Ron Schoonmaker held an impromptu news conference, withholding few details of
the day's discoveries. They could only hope that full
disclosure from the outset might impel somebody,
somewhere, to take a false step.

Meanwhile, Howard telephoned the two dentists referred by Mrs. Pindar. Marilyn had been treated by an
orthodontist in Ann Arbor as well as her regular
dentist, a Dr. Smeckert in Ypsilanti. It was the latter
who had on file the most recent dental chart on
Marilyn that Howard was looking for. Howard told
Dr. Smeckert to have the chart available the following
morning: it would be picked up and turned over to an
oral specialist at University Hospital to be studied during the autopsy. It might be the only means by which
Marilyn Pindar would ever be finally identified—or
not.

At 9:15 A.M. Tuesday, August 8, the autopsy was
begun by Dr. Bernard Naylor, a British pathologist in
residence at the University of Michigan Hospital. His
preliminary findings showed that it was a young
woman, perhaps twenty. She had sustained approximately thirty deep lacerations of the chest and
abdomen. Perhaps twenty of these punctures had been

inflicted by a knife or other sharp implement. The others might be attributed either to the ravagings of small animals or forceful escape of internal gases. Her feet had been severed at both ankle joints, the right hand above the wrist, the left thumb and parts of the other four digits on her left hand. It was not immediately certain, and might never be, whether these missing sections of limbs had been deliberately severed or been devoured by animals. Imprints of small teeth could be seen on some of the remaining exposed bones, but this in itself was not conclusive. And it did appear that the lower leg bones, just above the ankles, had been smashed rather than chewed or sawed.

Later, the pathologist reported having found the lower ends of both the tibias and fibulas shattered and the left fourth metacarpal bone fractured. Also detectable were lineal abrasions on the victim's chest and torso. These indicated that in addition to multiple stabbing the woman had probably been beaten.

In a community where petty crime and felonies were common enough but violence rare, this was the most unnervingly brutal crime most of these police professionals—and doctors as well—had ever encountered. And as yet they weren't even sure who had been murdered.

Probable identification was not long in coming, however. By midmorning Tuesday, Dr. Edward Haenick, the Medical Center's resident oral surgeon, had put together a tentative chart of the victim's dental structure. This he compared with Marilyn Pindar's chart supplied by her dentist and delivered by Lieutenant Howard and Sergeant Taylor. The comparison appeared positive; both showed an upper rear tooth missing on either side of the mouth, the result of extraction in each case, and similar patterns of identifiable fillings. Pending confirming examination, there was reasonable certainty that the dead woman was in fact Marilyn Pindar.

The State Police team that had returned to the
Carmody farm early Tuesday morning knew nothing
of these developments. Aided by a handful of uniformed troopers, for more than three hours Detective
Sergeants Ken Kraus, Ron Schoonmaker, and a fourth
member of the Ypsi DB unit, Juvenile Officer Bob
Johnston, had scoured the mass of underbrush, searching, so far in vain, for *something*.

Then, just before 11:30, Johnston lifted a large section of decomposing corrugated paneling, possibly once
part of a mover's packing crate, and found underneath
a moldy collection of feminine clothing. On top was an
orange dress with white polka dots. "Hey!" Johnston
yelled. "I've got something!"

The dress, dank and crawling with insects, had been
rent down the front from the neck almost to the bottom. Underneath it, discolored by the damp earth,
were white nylon panties, which had a small tear at
the waist, and a white brassiere with one strap torn
loose. The spot where they lay was only ten or fifteen
yards from where the girl's sandal had been discovered
the previous afternoon.

"I guess this about wraps it up for Vern Howard,"
Schoonmaker commented with a note of regret. They
liked the big, taciturn city policeman who they knew
had put so much of himself into the search for the
missing coed.

Howard could not bring himself to face the Pindars
again, so Ken Taylor and Ron Schoonmaker went
down to Willis Tuesday afternoon. The tight-lipped
detectives were braced for an emotional outburst, but
Charles and Margaret Pindar surprised them. Hearing
now, officially, what they already had acknowledged
to themselves, the couple was calm, as though all their
emotions had been long spent.

The father again asked: "Now may we see her?"

And, swallowing hard, Taylor had to say: "You'd
better not."

Mr. Pindar lowered his eyes, his arm going around his wife. "I understand . . ." was all he answered.

When the detectives drove off, they too were silent, drained. They spied the first contingent of reporters and photographers pulling up to the Pindars' neat brick home. That family's ordeal was not over yet.

Nor was their own. Having boned up on Vern Howard's month-long missing file on Marilyn Pindar, they realized bleakly that they would be starting from scratch in what was now an ugly homicide.

The remains were released by the police on Wednesday, August 9—one month to the day since Marilyn had disappeared—and by prearrangement transported to the Moore Funeral Home in Ypsilanti. There they were to repose in a specially ordered coffin with twin locks and a permanent seal.

The next morning, as Mr. and Mrs. Pindar were about to leave home for Moore's to discuss burial arrangements, they were intercepted by a telephone call from Sergeant Schoonmaker. He sounded businesslike:

"Do you know anybody with a bluish-gray Chevy? Say a young man, maybe twenty?"

Charles Pindar, surprised, could not think. "Not offhand that I know of. Why?"

"There was a visitor this morning at Moore's Funeral Home. A young fellow. Said he was a friend of the family. He wanted to take a picture of—your daughter!"

"A picture!" Mr. Pindar gasped. "Well, they didn't . . . ?"

"Of course not. They told him it was impossible. And he said, 'You mean you people can't fix her up enough so I could just get one picture of her?' And when the answer was no, he left and drove off in this blue-gray Chevy. Strange thing was, he wasn't carrying a camera. . . ."

"God Almighty!" Charles Pindar stared across the

kitchen at his wife. "There was that gray car the night Marilyn . . ."

"Yes," the detective said.

"What did this fellow look like? Maybe that would help me think."

Schoonmaker sighed irritably. "Bad luck on that. The one who spoke with the guy was just a dumb kid, a part-time handyman with about as much perception as a turtle. He's given us next to nothing. The guy was 'sort of' young, white, 'ordinary' looking, wore 'ordinary' clothes—probably sport shirt and slacks— no colors, features, distinguishing marks, nothing to follow up. Except the car, and we can't even be sure he's got that right. He never thought to get the plate number. . . .

"I just thought it might strike a bell with you folks —you know, somebody in the area, or a fellow your girl might have known."

Mr. Pindar glumly shook his head. "No, at this moment it doesn't register. I'll sure think about it— I'm sorry. *Really* sorry, because this must have seemed like a good lead, at last."

"You never know," Schoonmaker said kindly. "Keep your chin up. We'll be working on it."

"I know. Thanks." Charles Pindar hung up the receiver and went across to his wife and held her close.

A simple requiem mass was said for Marilyn Pindar on Saturday, August 12, at Immaculate Conception Roman Catholic Church in nearby Milan. Sprinkled amidst her family and neighbors and friends were half a dozen state policemen in plain clothes, watching for someone among the mourners who seemed not to belong, or someone who might betray inordinate curiosity or excitement. But there appeared to be no one like that. Nor was there a blue-gray Chevrolet anywhere near the church.

The girl was buried at St. Joseph's Cemetery in Whittaker. It was five weeks since Marilyn Pindar's family had last seen her.

The Ypsilanti P.D. sent out a bulletin:

WCT BC 34367 YPSILANTI PD TT 813   8/16/67
CANCEL MISSING GIRL
CANCEL WCT BC 30268 YPSI PD TT 737   7/12/67
MARILYN PINDAR . . .

CHAPTER 3

WEEKS PASSED, MONTHS, without anything further being turned up in the Pindar homicide. While officially remaining "open," gradually the case was relegated by the State Police to their inactive file. Through the winter and into the spring of 1968, there were no other notably violent incidents reported in the vicinity.

Washtenaw County had, in fact, known few crimes of violence. Quiet and peaceful, the county begins about thirty miles west of Detroit, with Ypsilanti situated on its easternmost boundary and Ann Arbor lying a few miles to the west. Residential and commercial growth between them has so overlapped, however, that the two communities could almost be taken for one, a homogeneous urban-suburban sprawl perhaps eleven to twelve miles wide and five to six miles deep.

Ann Arbor, the county seat, four times the size of Ypsilanti, is by far the more cosmopolitan, dominated by the University of Michigan, which is not so much *in* Ann Arbor as it is the very core of both the city's anatomy and its manner. Ann Arbor likes to regard itself as "the research center of the Midwest," and indeed a full 75 percent of its adult residents are white-collar professionals employed by the many sophisticated research-development firms that flourish there. The U. of M. itself attracts scholars from all over the United States and abroad.

Ypsilanti (called simply "Ypsi" by most) by comparison is more of a blue-collar town, projecting images of leathery faces and callused hands, whiskey and beer in tiled saloons, well-worn rockers on weatherbeaten porches. Where Ann Arbor entertains frequent concerts, plays, art films, Ypsi's only downtown movie theater features mostly bawdy skin flicks. Its populace ranges from stolid German farming stock to a sizable element of transplanted Southerners, descendants of a huge labor migration during World War II, many of whom work either at the big Ford plant at Willow Run or in smaller auto and machine parts factories clustered nearby.

Ypsilanti has its own university, of course; and Eastern Michigan—one of four such regional state institutions, specializing in turning out public-school teachers —has earned increased academic stature in recent years. But where in Ann Arbor the University of Michigan is almost indistinguishable from that city's total being, in Ypsilanti E.M.U., even after 120 years, seems tucked off, still a tenant, on its 450 acres north of town. In Ann Arbor, university security is administered by the city police. In Ypsi, Eastern maintains an independent uniformed campus force, deputized by the county sheriff. But both campuses are on the whole quiet, and security enforcement is generally of a routine nature.

All things considered, then, Washtenaw County seemed an unlikely stage for the ugly scene of violence of the summer of 1967. Most residents had in fact all but forgotten the brutal Pindar murder, when, shortly after midnight on July 1, 1968, a second Eastern Michigan University coed was reported missing.

The first call came into police headquarters at 1:47

A.M. that day, a Monday. A young woman named
Sharon Cooper was worried about her roommate, Jill
Hersch, a twenty-year-old art major who had just completed her sophomore year at E.M.U. Her home was
in Plymouth, but she rented an apartment near the
university with Sharon because both girls had jobs for
the summer in Ypsi. Now Sharon was worried because
Jill had hitched a ride to Ann Arbor late Sunday night
and had not yet turned up at a friend's apartment there
where she was to spend the night.

"How long exactly has she been gone?" the police
officer asked wearily.

"About two and a half hours now. But God!" Sharon
added, "she was only going over to Ann Arbor, why
shouldn't we have heard from her by now?" She had
another urgent thought: "There were these three fellows in a car—"

"Hold it, hold it," the flat voice on the other end
broke in, though the tone was not unkind. "Why don't
we wait just a while longer. There may be a simple
explanation to this after all. Let's wait until morning,
then if you still haven't heard anything you call us
back. Okay?"

At 7:38 A.M., Sharon Cooper telephoned the police
again. She was growing frantic.

Ypsilanti officers Moran and Savage were dispatched
to interview Miss Cooper at 703 Emmet Street.

The girls' apartment, at the end of a long, ill-lit corridor on the second floor of an old boardinghouse, consisted of a small, cluttered living room and a cell-like
bedroom, separated by a narrow alcove into which
were jammed a range and refrigerator and a commode.

As the officers perched on the edge of a battered
settee, notebooks on their knees, Sharon Cooper, a tall,
robust young woman with horn-rimmed glasses, reconstructed the girls' recent activities.

Clearly nervous, she told the officers that they had
both gone home for the weekend. Sharon returned to
Ypsilanti late Sunday afternoon. Jill was driven back
that evening by her parents and arrived about 9:15

P.M. They chatted for a while, then Jill spoke on the telephone with a friend in Ann Arbor, Celia Ennis, who had called earlier, and Jill decided to take a late bus to Ann Arbor and stay the night with Celia. She checked with the Short Way Line, which had a regular run between the two communities, and was told that the last bus would depart the downtown Greyhound station at 10:30. Jill threw some personal things into a large carryall and hurried to catch the bus at its next stop, nearer their house, in front of E.M.U.'s Welch Hall on Cross Street. Sharon went with her for company.

They were at the bus stop by about 10:30, but by 10:45 there was still no sign of the bus. At 11:15 Jill decided she would try to hitch a ride to Ann Arbor.

Sharon tried to talk her out of it but Jill was stubbornly determined. They strolled the curbside along Cross Street between Welch Hall and McKenny Hall for about ten minutes. Then around 11:25, a car that they'd noticed a few minutes earlier, when it had slowed as it passed them, came by once again and pulled to a stop ahead of them in the cut-in lane to McKenny Hall. There appeared to be three men in the car, which was a late-model coupe, two-toned with a red body and black vinyl top.

One of the men got out of the front passenger side and called pleasantly to the approaching girls: "Hey, you want a ride?"

In the reflected glow of indirect spotlights beamed onto the front of McKenny Hall, he looked to be twentyish, about six feet tall, trimly built, clean-cut and good-looking, with neat dark hair; he wore a green T-shirt with the letters E M U across the front, light-colored dungarees, and white tennis sneakers.

Jill called back "Yes!" and ran to the car and started to climb in; then she turned to Sharon to say she would telephone as soon as she reached Ann Arbor. With a wave she ducked into the back seat, the young man got in and slammed the door, and the car pulled away. Sharon watched as it continued along the driveway of

McKenny Hall, turned right into the parking lot, and disappeared behind the building. After a few minutes, Sharon, oddly depressed, started walking slowly back to the apartment.

She got undressed, washed and brushed her hair, and sat in a robe, reading, waiting for Jill's call. A few minutes past 12:30 A.M Celia Ennis called: What had happened to Jill, wasn't she coming?

Sharon's heart turned cold. She told Celia about Jill's driving off with the three men in the red and black car, and Celia became excited and said she would contact some friends and they all would keep their eyes peeled for Jill and such a car. Maybe one of Celia's friends would spot her, or she would phone in. Celia would stay in touch with Sharon.

It was nearly 1:45 A.M when the telephone rang again. Celia's voice was thin with concern. There had been no sign of Jill and no word.

That was when they had decided to call the police.

Jill Hersch was described as about five feet five, quite slim, weighing perhaps ninety-eight pounds. She had hazel eyes and wore her dark hair long and "natural," almost to her waist. When she left Sunday night she was wearing a dark blue mini dress and tan woven sandals and was carrying an oversized red burlap handbag, containing a purple beaded purse (with her student ID in it) and probably some personal things for overnight. Sharon thought she had on her gold ring with a small pearl in its center and also a pair of circular gold earrings, the kind for pierced ears.

Moran and Savage took all this down dutifully, adding Jill's home address and telephone number in Plymouth and those of Celia Ennis in Ann Arbor. Neither officer was unusually stirred by Sharon's anxious account. Still, their report would be turned over to the Ypsi P.D.'s Detective Bureau for whatever follow-up was considered advisable.

As the men drove away from 703 Emmet Street, however, Officer Moran noted thoughtfully to his partner: "You know, I just realized, that little gal they found out at the old farm last summer lived only about three blocks from here. She was a college kid, too."

Monday afternoon, when there still had been no communication from or about her roommate, Sharon Cooper felt it was her personal duty to advise Jill's family. Yet she could not bring herself to upset Jill's mother, whom she knew to be in delicate health from a heart condition, so she called the Detroit department store where Mr. Hersch was an assistant manager.

Jerome Hersch listened, with mouth set, to the hesitant account from his daughter's roommate. When he put down the receiver, his first thought was of Jill's boyfriend, Dickie Shantz.

The Hersches had never approved of young Shantz in the three years that he and Jill had been going together. A year younger than Jill, the boy was clearly less mature than Jill and her peer group. He seemed unstable, mercurial, rebellious.

Graduated from high school a year after Jill, Shantz had followed her to Eastern Michigan, dropped out before completing his freshman year, and then contented himself with bumming around between Ypsilanti and Plymouth. On two separate occasions, he'd got into trouble with the police and in fact the only way he'd escaped prosecution the second time, on a breaking-and-entering charge, was by accepting the court's alternative of enlisting in the army for a three-year hitch. But Shantz already had gone AWOL twice —once the past April, when he'd quickly been picked up in Plymouth and served time in the stockade, and again in early June, when he had taken off from Fort Gordon, Georgia, and made his way to Ypsilanti for a weekend with Jill. That time, however, Shantz had returned to camp voluntarily.

As far as anyone knew, Shantz was still at Fort Gordon. Had Jill now gone to *him?*

When the report of the missing girl came in to Ypsilanti police headquarters, Lieutenant Vern Howard turned it over to Detective Sergeant Bert Maxwell. The memory of last summer's missing coed was etched deep in Howard's consciousness, and the details of this new case appeared so like the other that he would not chance just logging and spiking it without an immediate preliminary checkoff.

Besides, there were aspects of this latest report that triggered a connection in Lieutenant Howard's mind with an incident the week before. The night of June 23, an eighteen-year-old local high-school senior had failed to come home, and her parents had called the police. It was soon learned that she had been seen that evening with three young males, in a red car with a black top. The next morning, the car was located outside the Huron Hotel, where they'd spent the night having sex, each of the youths taking turns with the girl. She was body-worn and a little frightened, but she would not admit to having been abused. Although never having met the three before, she indicated she'd gone with them—and participated—willingly. The police decided to pursue it no further than to deliver the girl home and send the others off with stern reprimands.

Now Lieutenant Howard ordered that the car's owner be picked up along with his two friends. Then Sergeant Maxwell was dispatched to escort Miss Sharon Cooper to the station for an ID test. The three young men were placed in a lineup with a number of other unrelated suspects, and Sergeant Maxwell brought Miss Cooper in. From the darkness she scanned the faces peering out, some sullenly, some blankly, from under the fierce white lights over the lineup platform. She turned, finally, to Maxwell and shook her head. Then she was taken outside and asked to examine the car. After studying it only a few seconds, she said no.

Further questioning revealed that each of the boys could account for his whereabouts on Sunday evening, and they were quickly released.

A little later Maxwell sat down with Sharon and reviewed her entire statement as given the day before to the uniformed officers. The sergeant wanted to know about her friends—particularly, did she have a boyfriend?

The girl's face flushed. "Well, Jill hasn't really talked about him all that much, not lately anyway." She saw the policeman's eyes narrow a bit. "I think his name was, is, Rich or Dick something. . . ."

"And where is this Rich or Dick now?" Maxwell pursued quietly.

"I—I don't know."

While Maxwell next went off to poke around E.M.U.—hoping to find anybody else who might have seen Jill Hersch Sunday night or Monday—Detective Don Howell, armed with a précis of Maxwell's interview of Sharon Cooper, drove over to Ann Arbor to talk with Celia Ennis. He got to the point quickly.

"Tell me about Jill's boyfriends," the detective demanded.

"Well, I . . ."

"Wasn't there one that she sort of went steady with?"

"I don't—think . . ."

"Well, you two were friends in high school, in the same class, and you've stayed close since then. You must know who she dated." Howell paused as the girl fingered a strand of hair uncertainly. "Okay," he said, "we can get it from her parents. We know his name is Dick."

Celia sighed. "Dickie Shantz."

Tuesday afternoon, the Plymouth Police Department received a wire from the provost at Fort Gordon, Georgia. Pvt. Richard Shantz of Plymouth had been absent without official leave since Saturday, June 29, and was now considered a deserter. Shantz's family had had no word of him. The Plymouth police were referred to Ypsilanti.

That evening in Plymouth, Jerome Hersch, who had so far resisted upsetting his ailing wife by telling her of Jill's disappearance, finally decided it would be better if the two of them faced the situation honestly—including his suspicions that she might be with Dickie Shantz. He was deliberating how to go about this when Sergeant Bert Maxwell called from the Ypsilanti P.D. Maxwell explained that the police had been reluctant to contact the family sooner, for fear of worrying them prematurely, but now . . . Had there been any word from their daughter?

Not yet, Mr. Hersch said.

Who is Dickie Shantz?

Mr. Hersch was startled.

Did they know that Shantz was being sought as an army deserter? Could she be with him?

Mr. Hersch painfully acknowledged the possibility. When he hung up, however, he was more pessimistic than ever. What if Jill *hadn't* gone off with Dickie Shantz?

On Wednesday, July 3, the Ypsilanti *Press* was given the go-ahead to run a story about the missing coed, with a photograph secured from the Hersches. At the moment, the best hope seemed to lie in someone's memory being jogged by the declension of circumstances, of time and place, as well as by the girl's likeness in print.

Jill Hersch was the second youngest of four daughters. An intelligent girl, she was studying art at E.M.U. where she seemed to have blossomed, revealing a strong, sensitive flair. While at times impulsive, more often she tended to be a passive, wistful dreamer. Her upbringing had been wholesome, small-townish comfortable, free of serious discord or evident dissatisfactions. She was not known to have experimented with drugs.

There simply was no reason why she should have dropped out of sight.

It remained a strong probability that the key to the mystery was held by AWOL Pvt. Dickie Shantz. Shantz still had not been spotted nor, so far as anyone was saying, heard from. The newspaper appeal, which named him, just might be the prod.

The tactic did draw a response, but not quite as hoped. Wednesday night, Dickie Shantz telephoned Jill's parents in Plymouth. In a voice tremulous with tension, he begged Mr. Hersch to believe that Jill was not with him, he'd not seen her. He, too, was worried sick over her. Please, wouldn't Mr. Hersch try to make the police understand that he didn't know where Jill could be? Through his own anguish, Mr. Hersch thought to ask where Dickie was calling from, but Shantz would not say, and hung up.

Mr. Hersch sat immobile by the silent telephone for a long time, trying to control the spasms of despair that wracked him. All the worst fears that he had almost succeeded in quelling had burst to the surface. He picked up the receiver and dialed Sergeant Maxwell in Ypsilanti.

"If he saw the newspaper, especially this soon," the detective commented, "then he must be in the area."

"Yes. But he insists that Jill is not with him. I'm inclined to believe him."

"Maybe so," replied Maxwell. "But when we bag him, he'll still have a lot of questions to answer. And he is still wanted by the army."

"All right," Mr. Hersch said wearily. "But my only concern is finding my daughter."

"Of course, sir."

Mr. Hersch said he would like to make an appeal on television—to Shantz, to *anybody* who knew his daughter, to please come forward with any information about her . . . a father's appeal. "Maybe even Jill herself might see it, somewhere," he added, a catch in his voice. "Maybe it would persuade her to come home." Maxwell said he thought it could be arranged.

Channel 4 sent a crew from Detroit to film the emotional plea. It was shown Thursday on Channel 4's news programs. But there was no response from either

Jill Hersch or Dickie Shantz or anyone else who might have seen the girl since late Sunday.

The media stories did, however, draw corroboration of Jill's last known movements. One of the first to contact police was an elderly black man who had also been at the E.M.U. bus stop Sunday night. His name was Ralph Morton and he was a maintenance man at a small, cheap hotel in downtown Ann Arbor, who had been returning after spending his night off with friends in Ypsilanti. After waiting awhile for the scheduled bus, he had gone to telephone the depot from a public booth and got no answer. As he was walking back toward the bus stop he saw the one girl standing by a car with a young white man; then she got in, and the car moved off and around behind the school hall, and the light-haired girl walked away alone.

That was all he could say. He hadn't been close enough to identify anybody. And he hadn't seen the car again. He'd taken a cab to Ann Arbor.

The scene had also been observed by a sixteen-year-old girl from her front porch directly opposite McKenny Hall. Eleanor Evans told police she'd come out to get a breath of air some time around 11:30, and as she sat there idly watching and counting cars going by she noticed the two young women who seemed to be looking for a lift. She didn't pay much attention to them except to note that one was taller, a blonde with glasses, the other dark and toting a big red carry-all bag. She remembered the bag.

Then, a minute or two later, her attention was drawn to them again when a red car with a black top pulled over and the two girls went up to it. There were several men in it, but Eleanor did not recollect one getting out. However, after a few moments the dark-haired girl did get in, leaving the blonde, and the car went around behind McKenny Hall. She saw it turn right again out of the parking lot and go east on Forest Avenue. (That would be the opposite direction from Ann Arbor!)

An E.M.U. campus patrolman, Fred Williams, remembered that, as he'd made his rounds Sunday night, sometime after 11 P.M., he was near McKenny Hall when a red and black car pulled away from in front of the building. There were several people in it, but he couldn't make out how many or if they were male or female. He'd thought nothing about it, naturally, until the news stories gave some of the details.

Two men who worked at McKenny Hall came forward with further verification and a bit more. Isaiah Diamond, a janitor, reported that late Sunday night—it could have been between eleven and midnight, but maybe it was earlier—he had come upon three young men *inside* the building, which was supposed to be locked. One of them, wearing a green E.M.U. T-shirt, was talking on a pay telephone near the front entrance. Diamond told them he didn't know how they'd got in but they did not belong there at that hour, and he ushered them out through the main doors.

The night custodian, Jack Pitts, confirmed that he had seen the janitor hustling three youths out of the building sometime Sunday night. After the three had been let out of the building, Pitts went up to the second floor and happened to look out a window. In the driveway below was a red and black car. It sat there awhile, engine idling, then drove away. He couldn't tell who was in it, but he assumed it was the same boys. He didn't notice any girl.

What the police got from this was little more than an assumption that, since later examination of McKenny Hall showed no evidence of forcible entry, the three young men must have had a key to the building. But what did that mean? Why would they have gone to the trouble to slip into a locked, empty Student Union? To make a phone call? Nothing had been stolen or vandalized. And what, if any, significance did this episode have with the disappearance of Jill Hersch?

All that seemed reasonably sure was that these were the same three described by Sharon Cooper, with whom Jill had ridden off. But that red and black car was yet to be found. Without that, they were at the same dead end.

And what of Dickie Shantz?

CHAPTER 4

AT MIDAFTERNOON ON Friday, in the sparsely inhabited northeast section of Ann Arbor, two construction workers became aware of something odd.

It was a muggy, hot day, and the men were taking a five-minute water break from the sapping toil of excavating storm drains for a new subdivision off Glacier Way. Slouched along the edge of the trench, their bare torsos running with sweat, breathing deep, they were silent until one, Tony Cola, cocked his head a moment, then said to the other: "There must be something dead around here."

Caleb Freeman groaned, "There sure is. And I'm sitting on it."

"No, really," Cola insisted. His nose lifted again, testing the air. "Smell. . . . Do you smell it?"

Freeman sniffed and his face began to pinch up. "Christ! Did you lay one?"

"Up yours." Cola got to his feet. "I tell you, there's a dead thing around here someplace." He started prowling tentatively through the high browned-out grass and weeds along the shoulder of Glacier Way. Freeman, bemused, tagged behind.

After a dozen yards, Cola halted stiffly. When he turned back to the other, his features were contorted. He pointed toward a clump of growth a few feet ahead of him. Freeman couldn't make out anything at first. He moved closer, and then he saw it: part of a bare arm protruding from the grass, elbow bent at an awkward angle, skin grayish, slack, lifeless.

Freeman edged past Cola to the spot. The arm was part of a body, which appeared to be nude. The stench was awful, but Freeman made himself bend and part some of the tall grasses. Almost instantly he had to recoil.

It was a woman. It was hard to tell how old, because not only was much of the thin, pale body slashed and caked with blood but from the bosom and upper arms to the head the skin was black, peeling with rot. Where the face would have been was a fearsome charcoal death mask, the mouth frozen open in a wide, silent scream, the teeth huge and sneering like a skeleton's because the lips were gone; the sunken eyes were also open, showing only blank whites.

Freeman and Cola ran to find their foreman, back down the road. Lane Beasley, who for a brief recent period had tried his hand as an Ann Arbor police officer, listened to the two panting men with some curiosity. Were they pulling his leg?

He saw soon enough that it was no joke. Beasley examined the scene with what he hoped was the care learned as a policeman. The dead woman's muddy clothing was bunched around her neck—white undergarments and a blue dress of some type—like some grotesque clown's collar. The body lay on its right side, arms thrown out from the trunk. The face was horrible, unrecognizable. In the black, swollen left ear lobe was a round golden earring. Beasley noticed that some of the damp grass around the corpse appeared to have been trampled, indicating that some other person or persons had been there recently. Yet, though the body was mottled with dried blood, there were no traces of blood on the grass or ground.

Beasley rose, faintly sick from the sight and the smell, and said to Freeman and Cola, who had held back: "You stick by and don't let anybody near. I'll go call the police."

It was 2:57 P.M. when the call came in to Ann Arbor police headquarters in the new City Hall. Lieutenant Marvin Dann took down the information, then hurried into the office of Captain of Detectives Harold Olson. A few minutes after three, Captain Olson himself and Lieutenant Ray Woodruff were speeding north to Glacier Way. En route, Olson used the car radio to alert the county medical examiner and also the Sheriff's Department. From the location given of the body, it could be either just inside the Ann Arbor city limits or across the line in Ann Arbor Township, which would make this officially a Sheriff's Department case.

When they got there, awaited tensely by Beasley and the two workers, a quick survey showed that the corpse did lie just inside the city boundary—on the south bank of Glacier Way about one hundred yards west of Earhart Road. Olson sighed. He was a thorough professional, but no cop relishes being thrust into investigation of mysterious homicides. And this one looked particularly nasty.

Olson, at forty-four a police officer for twenty-two years, could not remember having seen a victim in so macabre a condition: The advanced decay of the upper third of the body certainly meant that she'd been dead for some time; it was obvious that maggots and insects had had many days in which to grub away at the rotting flesh. But how then could the rest of her appear virtually fresh-killed?

It also appeared that the woman had been murdered—and kept—elsewhere and dumped at this spot only today. This was reinforced by the lack of blood under or near the corpse, also by the signs of trampled grass around it. It probably had been left there before dawn or soon thereafter; for no body would have been deposited here after 8:00 A.M., when Beasley and the others had arrived on the job. And none of them had seen anybody or anything unusual all day.

In questioning the men, Olson established that they were employed by the Hannagan Construction Company, which had been working the site for about three months, so far mostly digging out drainage trenches. It was Beasley's first job back in building work, which he'd done for many years previously, after having spent a year as a patrolman. All three, including Beasley—former cop or not—would be carefully checked out.

Two sheriff's deputies appeared, Detective Sergeant Joe Hall and uniformed Sergeant Ron Ritter, followed shortly by Ron Schoonmaker of the Ypsi State Police post. Olson asked Schoonmaker if he would request assistance from the State Police crime lab near Plymouth. Additional officers were already on their way from the Ann Arbor P.D.

An ambulance arrived from University Hospital, and within an hour of discovery the dead woman's remains were being delivered to the Medical Center for autopsy.

Soon the area was crowded with patrol cars from the various police units and they all fanned out for a foot-by-foot examination of Glacier Way, its grassy shoulders and the tangles of acreage adjoining. But hardly had the search begun than ominous thunderheads eclipsed the sun, and minutes later a rolling clap from the sky unloosed a pounding rain that scattered the men to their cars. They sat, drearily watching the downpour through fogged windshields. If there *had* been any useful tracks of any sort, they would be washed away by the time this was over.

In Ypsilanti, Sergeants Bert Maxwell and Don Howell got the two messages only minutes apart.

First, it had come over the police radio that a woman's body had been found in Ann Arbor, that she was partially decomposed and thus deceased for a length of time yet to be determined. The detectives looked at one another, each with the same automatic thought: Jill Hersch.

Then, as Howell was trying to get information from the Ann Arbor P.D., a call came in for Maxwell. The young man's voice was hesitant, sounding distant and hollow: "This is Dickie Shantz . . ."

Maxwell snapped his fingers to get the attention of Howell, who was on the telephone across the squad-room. "Where are you, boy?"

At 4:35 P.M., Dickie Shantz was picked up by two Ann Arbor detectives at Celia Ennis' apartment and went quietly with them to the county jail.

The Ann Arbor police had previously been alerted, of course, to Shantz's fugitive status as an AWOL soldier, but the Ypsi P.D. also had advised them that they were looking for him in connection with the disappearance of an E.M.U. coed. Ordinarily, then, Ann Arbor might have cooperatively handed Shantz over to Ypsilanti. But now that Ann Arbor had found itself with a fresh unexplained homicide—whether or not it should turn out to be the missing coed—self-interest decreed, not unreasonably, that the Ann Arbor P.D. warranted first crack.

Detective Sergeant Bill Canada led the interrogation, attended by Bert Maxwell of the Ypsi P.D. Dickie Shantz was a slight, black-haired young man, sallow complexioned, with a narrow face and almost delicate chin, on which there was now a bristly outgrowth of beard. He wore blue jeans and scuffed sandals on bare feet. His hair, still relatively short from the army, was tousled as though he had a habit of combing his fingers through it. He appeared worried, distracted, his small, moist eyes darting warily from one to another of the officers.

They'd recited to him his rights, and he'd waived an attorney, and then Canada demanded:

"Do you know why you're here?"

Shantz answered hesitantly: "Because I'm AWOL . . ."

"Sure, there's that. And we're holding you for the MPs. But anything else?"

"I guess—" Shantz faltered, glancing about him.

"You are also charged with possession of a concealed, unlawful, dangerous weapon," drawled Canada stonily.

Shantz looked surprised.

Canada produced a set of tarnished brass knuckles. "This is yours, isn't it? It was found in your room."

The prisoner blushed and slid a little lower into his chair. He had been taken from Celia Ennis' flat, but he'd given the arresting officers as his actual address a boardinghouse south of town near the U. of M. football stadium. His room there had been searched immediately. The knuckles actually had been the only incriminating item found. Still, it was enough to hold him for a while.

"What else?" resumed Canada.

"Well"—the young man moistened his lips—"I guess about Jill . . ."

"Jill Hersch? What about her?" the detective demanded.

"About—her being missing." Shantz's voice cracked. "I—you know, we were going together. . . ."

"Do you know where she is?"

"No. God, I wish . . . !"

"When did you see her last?"

"I don't know. A couple of weeks ago . . ."

"The last time you were AWOL?"

"Yes."

"When did you get back here this time?"

"Saturday night—early Sunday."

"And you didn't contact Jill?"

"I couldn't. She was back in Plymouth, at a wedding."

"What about Sunday night?" Canada bored in.

Shantz drew a long breath, then, slowly, told what he knew of that night. It was *he* who'd phoned Jill after her return from Plymouth and arranged to meet her at Celia Ennis' apartment. When she'd not shown up, he'd phoned back and heard from Sharon about Jill's having driven off with three men. At first that had made him sore. But then, as time passed without word from her, he and Celia had started to worry. Celia got a friend of hers to lend them his car, and they cruised back and forth between Ann Arbor and Ypsi for an hour or more without spotting a red and black car. Finally, he'd called Sharon and asked her to notify the Ypsi police. Being AWOL, naturally he wanted to avoid drawing attention to himself. That was also why, even in the days that followed, both Celia and Sharon had continued to conceal his presence in the area. They had all kept telling themselves that Jill would turn up eventually.

But each passing day, Shantz said, it had become harder and harder to put down the growing premonition that something awful *must* have happened to her— that she was in trouble somewhere, in danger, hurt— even . . . His eyes filled, and he had to blink. He was trembling.

There was silence in the room. Canada broke it: "Dickie, we found a body this afternoon."

The youth looked up, startled.

"It may be Jill," Canada said.

Shantz stared at him, then, as though suddenly, finally drained, he sagged back limply and wept, a hand shielding his eyes.

The autopsy had been completed at the U. of M. Medical Center by Dr. Robert Hendrix, professor of forensic pathology at the university and assistant county medical examiner. The victim was listed as a young female of about twenty. Height: five feet, five inches. Approximate weight: under one hundred pounds (not precise due to considerable loss of body fluids). There were twenty-five stab wounds in her torso, twenty-two in the front and three in the back. The weapon used —probably a knife about four inches long—had punctured her right lung and liver, severed the carotid artery on the left side of her neck and, by a vicious thrust into her head from behind the left ear, fractured her skull. Vaginal swabs revealed traces of male seminal fluid.

The young woman, who had pierced ears, had on one small circular gold earring when brought in, and on her right hand she wore an imitation gold ring with a pearl setting.

Dr. Hendrix estimated she'd been dead between four and six days—since some time the past weekend. Internal examination disclosed bits of meat, identified as beef; green leafy material, such as from a salad; and potato. These were still in her stomach, only partially digested, and from this Hendrix deduced that she had expired—or at least been in a climactic state of mortal fear—some three to four hours after her last meal.

The doctor and his associate pathologists had no ready explanation for the extraordinary condition of the body. The lower two-thirds appeared to have been kept in an almost ideal preservative state, at about a forty-degree temperature, and they estimated that it had been by natural cooling, not refrigeration.

Where would such a situation be found in July? Perhaps a storm or flood cellar, as many a farm had, or one of those old-fashioned southern springhouses. But why then the marked deterioration of the rest of the body? One possibility was that only the lower parts had been protected, while the upper torso and head had somehow been outside, exposed to the elements. Another was that wherever she'd lain had a window, and the position of her body was such that sunlight had touched only the upper part; or that some sort of covering, like a sheet or tarpaulin, had protected the lower parts.

In any case, everything about the victim matched the description of the missing Jill Hersch that Ypsilanti's Bert Maxwell had been going on: her clothing, jewelry, age, general appearance, height, weight; even the food found in her stomach—Jill's parents having said that at dinner on Sunday evening she'd had a steak, French fries, and a salad. Positive comparison of dental charts the next day clinched it.

Thus it became Sergeant Maxwell's unhappy duty to drive to Plymouth to inform the Hersch family officially. The mother collapsed; the family physician had to be called to see to her already overburdened heart. The father, though badly shaken, visibly willed himself to retain control. After listening in silence to the details from Maxwell, he sat and stared off vacantly. When his eyes began brimming, the policeman excused himself and quietly left.

Monday morning, July 8, a meeting was held in the office of Washtenaw County Prosecutor William Delhey at the county building in Ann Arbor. Present were two of Delhey's assistant prosecutors, Booker Williams from Ypsilanti and Thomas Shea, and representatives of the five police agencies in the area: Chief Walter Krasny of the Ann Arbor P.D.; Chief Ray Walton, Ypsi P.D.; Sheriff Doug Harvey; John Hayes, chief of Eastern Michigan's campus police; and State Police Sergeant Ron Schoonmaker, senior detective at the Ypsi post.

Delhey was a tall, handsome, well-turned-out man with graying hair and courtly manner, who had held his office since 1956 and was widely regarded as one of the most thorough and ablest prosecutors in Michigan. He had called the meeting to set up guidelines for some sort of coordinative investigation of the Hersch murder.

The police officers reviewed information compiled to date and what efforts were currently in progress. Following verification that the victim was Jill Hersch, her roommate, Sharon Cooper, by now a very frightened young woman, had been secretly moved from the Emmet Street apartment to another on the far side of Ypsilanti and kept under close protective surveillance. Although not relocated, Celia Ennis also was being watched closely. And the police in Plymouth had been asked to keep a vigilant eye on the Hersch family, lest there be some personal vendetta connected with the killing (although this last was regarded as remote).

Meanwhile, there had been no success as yet in tracking the red and black car. Since the exact make and year of the car were still undetermined—the only information they had to go on was that it was a two-door hardtop, a late model, probably a Pontiac but possibly a Ford, perhaps with three taillights—it was agreed that this exercise could be simplified if photographs were obtained from the auto manufacturers of every such model produced by each in the past three years, and shown to the few witnesses for more positive identification.

Pending that, they endorsed a suggestion that the dead girl's roommate, Sharon Cooper, be accompanied by officers at night to the spot on Cross Street in Ypsilanti from where she had last seen the vehicle in question, and there watch cars go by until she might spy one, under similar conditions, that most resembled the other. (This was done that very night. After several tedious hours, Miss Cooper thought a passing 1967 Pontiac Le Mans, though not of the same colors, looked like the one she remembered.)

Meanwhile, also based on Miss Cooper's memory of that night, the Ann Arbor P.D. had put together a composite sketch of the young man she'd seen wearing the green E.M.U. T-shirt, and copies were being printed and distributed on the chance that something lucky could come of it.

On another front, police details were scouring the countryside, trying to pinpoint a location where Jill Hersch's curiously decomposed corpse might have been stored. Officers were going from farm to farm, residence to residence, looking for culverts, springhouses, storm cellars, even house basements, where climatic conditions—constant temperature about forty degrees and some limited exposure to outside light or air—matched those theorized by the pathologists. Several such places were found, but in each the one other essential component was lacking—the dead girl's blood. It figured that wherever the body had lain would have to be heavily smeared with blood, if not other telltale evidence. But so far none had been found.

As for possible suspects, officially Dickie Shantz still was considered one, although his story had been verified, as far as it went, and most of the investigators seemed to feel it unlikely that he had done harm to his girl friend. Shantz had agreed to take a polygraph test, and the military police had agreed to delay their arrival.

The three construction men who'd found the body had been checked out and written off, and Jill's friends, Sharon Cooper and Celia Ennis, were held to be in the clear. At the moment, there was no one else.

The meeting adjourned with an agreement that henceforth any information acquired by any of the five agencies represented be channeled to Delhey's office through Assistant Prosecutor Tom Shea. That way, instead of having to sift through five separate investigative reports, the prosecutor's office could collate evidence quickly in a single file.

As they were leaving, Ypsilanti Police Chief Ray Walton struck a somber note that gave the others pause. "I don't care how you slice it," he commented drily, "but this case sure has the same smell as the one last summer, the Marilyn Pindar homicide."

Jill Hersch was buried the next day in Plymouth at quiet services attended only by family and a few close friends. Dickie Shantz was allowed to attend, accompanied by police officers. At the burial site Mr. and Mrs. Hersch ignored Shantz as though he were not there. The mother looked wan and unsteady and needed support from her two older daughters, but she managed not to weep. The father stood stiffly erect, his face an impassive mask, eyes focused on nothing. Shantz, handcuffs removed for the funeral, covered his face and sobbed throughout the burial service.

Returned to the Ann Arbor jail, Shantz took the lie-detector test and was adjudged by the polygraph examiner to be clear of any participation in or knowledge of the death of his girl friend. On Thursday, the eleventh, he was released to the military police, who took him to an army prison receiving station in Detroit, whence he was remanded to a stockade to await punishment.

Eastern Michigan University's student newspaper, *The Eastern Echo,* announced the first offer of a reward—$300 for information leading to the apprehension and conviction of Jill Hersch's murderer. By August the reward fund was up to $7,800: to the *Echo*'s original $300 had been added $2,000 by the Detroit *News,* $5,000 pledged by a group of local merchants and businessmen, and $500 voted by the Ypsilanti City Council.

To the police, all of this became more and more academic as time went on. The rewards so far were evoking not a single promising nibble. "It makes you lose faith in human greed," noted one cynical Ann Arbor detective.

In mid-August, though, the police got a lead that seemed a little more substantial than most. Allegedly there were two students at E.M.U. who had been heard to claim that they had seen Jill Hersch on the night she disappeared, in the company of another male student whom they could identify.

Sergeant Bill Canada went to interview the two, assisted by Lieutenant Mel Fuller of the E.M.U. campus police. Both worked at the McKenny Union cafeteria, as Jill had. One was the student manager, twenty-year-old Ted Shaefer, a junior from Jackson; the other was one of the cashiers, whom Shaefer dated steadily, Eileen Gaffney of Ypsilanti, also twenty and a junior.

Canada and Fuller interviewed them separately, starting with Shaefer. Shaefer protested that he didn't want to get anybody in trouble. At first, all he would say was that on that Sunday night he and Eileen and a friend of his were riding around Ypsi, and near the university they'd noticed a couple walking together who might have been Jill Hersch and a fellow Shaefer knew from his fraternity. He couldn't swear to the identity of either one. After all, they were just passing by, and it was a dark street, and the three of them had been doing some drinking.

"Who was it *might* have been with Jill, *if* it was Jill?" Canada cut in sharply.

Shaefer looked miserable. "Look, I told you, I don't want to make trouble for . . ."

"What's his name?"

He swallowed. "He's a fellow I pledged with, a good guy, really . . . James Armstrong. But . . ."

"Where does he live?" Canada pressed.

"I don't know. He used to room at the frat house, Theta Chi, but he moved out and got his own room somewhere. But what I was going to say; it probably *wasn't* James, because I mentioned it the next time I saw him, and he said he didn't even know that particular girl. So you see, I was probably wrong about it being James. Or else, it wasn't Jill Hersch I saw with him."

"You knew Jill well enough to recognize her?" Canada asked.

"Well, yes, I think so, sure—we worked together here, you know."

"How about Eileen Gaffney? She knew her pretty well, too?"

"I suppose so, but . . ."

"What about the other fellow? Did he see anybody?"

"I don't know. He was driving. But he wouldn't know them anyway. He's just a friend I'd met around Ypsi, not from college. Please don't drag him into it."

"We'll get to him if we have to," Canada said. "Where was it that you saw this couple?"

"It must have been . . . I'd say about where Emmet Street crosses College Place. They were on the corner." Just a few steps from Jill's rooming house.

"And what time was this, about?"

"Oh . . ." Shaefer frowned, as though doing hasty mental calculations. "I guess it was around nine thirty."

Canada and Fuller exchanged glances. According to Jill's roommate, the two had been in the apartment then and neither had gone out until they'd left to walk to the bus stop. Unless Shaefer was in error, and it had actually been fifteen or twenty minutes earlier, about the time Jill was dropped off by her parents.

The detectives talked next with Eileen Gaffney, a pretty, sprightly girl. She spoke a bit more freely than had Shaefer, but, except for a couple of significant points, her story was the same as his. She and Ted and Dana Wilson—she volunteered the other fellow's name —had been drinking beer at her apartment, which she shared with Diane Sandstrom, who was dating Wilson. Diane worked nights as a waitress, and the three were to pick her up when she finished work.

They were on their way to the restaurant when they saw the couple at the intersection of Emmet and College Place. Eileen was sure the girl was Jill Hersch, but she could not be certain about the man with her. It *could* have been James Armstrong—Ted had seemed to think it was—but she hadn't got a good look at him, and she knew Armstrong only slightly. In any case, none of them gave it much thought at the time. They went on to meet Diane, and the four then went to Ted's fraternity house on Cross Street and drank some more beer and watched a late movie on television.

"Do you recall the approximate time you saw Jill and the fellow with her?" Canada asked.

"Well, let's see. Just before we picked up Diane— that must have been about eleven fifteen or eleven thirty."

Oh, fine, the detective thought: Here we have two individuals who semi-identify a subject, then each try to cover up for him, and wind up laying a two-hour time differential on us. And to top it off, at the time the second witness says she saw her, Jill was supposed to be on Cross Street about to get a ride in a red and

black car. In any case, the next step seemed to be
Armstrong.

James Nolan Armstrong, twenty-one, a senior at
E.M.U., had a room at 619 Emmet Street, on the
corner across College Place from 703 Emmet. He was
from Center Line, a suburb north of Detroit. An education major, he was taking summer courses to make
up credits. Canada and Fuller found him a wiry but
muscular, quite handsome six footer with clean-cut features and neatly trimmed dark hair. He seemed somewhat surprised by the policemen's inquiries but was
unhesitant and open about answering them.

He had a part-time clerical job at E.M.U.'s Mc-
Kenny Union, but he did not know the slain girl either
from the school or from the Emmet Street neighborhood. He'd lived there, in a room by himself, since
the spring. (Jill Hersch had moved into the house
across the street only three weeks before her death.)

Sunday evening, June 30? No, he'd not been in
Ypsilanti that entire weekend. He had spent it at home
in Center Line—they could ask his mother about that
—and returned well after midnight Monday morning.
They could check with his friend who lived across the
hall, Donald Baker, about the time he got in; he had
dropped in to rap with Donald for a few minutes before going to bed.

What kind of car did he have? Armstrong chuckled:
an old DeSoto, a real bomb that barely ran. But he
had a fairly new motorcycle. He could not think of
anybody he knew who drove a late-model black and
red car of any make.

Of course he knew Ted Shaefer, a frat brother, and
Eileen Gaffney, though less well. And he held them
no grudge for having brought his name up. Anybody
could make a mistake. And after all, they hadn't exactly gone rushing to the police to accuse him, had
they?

Armstrong had an engaging quality—although Mel
Fuller could not dismiss a vague sense that the young
man had worked just a little hard at being unabashed.

bag's contents. There was a gift inside, about the
shape of a shoe box, wrapped and tied with ribbons
and a bow. Taped to the wrapping was an unsealed
envelope with a birthday card; written inside was
*Dearest Mom—Sorry I'm late, but in a hundred years
you'll never know the difference. I love you, Jeanne.*
There was also a folder thick with typewritten pages,
apparently a student's themes and worksheets. Rif-
fling through them, Mrs. Stowe found no indication of
the owner's name. She didn't recall any "Jeanne" in
the neighborhood.

Remembering the time, she shooed Matt out before
he missed his bus. Then she sat back and looked the
bag over again. Odd to misplace something like this,
especially so out of the way. Her finger felt something
sticky near the bottom of the bag. Raising it, she saw
two dark red stains close together, each about the size
of a nickel. They weren't quite dry. She bolted upright. Blood!

Suddenly frightened, she dropped the bag and ran
to a window to watch after Matt. Some undefined
instinct told her to get the car and go after him, make
sure he got safely to school. Throwing on a coat, she
hurried outside, and backed the car out of the driveway.

She'd gone less than fifty yards when, abreast of
the cemetery gate across the road, her eye caught a
splash of yellow on the turf just inside the gate. She
stopped and peered over at it. Long and bulky, it
could almost be the outline of a body under some
kind of covering—but that was ridiculous! Cemeteries
don't just leave bodies lying around!

She got out of the car and approached cautiously.
It *was* a human figure! Female, three-quarters covered,
partly by a yellow raincoat and partly by a gray
blanket or burial sheet, she lay on her back, the left
arm bent, forearm resting across the eyes, the right
arm stretched above the head. Penny Stowe screamed.

Stumbling back to the car, she somehow got it into
gear and screeched off up Cross Street, blindly think-

ing only of her son Matt. But the school bus had gone;
he must have made it. She wheeled the car around
and raced back to phone the police.

They arrived in about twenty minutes, a patrol car
with a pair of uniformed troopers. As they bent over
the corpse, Penny Stowe put on her coat and, with a
shudder, went outside accompanied by her husband,
Jim. After a little while, a man in civilian clothes
joined the two troopers and examined the corpse.

Flipping open a small wallet, with a gold shield
and an ID card, he walked over to the Stowes. "I'm
Detective Sergeant Taylor, State Police. I understand
you discovered the body?"

"Yes," Mrs. Stowe said shivering. She gripped her
husband's arm.

Ken Taylor noted their names and address, then
asked Mrs. Stowe to relate exactly what had taken
place. He was very interested in the shopping bag that
the boy had found, and the Stowes led him into the
house. The gift box contained a pair of fluffy blue
bedroom slippers. The papers in the folder comprised
mainly legal themes and notes, such as a law student
might be assigned. Taylor studied the birthday card.
"Jeanne . . ." he mused. Then he asked to use the
phone.

"When I got in this morning, I noticed a TWX on
a missing girl out of Grand Haven. I had to leave
right away to come over here. Look it up for me,
will you?"

He glanced over his notes as he waited. Then:
"That's it . . . Jean Holder? J, E, A, N? . . . double-N,
E. Right. . . . Twenty-three . . . five-four, weight one-
ten. Short brown hair. . . . First-year law student at
U. of M. And she graduated from there, right? . . .
Okay, look, send a car over to the university and pick
up a copy of the last yearbook, and shoot it right over
to me here. . . . Yeah, it could be. Anybody else com-
ing from the DB? . . . Max is on his way? Good.
Thanks."

Taylor came back to the living room and questioned

the Stowes about whether they had heard or seen anything unusual in or around the cemetery during the night or early morning.

Jim Stowe only shook his head. His wife, however, volunteered that she had seen a car pull out of the cemetery about midnight. She had gone out to get a hamburger with a friend, and on the way back, as they passed the cemetery gate, a white station wagon pulled out and turned in the opposite direction. She couldn't distinguish the make or the occupant or occupants, but she had not paid much attention. Kids often parked around there at night.

When Taylor returned to the cemetery Detective Sergeant Max Little had arrived, and so had a handful of technical people from the Plymouth crime lab, who were going over the body and every inch of the ground around it. Little, a powerful figure the size of a defensive lineman, was clapping and massaging his bare hands, shoulders hunched against the damp cold, a giant, good-natured bulldog. "Beat me to the punch again," he greeted Taylor.

"I keep telling you, a good little man—"

"Any line on her yet?" Little asked, jerking his head toward the cemetery.

"I think so." Taylor told him about the birthday card signed "Jeanne" and the missing-girl bulletin on Jeanne Holder.

"Sounds good," Little said. "She was also wearing an ID bracelet with the name Jeanne."

"I've sent up to the U. of M. for a yearbook picture. That might nail it down." Taylor went back to examine the body. The raincoat and blanket had been removed and now she was revealed fully clothed except that her skirt was bunched up around her waist, perhaps from having been dragged to the spot, and the top of her panty hose was rolled down a few inches over the buttocks. One of her shoes rested on her lower abdomen, the toe on the pubic mound.

She probably had not been a bad-looking girl. Her shape was respectable, trim and small-boned, and her face must have been pleasant, with a perky turned-up nose. But it was hard to tell now, because her throat was grossly bloated from something knotted around it deep into the flesh. Her head lay at the foot of a low upright gravestone, and the forehead had a small brown hole in it.

"Which killed her?" Taylor wondered.

"Take your pick," said Little. "That's a nylon stocking around her neck. Could've choked a moose. But she also took two shots in the head, front and back. No gun around, but it looks like a twenty-two."

"Find anything else?" Taylor asked, glancing about.

"A tan overnight case with women's things in it— a few clothes, toilet stuff. She was on her way somewhere or coming back. No monogram. Also this, next to her." Little pulled a paperback copy of *Catch-22* out of his overcoat pocket.

"How long do you figure she's dead?"

"We've got the medical examiner on his way. But just by looking, I'd say no more than a few hours— sometime before dawn."

One of the crime lab detectives joined them. "Well, we've come up with a couple of things. No telling if they mean anything. A man's shoe print in a muddy spot near the body. And some fairly fresh tire tracks right outside the gate. We're making plaster casts." Little and Taylor did not show enthusiasm.

"The tire tracks could be anybody's," Taylor complained, "and I'll lay odds the footprint turns out to be one of our own."

A trooper who'd been holding back some on-lookers strode toward them. "Excuse me, sergeant," he said to Little, tossing a thumb over his shoulder, "there's a newspaper reporter back there wants to get in. Ypsilanti *Press*. He's been dogging me."

Little looked past him up Cross Street, frowning. "I've been expecting the vultures, but this one's an early bird. Must be hungry."

Taylor grinned. "Must be the new police reporter the

Press took on—Cobb. His first homicide. I'll bet he can taste it. Maybe he's earned first bite."

"Sure, why not." Little blew on his huge hands. "Christ, we're freezing our cookies, we might as well have company. Okay, send him down," he ordered the trooper. "And hey," he called after him, "check on the damn meat wagon. We don't want to be standing around here all day."

Once the local medical examiner had made his examination and an ambulance finally had come and removed the body to the U. of M. Medical Center, the policemen—joined now by some Wayne County sheriff's deputies—spent the remainder of the morning canvassing the neighborhood adjacent to Pleasantview Cemetery, which consisted of not much more than a few lightly inhabited square blocks east of the Stowe house.

No one reported hearing or seeing anything unusual. The only thing worth noting came from some youngsters who had noticed a late-model green station wagon cruising slowly around the perimeter of the cemetery at dusk the previous evening. But they hadn't seen who was in it or noticed, later, where it had gone.

So the police had two ephemeral station wagons, one white, the other green; an overnight case; a shopping bag; a paperback book; and a footprint and tire tracks—all probably useless, except that which may have helped identify the victim. A trooper had brought the 1968 University of Michigan Yearbook, and the smiling likeness in it of graduating senior Jeanne Lisa Holder of Muskegon, Michigan, did bear a resemblance to the puffed face of the young woman stretched out lifeless in Pleasantview Cemetery. For the moment, that was as much as they had.

The autopsy at the U. of M. Medical Center, by pathologist Robert Hendrix, determined that the girl had died of the gunshot wounds in the head; and the weapon was a .22—two slugs were removed from her skull, although they were too misshapen to serve any

ballistics purpose. The garroting had come after the
fatal shots. The stocking used, he noted, was probably
not her own, judging by (a) its size and (b) the fact
that she wore panty hose. A sanitary pad was found
still in place, so the girl probably had not been sexually molested.

The pathologist put the time of death at no earlier
than midnight, no later than two or three hours thereafter. From this the police could only conclude that,
inasmuch as the two gun shots had ended her life, it
had to have been done elsewhere than in that quiet
cemetery. And that her body had been delivered and
laid out there sometime after 2:00 A.M Friday.

Jeanne Holder had been expected in Muskegon early
Thursday night. It was a brief semester recess at the
University of Michigan Law School, and she'd planned
to spend a long weekend at home, partly to make up
for having forgotten her mother's birthday. Jeanne had
called long distance the previous night to say that she
had been lucky to line up a ride—Muskegon being
some 165 miles northwest of Ann Arbor—and depend-
ing on what time Thursday they left she might even
make it home for a late dinner. She didn't say who
was giving her the ride.

When Thursday evening passed without word from
her, however, the parents grew restive, and after 11:00
P.M., her father, Dr. Donald Holder, a dentist, put in a
call to her room at the U. of M. Law Quadrangle.
There was no answer. Then he placed another call to
Jeanne's steady boyfriend, Paul Weiskopf, a thirty-
five-year-old graduate instructor at U. of M. Law
School.

Paul answered. "Dr. Holder! Hello! Did Jeanne get
there all right?"

"Not yet, Paul. And she hasn't called. We're starting
to get a little worried. I hoped you might know something."

"I'm sorry, sir, I don't." He paused to think. "She
was still here about six this evening. I dropped by the

Law Quad to see if she'd left yet, and she was all ready, packed and everything, waiting for her ride. She was looking forward to getting home," he added.

"Do you know whom she was getting a lift from?"

"To tell the truth, I never asked. You know she had put up a notice in the Student Union a few days ago, requesting a ride to Muskegon, and all she said to me was that it had worked out fine, she'd heard from someone who was driving out that way. I guess I should have asked who. Sorry."

"But she *was* set to leave around six?" Dr. Holder pressed.

"Right. When I left her—I had a tutoring session— I figured she'd be taking off any minute. I wouldn't worry, sir. They probably just fell behind schedule, and of course it does take a few hours from here to Muskegon. And what with the rotten weather and all—I'm sure she'll be there any time now."

"Yes . . . well, thank you, Paul. Please let me know if you hear anything. We'll do the same, if you like."

"I'd appreciate that. My best to Mrs. Holder."

"Yes, of course. Good night."

Dr. Holder had never felt easy with Paul Weiskopf. It wasn't that he and his wife actually disliked him— he was intelligent and, with them, always pleasant and a complete gentleman—but somehow, for reasons they never could quite isolate, they disapproved of Jeanne's growing attachment to the man. And of his obvious influence over her. They were sure it was Paul who had led Jeanne from serious study of law into the troublesome radical-left politics boiling up in Ann Arbor. They'd told themselves that he was too old, too worldly for Jeanne. But both knew there was something else about him that they were pained to articulate, that was part of it—that eastern liberal, somehow superior, irreverent Jewishness of his.

When Paul Weiskopf had finished talking with Dr. Holder, he found himself unnaturally depressed. He knew it would never be easy for him with the Holders. They never seemed to bend beyond civility. He'd sensed why, and he wouldn't have stood for it but for Jeanne. Such a marvelous woman—such depth, such a capacity for giving, for loving! She would need all that will and strength to tell her parents that she was going to *marry* Paul Weiskopf! This was to have been the weekend—the moment of truth. The two of them had been working up to it for weeks. Had her resolve finally crumbled en route?

Weiskopf reached for the telephone again and dialed Jeanne's room at the Law Quad. It was just midnight. After many rings, he hung up.

At 1:30 A.M. Friday morning, Dr. Holder telephoned the Muskegon police. The officer who took the call listened to the problem, then suggested that Dr. Holder contact the nearest State Police post, which was at Grand Haven, about fifteen miles south of Muskegon. They had better facilities there. But they would put out something on their own radio cars, he assured the anxious father.

Dr. Holder rang the Grand Haven post. The trooper on duty, Sergeant Ferguson, took down the information with only pertinent comment, then explained to Dr. Holder what would be done.

His daughter's name and description would be fed into the post's L.E.I.N. computer—a link in the new statewide Law Enforcement Information Network, which stockpiled data from and for all police agencies throughout Michigan in a master computer at the State Police headquarters at East Lansing. Should any subsequent report regarding the girl come in from anywhere in the network, it would be correlated and pinpointed. Further, Sergeant Ferguson said, direct messages would be sent from Grand Haven via either radio or teletype to all State Police posts between Muskegon and Ann Arbor-Ypsilanti, to be on the alert for the young woman.

So it was that within an hour the known facts about Jeanne Holder had been stored in the state capital computer and alerts about the missing girl were jammed onto desk spindles at posts across the state . . . including Ypsilanti, where Detective Sergeant Ken Taylor had glanced at it when arriving for work at 7:30 A.M., and remembered it a short while later at a small, sad cemetery in Wayne County.

By midmorning, when identification of the dead woman as Jeanne Holder was reasonably certain, the Ypsi post so advised Grand Haven. The post commander there, Lieutenant Art Baker, took it upon himself to drive up to Muskegon to inform the Holder family.

Nothing could be more crushing to any family than to have a police officer appear at the front door and grimly announce that a beloved child has been taken. Jeanne Holder had been just twenty-three. She'd been graduated in 1968 from the University of Michigan in the top 10 percent of her class and a week ago she'd been admitted to the Phi Beta Kappa national honor society. She'd always wanted to be a great lawyer. But now—she'd been not only taken, but destroyed. How could any father and mother, wondered Lieutenant Baker, ever be prepared to defend against such horror?

And yet, after reeling from the first shock, Dr. and Mrs. Holder managed to make Lieutenant Baker's job easier. Somehow they collected themselves; seeming to draw reserve strength from one another, they regrouped and retained control. It happened in a matter of seconds, before the policeman's eyes, and it was marvelous to behold.

The police naturally concentrated initial attention on Paul Weiskopf. Though few cops might admire his politics, his interrogators could not help being impressed with him personally. He was tall, erect, dark but clean-cut, straight-spoken. Possessed of an unselfconscious clarity, he was forthright and patient, even with the gruff, suspicious Max Little of the State Police, in telling of his deepening relationship with Jeanne and of his acute awareness of her parents' objections.

As they talked, Sergeant Little tried, with veiled
questions, to sound the depth of the man's emotional
reaction to the sudden, violent loss of his fiancée. Had
he submerged great inner turmoil? Was he torn up inside? Would he not rest until Jeanne's slaying was
avenged? But Weiskopf maintained full composure,
never wavered, in fact gratuitously reminded the policeman about his responsibility not to let righteous
zeal trample on the constitutional rights of whoever
might finally be accused, whenever.

Sergeant Little was left, in spite of himself, with a
curious mixture of admiration and disapproval. Strange
breed, these egghead liberals.

In any case, Weiskopf's stated movements checked
out satisfactorily—as did his previous background,
which was found to be without taint—and, while not
yet discharged as an official "suspect," Paul Weiskopf
generally was viewed as an unlikely killer.

The key to the puzzle seemed to be the identity of
the person for whom Jeanne had been waiting to pick
her up. It was disconcerting that she had not mentioned
her benefactor's name at least to her fiancé. Neither
had she confided in any of her fellow students. All any
of them who were interviewed knew was that Jeanne
had posted her handwritten notice requesting a ride a
few days earlier on the bulletin board in the Student
Union Building, and that later she'd been happy
about having received an affirmative response—but
without ever, as far as anyone could recall, mentioning
a name.

As at most universities, the Michigan Student Union
was the hub of campus activity. A constant flow of students and visitors passed in and out every day, just to
while away time, to snack, to study, or to meet. The
person-to-person communications center was the four-
by-eight-foot free-standing bulletin board in the lower
lobby, both sides of which were festooned with notices
and personal messages. Almost everybody on campus
checked this board periodically, and one of Jeanne's
friends even remembered seeing the notice she had put

up: *Would appreciate hearing from anyone who might be driving to Muskegon or vicinity, any time Thursday (3/20/69)*, with her name, Law Quad dorm, room number, and telephone extension. Any one of thousands of board watchers could have responded.

The Law Quadrangle was an impressive enclave within the campus, fine old Gothic-style buildings constructed around a square of pleasant lawn and trees and crisscrossing walks. The outer flanks of the Quad included the dining hall, imposing law library and main classroom building, and L-shaped in the interior corner were the three-story stone dormitories. Jeanne Holder had had a single room on the third floor of C section.

Nobody had seen her leave the dorm Thursday evening—indeed, the police could find no one but Paul Weiskopf who had seen or talked with her since early afternoon that day. Loretta Fowles, also a first-year student who lived on the ground floor of C, had chatted briefly with her classmate after lunch at the State Street entrance to the Quad. Jeanne had appeared in a bustling good humor, saying that she still had so much to do before getting away for home. Another student, Lynn Goldman, whose room was one floor below Jeanne's, had played bridge there with three friends from seven until about ten Thursday evening, and they'd not heard so much as a sound from upstairs the entire time; it was only after the others had gone—maybe an hour or two later, as she'd lain in bed reading—that Miss Goldman had heard Jeanne's telephone ringing, two different times, she thought; both times unanswered.

So it seemed plausible that Jeanne must have left her room some time after six, when Weiskopf had kissed her good-by, and before seven, after which the foursome below had detected no movements or other sounds above. She would certainly have been alive then, according to the postmortem hypothesis of time of death.

Had she left in the company of the one who had answered her notice—and if so, of her own volition?—

or had he (she?) telephoned or sent arrangements for meeting elsewhere?

Although the police had made an early, perfunctory check of Jeanne Holder's room, detectives returned on Friday night for a more minute examination, searching for any clue that might point toward the mystery person. Sergeants Little and Taylor were joined by two of Captain Olson's men from the Ann Arbor P.D.

Hardly had they begun scratching about than it seemed they'd struck paydirt.

"Ooo-eee!" yipped Taylor, bent over a small desk against one wall. "Lookee here!"

Lying open across the top of a neat desk was the Ann Arbor-Ypsilanti Area telephone directory. Hidden underneath it Taylor had found a small square of white notepaper, and on it was scrawled in pencil: *David Hanson, Lvg. 6:30 pm.*

"Oh, beautiful!" breathed Little over his partner's shoulder.

"Wait," said Taylor expectantly, "it may even be better!" Bending closer, he scanned the small type of the directory pages. The book was open in the Ann Arbor section, in the *H*s; in the upper left corner of page 50 was *Hancock—Harris.* His forefinger raced down the list of names and stopped in the middle of the second column. "Hanson, David!" Taylor cried. "Look, it's even got a check mark next to it!"

The address and number were that of a fraternity house on South State Street, little more than a block from the Law Quadrangle. The name was the only David Hanson. There were no Hansens with an *e.*

"How about this, Max!" Taylor grinned. "It has to be clean living. We've got it made!"

"Could be," the burly detective allowed with a smile. "Let's see, though."

Though a Friday night, because of the school midterm recess there were only a scattering of members and some of their dates lounging about the sitting room of the two-story, Victorian-style frat house when just before 11:00 P.M. the four men burst noisily through the unlocked entryway. The startled young people leaped up with shouts, a girl shrieking, a beer can clattering to the hardwood floor, a glass breaking.

Amidst the confused hubbub of protest, the intruders' leader, a massive figure, made himself heard: "Police! Everybody just stay put!" Max Little held aloft an open wallet from which glinted a gold badge.

The "storming" had been decided upon so as to minimize both planned alibis and the opportunity for anyone forewarned to make himself scarce—specifically one David Hanson. If Hanson *was* lingering about, perhaps feeling complacent, the surprise might just jolt him into some precipitous giveaway.

As the other detectives fanned out through the ground floor, Little watched the faces of the young men and women. Most were bewildered, some frightened, some already beginning to turn resentful. Little had taken the precaution of securing a bench warrant, which he now slipped out of his jacket pocket and exhibited.

"We're looking for someone named David Hanson," Little announced.

There was some excited murmuring, then a young male voice said: "He's not here."

"Where is he?"

"He's in a theater group, and they're doing a show tonight."

"Where?"

"Up on campus—I think." The speaker hesitated, looking around.

A girl picked it up: "The Trueblood Theater."

Little glanced at one of the Ann Arbor detectives, who nodded and went outside. "Okay," Little said, "we'd like to see everyone's ID, please."

When it was established that no one present was David Hanson, while the remaining detective and an Ann Arbor uniformed patrolman who had been summoned began to search the rest of the house, Little and Taylor were directed to Hanson's room. It was small, not overfurnished yet not uncomfortable, the walls colorfully decorated with theatrical posters, and the two experienced investigators "tossed" it from top to bottom within minutes. They found nothing remotely connecting David Hanson with Jeanne Holder. (Having sifted the contents of Hanson's personal wastebasket, Taylor thought to direct another patrolman standing by on the street to go through the frat house's trash cans in a side alley. That also produced nothing.)

Downstairs again, Little broke into the buzz of speculation by asking if anyone there was particularly close to Hanson. Once more there came a chorus of murmurs, before one tall young fellow spoke out firmly: "We're *all* friends of Dave's—but like, I don't think any of us here is *particularly* close to him, I mean, more than anyone else."

"All right." Little tried another tack: "Were any of you with Hanson last night?"

There was a pause, then somebody else said, "I had a couple of beers with Dave, late—"

"What time?"

"Oh, midnight, maybe later. We rapped for a while, till about one, then we packed it in."

"How about earlier?" the detective asked the group at large, his spirit a little deflated.

They looked at one another uncertainly, and it was the tall one who'd spoken earlier who answered again: "I saw him as he was leaving after supper. That was a little past six thirty."

David Hanson, Lvg. 6:30 pm. Little's hopes stirred again. His practiced eye sized the fellow up. Direct, not antagonistic, concerned—probably reliable, more or less. "Why are you so sure about the time?" he asked.

"Because just after he'd left there was a call for him, and I took it. Actually, it was a wrong number. I mean, they wanted a David Hanson, but obviously it was the wrong one."

"How's that?"

"Well, it was this girl, and she said David Hanson had promised her a ride home—I forget where she said, but I remember thinking it was quite a ways—and he was supposed to pick her up at six thirty and it was already past that. My watch said about twenty-five to seven. But the thing was, I told her she must mean some other Dave Hanson, because I knew *our* Dave was out for the evening and there was no way he could have promised to drive anybody anywhere."

"Why not?" asked Little, brows knitting. "Where did he say he was going?"

"Well, I knew where he was going—like tonight, to the theater. The show he's in is on every night, through the weekend. Last night was their second performance, I think. Dave's nutty about theater. He wouldn't stand that up."

The one who later had drunk beer with Hanson now chimed in: "That's where Dave had just come from when I met him."

Little and Ken Taylor exchanged losing glances. Little sighed. "Have any of you ever heard of a young woman named Jeanne Holder?"

Heads shook slowly. But then: "I think that's what the girl on the phone said," the tall fellow volunteered. "The 'Jeanne' sounds right, at least. I'm not really sure of the second name. Anyway, I'd never heard of her and I don't recall Dave ever mentioning the name."

It was not easy to give up summarily. Taylor asked: "What kind of car does Hanson drive?"

"A green Volkswagen."

The *coup de grace* to the sudden collapse of this phase of the investigation was applied when the Ann Arbor detective returned alone from the Trueblood Theater. Hanson *had* been at the theater, and on stage, all the previous evening. The group was the university's Gilbert and Sullivan Society, and they were putting on *Iolanthe* Wednesday through Saturday. Hanson had the role of Private Willis. The director said he was one of their hardest workers. Hanson himself, who was an undergraduate senior from the Detroit area, said he did not know a Jeanne Holder, nor anyone in the Law School, and had not answered any request for a lift to Muskegon.

The policemen departed the fraternity house with apologies. "So much for clean living," grumbled Max Little to Ken Taylor on the way out.

Other than "David Hanson," the police had not one clue. Despite tedious legwork, from the Law Quad to the Student Union and across the U. of M. campus, into the contiguous streets of Ann Arbor proper, no one could be found who had seen Jeanne Holder, by herself or with anybody else, after 6:00 P.M. Thursday —it was as though the girl had left the university in a puff of smoke and materialized again, in a heap, the following morning a dozen miles to the east.

Still, on the face of it, this David Hanson did not seem a bad lead, even after the first bid had been shot down. "David Hanson" was not guaranteed to be Jeanne Holder's killer, but how many times does a victim-to-be leave a note naming one who *might* be her assassin? The fact that she had telephoned the only listing of that name in the Ann Arbor directory, and had found *that* David Hanson not to be the one she was looking for, made it plain that she herself did not know the man, beyond his name, and that locating *the* David Hanson would not be quite so simple as the police, naturally, had been ready to wish.

Now the field of inquiry had broadened—to what extent was yet to be seen. There were three other David Hansons in the local telephone directory, which included listings for eight peripheral towns and villages in addition to Ann Arbor and Ypsilanti: Two of these were in Ypsi and one in Milan, a few miles south of Ann Arbor. Also, a rundown of the University of Michigan enrollment turned up a dozen more David Hansons. So far that made fifteen in the immediate area. Still to be canvassed was Eastern Michigan University . . . and—perhaps—the rest of Washtenaw

County . . . Wayne County (after all, that's where the girl's body had been found!) . . . and, God forbid, even the whole state of Michigan?

The chances were, of course, that pinning down *the* David Hanson would not be as unmanageable as all that. Whoever had answered Jeanne Holder's appeal for a lift in all probability had learned of it from her note on the bulletin board, which did seem to narrow prospects down to someone with access to the U. of M. Student Union. This still did not assure that the subject had to be a U. of M. student or a local resident: It was common for itinerant students from anywhere to home in on the Student Union. Or it could have been *anybody* passing through. But the odds did seem to favor the logical assumption.

The only problem with all this rationalization was, as the suspicion even now lurked in the backs of the investigators' minds, that the name "David Hanson" might be a phony.

Nonetheless, it was the one solid lead they had to start from, and so over the weekend they launched the painstaking quest.

As for the type of individual they were looking for —the killer, whatever he called himself—there was little enough on which to base sound speculation. Either he'd chosen the Holder girl at random; or he did know her or knew of her, and perhaps she him (although doubtless not as "David Hanson"). Either it was his intent from the outset to destroy his prey— which certainly made him a dangerous psychotic; or his initial compulsion had been the need for self-gratification with a female, but somehow he'd lost control—which made him no less psychotic. Or perhaps he'd really intended to give the girl a ride west to Muskegon (but then, how did they end up in Wayne County, to the east?), and something had transpired en route that set him off—which made him no less dangerous, maybe more so. Had the killer been prepared to force intercourse upon her, only to abandon the effort upon realizing that she was in her period?

The question that this reasonable deduction did not answer was whether she was already dead at the moment, or it was this discovery that drove him to murderous retaliation. And what was the meaning of the nylon stocking tied so savagely around the girl's neck *after* she was dead?

The police had to consider whether such perversities could have been ritualistic, indicative of some type of sadism or sex fetishism. They would start plumbing statewide files of previously arrested deviates.

And was there any significance in Jeanne Holder's head having been positioned at the foot of that particular grave marker, of one William Downing, Sr., dead more than half a century? One member of the Downing family of Denton Township was found to survive, an eighty-five-year-old daughter of William, Sr. and Leona, but she could conjure no memory of the name Holder out of the past.

Finally, the killer owned, anyway had used to kill, a .22-caliber pistol. (Ballistics were of no help in identifying the flattened slugs removed from the victim's skull, but here again, at least Michigan gun registrations could be checked at East Lansing for a "David Hanson.") Two shots had to have been fired from that weapon someplace in the vicinity between Ann Arbor and Denton Township, late Thursday night or early Friday morning. It was always possible that news coverage of the slaying would prompt some citizens to come forward who might remember having heard any explosive reports during those hours.

That was about all the police could do: Put in the required legwork, follow standard procedure as far as it would take them, and hope for a break—or an informant.

A funeral service for Jeanne Holder was held in Muskegon Monday afternoon, March 24. Almost four hundred persons crowded into the small Clock Chapel, including a number of her friends from the University of Michigan—among them, alone, an ashen

Paul Weiskopf. The pastor of the First Presbyterian Church told the Holder family and the assemblage that only their faith could afford any comfort "in this irrational act of violence. This girl, while she lived," he said, "did become part of each of our lives, and that at least can never pass away."

Less than twenty-four hours later, back in Ann Arbor, the debauched corpse of another young female was discovered in woods in an outlying section of the city —not a quarter of a mile from the spot where Jill Hersch's body had been dumped the previous summer.

The girl was nude, her clothes piled neatly by her side. She had been beaten to death.

CHAPTER 6

ANN ARBOR HAD been soaked by freezing rain most of Monday and through the night. By daybreak of March 25, the rain had stopped, but the sunless air stayed dank and chill.

Out in the still rustic northeast corner of the city, a construction survey crew glumly returned to work in a heavily wooded section off Earhart Road, between Glacier Way and Geddes Road. Planned as an exclusive colony of custom-built homes, a network of paved lanes and access drives already curled through the half-mile-square area, and storm sewers were in; but only one homesite so far had been completed, and it was not yet occupied.

At about 11:15 A.M. one of the surveyors, Adam Tendler of Saline, was picking his way through the dense wet brush of a slope some seventy-five feet to the rear of the lone house, measuring a marking point to be aligned with a mark previously set at the next homesite one hundred yards across Waldenwood Drive. Intent upon his perspectives, he stumbled over something bulky obscured among the thick layer of soggy leaves. Reflexively he glanced back at the ground behind, started to look away, then jerked his head around again.

It was an arm.

Tendler edged back, his heart leaping. He swiped away the clustered leaves at his feet, and was gripped by spasms of nausea. It was the corpse of a girl, the flexed left arm, which had tripped him up, raised above the head. The head was horrible, swollen out of proportion, and oozing like a diseased melon. The face, turned away from him, appeared bluish and the cheekbone looked crushed in. Her naked torso was covered with ugly welts. Between her legs, which were spread wide, the right one outstretched, the other bent at the knee, protruded a gnarled branch of a tree. Blood was caked all over the torn loins. . . .

Tendler stumbled down the slope, and when he reached the road he started running. He didn't give a thought to the others of the survey crew, he wanted only to get away from there. He got to his car and gunned it down Earhart Road, with no conscious idea of where he was going.

He was almost to Geddes Road when his mind began to focus. The police. He ought to tell the police.

It was the Ann Arbor P.D.'s second homicide of this nature in just under nine months. And the apparent similarities between this and the Jill Hersch murder were disturbing. Different specific methods of killing, noted Detective Sergeant Bill Canada, but the general *modus operandi* was too damned similar. Young woman, sexually abused, nude (clothes piled nearby), found out in the sticks in the same part of town, practically in the same unfinished subdivision.

It had seemed to Canada, from a superficial once-over of the death scene when he and Sergeant Don Carnahan had first arrived, that the girl must have been killed elsewhere. There was no blood about, and no indication that she might have crawled there from any place nearby. The heavy rains could have obliterated such tracks, of course—there were no others of any kind in evidence except the fresh ones of surveyor Adam Tendler—but signs of blood would have remained.

Canada's surmise was soon confirmed by the State Police crime lab people and by the early findings of the county medical examiner. The girl, who was in her mid- to late-teens, was five feet four, slender, about 115 pounds, with long light-brown hair. She had been dead twenty-four to thirty-six hours—putting the time of death at roughly between Sunday night and mid-morning Monday. She had taken as bad a beating as any of them had ever seen. Her crushed skull was a massive compound fracture, caused by continuous battering by some heavy, blunt instrument, as yet undetermined. Her torso and upper legs were covered with raw welts, as though she had been flogged by a belt with a large buckle. Imprinted across her breasts were the marks of what could have been straps, indicating that the victim had been bound tightly and was immobile during the vicious flogging. The investigators were aghast to find, stuffed deep into the girl's mouth, back almost to the windpipe, a piece of dark blue cloth.

But the most atrocious feature of the savagery remained the rough limb, apparently ripped from a small tree, and jammed into the girl's vagina. It had been driven some eight inches up her vaginal canal. Sergeant Canada hoped she'd been unconscious, or dead, before that had been done to her.

Her clothes lay near and partially under the corpse: a blue T-shirt, faded hip-hugger dungarees, beltless, dark blue zippered windbreaker, scuffed brown loafers, each of these next to the proper foot as though placed so. There were no undergarments.

There being no inhabitants in the near vicinity and little traffic around there after dark, the police did not expect to learn much by reconnoitering local residents. The closest was about a half mile away. But they went ahead anyway and did manage to pick up a couple of notes, however questionable their worth at the moment.

A University of Michigan student whose home was on Geddes Road said that on Sunday night between nine and nine thirty, as he'd been walking his dog, he'd heard in the distance—from the general direction of the subdivision site—an eerie cry, like a long screech, possibly a human scream. Just the once; he'd heard nothing more and seen no one.

And another resident, a woman, whose home across Geddes Road had an unobstructed view of Earhart Road where it ended at Geddes, where vehicles coming down Earhart had to turn right or left, reported having noticed two cars come to that T Sunday night: One was a red sedan, a Pontiac she thought, and the other a small white coupe, some foreign make; the red one had turned onto Geddes, the white one right. She'd had no reason to note the plate numbers, and was not sure about the time, though it was before she retired, sometime between ten and eleven.

Almost from the discovery of the victim, Sergeant Canada had a fair idea who she might be. The previous day, the Wayne County Sheriff's Department had distributed a bulletin describing a sixteen-year-old girl (formerly of Romulus, eleven or twelve miles east of Ypsilanti) who had been reported missing over the weekend.

Her name was Mary Grace Clemson, and she was known to the police as a narcotics user and small-time pusher. Her favorite haunts were around the campuses in Ypsi and Ann Arbor. Sergeant Canada and the Ann Arbor P.D. and some of the other local police agencies also were aware that Mary Grace Clemson had been used as an informant by Wayne County sheriff's investigators.

The body now lying in the University of Michigan morgue seemed to fit the description in the Wayne County bulletin—the physical dimensions, coloring, and age were about right, and the apparel pretty much

matched what Mary Grace Clemson reportedly was
wearing when she left home for Ypsilanti on Saturday; unaccounted for were only some jewelry—a pair
of earrings and a cheap "engagement" ring—and a
fringed buckskin purse.

Ann Arbor notified Wayne County, and on Tuesday
afternoon two detectives drove out from the Westland
sheriff's station to make formal identification of the
victim. They were policewomen who had known Mary
Grace Clemson: Detective Beverley Scannell and her
young black partner, Detective Rosemary Newsome.

Beverley Scannell, an attractive, outgoing woman
of thirty-five, who after thirteen years' service had
mastered an on-duty police manner of crisp assurance,
was surprised to find herself so moved by the ghastly
condition of the girl's body.

She, more than Rosemary or any of their colleagues,
had gotten close to Mary Grace in the past five months
—or as close as anyone of authority had been permitted to get. Although she had harassed the girl, even
pressured her into turning informant, Beverley had
felt that a certain empathy had developed between
them. Mary Grace, for a while at least, had seemed
to sense that the policewoman sincerely wanted to help
her as a fellow human being.

But there had not been enough time. Now, whatever good had been in her lay without life, crushed
out mercilessly. On the way back to Westland late
Tuesday, as her partner drove, the detective quietly
wept.

Beverley Scannell had first encountered Mary Grace
Clemson in the fall of 1968. She had taken a call at
the Westland station from a counselor at nearby
Romulus High School. The teacher and the school
nurse had a girl student, a fifteen-year-old sophomore,
who, after progressive troublemaking and truancy, had
admitted to them that she had serious problems with
drugs and was now asking them for help. Would Detective Scannell come over and talk to her?

The girl was afraid to be seen with any police person in or around the school, so they met at a county office building a few miles away. Briefed by the two women, Beverley learned that the girl, with a superior intelligence rating, an IQ of 123, had been a better-than-average student, but lately had utterly changed character, becoming more and more unreliable, irresponsible, hostile; she had missed so many classes she was in danger of being chucked out of the school altogether. And now this terrible business with drugs.

The detective sent the two away and took Mary Grace into a vacant office. She was physically well developed, rather pretty in a poutish way, but it didn't take long to determine that the girl, even at her age, was well on her way to becoming a hard case. She admitted readily to Beverley that she'd used pot and acid since she was thirteen, and that now she was also into pills—speed, uppers, downers—and occasionally mescaline. It had all been fun and games, just kicks at first, but now, she said, she was getting worried about herself. She didn't want to get hooked. She needed someone who knew the score to lead her out of the trap.

What about her family? Mary Grace had frowned, grown morose. She didn't have much family life. Her parents were older, square; they didn't understand her, they didn't pretend to try. And she hated where they lived. Romulus was a nondescript village about midway between Detroit and Ypsilanti, jammed in amidst large industrial plants.

With increasing frequency, the girl would leave home and stay with friends in Belleville or Westland, or Ypsilanti, or even Detroit. Yet not once had her parents found her waywardness disagreeable enough to take a firm stand. She was canny enough to keep in touch with them usually, to say that she was "just visiting" here or had "taken a job" there, and she was fine and behaving herself and don't worry about her. And, it seemed, they had accepted her flimflam, if not without some questions then evidently without serious reservations.

From what Mary Grace told her—plus what she herself was to find out independently—Beverley was able to piece together a graphic picture of the girl's accelerating involvement with drugs. It had started around the high school, and up at the huge Westland Shopping Plaza where a lot of kids hung around— first with a little grass and then maybe a few pills, the amphetamines that seemed so easy to come by.

Then Mary Grace, whose tastes and capacities were further advanced than her peers', had broadened her horizons—branching out to Ypsilanti with the Eastern Michigan University crowd. There she found older, hipper kids, who knew what was happening. Some of them had communal pads in Ypsi or Ann Arbor, where a bunch could crash for a night or a weekend and trip out in a kind of atonal harmony.

Mary Grace's tutor in her conversion to this new life style had been her friend Sherry, a seventeen-year-old girl from Belleville who'd dropped out of Belleville High at the start of her senior year and married her nineteen-year-old boyfriend, Jerome Fantosi. Jerome was usually unemployed, but they managed to scrape by in a dingy little flat in Ypsilanti. Sherry and Jerome had introduced Mary Grace to their friend Miller Agee, one of the hip crowd they ran with. Agee, seventeen, also a high-school dropout, was tall and dark, intelligent, introspective, and his attitude was the hell with the world. He and Mary Grace believed they'd fallen truly in love.

Yet even this desperately needed emotional attachment had not halted Mary Grace's slide into drug dependency. By fifteen, she had diverted her natural ingenuity and boldness into dealing—on a relatively modest scale, but enough not only to keep her and her new friends supplied, but to turn an occasional profit as well.

Detective Scannell felt a certain sympathy for the girl, and over the next several months she tried to help Mary Grace out of her destructive cycle. But each time she thought she had broken through the girl's defensive barrier and convinced her to go straight, Mary Grace would slip back into her old patterns.

In January 1969, Mary Grace was hospitalized with what her parents believed to be a severe case of flu. Beverley found out easily enough that it was actually an overdose of narcotics, either heroin or cocaine. She tried to convince the Clemsons at last that their daughter had a serious problem. They refused to believe any such thing; they were outraged at the detective's "meddling."

In March, Detectives Scannell and Newsome again were called to Romulus High School: Mary Grace Clemson was suspected now of selling dope to other students. They confronted her and found amphetamines in her wallet. That was it for Beverley. She arrested Mary Grace.

Mr. and Mrs. Clemson pleaded for her. They were selling their house in Romulus and moving north to Flint. It was a chance for Mary Grace to make a fresh start. Couldn't the policewoman give her a break this one time? Beverley considered. She doubted Mary Grace would ever straighten out, but at least a change of environment would remove her from the poisoning influence of the pack she traveled with. Beverley agreed to drop the charge with one provision: If Mary Grace were ever again picked up in Wayne County, they would throw the book at her.

The Clemsons moved to Flint at the end of the second week in March.

Almost at once, however, it became evident that the Clemsons were not going to be much more successful controlling their wayward daughter in the new location than in the old. Mary Grace had no intention of being cut off from her friends—especially from Miller Agee, who was now her fiancé, having given her a plain gold-plated ring the day after her sixteenth birthday. Three times during their first week in Flint, Mary

Grace made her way down to Ypsilanti. The third time she did not come back.

As investigators subsequently traced the slain girl's last known movements, it was learned that Mr. Clemson himself had transported Mary Grace from Flint that last time. It was Friday evening, March 21. Alf Clemson had driven a rented U-Haul truck down to Romulus to retrieve some furnishings left behind at the old house, and his daughter had gone along to help him.

They'd got to the Romulus house after dark and as her father rummaged about, Mary Grace went out to look up, as she put it, some of her former neighborhood chums. Instead, however, she managed to hitch her way to Ypsilanti.

Unable to find Miller Agee or the Fantosis at their usual haunts, she went to the Woodland Hills apartment she and her friends so often frequented, occupied by two young men, Ed Carroll and Al Tabor. This was a kind of safe house for Mary Grace and the others, snug and secure and off the beaten paths. More than anywhere else, it was there that Mary Grace felt part of her "family."

Alf Clemson was asleep by the time Mary Grace got back to Romulus that night, and when he awakened her in the morning he was not in a cheerful mood. To his demands about where she'd been so late, she would answer only "around."

Mary Grace was not much help that morning. While her father crated and lugged things into the truck she went across the street to a girl friend's house to phone Miller Agee. But he was not in, and she told his mother that she would try again later. Then she phoned a boy named Robin Hobby, a friend and neighbor of Miller's, asking him to get word to Miller that she hoped to be around later in the day and would be in touch about plans for that evening. "Tell Mil I expect my old man to give me a lift," she chortled. "*My father!* Isn't that a kicker!"

By the time Mary Grace returned, most of the packing and loading had been done, and her father had isolated himself behind a wall of angry silence. From midmorning into the afternoon, only a few words passed between them. Mary Grace didn't care much, though she made a token effort to be cheery so as to work up to the favor she was going to ask.

It was nearly 3:00 P.M. before they were ready to leave. Mr. Clemson drove the van onto Interstate 94, westbound, then north on US 23. Mary Grace tried to make small talk, but he remained uncommunicative. As they neared the Washtenaw interchange, where US 23 divides Ann Arbor and Ypsilanti, Mary Grace asked quietly, "Would you mind dropping me here?"

He looked at her, his lips tightening.

"Some people I promised to see," she explained.

He turned away from her and eased the truck over onto the road shoulder, stopping just beyond the off ramp. He did not speak; he kept staring straight ahead.

"Thanks," Mary Grace said and got out. As she shut the door she added, like a dutiful afterthought, a flat "So long," and turned and strolled off.

Alf Clemson ground the truck into gear and pulled out into the freeway traffic. He did not look back at his daughter.

It was a few minutes past four when Sherry Fantosi got a call from Mary Grace. She was in a phone booth outside the giant Arborland shopping center on Washtenaw Avenue, just off US 23. She asked if Sherry could drive out and pick her up, but Jerry had the car, so Sherry suggested she get a lift in to the McKenny Union, and she would meet her there. Jerry would join them and Ed Carroll said he might be around.

Mary Grace asked if anybody had seen Miller Agee. Sherry said no, but she'd phone him and tell him, or leave word, to meet them at Eastern. Mary Grace said fine, she'd be there in about fifteen minutes.

Sherry called the Agee house. Miller was out, but Mrs. Agee expected him back any time and would give him the message. Then, leaving a note for her husband, Sherry walked to the E.M.U. campus, reaching McKenny Union a little past 4:15. Jerry Fantosi arrived ten minutes later. The lounge and snack bar were not crowded, and there was only a handful of kids they knew. Ed Carroll was not there.

They waited for over an hour and a half, and Mary Grace did not show up. Puzzled, and beginning to feel concerned, they phoned Ed Carroll's place in Woodland Hills. Al Tabor answered and said that Ed was out somewhere, and that he himself had neither seen nor heard from Mary Grace that day.

They called Robin Hobby. He'd had no word since the morning. They drew similar blanks with the few others in town who knew Mary Grace.

Where the hell could she be, then? It was unthinkable that she could still be thumbing out on Washtenaw. Hitching between Ann Arbor and Ypsi was as reliable as a shuttle system; it would never take so long to hitch the three miles or so from Arborland —especially for one so road-wise as that girl. It was nearly 5:45 now.

The only place left to try was Miller Agee's again. Miller himself answered the phone. He'd just walked in and hadn't even got the earlier messages yet, but he didn't seem overly anxious.

By ten o'clock, however, when there was still no word, he asked his father if he would drive him over to Romulus. Maybe, for some crazy reason, Mary Grace had gone back to the old house. But the place was deserted. Then he decided to call the Clemsons in Flint. Mrs. Clemson answered.

"Is Mary Grace there?"

"No, isn't she with you, or Sherry?"

"No, she is not with me. *Nobody* here has seen her. We've looked for hours. *You* haven't heard from her?"

"Why, no—"

Ellie Clemson sat staring at her telephone. She was shivering.

A little past 12:30 A.M. Sunday, Sherry Fantosi put in

a call to the State Police post in Ypsilanti. A sergeant took down the particulars, wrote up a report and stuck it, with others like it, on the "wait-and-see" spike. These held the doubtfuls down to the far-fetched.

The rule was to act on missing reports only if filed by the person's nearest kin. He'd checked the night's reports, and there'd been nothing on a kid from Flint from her own family.

It was more than twenty-four hours later, a little after two o'clock Monday morning, before Ellie Clemson finally made the decision to report her daughter as missing. And then she did not contact the State Police post in Flint; she put through a long-distance call to the Wayne County Sheriff's Department at Westland —to Detective Beverley Scannell.

Lieutenant Gene O'Grady took it. Detective Scannell would not be in until 8:00 A.M., but O'Grady assured her that a notice would go right out. He typed up a missing-girl bulletin, with a supplement signed by himself, and put it on the teleprinter. He left a separate copy on Detective Scannell's desk.

The report was upsetting to Beverley. For some reason she thought of the young Holder girl found murdered in the Belleville cemetery just Friday: That was not far from Ypsi, and her recollection was that it was the third violent homicide in the area in the past year or two.

She immediately sat down and typed a letter to the Washtenaw County Sheriff's Department, telling what she knew about the missing Clemson girl and making a special request to be on the alert for possible foul play in this case. Her letter was received in Ann Arbor the next morning, Tuesday, March 25. Hardly had it been distributed to sheriff's detectives than the first report came in on the corpse of a young female found out in the lonely northeast sector of the city, and Beverley Scannell was called in to identify the tortured body of Mary Grace Clemson.

The first person brought in for questioning, late Tuesday afternoon, was Miller Agee.

Young Agee was not unknown to authorities in Washtenaw County. Within the past year he had been convicted of a felony, possession of stolen property, and as a first offender had drawn five years' probation. Officially, according to the Probation Department, his record had since been satisfactory; but unofficially, he was suspected of using and associating with others who used and sold narcotics.

Miller looked unkempt and bewildered—almost as though coming down off a high—when brought in by a pair of Ann Arbor detectives about 4:30 P.M. They'd found him at home in Ypsilanti, in bed. His eyes were cloudy and his speech awkward as he answered questions from the officer in charge, Sergeant Bill Canada, joined by the two Wayne County detectives, Beverley Scannell and Rosemary Newsome.

Canada asked if Miller knew why he was there.

He said he guessed it had something to do with Mary Grace.

What about Mary Grace?

On account of her—well, being missing.

When did Miller first know that the girl was missing?

The youth haltingly related his activities of the past few days, from time to time pausing in mid-expression to grope for continuity of thought. Sunday, he'd just hung around all day, part of the time with a neighbor, Tommy Hyers, part with another friend, Phil Nader. That night, Jerry and Sherry Fantosi came by in their car and the three of them drove around looking for Mary Grace—even in to Detroit. Nobody knew anything. It was unreal. Monday, he and the Fantosis were together most of the day, driving to different places in Ypsi and Ann Arbor. Still nothing. Miller went to bed sometime after midnight, and he didn't wake up until the police had come for him.

Sergeant Canada shuffled some papers. "So, you have no idea where Mary Grace might be right now," he said.

"No, sir."

"You and she didn't have a fight, did you?"

"Us? No, sir. We got along real good. We were engaged, we wanted to get married."

Canada eyed him straight on. "Why do you say *got* along, *were* engaged, *wanted* to get married? Do you think she's dead?"

Miller blanched. "No, I—I don't know. God! . . ." His voice choked off.

"You do know she's dead, don't you?"

"No!" Miller pleaded.

"She is." Canada's voice was soft, but it still seemed relentless. In a few words he described the finding of her body earlier and the subsequent identification. "When did you see her last?"

The boy was sniffling, trying to hold back gulping sobs. "Last week. Wednesday, I think."

"Were you having relations with her? Sex?"

"Yes," he said weakly.

"When was the last time?"

"Last week."

"Do you use, have you used, narcotics?"

He swallowed. "Yes—some."

"How long?"

"Maybe a year. Since about last summer, I guess."

"What are you on?"

"I'm not *on* anything, not regular." He took a deep breath. "Grass once in a while. A little speed . . ."

"No hard stuff?"

He looked down at his shoes. "I've tried it a couple of times."

"Did you turn *her* on to dope—Mary Grace?"

"No, sir. When I met her, she'd been using like a year already. That's what she told me."

"Do you know of anyone who had reason to be angry with Mary Grace? *This* angry?"

"No," Miller said. He paused. "The only one I could possibly think of would be a guy named Robert—I don't know his last name, I never met him—a black guy from Detroit. Mary Grace said she owed him money, thirty or thirty-five dollars. He was pressing her, so Mary Grace gave him a ring that some aunt

had given her that was supposed to have a small diamond in it. But when he took the ring to a hock shop,
they told him the 'diamond' wasn't worth a nickel, it
was a zircon or something. So I guess this Robert
wasn't too happy about that. But I don't know whatever happened there. . . ."

"When was this?"

"Oh, a couple of months ago."

Canada looked at some papers, then asked: "Any of
your friends drug addicts?"

Miller flushed. "No, sir."

"Any hung up about sex—sex fiends, or deviates?"

"None that I know of."

"Do you know the name Jill Hersch?"

Miller hesitated. "Yes—I think so."

"In what connection?"

"Wasn't she the Eastern girl who was—murdered
last summer? The second one?"

"That's right. Did you know her?"

"No. I just remember she got killed. She lived in
Ypsi."

"You don't know who killed her?"

The boy started. "Me? Hell, no!"

"Do you know who killed Mary Grace Clemson?"

"No, I swear." Tears again rushed to his eyes.

"Did *you,* Miller?"

"Oh, God, no, I didn't . . . I couldn't . . ." He bent
over and hid his face in his hands. They had to help
him as he left.

The Fantosis and Ed Carroll and others of Mary
Grace's friends interviewed next all told much the
same stories, and vouched for one another and for their
respective movements the past weekend. They all
seemed genuinely stunned by the calamity befallen
their friend. Their stories generally were verifiable. And
further, Miller Agee, Jerome and Sherry Fantosi, and
Ed Carroll and several of the others agreed to undergo
polygraph tests and all were rated guiltless—both of
the crime itself and of knowledge of it.

Police in Detroit were asked to check out "Robert" and a number of others whose names had come up in the Ann Arbor interrogations. For all practical purposes, however, these avenues of inquiry also led to a blank wall. Several of the individuals sought never could be located—not by the identities given, at any rate. And of those able to be traced, all produced acceptable alibis, or at worst gave no cause for suspicion in this particular case.

All hard leads apparently having been quickly depleted, the investigators in Ann Arbor turned to beating the bushes. The Ann Arbor P.D. publicized a special telephone number—663-4112—through which any tips about the slaying, anonymous or otherwise, could be channeled. By the end of one week, more than eight hundred alleged tips had been received.

A few seemed promising. One had a girl hitchhiker getting into a blue minibus late Saturday afternoon outside the Arborland shopping center on Washtenaw Avenue just off US 23. Another put her at a house party Saturday night in Ypsilanti, only a block from Ypsi P.D. headquarters. Yet another claimed that such a girl was in a diner near Romulus as late as Sunday night or early Monday. But none of these could be verified.

Among all the tips being received, a persistent suggestion as to the motive—which quickly grew into a widespread rumor—was that the Clemson girl had been "hit" by vengeful narcotics traffickers for having turned police "stoolie." The Detroit *News* went so far as to publish this only a day after discovery of the body, the information attributed to "informed sources."

The police never could corroborate this. It was certainly a possibility to be considered, but, after weighing all factors, the majority of investigators tended to doubt that so insignificant a conspirator as Mary Grace Clemson would have rated such an extreme show of retaliatory force. (Beverley Scannell, for one, who knew more than anyone else the extent of Mary Grace's "cooperation" as well as the level at which she'd handled dope, simply rejected the liquidation theory without reservation.)

Nonetheless, nothing could be discounted out of hand, and in the succeeding days local police swooped down on all known or suspected drug users in the Ann Arbor-Ypsilanti area—many of them university and even high-school students nesting in drug-oriented communes. Hauled downtown for questioning, dozens of these wound up busted for possession. As far as advancing usable information about the Clemson homicide, however, the return was zero.

In the midst of all this activity, Mary Grace Clemson was quietly returned to Wayne County. Friday morning, March 28, a private funeral service was held in Romulus, attended only by the several immediate members of her family. Morticians had prepared her broken body admirably, lying her on her side so that the crushed half of her face and head could not be seen when the family viewed her. She wore a girlish, frilly pale yellow chiffon dress, selected by her mother, and pink and yellow rosebuds were sprinkled on the coffin, also at the request of Ellie Clemson, who was determined to remember her daughter the way she had always wished to think of her.

Miller Agee, with Jerome and Sherry Fantosi, none of whom had been invited to the service, were waiting at the Tyler Street Cemetery. They stood apart as the girl was buried—unnoticed, or more likely ignored, by the Clemsons. The three of them wept silently, helplessly, and then went away.

If little attention was given elsewhere to an inconspicuous funeral in a nondescript village in eastern Michigan, there were more than a few thoughtful citizens in the Ann Arbor-Ypsilanti area for whom it assumed unusual significance. For a shadow of dark foreboding was beginning to creep across the community, a gathering realization that over a period of twenty-one months, four young women from the area had met violent death, each in still unexplained fashion.

For the first time, there was in the air a growing anxiety, along with a simmering of outrage, that individual safety was under threat from some spreading, unseen evil.

CHAPTER 7

AREA NEWSPAPERS, NOT too surprisingly, did not hesitate to play up the numbers game. As early as Jill Hersch's death the previous July, typical headlines had read 2D E.M.U. COED SLAIN; then, after Jeanne Holder, 3D COED MURDER VICTIM; and now, 4TH GIRL FOUND IN ANN ARBOR!

Heretofore, the police had disregarded this approach as the usual media hokum. With only a few exceptions, the various investigators involved in the first three homicides had not thought of them in terms of a "series," as the news accounts implied. They were three distinct cases, each dealt with in turn by the appropriate jurisdiction. And while all three had remained unsolved to date, among the professionals there had seemed little reason to indulge in any fanciful speculation that the crimes might be connected in some sinister way.

It was true that several aspects of the Hersch case had borne disturbing similarities to that of Marilyn Pindar: Both were E.M.U. coeds of about the same age, each with a summer job at the university, each having lived off campus a few blocks apart (yet each of whose families resided within a short drive of Ypsilanti), and of course both killed in much the same manner. But their deaths had been separated by nearly a full year. It had not been reasonable to conclude a "series" from such scattered incidents. Thus, the Hersch murder had been logged only as a second homicide, not *the* second in some fearful progression.

The slaying of the Holder girl, almost nine months after the last, had, if anything, directed reason farther away from any one, two, three concept. The MO was different—a pistol used instead of a knife, the victim not known to have been abused sexually. She was older and more mature than the previous two, a graduate student and from a different school, who'd lived on campus and whose home was in a distant part of the state.

So, melodramatic headlines to the contrary, the respective police agencies had continued to plug away separately. Except for the one joint conference with the county prosecutor and his people, following the 1968 Hersch killing, plus informal and haphazard exchanges of information in the months thereafter, local investigators had not been notably coordinated in their efforts; they had not even compared notes with any regularity.

Until Mary Grace Clemson. Now, all at once, everything seemed different. This homicide, smack in the wake of Jeanne Holder, had brought everybody up short. The pendulum of educated conjecture began swinging the opposite way. Now policemen, too, were starting to talk of *the* murders.

This shift in official perspective was first given substance a week into the Clemson investigation, when Ann Arbor's Detective Sergeant Bill Canada held a briefing session with newsmen. Responding to a query as to where the probe stood, in his direct manner Canada said:

"Where it stands is, we've got four homicides, and investigations continue into each. That's it."

Were any of the murders thought, in fact, to be linked? Did the police feel that if they solved one they might clear up all four?

"I didn't say that. And I would say there is nothing definite to indicate that at the present time." Canada paused and eyed his questioner evenly. "But we're looking into every possibility."

The Ann Arbor Police Department having been thrust to the forefront with its second case, Detective Captain Harold Olson personally took full charge of stepped-up investigations. Olson, forty-five, was tough, dedicated, and efficient. A former army top sergeant in the World War II African and Italian campaigns, he'd been a cop almost since his discharge from the military. He'd been selected for special training at the FBI National Academy, and now he was number-two man in the Ann Arbor department under veteran Chief Walter Krasny. Back in the early 1950's, as a sergeant, Olson had helped crack the city's last major homicide, when three youths from Ypsilanti had beaten a young nurse to death. There had been nothing like that in Ann Arbor in sixteen years—until now.

Olson reassigned a half-dozen "dicks," as he called his detectives, to the homicide detail, along with two patrolmen who'd had some investigative experience. Also drafted from the Detective Bureau was a bright female secretary, to work full-time until further notice for the captain's special squad. Their first task was to set up a universal system of filing all available information on each of the homicides to date, cross-indexed and coded to the individual case, which would also be available to any of the other police agencies concerned.

Not even Captain Olson could have imagined at the time how helpful this organization would prove in the months ahead when the local situation reach a crisis pitch.

By the beginning of April, from among the area's law enforcement agencies—six, counting the Ann Arbor

and Ypsilanti police departments, the State Police, plus
the Eastern Michigan University campus police—some
twenty investigators were devoting themselves more or
less exclusively to the four unsolved homicides, coordinated loosely by the prosecutor's office.

Among other things, they determined to stay abreast
of unsolved violent crimes in other locales. They began by querying law enforcement agencies with kin-
dred problems and inviting inquiry in return, in hopes
of detecting some link between like crimes, no matter
how tenuous or how far distant, at one end or the
other.

Ongoing investigations in two other widely separated
localities drew immediate mutual interest. One was in
southwestern Michigan, in lakeshore Berrien County,
where for more than four years authorities had been
frustrated in trying to solve the vicious slayings of four
females.

Early in February of 1965, the mutilated body of a
nineteen-year-old girl had been found in a vacant
building in the city of Benton Harbor. Then, that April,
in a pine forest ten miles outside Benton Harbor, three
more corpses were discovered, all also mutilated. Two
of these, a seven-year-old child and a sixty-year-old
matron, had been abducted from different places several days before. Lying close by the others were the
badly decomposed remains of the third, a thirty-seven-
year-old woman who, it turned out, had been missing
for two months but had not been so reported. Of all
four victims, only the child appeared to have been sexually molested.

There never had been a hard suspect in any of these
killings—which had come to be commonly sensation-
alized as a "multiple slaying," although not all investigators there were fully convinced of that. Now, Berrien
County officials, impressed by a similar element of
"overkill" evident in recent events around Ann Arbor,
asked for an exchange of information on the recent
"coed murders" (as the press had begun tagging them)
and these older cases.

At the same time, a second, more distant locality was burdened with its own rash of ugly killings—Cape Cod in Massachusetts. There, during February and March of 1969, the decimated bodies of four young women had been unearthed from shallow graves near the village of Truro, on the northerly hook of the Cape. Each had been hacked to pieces with either an ax or a brush hook. At least two also had been shot by a .22-caliber weapon; about the other two, there was no way of telling, they had been so mutilated.

Massachusetts and Michigan also exchanged confidences on their respective brutalities. Anything was possible.

Dr. Ames Robey of Massachusetts had been appointed director of Michigan's new Center for Forensic Psychiatry at the Ypsilanti State Hospital—actually located in York Township, south of Ann Arbor—in July of 1967. Previously Dr. Robey had for several years been medical director of the Bridgewater State Hospital near Boston. It was there, during the 1963–64 height of the "Boston strangler" investigations, that he had personally examined some of the prime suspects of those murders, including the confessed Albert DeSalvo.

Only thirty-five when chosen for the prestigious Bridgewater post, Robey at forty-one had lost none of the galvanic assertiveness that had characterized him there. A tightly wound six-foot-four beanpole, he was a fussy man of hair-trigger intuitions and opinions, which almost obscured his real expertise in his field, forensic psychiatry, the application of psychiatric methodology to criminal behavior and the law. Dr. Robey had not endeared himself to law-enforcement people in and around Boston by his persistent dissent from their accepted belief that they had found the strangler. His opinion had been—and still was—that in fact Albert DeSalvo probably had not murdered any of the thirteen women in that skein; moreover, he believed it likely in any event that only the first five—all elderly matrons who lived alone, killed between June and Au-

gust of 1962—had been murdered by a single individual, that the rest were later victimized by persons unknown who (as Robey put it) "cashed in on the
earlier publicity."

The authorities, relieved to have been blessed with
DeSalvo's detailed confession, hardly appreciated Dr.
Robey's outspoken repudiation. Nor was their disaffec-
tion with him lessened by his insistence that he was
reasonably sure who one of the *real* stranglers was.

Robey's suspect was a brilliant but, in his view,
dangerously psychotic former Harvard undergraduate
named David Parker.* Robey had first encountered the
young man in January of 1964, when he was ordered
to Bridgewater for observation after having been arrested while assaulting a young woman—who turned
out to be his pregnant wife of two weeks—in the middle of Harvard Square, Cambridge. At the time, the
slender, six-foot, handsome bearded youth was made
up like the Moor Othello—natural blond hair dyed
jet black and curled in ringlets, fair skin darkened a
nut brown, wearing one gold earring, sandals on his
feet, and a dagger in his belt.

Despite an IQ of somewhere between 150 and 170,
by age twenty-two Parker, a New Yorker, had been in
and out of trouble with Boston-area police on charges
ranging from disturbing the peace, to making pipe
bombs, to selling hallucinogenic drugs (homemade in
his own laboratory), for which he'd been dismissed
from Harvard. He was a frequent user himself of the
so-called mind-expanding drugs and recently had been
treated at another hospital for what was diagnosed as a
"personality disorder," which one attending physician
specified as acute schizophrenia.

Parker was feared among his friends as having a
tendency toward sudden and extreme violence. And, as
Dr. Robey discovered during the weeks he observed
him, most of that violence was directed toward women.

* "David Parker" was the pseudonym given this individual by author
Gerold Frank in his book *The Boston Strangler* (New American
Library), and it will be continued here.

He would rant incessantly, with mounting intensity, of his aim to "save the world" by destroying its women. Robey did not feel that it was a severely aberrative strain of either male chauvinism or homosexuality that consumed this young man, although Parker did admit to having had homosexual experiences. The doctor read it as a deep psychosis probably of primal origins, indicative of a child's helpless, agonized unfulfillment of basic needs and desires at the hands of either or both parents.

An individual so possessed, Dr. Robey knew, could be quite capable of rape and murder; he could even be a necrophile. He could be prone to castration anxiety as well, in which women appeared as threats to his virility.

Dr. Robey, armed with relevant insights into David Parker's recent behavior as well as his personal history, had argued to the Boston authorities that here they had a powerful suspect in the strangler killings. And for a time Parker had been so regarded. But then Albert DeSalvo had enthralled everybody with his remarkably precise accounts of so many of the crimes, and active interest in Parker waned and finally died. He was ordered released from Bridgewater, and the last Robey had heard of him—four or five years ago—was that he'd resumed studies at a small college near Albany, New York.

The psychiatrist was startled, therefore, when a week or so following the murder of Mary Grace Clemson he picked up the Ann Arbor *News* and on the front page saw the face of David Parker. It was in a photograph of a group of University of Michigan students who were agitating for a rent strike of privately operated off-campus housing. Parker was identified in the caption and accompanying story as a graduate student of U. of M. and a leader of the activist group, which Robey recognized as representing a coalition of some of the more radical campus organizations.

David Parker in Ann Arbor! Robey was excited.

He dialed the Ann Arbor Police Department and was put through to Detective Captain Harold Olson. He identified himself and told Olson his suspicions. "I don't mean to butt into police business unasked," he said, "but if there's the slightest chance that this Parker fellow—well, I felt it was my duty . . ." Olson said of course and asked if the doctor would mind coming in to headquarters to give them a complete fill-in.

The next morning Dr. Robey was interviewed at length by Captain Olson and Sergeant Bill Canada. He told them everything he'd learned and observed about David Parker at Bridgewater, then threw in an additional theory. It had come to him just the previous evening as he'd briefed himself from recent newspaper clippings about the two latest homicides:

"After the third death, that is, Miss Holder, the police were said to be looking for a man named David Hanson. If I'm correct in guessing that you have not found this person yet," the psychiatrist propounded, "I leave you with these thoughts: the book *The Boston Strangler* has been out several years. Unquestionably our friend is fully aware that in the book he is called 'David Parker.' *David*. Do you see? There is no doubt in my mind that this fellow is quixotic enough, has the sense of irony, to brazenly adopt the fictitious name David in the commission of yet another crime under another set of policemen's noses. *He* could be your 'David Hanson'!"

The detectives glanced at one another, then stood and thanked Robey, and told him his information was most valuable. They would be in touch.

A lot of what the doctor had told them did fill in a number of blanks. For they already knew of this Parker, and in fact an urgent check had been initiated into his recent past.

David Parker originally had come to police attention by virtue of his activities in and around the university—including a sometime association with the local drug culture "revolutionist" James Upton and his cadre—and already was being monitored under partial surveillance. Even now the *Strangler* book was being studied minutely, not only for all pertinent material about Parker but for any suggestion of a pattern in those murders and these recent crimes. (Parker himself had recently been bragging about being a key figure—and key suspect—in the book.) Massachusetts was queried for more official background on Parker and whatever information was available about his movements since he'd left there. And sources in Ann Arbor, specifically those connected with the university, were being tapped to supply a schematic of Parker's existence since his arrival. But there had been disappointments.

The first had been in learning that Parker had not come to Ann Arbor until the *fall* of 1967—which seemed to eliminate him from consideration in the Marilyn Pindar case. The next had been verification that Parker had spent the entire summer of 1968, when Jill Hersch was killed, far from the immediate area, at home in New York and then on a European trip. Finally, so far no indication had been turned up linking Parker with Jeanne Holder—although this would not be dismissed if only because both were U. of M. graduate students. As for the young Clemson girl there was a remote connection at best, whose only basis lay in the fact that each had moved, in one way or another, through the underground world of James Upton.

They had resisted questioning Parker directly as yet. They knew where to find him—he was being watched closely now—but for the moment they simply had nothing on him. If the man *had* killed, he was bound to make a slip; there was no point in putting him on alert before complacency might cause him to grow careless.

Captain Olson and Sergeant Canada had told Dr. Robey none of this during their interview. Nor did they mention that, in fact, they had been about to call on *him* when he contacted them first. They'd wanted

to get the doctor's full views without his being in-
hibited by an awareness that the investigators had
prior knowledge.

But something else had struck the two veteran officers: David Parker was not the only one who'd
been closely tied to the Boston murders and now happened to be in Ann Arbor. Another was Ames Robey.
He seemed to have a fixation on the Michigan murders.
And he'd been here since July of 1967!

Maybe it was silly, but they would take a long discreet look into the psychiatrist's own background and
activities as well as his patient's. After four clueless
homicides, hardly anything was too far-fetched anymore.

While inquiries continued into the Clemson killing, the
hunt had gone on for the David Hanson apparently
implicated in the Holder case. By the second week of
April, a list had been compiled of sixteen men by
that name who had lately attended any of the area's
schools or otherwise had ties to Ann Arbor-Ypsilanti.
There was a flurry of interest in one, a recent E.M.U.
graduate who had been residing at 619 Emmet Street
in Ypsi, a boardinghouse on the corner opposite 703
Emmet, where Jill Hersch had roomed.

This David Hanson, upon graduation the past January, had taken a government job in Washington.
Detectives were sent to talk with him there. He professed ignorance of any wrongdoing, said he had not
been back to Ypsi since leaving, never knew anyone
named Jeanne Holder, had not even known Jill Hersch.
He seemed honest and sincere, and his statements
checked out favorably. The detectives wrote him off
and flew home.

Nine of the other fifteen David Hansons also had
been located. All were questioned, all voluntarily took
polygraph tests, all were cleared. Detectives were
tracking down the remaining six as the search for
Jeanne Holder's killer continued.

Easter had come and gone, the students were back—
and the hitchhikers. On the heels of two murders, the
police issued strong warnings against hitchhiking, especially by females. And it appeared to have a certain effect for a time. But by the middle of April, as the
days grew warmer, the hikers began reappearing as
if by seasonal ritual between Ann Arbor and Ypsi.

On the morning of Wednesday, April 16, police reporter John Cobb of the Ypsilanti *Press* was on his
way to Beyer Memorial Hospital to pick up overnight
admission reports before going on to the office. As he
neared the hospital, a siren and flashing red lights
came up fast from behind, and Cobb pulled over.
It was not the expected ambulance that flew past,
however, but an unmarked automobile, and Cobb recognized the familiar blond crew cut of Washtenaw
County's youthful, hard-boiled sheriff, Doug Harvey.

Where the hell was he racing to at this hour? It
wasn't yet 7:00 A.M. The young reporter switched on
his police radio monitor, and two minutes later he
was slamming his '68 Chevelle north out of Ypsilanti,
in the same direction Sheriff Harvey's car had headed.
Another girl's body had been found on Gale Road in
a remote section of Superior Township.

Gale Road was little more than a country lane less
than two-and-a-half miles long, running between
Geddes Road and Plymouth Road. Medium-expensive
homes were scattered along one side, many of them
set well back and almost hidden among dense trees
and foliage. The opposite side was lined much of its
length by a high chain-link fence, beyond which
stretched the rolling fairways of the University of
Michigan's Radrick Farms golf course.

Cobb's was the third car at the scene, the sheriff's
sedan having been joined by a white and blue patrol
car. Cobb skidded to a stop and, grabbing his Rollei-
flex, hustled toward the knot of men bent over a
figure sprawled on the roadside, which appeared to
be covered with a red blanket. In addition to the sheriff
and his driver, both in civilian clothes, there were

two uniformed deputies and also an older man wearing a figured bathrobe. Good, thought the reporter, he must be the one who found it.

Sheriff Harvey looked around abruptly and strode toward Cobb. "Police business," he snapped. "You'll have to leave."

"John Cobb, sheriff. The *Press*."

Harvey's eyes narrowed. Cobb was still new to the area, having come to Ypsilanti from a paper in upstate New York only in mid-March. "Oh, yeah," the sheriff muttered, looking the reporter up and down. "How the hell'd you get on this so quick?" he demanded.

Cobb nodded back toward his car. "Picked you up on my monitor."

The sheriff glanced at the white Chevelle. It had a pair of tail antennae growing out of the rear. "Authorized?" he growled.

"Absolutely."

"Hmm. Well, you can take off anyway. We don't want no reporters around now. We got work to do." Harvey made a gesture of dismissal.

"Wait a minute, sheriff," Cobb spoke up. "You can make me stand by, but I'm not going anywhere. I know you've got another homicide here, and I'm staying until I get the facts. The other news guys will be all over this place soon enough."

Harvey scowled at him, then shrugged. "Just stay out of our way."

Cobb waited off to one side, snapping pictures of the general scene. Soon another patrol car came into view, then another from the opposite direction, and these were directed by Harvey's assistant to seal off Gale Road at the nearest access streets. Here and there residents had come out of their homes and, hastily dressed or still wrapped in night clothes, were huddling at the entrances to their driveways, observing the scene down the road.

Then Harvey came over to Cobb and said, to his

surprise: "Okay, you been a good boy, I'll give you a
break. Here's the rundown."

As Cobb scribbled notes, the sheriff related that the
victim was a young female, maybe seventeen. No positive ID yet. Reddish hair, like strawberry blond. Dead
less than twelve hours. Strangled with a length of
black electrical cord. Also slashed repeatedly across
her torso. It looked like she'd been raped. Probably
killed someplace else and dumped here during the
night or early morning—she had on only a bra and a
blouse; the rest of her clothes were not around.

About 6:35, Harvey went on, a man driving north
on Gale had spotted the body. He drove to this man's
house just up the road—the sheriff indicated the man
in the bathrobe, Victor Barrow—and they phoned
the Sheriff's Department. Then Mr. Barrow came down
with a blanket and covered the body and waited for
police. The other man continued on to work, but they
had his name and address, which would be kept confidential at this time. That was it, so far.

"You can say," Harvey concluded, "that Sheriff
Douglas Harvey led responding officers to the scene
within twenty minutes of the alarm." He flashed an
engaging grin, rarely seen by newsmen, with whom he
kept up a running skirmish. "*You* know that, you
were right on my tail." Harvey then asked if he wanted
to take a look at the corpse.

"Sure," Cobb said, unslinging the camera from his
shoulder. "Pictures?" he asked.

Harvey said, "Why not. Come on."

The blanket had been removed from the body. The
girl was on her back in grass and weeds just off the
roadway. She was exposed from the chest down, her
bare legs straight out and spread wide, white arms
bent above her head. A torn white blouse and a white
brassiere were bunched over the tops of her full
breasts, which were bloody, crisscrossed with ugly red
grooves. There was still some baby fat at the hips and
inside the thighs. Her face probably had been cute, but
it was hard to tell how she had really looked in life

because the features now were discolored and bloated from the pressure of the loop of black wire cutting into her neck. Cobb heard somebody say that a piece of the blouse had been recovered from her throat, where it must have been jammed to prevent an outcry.

The reporter felt his stomach turn queasy. In Ypsi only a month, and already he was covering his third obscene murder. Lowering his camera, he turned away a little unsteady.

"Save some of those prints for us," Sheriff Harvey said behind him, the amiability still in his voice.

With a nod, Cobb made his way back to the Chevelle. As he maneuvered through the cordon of police now isolating Gale Road, he recognized Prosecutor Delhey arriving, followed by newsmen. It would be another big story. Each one got bigger.

CHAPTER 8

BY THE TIME the early stories appeared in the afternoon papers—John Cobb's was the first—the dead girl's identity had been affirmed. Her name was Dale Harum, of Ypsilanti, who had been reported missing late the night before. She was thirteen, and she was in the eighth grade at West Junior High School.

She was officially identified by Lieutenant William Mulholland of the Sheriff's Department. His own thirteen-year-old daughter had been one of Dale Harum's best friends; the girl had slept over at the Mulhollands' only two nights before.

Shortly before midnight Tuesday, Bill Mulholland had received a telephone call at home from the child's worried mother, Clara, a widow, wondering if she was there again. Dale had gone out after supper, a little past six, to see some friends, was supposed to have been home by dark, but had not returned or called to say where she was. And she had school the next day.

Mulholland knew Dale as a good girl, level-headed and dependable, and this did not sound like her. He advised Clara Harum to keep phoning everybody she could think of at whose house Dale might have stopped

off to stay the night; if that didn't turn up any word of
the girl, he told her, it wouldn't hurt to give the
Ypsilanti city police a call.

At 12:45 A.M. Wednesday, the sixteenth, night duty
Sergeant Bill Stenning at the Ypsilanti Police Department took a call from Mrs. Clara Harum of LeForge
Road, Ypsilanti, that her daughter was missing. He
logged the details for follow-up in the morning. By the
time Sergeant Stenning was making his notes, Dale
Harum was already dead. Preliminary medical examination indicated that the girl had died ten to eleven
hours before her body was found—which would have
been between 8:00 and 9:00 P.M. Tuesday evening.

According to her mother, Dale had left the house a
few minutes after six. She was wearing an orange mohair sweater over a white blouse, blue denim stretch
pants, black shoes with straps. She went next door to
her sister's and asked her brother-in-law, Richard Best,
if he would drive her to "Depot Town"—a dilapidated
factory section of Ypsi near the abandoned Penn Central depot, a mile or so from the Harum residence,
where many of Dale's friends were in the habit of
gathering. Richard Best dropped her there, at the intersection of Cross and River streets, east of the Huron
River, at 6:20.

Dale was with friends in that area until a little after
seven, when, as dusk gathered, she started home on
foot. One of the crowd, Arthur Childs, walked with
her about three blocks as far as the railroad crossing
on Forest Avenue, where she continued on alone, intending to follow the tracks homeward, as she often
did.

A few minutes later—the police were able to trace
back—Dale came upon two teen-age boys whom she
knew, fishing from a small footbridge over the Huron
River where it snakes beside the railroad right-of-way.
The girl watched them, and they talked some, and after about ten minutes she asked if they would walk
her home. Both declined, saying they had to get started
home themselves and they lived in the opposite direc-

tion. The boys watched her go on, walking briskly alongside the tracks in a northwesterly direction.

It was almost 7:30 when a man standing on a knoll overlooking the westbound tracks saw a young girl hustling along the roadbed toward him. The man, thirty-one-year-old Francis Timmons, was a train buff who lived with a maiden aunt in a house on nearby Railroad Street, and he had come out five minutes or so earlier, as he did each evening, to clock the *Wolverine*. This was one of the Penn Central's few remaining passenger trains, which lumbered into Ypsi at 7:25 P.M. daily and ground to a brief halt on this stretch of the track while rails were switched. The *Wolverine* had been right on time this evening. Timmons, a familiar figure by now to train crews passing through, had gotten a friendly wave from a white-hatted cook in the open door of the dining car. (The cook also had a glimpse of the girl as she hurried by his car a moment later.)

The girl left the roadbed, and Francis Timmons watched as she made her way between the clumps of scraggly bushes and weeds, until she reached Railroad Street, where she resumed walking swiftly west toward LeForge Road.

Then the *Wolverine*'s whistle and the clank of the cars as they started moving again recaptured Timmons' attention. It was 7:35—still on schedule. He waved to the trainmen, forgetting the girl.

So Dalé Harum apparently had vanished between Railroad Street and her presumed destination, home— a distance of less than half a mile—and between 7:35 and 8:00 P.M., or 8:30 at the outside. The only reasonable conclusion, then, could be that at some coordinates within that brief span of space and time, the girl had been picked up, or at any rate had gone off with someone. The problem was that no one, either residents or infrequent passersby, had observed the girl, much less such an occurrence.

No one who knew Dale Harum believed for an instant that she would have accepted a lift. Stacy Tanner (who'd known Dale since birth and whose own children had grown up with her) later told police that there had been occasions when Dale had refused offers of rides from *him*. It was something the girl just happened to be very firm about.

A couple of hours after discovery of the body, there still was no trace of the victim's sweater, pants, and shoes. But then a sheriff's deputy found one of the missing strap shoes in brush along the golf course fence on the west side of Gale Road, only about fifty yards south of the scene. And less than an hour after that, another deputy came upon the second shoe in a ditch on the east side of Gale, well back down toward Geddes Road.

There seemed no doubt that the shoes had been discarded from a vehicle bearing the dead girl, one tossed out of the presumed killer-driver's window, probably on his way to dumping the body, and the other on his way back.

The question remained, Where had the killing taken place? In the vehicle itself? In a dwelling? Out in some field or wood? And where had the body been kept before finally being disposed of? There was almost no possibility that the actual slaying had taken place at the spot where she was found. The probability was only slightly less remote that her corpse had been dumped there immediately after death. Considering that no attempt had been made to conceal the body, surely *somebody* would have happened upon it. Nor did it seem logical that the killer would have driven around for hours with a corpse for a passenger. No, she had to have been kept in some *place,* and the odds were it was the same place at which the killing took place.

Sheriff Harvey held a news conference in midmorning—waiting until the big-time Detroit correspondents had had time to join the locals. Doug Harvey knew the uses of media. The youngest sheriff ever elected in Washtenaw County, he was only thirty-two when he took office in 1965, with less than seven years' police experience, most of that with the Ypsi P.D. The past fall he'd won reelection by a three-to-one plurality and was feeling his oats. He knew how to provide reporters with good copy—not necessarily always favorable, but colorful. Harvey was a law-and-order hardnose, which tended to antagonize segments of the press as well as part of his constituency, the "liberal" university quarter. But they were a distant minority amidst an essentially conservative electorate, and Harvey made no concessions to appeasement.

Now he rattled off most of what was known of the latest slaying (and somewhat less of what he and some of his colleagues thought at this point), and added:

"We figure the girl's body was dumped here not too long before we found it—while it was still dark, say anywhere between three and five o'clock this morning. Naturally the killer didn't want to risk being seen *doing* it, so he picked the quietest time. *But*"—he laid dramatic emphasis on the word—"it's plain to us that he *wanted* her to be easily found.

"The way the body was left right by the side of the road, so exposed that anybody driving past would have to spot it, even before dawn with headlights on.

"So it looks like this guy, the murderer, is starting to play games with us. . . ."

The reporters stirred. One spoke up:

"Sheriff, when you say *the* murderer, do you mean that whoever did this had killed before—that you've found a connection between this homicide and some of the others?"

Harvey regarded his questioner benevolently. "I'm not *saying* that—yet. But I do say there sure seem to be similarities in the MO of this one and some of the other things that've been going on around here lately."

"Which cases, specifically?" another newsman pressed.

"Well, like that kid a few weeks ago . . ."

"The junkie kid?"

"Right. And that Eastern coed last summer. And maybe even the one before that."

"How about the one last month, the girl in the cemetery?"

The sheriff glanced at one of his aides before responding. "Well, that looks like a tough one. It doesn't seem to fit with the others. Anyway, I believe the State Police are handling that one." He made a sound like a competitive jab. Then, squaring his shoulders, he added: "This is the first crack my department's had, and we're going all out to get to the bottom of this."

Harvey's evident aggressiveness brought a new babble of questions: "Any leads so far? Any suspects?"

But the sheriff turned stolid. "No comment at this time."

"How about the man who found the body?"

"We're withholding his name. My people have already talked to him extensively, he's been checked out, and he looks okay so far. I'll only tell you he's a local resident, a family man, a good, steady workingman. I see no need to give him bad publicity that he don't deserve, not to mention his family."

"One more thing, sheriff? Have you *any* idea where the girl may have been killed?"

The emphasis, with its faint hint of needling, brought back the stern, rigid demeanor that reporters who pursued Harvey too hard had become familiar with. The news conference was about to be terminated. "Not yet. But we will," he snapped. *"This* time we will find it, and then some of the pieces might start fitting together. That's all." He turned and strode away from them.

As Sheriff Harvey had indicated to the press, for hours that morning a task force of deputies, state troopers, and officers from the several local police agencies had fanned out from Gale Road, looking for something that might indicate where Dale Harum had been murdered. Find that location and, as Harvey had also indicated, they might find out quite a few things.

They explored overgrown gullies and ravines, stream

beds, culverts, storm cellars, farmers' outbuildings, residents' garages, abandoned vehicles, and any parked vehicle that looked out of place in the countryside. They concentrated on the rural and lightly inhabited areas around Ypsilanti and Ann Arbor, because it seemed more likely that the girl would have been attacked in some remote place out of sight and earshot.

And then, shortly before 11:00 A.M., word was passed that electrified the police teams. A sheriff's deputy, Thomas Kelly, picking through rubble at the rear of a deserted farmhouse just north of Ypsi, had found a girl's sweater. It was a bright orange mohair. A security lid was ordered, and investigators raced to the location.

The long-abandoned farm site was off LeForge Road, near Geddes—less than a mile north of the slain girl's home! Car after car of police arrived, and they swarmed over the decaying property and through the crumbling buildings still standing—the stucco shell of what had been the main house, a partly demolished barn, the skeleton of a garage, the spindly remains of a tin-sheathed water tower. What wasn't choked with weeds was strewn with rubbish—countless beer and soda cans, liquor and wine bottles, food containers and wrappings, torn, yellowed newspaper pages, scraps of garments and upholstery, broken, rusty auto accessories, and, inside the house and barn particularly, scatterings of wrinkled condoms and dirty sanitary napkins; shattered pieces of wood and chunks of tile and plaster were everywhere. It seemed almost a miracle that Deputy Kelly could have unearthed the sweater from amidst all that.

But that was not to be the end of apparent miracles this day. In the littered, gloomy basement of the farmhouse, detectives of the State Police crime lab, hastily summoned, found fragments of a girl's white blouse. Then, under strobe lights, in a corner on the stone floor, they discovered traces of blood that was fairly fresh and, by tentative examination, human. On the rickety wooden stairs down from the main floor were particles of broken glass—and these matched bits of glass that had been ground into the soles of Dale Harum's shoes (one of the facts not released to newsmen earlier).

The clincher came a bit after noon. A searcher ran out of the barn excitedly. He'd come up with a long, curled length of black electrical cord. The cut ends compared with the strand used to strangle Dale Harum. They matched.

Finally! They had pinpointed a murder site! This murder, it seemed sure, and quite possibly some of the others—or all. The location, it was readily noted, was no more than a half mile from the other blighted farm out on Geddes Road at which the wasted remains of Marilyn Pindar had been discovered in the summer of 1967. Also, they'd never been able to determine where Jill Hersch's corpse had been stowed for the better part of a week the following summer, before it turned up only partly decomposed, as if having lain in some semicold storage—like the cool darkness of a deserted farmhouse basement. And still to be answered was where the two most previous victims, Jeanne Holder and Mary Grace Clemson, had actually met death. Why not this same bleak place? Another urgent call went out to the State Police crime lab to comb the area.

Sheriff Doug Harvey was jubilant. Hardly more than five hours after his department had taken over the latest probe, they'd landed feet first in what very well could be the one spot everybody had been going nuts hunting for. *All goddamn right!* Now to start putting the squeeze on the murdering sonofabitch!

The sheriff and Assistant Prosecutor Booker Williams had a plan. No one outside the police yet knew that the place where Dale Harum was murdered had been located. The killer was the only other one who would know it was the old farm. If a tight lid was kept on this news, it was just possible that the killer might return—

perhaps even feel safe enough to use the spot again for some purpose. So it was agreed to say nothing for publication, seal off the place with a discreet round-the-clock stakeout . . . and wait.

The news people were persistent, however, pressing hard for developments, and it soon became obvious that they would have to be told *something* before there was a leak. The question was, Should the key information be withheld completely, or should they be briefed off the record and asked to voluntarily embargo the key element of the story in the public interest? Booker Williams was in favor of the latter course. It went against Doug Harvey's instinct, but he agreed finally.

At four o'clock that afternoon, some two dozen newsmen were assembled in the sheriff's cramped office in the county jail at Ann Arbor. All the local investigative chiefs were present, they noted—and looking unusually keyed up. Something had to be brewing. Harvey assumed the role of spokesman. Without embroidery, he snapped off the essential facts. Just enough for effect—which was achieved. The journalists started buzzing appreciatively.

Then the sheriff laid it on them. "We've been more open and honest with you people than we'd planned. Actually we weren't going to let you in on any of this so soon. But then we decided you were entitled to a clear picture of what's going on, so you would be fully aware of the critical point the current investigation is at—so you would be prepared to understand the special request we now make of you." The room hushed as Harvey paused dramatically.

"Cooperation works both ways," the sheriff went on, building grimly to his punch line. "We believe we got a good shot at nailing this bird if we can lure him back to the farmhouse. The only way that can work is if he thinks we haven't found the place yet. And the only way he's gonna think *that* is if there's no publicity.

"So we're asking you fellows *not* to use anything we've given you this afternoon—"

There was a spontaneous outburst of surprise and protest.

"—not for a couple of days anyway," Harvey amended, "at least until it looks like—"

"Sheriff!" A tall young reporter from the Detroit *News* interrupted loudly over the babble, his arm raised high. Harvey peered at him.

"Sheriff, I'm afraid it's too late for that," the *News* man said.

"What do you mean, too late?" barked Harvey.

"I was talking with our office just before we came in here. We've had the farmhouse story on the street for an hour."

The sheriff stared at him, face reddening. "How in the hell . . . ?" He shot a sudden dark look at Booker Williams.

"It was me," the young *News* man explained. "I ran into one of your men before, out around Gale Road, and he was excited about finding the murder site. I got enough to phone in a bulletin. I didn't know—"

"One of *my* men?" Harvey roared. "Well, Jesus H. Christ!" he spat, clenched hands on hips in a graphic attitude of furious helplessness. Then, with an abrupt, "Okay, the hell with it, go ahead and print your fucking stories," he stalked out of the room.

Booker Williams quietly gathered some papers from Harvey's desk and followed. Time seemed just unwilling to wait, or work, for them.

In the weeks following Dale Harum's murder, the police got no further than they had the first day. They did have the edge over the previous homicide investigations, knowing the *where,* but they still had no more inkling as to the *who* or the *why.*

Dale Harum had been no more troublesome or scatterbrained a girl than any her age. Pop records. Basketball games. Tie-dyed jeans and wildly colored miniskirts. The telephone. Sweets. Newly painted fingernails. Pierced ears. Boys.

And boys liked her generally, both because she was

pretty and outgoing, fun to have around, and—up to a point—because she was athletic and could meet them on familiar ground. In the few cases where she was more agile or adept than some of them, there were mixed feelings. Still, she'd had no *problems* with any boys so far as the police could determine; nor had she got to the point of "going" with any. She was generally popular with her classmates in junior high, and no one knew of any lasting grudges against her.

Dale's father had died when she was seven, and she and her brother, Dewey, Jr., a year older, had been raised since by their mother and grandmother. Two older sisters, both married, also lived nearby. The mother, Clara, at forty-five was still an attractive blonde with a determined zest for life, and she had done well by her children—working full-time to support them, keeping a neat comfortable home (and paying off the mortgage), and managing to inculcate in her youngsters a sense of responsibility and worth. Dale had been her mother's pet—emerging, Clara thought, much in her own spunky image.

After the girl's death, Clara was in a state of collapse for almost a week, barely rousing herself to attend the burial. She dissolved again then, as six young classmates of Dale's bore her white coffin to the grave, and time had yet to stiffen her to the inexplicable loss of part of herself. . . .

Sheriff Harvey diverted every available man in his department, and the State Police brought in detectives and troopers from other commands, and this combined force made a house-to-house canvass of the LeForge Road-Railroad Street triangle within which it was assumed the girl had been accosted. They did not come upon anyone who remembered having noticed anything unusual in the neighborhood the evening of April 15.

Despite official pleadings through the media, the police in fact were receiving almost no help or comfort from the local citizenry. People had turned silent, withdrawn, as though benumbed by the overwhelming incredibility of it all.

The instrument that finally helped break through the lethargy came from an unexpected source. On Saturday, April 19—as Dale Harum was being buried —a twenty-year-old coed at Eastern Michigan University went to the Ypsilanti *Press* with a proposed open letter of appeal to the public, which she had composed that morning. The editors of the *Press* liked it: it had dignity and poignancy, and a dramatic relevance. For the writer was Sheila Pindar, whose own sister had been the first victim.

The letter was published on the front page of the *Press* Monday afternoon:

TO THE PUBLIC . . .

Have you ever walked from class to class on campus without looking over your shoulder for fear of someone watching you? I haven't!

Have you been able to sleep without awaking in the middle of the night from an endless nightmare? I haven't!

Have you ever had a stranger smile at you and want to smile back, but been too afraid to? I have!

Have you ever driven down Geddes Rd. without shedding a tear? I haven't!

For I am the sister of one of the five victims of the brutal, perverted murders that have taken place in this community within the last two years. My sister was the first—whose sister will be the last?

Many of you will read this letter and pass it off by consoling yourselves with "it could never happen to me." But I believe that after five of these slayings, it should be obvious that the murderers have no respect of persons and that any one of you could be the next!

I think it is time for the people of this community to exercise their rights as citizens and to do their part to see that justice is brought about.

I am, therefore, making a personal appeal, not only for myself but for all young girls who are forced to live in this constant fear for their very lives. This appeal being that you—the public— come forth with any information you may have, which in some way may be relevant to these murders.

Sincerely,
Sheila Pindar

This letter claimed considerable attention. It was reported in other newspapers. Area radio stations interviewed the girl. A Detroit TV channel brought her in to repeat her appeal before live cameras. Everybody seemed to be talking about it.

Sheila Pindar's moving plea unloosed the public reaction the local police agencies had looked for, and tips began to pour in again.

One of the first was bizarre. A writer-photographer of the Ann Arbor *News*, who specialized in outdoor essays, was roaming the countryside north of Ypsilanti when he came upon a life-size baby doll hanging from the barbed-wire fence—head down, reddish hair, torso bruised and scarred, and clad only in the tatters of a white blouse! Pictures he'd seen of Dale Harum's corpse as it had lain on the roadside flashed through the journalist's mind. Could this doll represent some macabre memento of the girl's murder? Had the killer himself placed it there? Shaken, he hastily took photographs of it, which were picked up by local papers.

The answer to the riddle came less than twenty-four hours later, when the Ypsilanti *Press* got a phone call from a housewife whose home was out in the country north of Ypsi. She said that her child had found the doll among some rubbish behind their garage and, having played with it awhile, had hung it on the fence. And that had been two weeks or more ago. So much, the police thought, for symbolism.

But on the heels of that came a more concrete piece of evidence. On Wednesday, the twenty-third, one week after the discovery of Dale Harum's body, Sheriff's Detective Chester Wilson was making a routine check of the abandoned farm. Down in the basement, the beam of his flashlight reflected off a shiny, small object on the floor near one stone wall. Wilson went over and squatted over a girl's earring; thinly gold-plated, dime-store stuff. Funny, he'd been in this basement maybe a dozen times in the past week, and he'd not noticed an earring before. As he examined it, puzzling, his eye was caught by something else on the floor a few feet away. It was a scrap of white cloth, soft, smooth, a synthetic material of some kind such as from a drip-dry shirt. *This* hadn't been here before either, he was sure. Could someone have got down here since the last time he or one of the other men had inspected the place?

Leaving the two items where he'd found them, Wilson went to do some inquiring. Headquarters had had no surveillance report in the past twenty-four hours of any trespassers at that scene. There was no need to check back farther: he'd been there himself more than once during that period. Then he telephoned the State Police crime lab in Plymouth and got the commander, Detective Staff Sergeant Ken Christensen, on the line.

"In your inventory of the farm on LeForge Road," asked Sergeant Wilson, "did you make a gold earring? Not real gold, a cheapie."

"Wait a minute." Christensen dug into his file. "No, some bits of costume jewelry, but no earrings. Why?"

"I found one."

"When?" The detective was interested.

"Today. Just a little while ago. In the farmhouse basement."

"Well, I'd bet my tin it wasn't there a week ago," said Christensen. "We put that place through a sieve."

"Your guys couldn't have missed a little thing like that?"

᠊ "Not a chance. Not in *this* kind of homicide, surely. It must have been left there since then."

"How about scraps of white material, like shirt cloth?"

"We cleaned the place out. That's how we got the matching pieces of the girl's blouse. There wasn't a scrap left behind."

"Then maybe you better get over there," Wilson said, "because I just found one of *them*, too. It could be from a blouse."

Sergeant Christensen drove the fifteen miles from Plymouth and, with Sheriff Harvey, examined Sergeant Wilson's finds. The piece of material definitely was from the same blouse that Dale Harum had worn. The earring was a little harder to trace. The girl was not known to have been wearing earrings. Then Christensen remembered something. He checked back on the compiled list of personal items missing in each of the homicides. Mary Grace Clemson had worn cheap gold earrings which had not been found. It had to be confirmed, but this looked like it might be one of them.

The implication was clear, and it was discomforting: The killer *had* returned to the scene of the crime— crimes?—to brazenly leave his calling cards for the police. He was smug, feeling superior.

Was he superior?

"Like I said, he *is* playing games," Doug Harvey growled. "Laughing at us. Well, maybe the cocky bastard will be funny once too often!"

"Maybe," mused Ken Christensen. "But how many other girls will it take?"

The investigators no longer had cause to complain about lack of communication with the public. The Sheila Pindar letter had loosed would-be leads by the score—all logged on tip sheets and doled out to the respective police agencies, each once more to be looked into irrespective of how farfetched or unsubstantiated or seemingly irrelevant. Not one panned out.

And there were the inevitable crank calls. The breathless ones: "I had a dream last night, and I saw the killer!" (This usually followed by the offer of a pencil sketch of the dreamed killer.) The stargazers: "The moon is not right this week to find the murderer. Give me nine days, and I'll wrap the whole thing up for you." The impatient: "Why don't you call in the FBI? I watch them on TV every week, and *they* always clear up their cases long before this!" And the mean, tantalizing calls, suggesting when and where the next murder would take place and sometimes even giving a clue to an unnamed target. Or the vicious or obscene threats in the middle of the night to policemen themselves, or their wives or children . . .

But nothing came of any of it. They still weren't getting anywhere. It was maddening. *Something* had to give!

And then, on May 13, something extraordinary happened. A mysterious fire broke out in the barn at the old farm on LeForge Road, and the remains of the place burned to the ground.

CHAPTER 9

IT WAS A little after 3:00 A.M. that a sheriff's deputy cruising in his patrol car along Geddes Road noticed the small yellow flames snapping up out of the blackness. He radioed the fire department, and by the time the blaze was under control there was only a smoldering heap of unidentifiable rubble.

Now what the hell was *this* all about? The barn had been where the matching coil of the electrical wire used to strangle Dale Harum had been found. Had her killer returned to see to it that whatever other secrets the place may have held would stay hidden forever? But then why had not the farmhouse been fired as well? More evidence had been discovered in its bowels than in the barn.

It didn't make sense. Yet the unnerving senselessness was to be aggravated still further within only a few hours.

Reporter John Cobb of the Ypsilanti *Press* got word of the fire over his car radio as he drove to work at seven that morning; he detoured to take a look at the scene. The farm site was deserted. Parking just off the road, he picked his way up the eroded driveway toward the smoking pile of debris that had been the barn. Suddenly he stopped short.

Before him on the ground, in an even row across the driveway, lay five plump lilacs. The purple blossoms, each the size of a man's fist, appeared to have been freshly cut. Cobb looked around. The nearest lilac shrubs he could see were up near the old farmhouse some twenty yards off. These must have been picked there and placed here deliberately. But *why?*

It struck Cobb like a blow. *Five* fresh lilacs. Five *murders!* A reminder from the killer! God, how sick!

Cobb, his adrenalin pumping, was deciding whether to look around some more or to hurry on to his office and get cracking on this twist, when he heard a car pull up on LeForge, and a sheriff's deputy got out.

"Deputy!" called Cobb.

The officer strode toward him, his eyes narrowed and his mouth set.

"What are you doing here, mister?" challenged the officer.

"I'm a reporter. Ypsi *Press.* I came by to check out the fire. But look what I—"

"It don't matter who you are, you still got no business here without official permission. This place is under police investigation."

"I understand. And I'm trying to tell you, I just found something here that needs to be investigated." Cobb stepped aside and drew the other's attention to the lilacs. "I came up the drive and these were lying here like this."

"So they're flowers. Lilacs." He looked at Cobb. "What about it?"

"Don't you see. *Five,* set in a row—and not too long ago, probably since the fire. Five lilacs, representing five homicides—the murdered girls! And this is where the fifth one was killed! Don't you think *that's* something?"

The deputy stared down at the flowers again, his expression changing. "I guess the DB *had* ought to know about this." He jotted a few lines. "And your name is Cobb? . . . Okay, I'll report this. You get along now. Somebody will probably be in touch."

At the sheriff's headquarters, there was indeed consternation—not only over the perplexing lilacs, but about this new reporter, John Cobb, as well. The young man seemed to have an uncanny way of turning up at just the right moment. And they had had other cause to give Cobb more than passing thought.

Only a week earlier, a citizen's complaint had been received about a "suspicious" automobile, with two persons in it, that had been parked for some time late at night in the driveway of a small radio station southwest of Ann Arbor. A patrol car in that sector was asked to investigate, but before it got there the subject car had sped away in a northeasterly direction. This was reported by the original complainant, the message transmitted to radio cars in the area, and within minutes they'd caught up with the car, which seemed to have slowed to a stop and was waiting for them to catch up. In the car were a young male and a younger female. The man got out and identified himself: John Cobb, reporter for the Ypsilanti *Press*.

What had they been doing parked so long in that driveway?

They'd had a date, Cobb said. They were—just talking.

Then why the hell had they run?

Well, Cobb explained, they'd heard the report of a "suspicious" car on his own police radio, had realized that it was *his* car, and he'd thought it just as well to avoid a hassle. When he'd realized that it was turning into such a big deal, he figured it was better to stop and straighten it out before anything regrettable happened.

The officers, after corroborating Cobb's story with his date, had let the couple go. But they'd reported it in full, with a few pointed remarks about civilians being so privy to police communications.

Cobb had been made aware of the repercussions

almost immediately. The very next morning a uniformed deputy appeared at the *Press* office demanding
to search his car.

"Do you have a warrant?"

The deputy glowered at him. "No, but we can get
one real quick. It'll be simpler if you just cooperate."

Cobb gave him the car keys and hurried back to his
desk to wrap up his story. When he got out to the
rear parking lot fifteen minutes later, he found that
the deputy and his partner had emptied the Chevelle
of everything movable. Arrayed on the asphalt behind
the open trunk were not only the spare tire, jack, and
other tools, but his pair of prized cameras, high-
powered binoculars, first-aid kit. Up front were stacked
various paraphernalia taken from the car interior: twin
radio monitors, a compact burglar alarm unit, a blue
beacon light from the rear window shelf; even a tin
auxiliary police shield from Chautauqua County, New
York, which he'd kept as a memento, had been removed from the windshield.

While the partner continued a minute inspection
into the glove compartment, the first deputy scrawled
the inventory on a pad. "Get rid of the siren on that
burglar system," he drawled to the dismayed reporter.
"It's illegal. So's the blue flashing light."

"It's a fire signal. It was okay back in New York
State."

"Not here. And you're not auxiliary police here,
either. Don't show that shield anymore, or you could
get in real trouble."

"The way it looks," Cobb grumbled, "you fellows
already think I *am* in some kind of trouble."

"Could be. You got State Police clearance for the
radio monitors?"

"The license is in the glove compartment."

The deputy found the radio license, studied it a moment, and dropped it back on the seat. "It's there."
He sounded disappointed.

"Now will you tell me what is going on?" Cobb demanded.

"As far as you're concerned," the deputy said drily as he shut his pad, "it's just a routine inspection. We got complaints you had too much official equipment in your car, unauthorized. We inspected and found the violations. You have been warned. If you fail to comply, next time you could be locked up. Okay?"

The deputy and his partner drove off in their patrol car, leaving Cobb to replace his own things in his car.

John Cobb thought he was just being harassed. He would have been amazed, however, to know that at the Sheriff's Department his name had been added to a list of tentative homicide suspects.

Since the night auto chase, they'd done some back-checking on Cobb. He'd come to Ypsi only in mid-March, and in rapid succession three girls had been slain. He had shown up at the Harum girl's body only minutes after the sheriff himself. When State Police Detectives Little and Taylor had been called to investigate the body in the Wayne County cemetery back in March, John Cobb had arrived practically on their heels. And Detective Sergeant Canada of the Ann Arbor Police Department recalled that the day Mary Grace Clemson's corpse had been discovered out in the uninhabited subdivision, John Cobb had been one of the first reporters at the site—possibly *the* first.

Although otherwise there were no complaints from area police about Cobb, these coincidences of his popping up out of nowhere at each of the latest murder locations bothered Sheriff Harvey and his aides. *Were* they mere coincidences? Nobody was above suspicion.

Then there were those police monitors that Cobb evidently kept on day and night—wouldn't it be invaluable to a killer to know practically every move of his hunters?

Now this business of his being discovered alone at the burned-down barn and "finding" a row of portentous lilacs! It was as though Cobb was *looking* for special attention. Well, he was getting it.

Attention remained focused on the fire. The Sheriff's

Department wanted very much to get to the bottom of that. The strange business of the lilacs was secondary. They felt strongly that if the arsonist were collared, they might also have their murderer.

But almost three days of intensive probing had got them nowhere. And then, late on Friday, May 16, Sheriff Harvey and his people got a shock. The State Police summarily announced the arrest of a twenty-one-year-old former E.M.U. student as the confessed arsonist.

Harvey didn't stay stunned for long. He turned furious. His department hadn't even been advised that the State Police were also working on the fire case! Not only did it show a damn lousy spirit of cooperation, but the uppity bastards were overstepping their prescribed bounds! The state was supposed to *assist* the local police, not take over. So where did they get off tippy-toeing around on their own private investigation of *this* local case? Like the Sheriff's Department had gone out of business!

All right. So what did they have in the arson case?

An Eastern dropout named Robert Gross, the arresting officers said, had admitted setting the barn fire while under the influence of alcohol. Further, he may have had one or perhaps two other accomplices. Gross had refused to implicate anyone else, but detectives were talking to certain individuals and they expected to make additional arrests imminently.

The State Police said that witnesses had spotted Gross and several other youths watching the firemen battle the blaze, and a subsequent house-to-house inquiry through the proximate area had uncovered the suspect. But perhaps the most intriguing factor was where Robert Gross had been found to live—on lower LeForge Road, diagonally across from, and within easy sight of, the Harums'.

Gross had told police that he and his friends had often whiled away time at the abandoned farm with their six packs of beer or pints of liquor, and sometimes—"when we got lucky"—with girls. In fact, he said, that night before the fire he'd had a girl up to the barn, but they had a fight over something and she walked out on him. He'd stayed, drinking bourbon, and got loaded, and decided to burn the place down. He just put a match to the dried-out hay in the barn loft and in seconds, *whoosh!* He ran out and waited across the road, and watched as it went up in flames.

But he insisted there'd been nothing else behind it. He denied vehemently—and with an evident sincerity that was disconcerting—having known any of the murdered girls, including Dale Harum, even though she'd lived just across the road from him. Sure, he might have seen her around the neighborhood at some time, but he doubted he'd have recognized her if he'd fallen over her—he didn't take much notice of thirteen-year-old grade-school girls.

That was the sum product of a weekend of intensive probing and grilling of Robert Gross.

On Monday, May 19, the State Police picked up a school chum of Gross's who lived in an adjoining apartment complex, charging him as accessory to the act of arson. The prisoner, a nineteen-year-old Eastern freshman named William Sterling, confessed that he had helped set the blaze. Otherwise, his story essentially matched the other's and checked out as factually.

The only gambit remaining to the disappointed investigators was the polygraph—if the cold-blooded lie detector could record no sign of subterfuge or conspiracy, then they would have to concede that, as far as the homicides were concerned, they'd struck out once again.

Gross and Sterling both agreed to be tested. In a day-long session, a top polygraph specialist separately tested each of the suspects twice over, alternating both the content and sequence of sets of carefully devised questions.

At day's end, the specialist emerged to inform waiting officers that he was convinced neither of the two knew anything about the Washtenaw murders.

Now that it had been determined that the burning of
the barn was unrelated to the murders, what was the
significance of the five lilac blossoms, if any? Both
Robert Gross and William Sterling had professed no
knowledge of the flowers placed on the farm driveway.
If *they* hadn't done it, who had? Had the actual murderer also been around the farm that night or early
morning? Or was the whole question still another red
herring, empty of any pertinent meaning? It was beginning to seem that the answers might never be known.

Spring lengthened into June, and the homicide investigations remained static. During the first week of
June, reports of attacks on females in three distant localities attracted the interest of beleaguered Washtenaw County lawmen. In Rockford, Illinois, a drifter
locked up on a drunk charge, telling police he wanted
to clear his conscience, made a startling "confession":
In the fall of 1967, either October or November he
thought, in woods about five miles outside Ann Arbor,
Michigan, he had stabbed a young woman and shoved
her body down a ravine. He hadn't waited to make
sure she was dead, but . . .

In Ann Arbor, police pored over their records of reported assaults during the stated time period. There
had been none such as the man described, and no
known violent deaths. Could there have been another
slaying that they hadn't even suspected?

But in Rockford, nothing more cogent could be got
out of the besotted derelict—no details about the alleged incident, not the beginning of a description of the
supposed victim, no more precise hint of the location—
and after medical examination it was concluded he was
just a dipso sunken to murky delusions.

Then came the news from Bay City, Michigan, on
Saginaw Bay about a hundred miles north of Ann
Arbor-Ypsilanti, of a twenty-four-year-old barmaid, an
attractive divorcée, having been attacked and raped
early one morning on her way home from work. Her
car had been cut off by another, she'd been carried off
into the next county, there raped, beaten, and stabbed,

then dragged a hundred feet down a forest trail and thrown into a clump of bushes, left for dead. Hours later, however, the woman was found wandering nude, bleeding, and in a state of shock, along a county lane outside of Midland, more than twenty miles from where she'd been abducted. She had eight knife wounds, her trachea had been severed, and her jaw broken.

This sounded frighteningly like the vicious crimes being investigated in Washtenaw County. And when, thanks to a description gleaned from the battered but surviving victim, Bay City police quickly picked up a man and charged him with the attempted homicide, there was a spurt of hope that they might have lucked into something: The prisoner was a Jesse Franklin, age thirty-one, currently of Bay City but formerly of Ann Arbor!

But the elation was deflated even before Washtenaw investigators could get on their way to Bay City to interrogate the man. Word came through that until only a few weeks before, Jesse Franklin had been an inmate of the Southern Michigan State Prison at Jackson, serving out his eleven-year sentence for a previous rape.

During the same week, interstate police teleprinters clacked out the report of a gruesome double slaying of young females in the shore area of southern New Jersey. The nude, mutilated bodies of two vacationing college students, who had been missing for most of a week, were found in shrubbery just off the Garden State Parkway near the ocean town of Somers Point. Both had been stabbed repeatedly with a small sharp instrument, probably a pocket knife.

The girls, both nineteen, were Sally Jefferson of Camp Hill, Pennsylvania, and Eleanor Mason of Excelsior, Minnesota, roommates at a women's junior college near St. Louis. They'd spent a week at Ocean City, New Jersey, then had left by car early on the morning of May 30 to drive to the Jefferson home not far from Harrisburg, Pennsylvania, some 135 miles distant. They'd got only about five miles.

The types of these victims and the way they'd been

killed also seemed to bear unusually strong resemblance to the Ann Arbor-Ypsilanti murders. The Michigan State Police dispatched two detectives to New Jersey to see if they could find any deeper implication. Perhaps the Washtenaw killer had moved east.

Thus the situation stood as June entered its second week—quiet, a little uneasy still, but less strained. It had been almost two months since the Harum death, the weather was glorious, and soon the bulk of students would be gone from the area for the summer holiday, which could only be a blessing. . . .

But the deceptive calm was not to last beyond June 9.

At about 3:15 that Monday afternoon, three teenaged boys in an open truck turned into the unused driveway of a deserted farm off North Territorial Road in Northfield Township, some six miles out of Ann Arbor. The three worked part-time for a landscaping contractor, and they were taking a familiar shortcut to a nursery beyond the empty farm. Suddenly one of the boys screamed out for the truck to stop.

They had almost run over a body lying in the path. It was a female, sprawled on her back, mostly naked, her torn clothes scattered about. There was blood all over her.

CHAPTER 10

LIEUTENANT BILL MULHOLLAND, who had been cruising in a radio car not far from the area, was the first police officer at the scene, followed quickly by Sheriff Doug Harvey. The farm site of about ninety acres obviously had gone untended for some years; the fields were withered and weed-grown, the remains of a house and two barns skeletonized, a yard between the house and outbuildings strewn with rusted machine parts, remnants of furnishings, and other accumulated refuse. It was in the midst of this debris that the body lay, fifty yards in from North Territorial Road.

After examining the corpse, Harvey snapped directions to Mulholland: the prosecutor's and medical examiner's offices were to be notified, and the State Police crime lab at Plymouth; then, of urgent importance, deputies were to be brought in to cordon off the area as soon as possible. No one unauthorized was to be permitted near the location—*no one*. The sheriff had a plan.

Less than an hour after the discovery, the bleak farm was sealed. Prosecutor William Delhey himself had arrived, along with Pathologist Robert Hendrix. They found the victim to be a rather large young woman in her early twenties, about five feet seven and 135-140 pounds. Her dark brown hair was twisted in a pony tail. A strip of sheer purple fabric was wrapped around her forehead like a headband. Apparently it came from the tattered purple garment, a blouse perhaps, that lay across her outstretched left arm. A blood-spattered white skirt covered her legs below the knees, and across her feet was folded a black-and-red-striped outer coat of rainwear material. On the ground near her were torn panties, a bright reddish orange; dark-colored panty hose, slashed through the crotch; a mud-stained yellow and white babushka. A few feet off lay a single shoe, a purple patent leather pump with an ornate bow at the instep.

It had rained heavily the night before, and from the sodden appearance of her, she must have lain there at least since then. She'd been stabbed many times over her entire body, as though her attacker had been in a frenzy. Two thrusts to her chest had gone squarely through the heart. And her throat had been cut in a grotesque semicircle extending from approximately one-and-a-half inches below her ear. But it appeared that these savageries had been inflicted after she was already dead.

The actual lethal force seemed to have been a gunshot high in the head, above the hairline. This deduction was drawn not as much from the deadly placement of the bullet itself—preliminary judgment indicated that it probably had pierced her brain—but from a secondary wound to her right thumb. The thumb had been shattered as by the impact of a deflected bullet, which suggested that the girl—still alive —had raised her hand instinctively to protect herself, and probably ducked her head at the same time, as the killer had fired at point-blank range.

In any event, Dr. Hendrix's first determination was that she had been dead some twelve to eighteen hours —which would put the slaying at some time between about nine o'clock Sunday night and three Monday morning. That left two key questions (other than the all-important, Who had done it?):

One, had the girl been killed at this place or, as in the other homicides, somewhere else and transported here? They again concluded the latter, because there was so little evidence of blood around or beneath her, and she had bled profusely. One of her shoes was missing, as well as two red buttons from the blood-soaked raincoat.

The second question was for the moment perhaps the more intriguing: Who was she? There was no ID on the girl—no handbag, wallet, personal letters. There were just a couple of slim leads: One was the label in the raincoat, which read *Ruby's, Kalamazoo*. It was the only identifying mark found in any of her clothing, but it indicated at least that she was from the western end of the state—and perhaps a student at one of the local universities. (But a quick radio check with all area departments was negative. No female of that description had been reported missing.) The second clue was a rhinestone clasp with the monogram *A* pinned to the yellow and white babushka. The only other distinguishing items were a pair of silvery triangular-shaped earrings, still clipped to her ear lobes.

Until they could nail down the victim's identity, it would be hard to know where even to begin looking for her assassin.

None of the frightened boys, all from Whitmore Lake, a few miles north, had ever seen her before. Nor did any local residents, brought in reluctantly to view the remains, know who she was. There were few homes in the area, the nearest several hundred yards east and across North Territorial Road. The family there—whose telephone the boys had used to call the police—said that the farm had been vacant and up for sale as long as six years. People did wander in and out occasionally, and some nights autos might pull in to park. But they hadn't seen or heard any activity over there Sunday night.

The body removed to the morgue in Ann Arbor, the farm site was left to the crime lab unit and a force of deputies and troopers combing the unplowed fields. Sheriff Harvey went into a huddle with Prosecutor Delhey. Harvey wanted to try again the plan that had misfired at the murder site on LeForge Road: clamp down tight security and see if they couldn't draw the killer back.

Delhey looked pained. "It's a good idea, Doug— but I'm afraid it's impossible now," he added apologetically. "The story's already out. I heard it on the radio news on my way here!"

The sheriff gaped at him, then exploded: "Already? *Again!* How in the hell—?"

The prosecutor only shook his head. And even as they stood there miserably, they spied the first reporters pulling up in cars, beginning to argue with the deputies trying to keep them away. In the forefront of them was John Cobb of the Ypsilanti *Press*.

Spotting him, Harvey swore: "*That* fucker again—!"

It wasn't long, however, before the furious sheriff learned that he could not pin the leak on Cobb this time. It had come from one of the teen-agers who'd found the body. The youngster had taken advantage of a lull in police questioning to phone in the scoop to radio station CKLW in nearby Windsor, Ontario, which had a standing offer of twenty-five dollars to any listener providing a news break (with $1,000 to be awarded later to the best such tip during the year). It had been the bulletin aired from the boy's information that Prosecutor Delhey had heard even while en route to the "blacked-out" murder scene.

The autopsy of the unknown girl, performed Monday

evening at the U. of M. Medical Center by Dr. Hendrix, added little information of direct use. It was confirmed that the primary cause of death was the bullet to the head; the slug retrieved from her skull was too mangled for specific ballistics identification, but it was of .22 caliber. The killer must have attacked his victim with the knife immediately thereafter. She had also been sexually assaulted, although there was no determination of whether that had occurred before or after death.

The MO was essentially the same as in most of the previous slayings—except for the use of a gun. Only Jeanne Holder among the others had been shot.

Well into Monday night they still had no line on the identity of the victim. Detectives pored through sheafs of recent missing persons bulletins from police agencies across Michigan, but none matched this young woman. The police in Kalamazoo were requested to give their files special attention, but the word that came back also was negative.

First news of the murder had swept through the community, though, and into Sheriff Harvey's makeshift command post—the cramped lobby of the jail—came inquiries from friends and relatives of young women who, though not having been officially reported as "missing," had run off or whose whereabouts were unknown. Half a dozen times during the night, grim-faced detectives raced out to escort anguished relatives to the morgue to show them the corpse. Each time, the sobbing response would be: "No, it's not her. Thank God!" So far she could only be referred to as Number Six.

First thing Tuesday morning, the State Police in Kalamazoo went to Ruby's, the department store whose label was in the raincoat. Ruby's had several outlets in the area. The only one that stocked coats of that type was located on Portage Street in Kalamazoo proper. There, photos of the slain girl were shown to employees, but none recognized her. Striped raincoats were fairly popular items. About all the inquiry produced was the strengthened supposition that she did come from that area.

Finally, Sheriff Harvey released to the media one of the less gruesome closeups of the girl—eyes closed, her face in apparent repose, taken from an angle that did not show any of the brutality done her. The picture would be published and televised widely. Perhaps somebody would recognize her.

Washtenaw County sheriff's deputies and State Police troopers had the painstaking task of scouring the rural countryside in search of the actual murder site. If they could find the spot, it might give them at least a starting point. There would likely be evidence of blood. The killer might have left a trail, if not of blood itself then of some other sign that could be pursued.

The wearisome hunt continued all day Tuesday, radiating from the farm across Northfield Township into adjoining Webster and Salem townships, up through Whitmore Lake to the north and back down toward Ann Arbor. And then, as dusk was falling Tuesday evening, the unlikely strike was made.

Deputy Earl Lewis, cruising in his patrol car north along Earhart Road, stopped just short of Joy Road, the dividing line between Ann Arbor Township and Northfield. He'd noticed something peculiar lying in a crude service road leading off Earhart into a large excavation, a commercial gravel pit desolate now after working hours. Lewis went to take a look.

It was a pair of women's shoes, side by side— matching brown loafers. The deputy looked closer. A few feet off he found a red button . . . then another. He studied the ground. There were dark brown stains splattered all around the pebbles and sand. Dry, but without doubt blood.

Lewis radioed headquarters and investigators rushed to examine the finds. The two red buttons matched those on the victim's raincoat. On a chance, the loafers were tried on the dead girl's feet—and they fit. (It had been assumed that she'd been wearing the purple pumps, matching her outfit . . . now why was one missing?) Preliminary tests also indicated that the dried blood matched the girl's, Type O, although that admittedly was a common type. Its present consistency put the time of its spilling at some time late Sunday night.

Through the operators of the gravel pit, the Washtenaw Sand and Gravel Company, police were able to contact workers and truckers who'd been in and out of the site the past two days. A few said they'd noticed the shoes lying discarded in the service road as early as Monday morning, but it didn't arouse any particular interest—litter from passing motorists, or nighttime parkers, was not uncommon out in that remote area. None had seen any buttons nor looked close enough at the ground to notice anything like blood.

In any event, this had to be the murder site—five miles by road southeast of where the body was left. It was also just a few miles north, along the same Earhart Road, of where first Jill Hersch's corpse and later Mary Grace Clemson's had been discovered. Indeed, of six victims, five now were known to have been slain and/or disposed of within, roughly, a twelve-square-mile area. The only one that still seemed not to fit the pattern was Jeanne Holder, found over in Wayne County, but she too might well have met her fate within the apparent death zone.

The latest victim's identity was still unknown late Tuesday when a young couple nervously entered Sheriff's Department headquarters on Washtenaw Avenue. They had seen the dead woman's picture in the evening paper, and they thought—they couldn't be sure—it might be the girl's roommate.

She identified herself as Betty Hart, from Battle Creek, a recent graduate of U. of M.'s School of Architecture and Design, as was her roommate. Both had stayed on in Ann Arbor for the summer to take additional courses, and they shared a flat in a private dwelling just off the campus. Miss Hart said she'd last been with her friend the previous Thursday, before leaving for a long weekend at home. She hadn't seen Audrey since her return. . . .

Her roommate's name was Audrey Sakol. She was from Kalamazoo.

A for Audrey. Kalamazoo.

Betty Hart said that when she'd returned Sunday night, the flat was empty but the lights were on. Nothing appeared out of place except for a shoebox lying open on the living-room floor. The box looked new.

Did she recall her roommate's having a pair of purple leather pumps with bows? No, Miss Hart said.

How about a sheer purple blouse, a white miniskirt, a red-and-black-striped raincoat, a yellow-and-white kerchief? Yes, she thought so.

Miss Hart's companion was Samuel Farrar, also an Architecture and Design graduate, who lived at home in neighboring South Lyon. He and Audrey were good friends, sharing a particular interest in photography. They'd been together only the past Friday, when he'd been at her place until about midnight, showing her how to use his enlarger. When he left, she was developing prints in her makeshift closet darkroom. She'd been in good spirits, looking forward to a party she was going to the following night.

Farrar said he'd telephoned her over the weekend but got no answer. He'd next gone to the flat on Monday evening to pick up his enlarger, and was surprised to find the prints Audrey had been working on still in the pan of hypo rinse. This struck him as queer, because she certainly knew enough about developing not to have left prints immersed like that for any length of time.

The sheriff's detectives suggested they go out to the morgue.

Betty Hart and Samuel Farrar managed a taut

control on the way to University Hospital. But when the sheet-covered figure of the dead girl was wheeled out from its refrigerated cubicle, they seemed to cave in. As the sheet was turned down to reveal the sallow, puffy face, Miss Hart whirled away, hands covering her eyes, crying: "I can't look! I can't look!" Her knees buckled and, faint with revulsion, she had to be assisted outside. Farrar had also turned ashen. "I don't know . . ." he gasped. "It could be her. . . ." He, too, had to turn away.

Hardly the positive ID hoped for. By now the detectives felt reasonably sure it *was* Audrey Sakol, but they wanted something more certain before calling in the girl's family. They'd learned that Audrey Sakol had worked part-time at the university library, so her supervisor there was contacted and brought to the morgue as well. A pale, conservative man of about forty, he steeled himself to gaze at the corpse.

After almost a full minute, he looked up, face drawn. "I think it is Audrey," he murmured.

At about that hour Tuesday, a hundred miles west in a neat Colonial house in Portage, a suburb of Kalamazoo, Marcus and Judith Sakol were settling down to a quiet evening of reading, as they often did now with all three children grown and away. Mr. Sakol, a chemist, absorbed himself in a technical book as his wife scanned the Kalamazoo Gazette. A front-page story reported another grisly homicide near Ann Arbor, and she shuddered. . . .

The Sakols, like many other parents, had grown increasingly restive about the terrible things happening where their daughter went to school. It was beginning to seem that it could happen to anybody. They'd hoped that Audrey would get away from there, come home finally, after graduation in May. But then she'd wanted to take this two-month summer course for a temporary teaching certificate. And now she was talking about staying on to work toward a master's degree. It made her mother vaguely uneasy. Of course Audrey constantly reassured them that she was in no danger; she was careful and she never went out with strangers. Just the day before, they'd had another letter from her, mailed Saturday, and it was typically breezy and cheerful. She was going to a big party that night. Her work was going well. She could hardly wait for August and holiday. Dad had better not forget he'd promised to buy her a Volkswagen!

Reading on in the account from Ann Arbor, Judith Sakol began to feel a strange chill. There was a description of the victim, as yet unidentified: five feet seven inches, about 135 pounds; dark brown hair; black-and-red-striped raincoat . . . the story was continued on page 2. There was a picture of the dead girl's face—

Marcus Sakol sensed his wife's silent horror. He leaned out from his easy chair to get a glimpse of the newspaper in her lap. "Oh, good God!" he cried out, springing to his feet. *"Audrey—!"*

By the time the authorities in Ann Arbor tried to contact the Sakols Tuesday night, the couple was already speeding east along Interstate 94. . . .

It was past midnight when Audrey's father and mother reached the Washtenaw County Jail. They were ushered past gathering reporters directly into Sheriff Harvey's private office. Marcus Sakol was a large, stout man of about sixty, white-haired and bespectacled, whose gait was heavy and somber. His wife, holding onto his arm, was gray and slight, almost frail-looking in a summer print dress that looked a size too large. The sheriff, choosing his words with care, filled them in on what was known to date. They listened blankly, saying little. Then Harvey drove them to the University Medical Center.

In the hospital the sheriff led the man and woman slowly down the long, bare corridor to the morgue. She walked with small and measured steps, as though uncertain with each that she could make the next. Her husband guided her by the elbow. They paused appre-

hensively before the heavy metal door to the morgue.
An attendant swung it open, and it closed behind them.

The Sakols looked upon their daughter's broken
body in silence for several minutes. Then the mother
murmured simply, "Yes," and leaned against her husband. She had no tears. The father kept staring down
at the still form, the muscles in his jaw working.

Suddenly he yelled: "No! *No!* I didn't come here to
see my daughter dead! I worked too damn hard to
raise her, to send her to this—" His face was wracked
with strangling helplessness. "I don't *want* her dead
body! I want her *alive!*" The fragile woman turned to
the big man and held him, her small hands patting and
caressing as he wept.

Once the girl's identity had been established, the police had managed to narrow somewhat the information
gap as to her last known movements.

A small task force of officers, led by Sheriff Harvey
and Ann Arbor's newly promoted Deputy Chief Olson,
earlier had swarmed through her rooming house, on
Thompson Street in the center of Ann Arbor, two
blocks from the main Michigan campus. It was a
three-story Victorian relic, hemmed in between a windowless municipal parking facility and a new high-rise
apartment tower. The three-room flat shared by
Audrey Sakol and Betty Hart was at the ground floor
rear. Guided by Miss Hart, the detectives found nothing of Audrey's apparently missing; not only were all
her clothes, except what she'd been wearing, still there,
but—puzzlingly—also her wallet-purse containing both
cash and personal identification, including a valid
Michigan driver's license. When did a woman go out
anywhere, one of the men wondered, without her
purse?

Yet there were no signs of unwanted intrusion, no
disruption—except for the empty shoe box on the floor.
It was from Jacobson's, a local boutique . . . and a
check there had disclosed that a young woman of

Audrey Sakol's description had purchased a pair of purple pumps on Saturday. It did not appear, then, that she had been abducted but had left voluntarily, perhaps with someone she knew. Interviews of other tenants produced no evidence either way. One elderly couple in the ground floor front apartment did say they'd run into Audrey around 8:30 Saturday evening; they were on their way out to a movie, and she was coming into the house with clothing over her arm. She'd greeted them cheerfully, as usual, and gone toward her apartment. When they'd returned a little before midnight, all was quiet in the rear flat.

Thus, 8:30 P.M. Saturday was the latest time, so far, that Audrey Sakol could be accounted for alive. Where had she been coming from at that hour? The answer to that might help clear up the other key questions: What time did she again leave the house? Where did she go then (or intend to go)? And was anybody with her?

Some answers came through sooner than expected. A U. of M. coed named Caroline Brown called the police to advise that Audrey had been with her much of Saturday afternoon and into early evening—until about 8:30, in fact. Interviewed at her apartment on Forest Avenue, across the university campus near the Medical Center, the distressed young woman said that Audrey had come over in midafternoon Saturday to iron a purple blouse and white skirt she planned to wear that night to a party. She seemed excited about the party, in honor of a popular local rock musician, which was to be held at the Depot House, a reconverted former railroad station in downtown Ann Arbor.

The two chatted all afternoon; they had snacks for supper; then, near 8:30, Caroline drove Audrey home. Audrey had said the party was to start about nine, but that she didn't want to get there too early. She mentioned nothing about going with a date or expecting to meet anyone in particular there.

Did Miss Brown know of any young men Audrey had been seeing?

No one current that she knew of, the young woman said. There had been one fellow she'd seemed to like quite a bit the last semester—a charming young Egyptian who'd been studying for his doctorate at U. of M. But he'd returned to Egypt. Audrey had been hoping that he could manage a teaching fellowship for her at the American University in Cairo, where they could be together again.

Otherwise, Caroline didn't think Audrey had dated much.

That left the party at Depot House.

Depot House long ago had been the main passenger station of the Ann Arbor Railroad. It had been restored several times in recent years by entrepreneurs trying to merchandise its turn-of-the-century quaintness—all without success. Lately it was mostly rented out for private social affairs.

The party Saturday night had been jammed—loud and late. Some two hundred young people had been invited to celebrate the birthday of musician Bleek Mundy. Many of the guests—the police learned—were from U. of M. and E.M.U., but just as many were nonuniversity locals. The party had wound on until nearly 4:30 Sunday morning.

Immediate indications were that Audrey Sakol had been there from about 9:30 P.M. until anywhere between 2:30 and the time it broke up. Bleek Mundy, who told detectives that he personally had invited Audrey—they'd met a few weeks earlier through mutual friends—said he hadn't actually noticed her there himself, it being so crowded and he so busy on stage, but that several people had told him they had. One remembered seeing Audrey on the dance floor. Another said that Audrey had still been there at 2:30 A.M., among a group at a table. And another thought she'd left the Depot House not long after that in the company of an unknown young man with long flowing hair. Finally came a report—from the driver of a

Deteroit *News* truck—that a female of Audrey's description had been with "a couple of hippie types" in Dunkin' Donuts as late as 4:00 A.M. Sunday.

But then, with the evidence seemingly marking a clear trail to the subject's movements that night and into early morning, the police were confronted by a sharply variant account. A U. of M. student named Art Wilkens, who said he'd known Audrey Sakol quite well, stated that he had been at the Depot House party from about 11:00 P.M. to 1:30 A.M., and he had *not* seen her there. Wilkens said he did spot one girl who bore an interesting resemblance to her, who might in fact have been mistaken for Audrey by some not so well acquainted with her. And following him, others who knew Audrey, if only by sight, told police interviewers that they could not say they'd seen her at the party; they tended to doubt it. Others were less sure, one way or the other.

The investigators did come upon a girl who'd been at the Depot House who, it had to be admitted, looked very much like Audrey Sakol. She was about the same age, size, and coloring, and in certain conditions— such as at a rock blast in alternately dim and flashing lighting—the two could easily have passed for sisters. The girl did not know Audrey Sakol and had not noticed anyone at the party who looked like herself.

Had *she* been at a table with friends at about 2:30 A.M.? Possibly. Had *she* then left with a young man with long hair? It could have been around then.

Back, suddenly, to uncertainty. Now it could no longer be assumed even that Audrey had *been* at Depot House. Back to 8:30 P.M. Saturday, the last point in time when she positively had been seen. Obviously, at some time she had left the house on Thompson Street. Either she had to have been taken by someone, or called a cab, or walked. There was no evidence as yet of the first conjecture. The second turned up a blank—no local taxi companies had logged a call to or from that address all weekend. That left,

for the moment, walking. Teams of officers fanned out
to retrace Audrey's probable route in every direction
from 45 Thompson Street—door by door, building by
building, block by block. But the exhausting exercise
produced not one person who recalled having seen
such a young woman, either alone or escorted, that
Saturday night.

Her trail, having started out so promisingly, had
ended abruptly. The police were stymied again. It
was like a recurrent nightmare.

Of course, there was the usual barrage of tips and
rumors—more than five hundred within days of the
murder. But even more disturbing now than the futility
of most of them was their unmistakable new tone of
meanness and paranoia. Many callers suggested a
significance in that each of the six victims to date had
been in her menstrual period when slain (not definitely
established); or that each had pierced ears (untrue;
four had); following which, in all too many instances,
such callers named acquaintances who should be investigated because they were known to harbor morbid
revulsion for menstruation and/or pierced ears in
women.

A dark rumor spread among the universities' more
radical element that none of the murder victims had
been allowed to be seen once in the morgue (false)
for a very sinister reason: secret scientific experiments
were being performed on their corpses—holes drilled
behind their ears and their brain fluids extracted, one
underground report insisted—as part of some ghoulish
research for the military-industrial establishment.

The relentless pressure squeezing the community
was bringing the real neurotics to the surface.

There were, of course, the usual "confessions" that
had to be looked into. Word came first from police in
Flint that a man in custody there was claiming to be
"the killer they're looking for down in Ann Arbor."
He was about thirty, seedy and coarse, with the furtive

manner of one who had been on the run. He seemed to know a lot about the Washtenaw slayings, but it soon became apparent that all he did know had been gleaned from published accounts. (Over the months, the prosecutor's office and the police had selectively released some false or incorrect information and withheld certain other facts about the crimes, for two sound reasons: one, to minimize the likelihood of other psychotics with homicidal bents knowing the exact MO's of any of the killings, perhaps to simulate the performance against some personal target and have that palmed off as another "coed murder"; and two, to be able to test just such inevitable confessions as this man's.)*

Another confession on the heels of this seemed to hold more promise. A prisoner in the city jail in Nashville, Tennessee, reported that his cellmate had told him he had killed "that wild kid" Mary Grace Clemson. The man was pulled out and grilled. He was a twenty-six-year-old Nashville native with a record of petty arrests, who had been for a brief period a groundskeeper at the Ypsilanti campus of E.M.U.

He said he'd picked up the Clemson girl near the big shopping center on Washtenaw Avenue late one Saturday afternoon, and they had driven around awhile. He took her to his room in town, and they smoked a couple of joints and then had a roll in the hay. When they were finished, she wanted to leave, but he didn't want her to and he had to belt her a few times. He tied her up and kept her there the rest of that night and most of the next day. But she kept crying and started to make a racket, and he figured he'd better

---

* Why he had lied became evident shortly. The man was a fugitive from Kentucky, where he was wanted on a first-degree murder charge. Having been arrested in Michigan, he faced extradition back to Kentucky, and there capital punishment was still in force. But the maximum sentence in Michigan was only mandatory life, with, moreover, a fair chance of eventual parole—and if charged and convicted of murder-one in Michigan, he not only would *not* be returned to Kentucky and probable execution but could even wind up a free man in the end.

get rid of her. So after dark he drove to a deserted spot outside Ann Arbor, and there he did a real job on her, so there was no chance of her ever fingering him.

The Michigan authorities, juices flowing hopefully, wired Nashville police some of their special confidential facts about the Clemson murder which only her killer would know. But the disappointing report came back that the man had failed to mention any of these revealing details. Then their fading hopes were dashed further by an official check through the suspect's criminal records: At the time of the Clemson slaying, the man had still been an inmate at the Federal Correctional Institution at Milan, Michigan. Just another psychotic showboat.

The man's own mother put the decisive stamp of mockery upon the episode. She told newsmen in Nashville that it was impossible for her to believe her son guilty of the confessed crime but not out of pure maternal faith: "That one," she said ruefully, "has never once told the truth his whole life."

Six homicides, not one real suspect. The police had been frustrated at every turn, and the community was up in arms. Reward moneys were up to $42,000. Politicians began to voice concern, promising swift action. At a news conference in Lansing, Governor William Milliken announced that the commandant of the State Police, Colonel Frederick Davids, had been instructed to give his personal attention to the homicides, and pledged that "no efforts or resources" would be spared to help local authorities. In Washington, Michigan Congressman Wayne B. Sackett of Portage suggested that it might be time to enlist federal support.

Continuous, relentless news coverage of the unsolved crimes aggravated the growing sense of police futility. The press contingent on the scene had swelled with each new violence. The two Detroit papers now had teams of investigative and feature reporters practically in residence. The big news services, AP and UPI, no longer filed rewrites by local stringers but had brought in first-string byliners. Area TV and radio crews were on hand almost daily. And an increasing number of out-of-state journalists had checked in: Both the *Tribune* and the *Sun-Times* of Chicago were represented, a *New York Times* correspondent had recently materialized, and word was that *Newsweek* and *Time* and perhaps even *Life* would soon descend.

Their problem was that, in the main, there was hardly anything to report. The reporters kept clamoring for news conferences with the investigating authorities, but the lawmen were as loath to keep talking about how much they still did not know as they were to reveal what little they did. It had become an impasse: "News" accounts of the crisis in Washtenaw County turned into repetitive rehashes of the ugliness that had gone before and speculative theorizing of horrors perhaps yet to come. And the lawmen kept looking worse day by day.

Sheriff Doug Harvey was beginning to feel the pressure. So was Prosecutor William Delhey, whose elective position designated him the chief law-enforcement official in the county.

And so on Monday morning, June 16, two days after Audrey Sakol was buried, Delhey called a high-level conference in his office of representatives of all police commands active in the investigations. Colonel Davids came down from State Police headquarters in East Lansing. Sheriff Harvey was there. And Ann Arbor Police Detective Chief Krasny; Chief Ray Walton of Ypsilanti; John Hayes, director of the Eastern Michigan University force; and Delhey's own lieutenants, Assistant Prosecutor Booker Williams and Chief Investigator Roy Tanner.

Delhey was blunt. "Six persons are dead. God knows who or when the next might be. There's a killer—or killers—roaming loose out there, and we've not come close to stopping him. The way we've been operating, we may never stop him. We've either been getting in each other's way or flying off in different directions. I say it's time we all start to pull together—it's no time for any of us to be heroes or prima donnas. We have got to make this an all-out joint effort from here on— and make it work!"

There was no disagreement from the somber police officials. Their jobs were all on the line.

CHAPTER 11

WITHIN FORTY-EIGHT HOURS, the new task force was operative. Space on neutral ground was secured for a joint command post, a vacated one-story building, once a Catholic seminary, in a semirural area midway between Ann Arbor and Ypsilanti. A variety of communications equipment—much of it supplied by the well-stocked State Police—was moved in and activated, along with steel desks, chairs, tables, file cabinets, message boards, maps. Each department allocated a quota of men to operate exclusively out of this "crime center," as it became known almost at once. At any given time, seven days a week, there might be twenty or more on duty, inside or out in the field. The location was given tight security; only working members of the task force were permitted entry.

All were to report to the prosecutor's chief aide, Booker Williams. All information pertinent to the homicides would be fed into the cross-indexed filing system set up by the Ann Arbor Police Department's

Deputy Chief Harold Olson to be reviewed regularly and updated as required.

State Police Sergeant Earl James was brought in from the Flat Rock post and assigned to compose a "documentary," or narrative profile, of each of the six homicides. Sergeant James was to cull his material from everything already known about each victim, as well as from personal interviews of every individual concerned. His aim was three-pronged: To dig up any relevant facts, no matter how small, that might have been overlooked in any of the previous investigations. To organize all known facts in lucid, comprehensible sequence. And, most intriguing, to try to detect any conceivable *pattern* in the murders—some as yet unrecognized thread that might link the crimes, something that, if picked out now, might just aid in forestalling yet another tragedy.

No sooner had the crime center been set up, however, than the law-enforcement agencies were confronted by a new crisis from another quarter that demanded maximum attention. Ann Arbor was rocked by a series of street riots that threatened to tear the city apart.

Tension had been building, growing more ominous for weeks, especially in the university area. The extended, bitter student conflict with local landlords had strained patience even before the successive shocks of unmanageable horror, and by now acrimony had fused with common frustration and anxiety to a dangerously explosive level.

The feared outburst came on the night of June 16th —triggered when two city policemen arrested a long-haired motorcyclist for "stunting" on a crowded thoroughfare near the U. of M. A restless crowd of young people gathered around the police car, and when the apprehensive officers, taking their prisoner, tried to maneuver the vehicle through the crowd, a couple of youths were sent sprawling. As the police car sped off, the gathering erupted into a mob.

Within minutes, they took over an entire block of

South University Avenue, defiantly proclaiming it a
"people's mall." Police quickly surrounded the area
but did not move in. The mob held its ground until
midnight, heaving, menacing, shouting incitements.
But they seemed divided, uncertain how to handle the
impasse they'd unexpectedly forced, and finally their
resolve splintered and they began to separate and the
street was cleared without incident.

But the next night was ugly. Before dusk, packs of
loudly belligerent youths coursed through the avenues
around the university. By nightfall there were fifteen
hundred of them, a marauding army, and they had occupied some ten city blocks. Cars were overturned,
windows smashed and some shops looted, merchants
and pedestrians manhandled. The invaders were dar-
ing the police to try to roust them.

Sheriff Harvey's response was quick. By 9:00 P.M.
he'd mustered two hundred armed men to the be-
sieged sector—every available deputy, Ann Arbor
city policemen, state troopers. Through a bullhorn
Harvey demanded the demonstrators retreat. The mob
hooted. Then a bottle flew from their midst and struck
an officer in the face; it was followed by a fusillade of
other missiles. "Move the bastards out!" roared
Harvey. The police charged.

It was a brutal war that raged five hours through
the night. Not until 2:00 A.M., with the stench of tear
gas hovering over Ann Arbor, were the streets finally
cleared. By then, twenty-five persons had been hospitalized—seventeen of them policemen—and seventy-
seven rioters dragged off to jail.

Of those arrested, many were found to be members
of such local extremist groups as the White Panthers
and Trans-Love Energies; a number of others were
not even from the Ann Arbor area. Only a dozen were
university students. This proved to be the key to restoring order.

While Sheriff Harvey geared his forces for a possible
resumption of hostilities the next night, concerned citizens among both the city and university administration

tried to reason toward a solution. U. of M. President Robben Fleming appealed to assembly after assembly of restive students to recognize that responsibility for the riots lay not with the police but largely with a reckless horde of *outsiders* whose motives were unclear except to exploit disruption for its own sake. Was the university, and its overwhelming majority of decent, thoughtful students, to be dragged down to the level of uninvited and unknown gutter terrorists?

Student leaders seconded the president. Ann Arbor Mayor Robert Harris, a liberal favorite of the academic community, added his own earnest appeals for sense and restraint.

Still, it was a long, uneasy day. Only the third night would tell the story.

By 7:30 P.M. some two thousand youths jammed the streets around the university. Tense police watched but kept their distance. The crowd's mood was uncertain—raucous, but more mischievous than aggressive. They sang and chanted and milled around, many waving bottles of wine or slugging down canfuls of beer, and the pungent aroma of boldly smoked marijuana thickened the air. But the night wore on, and there was no outbreak.

At 11:00 P.M. two scruffy motorcyclists, wearing leather jackets emblazoned *God's Children* and evidently high, started haranguing a segment of the crowd to get some action going. There was a long, anxious moment of indecision, some stirring . . . and then a knot of bearded young men hooted the agitators down. "Why don't we just cool it!" someone cried. There were cheers of agreement. The tension was broken.

By midnight, most had drifted off, babbling but spent. It was really over.

In thinking back, later, on those nightmarish few days, Sheriff Harvey was bedeviled by one thought above all else: How cruelly ironic it would be if one of the rioters who'd been locked up, and since released, had in fact been the elusive killer they were so desperate to find!

Three weeks after the Sakol murder, there still were
no new developments on that or any of the crimes.
The last week of June the new crop of summer scholars, make-up students, and incoming freshmen taking
advanced courses poured into Ann Arbor and Ypsilanti.
Many, especially the new, younger ones, did not seem
aware of the intense situation locally. Many, therefore,
were surprised, bemused or, in some cases, titillated by
the resolute security precautions in evidence around
them.

Since the last homicide, more uniformed police had
become visible at both Michigan and Eastern than
ever before. In addition, on both campuses military
veterans and R.O.T.C. students had marshaled volunteer patrols; a number of the male fraternities had
organized nighttime escort services for coeds; other
groups, on their own, were keeping constant watch on
the women's residence halls and campus parking lots.

With few if any hard developments to report, but
pragmatically unwilling to let the inherent drama go
unsustained, the press continued to offer a steady diet
of feature stories on the slayings. The approaching July
Fourth weekend seemed to a number of editors to
provide usable fodder. The Detroit *News,* for instance,
ran a long recap, bristling with both analysis and speculation, under a somber three-column headline:

MURDEROUS WEEKEND
ANN ARBOR, YPSI
DREAD 'DEADLY 4TH'

The article's hook was that it had been at about this
same time in éach of the previous two summers that a
young woman, a coed, had been murdered: Did July 4
have a "special, twisted significance to the 'Coed
Killer'?" It was recalled that the first had been
Marilyn Pindar, "murdered the Sunday following
Independence Day, 1967." (Actually, she had disappeared on July 9. There was no July 4 "weekend" that year, as the date fell on a Tuesday.) Jill

Hersch had been next, almost one year later—"killed the Sunday before July 4, 1968." (She was last seen on June 30. The Independence holiday was the following Thursday.) Thus fearfully, the writer brooded, did "Ypsilanti and Ann Arbor await another Fourth of July weekend."

As for the police, they laid no materiality to dates. Tragedy knew no calendar. July 4 was no more meaningful in this context than, say, June 9 or March 21—except, of course, that it *was* a holiday weekend, which always escalated the possibilities of some kind of trouble, and except for the increased possibility, now, that such damn-fool newspaper articles might actually program some lunatic into fulfilling the morbid conjecture.

As it happened, a heavy rain kept people off the streets much of Friday the fourth, and the holiday seemed to be starting out on a welcome note of quiet.

But a little after midnight, the Ann Arbor Police Department switchboard jangled an alert. An almost incoherent caller reported a young woman in trouble in a rooming house on North State Street. A Michigan student. She'd been shot.

Elizabeth Peters had been shot twice in the head at close range by a small-caliber weapon, but she was still alive. The police rushed her to Ann Arbor's St. Joseph Mercy Hospital.

She'd been discovered by another U. of M. student, who had heard the shots from her room next door. Lucy Barron had also heard something else: At about 11:30 P.M., lying sleepless in bed, she'd heard Beth Peters quietly let someone into the house. She'd made out murmurings of conversation from the next room—the visitor was a male, she was sure—and clinkings from the communal kitchen down the hall. And then, after the two loud reports, she'd heard soft footsteps hurrying out the front door.

The Ann Arbor P.D.'s top brass, Chief Walter

Krasny and Deputy Chief Harold Olson, took over this investigation personally. They found no signs of a struggle in Miss Peters' room. The victim's purse was on a chair, undisturbed, a wallet with cash and credit cards still in it; theft evidently had not been the motive.

For once there appeared to be some clues. On a table they found a ceramic mug about three-quarters filled with coffee. Olson dipped a finger into it; the coffee was still warm. This meant that it had been poured just before the shooting. Either the woman had been drinking it or her visitor had. The assailant's *prints* could be on the mug!

On the same table lay a newly opened package of Pall Mall cigarettes. Only one cigarette appeared to have been taken from it; but there was no stub in sight, nor in fact any ash trays in the room. Told that Miss Peters did not smoke, Olson examined the package more carefully. It was opened in a peculiar way: the tinfoil had not been torn off the top, as most smokers did, but slit and unfolded neatly along the edge of the tax stamp, forming a kind of cowl that could be refolded to protect the cigarette tips after one had been extracted. Olson had seen only a few people take such pains; it was idiosyncratic enough to stand out.

"The butts are his," he chirped to Chief Krasny. "Now we're starting to cook."

The State Police crime lab crew went through the premises until after dawn. They returned to Plymouth with a wide sampling of possible trace evidence from the victim's room—including the coffee mug and the package of Pall Malls.

At midday, Charles Peters, Beth's father, arrived, transported by the State Police from their home near Grand Rapids. He had been delayed because his wife had collapsed and had to be hospitalized herself. Mr. Peters went straight to St. Joseph Mercy Hospital and sat with his daughter, who lay in a deep coma but still clung perilously to life.

In the meantime, investigators had started digging into her background. Beth was twenty-five, a U. of M. graduate with a master's degree in sociology and currently working toward a doctorate. Serious, earnest, with few close friends, in recent months she had been almost totally absorbed with a complex thesis project for Michigan's Institute for Social Research, the subject of which she had been strangely guarded about, even for her, the friends said. Sheafs of notes and several hundred pages of rough typescript had been found in her room, and now detectives reading them saw that Beth's thesis amounted to a probing, intensely sympathetic examination of the causes and effects of social disenfranchisement in the ghettoes; it called for a bold commitment by society to regenerate those who, because of insufferable living conditions, had been forced to turn to crime.

What interested the police most about this was the disclosure that the young woman's research had taken her to some of the seamier urban areas, including Detroit, where she'd managed to get surprisingly close to a number of possibly dangerous individuals. One mentioned several times in her notes was an "Eddie," apparently an ex-con in whom she'd developed a special interest.

When detectives finally got a chance to talk with Beth's father, one of the questions they asked was whether she had ever mentioned working with criminal types as part of her research. This appeared to strike at a sore spot. Mr. Peters, a slight, pale man of fifty who was a bookkeeper in Grand Rapids, pursed his lips distastefully:

"She did mention something about it. The most exciting part of her project, she said, was how she was going to prove that a man who had gone wrong *could* be rehabilitated. She seemed to have one individual in mind—though she wouldn't say who he was or what he'd done. One of her professors had brought her together with this person—Professor Kayser, Theo

Kayser. I gathered he would be supervising the 'experiment.' "

He paused. "To tell you the truth, the whole thing never did sit right with her mother and me. . . ."

Detectives went to the university to ask Professor Kayser about the subject Beth Peters had been working with. Kayser, in his early thirties, was an aggressively "involved" sociological type with built-in suspicion of police, and he was reluctant at first to name the man. Finally, persuaded that it was in Beth's as well as his own best interests, he identified him as Edgar Hatton, Jr., a resident of Ann Arbor. He was black.

Hatton had served time for rape.

Inquiries at the address Kayser gave them, a shabby boardinghouse on Gott Street in a predominantly black neighborhood, disclosed that Hatton, who lived there alone, had not been seen for several days. "Junior," as he was called, came and went unpredictably. He used to work for the Ann Arbor Sanitation Department but hadn't been working lately. He was described as short, only about five feet five, and wiry; he was about twenty-eight years old.

Shortly after 10:00 A.M. Sunday, July 6, Elizabeth Peters died. Her father had sat by her side more than twenty hours, helplessly watching her life drain away.

An autopsy, performed immediately by Dr. Robert Hendrix, showed no wounds other than from the bullets; she had not been sexually molested. The chunks of metal recovered from her brain—determined to be from a .22 automatic—had caused such massive damage that she might never have come out of the coma even had she lived.

At noon, Ann Arbor Chief Krasny announced her death at a news conference.

The reporters' first question was spontaneous: Was this Murder Number Seven?

Krasny was prepared. "It's the seventh homicide of a similar nature in two years. I can't say yet whether it's part of a chain. If we can nail this one down quickly, maybe we'll find answers to some of the other questions, maybe not."

How close *were* they to breaking this one? Were there any clues? Did they have a suspect? When did he expect—?

"I can't go into particulars at this time," the chief said. "We're hopeful. We've got a line on the weapon. We've located a couple of witnesses—they're under wraps, naturally—who've provided a partial description of the assailant. And . . ." he paused dramatically, ". . . before dying the victim was able to give us certain information that could prove helpful. . . .

"That's all I'm at liberty to tell you at the present time."

It was plenty. The newsmen scurried to their telephones and typewriters.

Krasny had been bluffing. The only "line" they had on the murder weapon was its type. The only "witnesses" were Lucy Barron, who'd heard things but seen nothing, and one other young man, who, while sitting on his porch several houses away on the night of the crime, "thought" he may have seen the fleeting silhouette of a man running from the scene. As for Beth Peters' dying "information," she had never regained consciousness. What possibly helpful information investigators had picked up she *had* given them, but unknowingly—from the contents of her room and what had been learned of her associations. Edgar Hatton, Jr., for instance.

Krasny was shooting craps. He was hoping that when word got out that the police seemed to be closing in, the killer—Hatton or whoever—might panic and blunder into their arms.

It was worth the gamble. Something had to break right sometime.

Fortune smiled, for once, sooner than they could have dared hope. Sunday afternoon, State Police Sergeant Ken Christensen raced from the Plymouth crime lab with exciting news: Latent prints lifted from Beth Peters' room, including one on her coffee mug, had been identified. They belonged to an ex-convict named Edgar Hatton, Jr.!

Hatton was finally located late Sunday night. Two stakeout teams of detectives, stationed in parked cars at opposite ends of Gott Street, spotted a slim figure moving stealthily through trees toward his boarding-house. The cars converged and stopped him. The man admitted he was Junior Hatton. They took him down-town.

Hatton was a disappointment. Every police officer who had worked on the murder cases had formed a picture in his mind of "the" killer. Each one's visual-ization differed, of course, but each probably would have matched in certain characteristics: physical at-tractiveness, cleverness, confidence, glibness—and strength. Junior Hatton displayed none of these qual-ities. He had a furtive look about him. His inexpensive sport shirt and trousers were rumpled and soiled, as though unchanged for some time. His manner was shambling, his speech barely literate. He was not jaunty but forlorn.

"You want a lawyer, Junior?" Harold Olson asked him. They were seated at a table in an interrogation room at Ann Arbor P.D. headquarters, Hatton be-tween Olson and State Police Captain Walter Stevens. Four or five other detectives stood by or came and went. A stenographer sat in a corner.

"A lawyer?" Hatton's eyes widened. "What I need a lawyer for?"

"Among other things, you may be in parole viola-tion. You haven't worked in a couple of months, and" —Olson glanced at a sheet before him—"you quit the last job, right?"

"My parole officer know all about that. Ain't no vio-lation. My P.O. and me is cool. He *helping* me. . . ."

"You're still entitled to have a lawyer present. If you want, we can—"

"Don't need no lawyer," said Hatton flatly.

"Okay. But you understand that anything you

say . . ." Olson unhurriedly recited his rights. "Now, how's your P.O. been helping you?"

"He get me some work . . . with some of them U. of M. people."

"Great. Doing what?"

Hatton paused a beat. "Well, it ain't a *job,* you see. It's like volunteer. I'm helping with this kind of study they're into."

"Would that be Professor Kayser?"

"Yeah, that's the one." Hatton licked his lips.

"Who else?" Olson saw perspiration suddenly glisten on the man's forehead. The detective prodded: "How about Elizabeth Peters?"

Hatton nodded but his eyes flicked away from Olson. "Yeah, I see her sometime."

"How well do you know her?"

"We get along. She pretty nice. . . ." His voice had become a murmur.

"When'd you see her last?"

"I don't know . . . a while."

"Not this weekend?"

"No, man," Hatton said quickly. He forced a thin smile. "I been out of it for three days, man. Partying."

"Where?"

"All over. I don't even remember some of the places. Just balling with friends, you know?" He looked it. His eyes were red-rimmed and he needed a shave.

Olson studied him, then from his shirt pocket he took an unopened package of Pall Mall cigarettes. "Smoke, Junior?"

"I could use one," Hatton said. "My brand, too."

Olson tossed him the pack. Hatton slit the wrapper along the tax stamp, then carefully unfolded the tinfoil until it stood up like a cowl. Extracting one cigarette, he refolded the wrapper and slid the pack across to Olson.

The chief of detectives glanced at Walt Stevens, then asked: "When was the last time you did see Elizabeth Peters, Junior?"

Hatton exhaled and thought. "I don't know . . . a week, two. . . ."

"How about this past Friday night?"

"No, man! I told you—"

"Maybe you were too out of it to remember."

Hatton's mouth worked, but nothing came out.

Olson leaned toward him. "You do know she's dead, Junior? Murdered?"

Swallowing, he croaked, "Yes."

"How do you know that?"

"From the radio."

"Then why'd you let on you didn't know it?"

"I don't know. . . . Don't like to think about that, maybe."

"Because *you* killed her?"

"Me?" The man had gone rigid.

"You'd been partying, making the rounds, looking for a little action. But it was raining and the town was dead, and then you thought of Beth Peters. So you went to her place, and of course she let you in because you were her 'project' . . . or maybe even more—"

"Man, that crazy!" squealed Hatton. "I never—"

"—*but,*" Olson bored in, "she wasn't in the mood, it was late, she turned you off. I'll make you some coffee, Junior, she probably said, and then you go on home and sleep it off. So you get hot, and you say, Fuck you, bitch, and after she comes back with the coffee you stick a gun up that high-toned nose of hers and—*zap!*—blow her away!"

"I got no gun!" Hatton cried. "I was never there! How can you—?"

"I'll tell you how," said Olson, staring him down with icy assurance. "You left your prints all over the goddamn place—*including* on the fresh mug of hot coffee!"

Hatton stared from one to the other, every muscle straining, gagging on unuttered words. Then, all at once, he slumped back, limp as a discarded rag doll.

He shut his eyes and breathed out a long sigh and nodded dumbly.

"Why did you kill her, Junior?" asked Stevens.

Hatton shook his head in a pained wonderment. "I don't know. I didn't have nothing against that girl. I don't even know why I went there." He fell silent, eyes still shut, reaching back. "Seem to me I—I must have just wanted to see somebody *die. . . ."* His eyelids flickered open then, as if to see if *they* understood the self-posed enigma that he himself found it impossible to grasp.

"Junior," asked Olson, "is Elizabeth Peters the *only* young woman you've killed?"

Hatton looked at him curiously. "Yes. The only—" His eyes widened as the implication sank all the way in. "Oh, no! Not them others! *Believe* it, man!"

They did believe it. By this point they'd given up expecting any more. For one thing, they'd found that Hatton had been serving his time on the rape charge during 1967 and 1968—which let him out of the first two murders. But in any case, their long-tested instincts had already told them that the one they were after would have to have more substance, however diseased, than an Edgar Hatton, Jr.

Additional evidence was quickly logged to back up the confession. From a friend named Clarence Boatwright, a nervous twenty-four-year-old who Hatton said had been his companion through his three-day binge, came substantiation of his movements Friday night. The pair had started celebrating the holiday the day before, drinking heavily at friends' houses from Ann Arbor to Ypsilanti. Friday, still at it, Hatton decided to liven up the rain-soaked Fourth. He produced a pistol he'd had stashed away, and they drove around in Boatwright's car looking for a good place to shoot it off. But by Friday night, after hours of cruising Ann Arbor streets deserted in the driving rain, swigging cheap rum and vodka, Hatton had grown morose. On South State Street, just off the U. of M. campus, he abruptly ordered Boatwright to let him out of the car. Mumbling about somebody owing him something, he staggered off into the rain, taking the gun.

That was about 10:30. Boatwright saw him again two hours later, when Hatton came to his door at home. He looked a mess—drenched and frightened. He told Boatwright they had to go for a ride again but wouldn't say why or anything about where he'd been. He remained silent as they drove out US 23. Then, nearing an overpass crossing the Huron River, Hatton cried for Boatwright to stop. Taking the gun from under his sopping sweater, he got out and pitched it far out into the dark river.

On the way back into Ann Arbor, Hatton kept murmuring incoherently about some girl who'd been going to college practically all her life . . . seven or eight years . . . about seeing small black holes instantly appear somewhere. It scared Clarence. Turning into North State Street, they could see a flurry of activity around a corner house—police cars with beacons spinning, knots of people outside. Hatton stared, then as they passed, slumped down low in his seat. "That's the house!" he rasped.

He hid out at Boatwright's house the rest of the weekend, most of the time listening tensely to radio news reports. Late Sunday, suddenly he decided to leave. . . .

It took a State Police skin-diving team four days, even using electromagnets, to fish the gun out of the silt of the Huron River—a seven-shot semi-automatic Bernardelli small enough to fit in a man's palm, the cartridge clip missing. It was identified by Boatwright, and others, as the pistol seen in Hatton's possession. And in the lab it was certified as the instrument of Elizabeth Peters' death.

Edgar Hatton, Jr.'s preliminary examination took less than three hours. Prosecutor Delhey's presentation to the court was complete, compelling, damning. The court-appointed defense counsel could not offer a

168 THE MICHIGAN MURDERS

single alibi witness. Judge Sanford J. Elden swiftly
remanded Hatton to the county jail to await trial for
first-degree murder.*

So it looked like they had a murderer—but not *the*
murderer. A check of Hatton's gun, a foreign make,
and the type of bullets used, established that it was
not the same .22 used against either Jeanne Holder
or Audrey Sakol. It had already been established that
he was in prison when both Marilyn Pindar and Jill
Hersch were slain. And absolutely nothing had been
uncovered to connect him with any of the other coed
murders.

The older, larger menace remained. Assuming that
they *were* after a single individual, they still could
only guess about what *kind* of person they should be
looking for. Young or old? White or other? Male or
female?

There was no shortage of gratuitous advice on the
subject. *Everybody* seemed to have a pet theory to
contribute—not the least of the donors coming from
among the host of practicing and teaching psycholo-
gists abounding in the academic community:

*A young man suffering deep, perhaps psychotic,
fears about his masculinity* was how one analyst
characterized the subject; while a second saw him as
*a smooth operator who digs chicks, highly intelligent
and glib enough to appeal to innocent and idealistic
young women and elicit their trust—right up to the
instant of his lethal assault.*

Another: . . . *supremely self-centered, a self-styled
"colorful figure" with a consuming appetite for the
limelight and attention.* Yet another: . . . *may see*

---

* Hatton's trail was first set for December 8, then set back to January
8, 1970. During the trial, a defense psychiatrist testified that Hatton
displayed definite signs of mental illness, that he had told the doctor
of having heard "voices" urging him to "kill! kill!" and that the
defendant's violent action had been the result of "irresistible impulse."
A hung jury—at one point 11-1 for conviction—finally acquitted Hatton
on grounds of insanity, and he was committed for an indeterminate
period to the maximum security mental institution at Ionia, Mich.

*himself as a "hero"—with an unshakable, symptom-
free, and fully self-justified conviction that he is fulfilling a far greater mission than his own personal
pleasure. And, as an extension of that, possibly an
extremist of some quasi-political camp . . . contemptuous of a "despotic establishment" . . . imposing himself as the merciless executioner of any supposed
"enemy" to his cause.*

All of which was regarded as high-flown and, at
best, of little practical help to earthbound homicide
investigators. They didn't question that the killer more
than likely *was* disarmingly attractive or innocent
looking, and facile enough to be able to lure his victims without arousing initial suspicions. (A threatening, or loathsome, predator could only have snatched
them by force; and it did not seem reasonable that
such could have been done no fewer than six times—
keeping in mind the circumstances of each crime—
without once having caused some kind of ruckus, without ever having drawn *some* bystander's attention.)
The question that *had* begun to intrigue the police was
whether the killer perhaps used different guises in approaching prospective victims. In order to lull apprehension, gain trust, indeed evoke sympathetic response,
had he represented himself as someone familiar and
safe—say, a clergyman, or a teacher, even a police
officer?

But as for the killer's unknown hangups, neurotic
thought processes, behavioral compulsions, the investigators had about given up hope that they might close
a trap by anticipating him, psychoanalytical guidelines
notwithstanding. As Prosecutor Delhey by now had
concluded: "We might *never* find an answer by trying
to dope this person out. Our problem has been in at-
tempting to ascribe logical lines of reasoning and behavior to one who is unpredictably *il*logical and savage.
We just have to come up with something solid—hope
to be at the right place at the right time."

For all the painful theorizing, then, the situation—
more than a month since the slaying of Audrey Sakol—

was unchanged, the prospects still bleak and chilling: It would likely take another murder, or attempt, before the police could make any real move to stop the murders.

CHAPTER 12

THE ULTIMATE INDIGNITY, it seemed to the hapless lawmen, was visited upon them in mid-July. A citizens committee in Ann Arbor announced that it had persuaded Peter Hurkos, a controversial Dutch-born "psychic" (who had gained a certain notoriety in, among other cases, the earlier Boston strangler investigations), to come in from California to help solve the local murders. Police reaction ranged from skepticism to outraged incredulity.

Prosecutor Delhey grumbled something about being unwilling to "give this Hurkos a nickel for five pennies." Sheriff Harvey was even less charitable. "A goddamned mind reader?" he said. "I wouldn't piss in his ear if his brains were on fire!" Only Ann Arbor Chief Krasny expressed a reluctant willingness to receive the visitor. "We've certainly nothing to lose," he said.

It took unflappable Booker Williams, Delhey's chief assistant, to put the development in perspective. "Either this man Hurkos is going to come up with something we haven't—in which case we'll be ahead of the game," he said drily, "—or he's not, which is what I personally expect. But either way, I've a strong hunch we *can* look forward to something else. With all the publicity about a 'wizard' coming in to expose the killer, unless I read our man wrong he's going to have to kill again very soon—maybe even while Hurkos is here, to show him up, right under his nose."

Peter Hurkos' career had waned since his inconclusive participation in the Boston strangler investigations five years earlier. Now, in 1969, he was enjoying what might be termed a comeback.

The uneducated onetime merchant seaman had been a psychoscientific wonder since 1941, when, at the age of thirty, after surviving a four-story plunge from a painting scaffold in The Hague, capital of his native Netherlands, he was found newly possessed of an unexplainable cerebral phenomenon often referred to as "sixth sense" or "ESP." In his case, the strongest influence seemed to be psychometric—an ability to "sense" facts about an unfamiliar person merely by being in close physical presence or by touching some object connected with the individual.

Although mystified by his occult "gift," in the decade following World War II Hurkos managed to make it work for him. By the mid-1950's, he had realized acclaim on the Continent and in Britain for his public performances and uncanny private consultations, and for certain help he had apparently provided in a number of missing persons and criminal investigations.

In 1956, Hurkos visited the United States for the first time under the sponsorship of a psychical research foundation. He soon decided to forsake Europe for the fresher prospects of faddish America. Adroit application of the mystic's powers soon turned him into a bona fide celebrity. High-placed individuals and business organizations began to seek his counsel. Predictably, the show world raised him into its firmament: He became a prize guest on TV talk shows, cabarets vied to book him, magazines profiled him. He moved to the West Coast, where he was befriended by one insecure or superstitious luminary after another, from screen idols to tycoons, who offered to pay him handsomely to be, in effect, their soothsayer.

And more and more law enforcement agencies came to find it possible to swallow professional antagonisms and permit him to explore hitherto unfathomable cases—in Florida, Virginia, California, Nevada. His deductions (the psychic "vibrations" he experienced from clutching an article of clothing of a victim or suspect, concentrating on a subject's photograph, prowling a key location like some preternatural bloodhound) were not always on target, but his percentage of accuracy or near-misses was high enough to make the most cynical cops pause to watch and listen.

Thus Hurkos was riding something of a crest when, early in 1964, he was called in on the eighteen-month-old homicide investigations in Boston. After a week of roaming the city under a protective umbrella of police, at last Hurkos zeroed in on one wispy, effeminate, fifty-six-year-old shoe salesman with a history of mental disturbance, who had only recently come to attention after having written a suggestive letter to the Boston College School of Nursing. Hurkos shut out all other possible suspects: *This* was the multiple killer sought so desperately, he assured the professionals; there was no need to look further. Whereupon drained but satisfied, he abruptly packed and left Boston.

But the police were not satisfied with Hurkos' "solution." Exhaustive investigation of the shoe salesman confirmed only that the man was sick, all right— enough so as to warrant his commission to a state institution—but that he could *not* be the homicidal strangler.

And then, not too long after, came the sensational confession of Albert DeSalvo.

From that point, having lost credibility, Peter Hurkos' fortunes declined—especially in mercurial Hollywood. Finding himself shunned by those who had sworn by him, who had, indeed, helped fashion the very mystique about him that had nourished his career, he retreated into disillusionment and melancholy. . . .

But by 1969 Hurkos appeared to have regained direction—under the twin prods of a new, aggressive business manager and a new, ambitious young wife. His talents were coming into demand again: $2,500 for a weekend at a Lake Tahoe night club, $10,000 for a week at a Los Angeles theater. He recaptured attention in the newspaper columns, in magazine features, on TV guest spots. Lost status was returning.

This, then, was the "psychic detective"—now aged fifty-eight, but renewed and reassured—who was on his way to Michigan to exorcise the demon of Washtenaw County.

Hurkos had been first drawn into it by an enterprising Detroit journalist. Back in June, following the sixth slaying, Arnold Rosenfeld, thirty-six-year-old editor of the Detroit *Free Press*'s Sunday magazine, had got an inspiration: With local police still at an embarrassing loss to track down the murderer, it could be engrossing to ask the nation's most celebrated clairvoyant to conjure a likely suspect—from two thousand miles off, no less. Rosenfeld contacted Hurkos' manager and arranged a weekend's interview with the psychic at his Studio City, California, home.

Rosenfeld brought photographs of the six victims to date and a handful of personal items he'd managed to secure from friendly police sources. Hurkos knew nothing of the Michigan murders as he never read newspapers, he said, but requested only a scant briefing from the editor on the overall situation there. From this, in two intriguing sessions he gave Rosenfeld a telepathic "composite" of the killer:

A young man, under twenty-five, not big—five-six or five-seven, maybe 140 pounds . . . light-colored hair, a mustache . . . but not always the mustache; sometimes he dresses in women's clothes, very mixed up about sex . . . he loves dolls, teddy bears . . .brilliant, maybe a student, but not only a student; he

has a job, works days, goes to school at night; salesman, maybe . . . lives in an apartment, not at home
. . . good with his hands, with machines; loves cars;
drives a motorcycle . . . name Rick, or Rich; Richie,
Rickey; very strong . . . left-handed . . . hair curly
. . . beautiful face, but strange eyes; one eye possibly
bigger than the other . . . takes dope sometimes . . .
wears dark leather jacket, or sweater, brown, dark
brown . . . old car . . . moves bodies to different
places; kills, then moves bodies . . . gets thrill, sexual pleasure from killing girls; from watching dying
faces . . . does not sexually attack every girl; not his
thrill—just the killing . . . has a knife, maybe four or
five inches long . . . at one time he worked in gar-
dens, or with trees; a nursery . . . police are not sure
if he killed every girl, but yes, he is the one . . .
there will be more, another . . . maybe a colored
woman. . . .

The timing of Rosenfeld's subsequent feature
story was fortuitous from a journalistic standpoint. It
ran in the *Free Press*'s Sunday edition of July 6, only a
day after the fatal attack upon Elizabeth Peters, then
thought to be the "coed killer's" seventh victim.

Out of that was born the "citizens committee." It
consisted, actually, of just two persons, a young
married couple: Alex Archer, twenty-seven, a Michigan alumnus with a small real estate business in Ann
Arbor, and his twenty-year-old bride of only a few
weeks, Naomi. Through Rosenfeld, they reached
Hurkos' manager, Barbara Silver, in Los Angeles and
asked how much Peter Hurkos would charge to come
to Michigan and solve the murders. They were told
$5,000 plus expenses . . . *plus* a commitment be-
forehand from the police that the psychic would
receive their full cooperation.

The Archers didn't have $5,000, so they mounted
a public subscription campaign, earnestly going about
to every area newspaper and broadcasting outlet imploring the citizenry's financial investment toward end-
ing the common horror. At the same time, they

approached the local police-agency heads seeking the pledge of acceptance that Hurkos required. The State Police wouldn't talk to them at all. The prosecutor's and sheriff's offices were openly contemptuous. Only the Ann Arbor Police Department listened with any equanimity.

Chief Walter Krasny was sensitive enough to the current mood of his community to recognize that fires of discontent might only be fueled anew were the police, having already lost so much face, now arbitrarily to scorn a desperate move by troubled citizens to put an end to their nightmare, however unlikely the assistance sought. Besides, Krasny knew a little about Hurkos' work for other police agencies, and he was not so sure that the man *was* a crackpot or charlatan.

So he told the Archers that, while it must be understood that no one in authority, including himself, could officially endorse Hurkos' participation in the homicide probes, should he come to Ann Arbor under legitimate sponsorship he would be treated courteously at least, and—the only concession the chief could make— might even expect *some* cooperation, to the extent perhaps of certain factual orientation on which to base whatever investigation he chose to undertake.

The Archers were distressed; that was hardly an unrestricted commitment. Moreover, their subscription campaign was going badly—to say the least. Despite all the publicity their appeal had received, after several weeks only $10 had come in, two $5 money orders. Unhappily, they relayed word to the coast: they just weren't going to be able to meet Hurkos' terms.

But Hurkos surprised them. He'd been giving the Michigan situation much thought, and the challenge now stirred him personally. He *would* come, waiving his fee, if only travel expenses were underwritten for himself and an associate. The delighted couple said that they would find a way to handle that.

The media played the announcement up flamboyantly, as though a liberator were coming at last to loosen the anxious people of Washtenaw County from their long bondage in fear. . . .

Hurkos arrived at Metropolitan Airport on Monday evening, July 21, amid a hurly-burly of shouting reporters, glaring lights, and television cameras. An unsmiling, rumpled bear of a man, the Dutchman was hobbling on crutches (the result of a fall in California's ice-bound Sierras a month earlier, as he'd led a search expedition for a lost hunter). But now he rose to the clamorous occasion, growling in a heavy accent to the battery of microphones and cameras: "This killer knows I come for him. And I *get* him! Maybe he comes after me, so. But Hurkos is not afraid! Let *him* be afraid now! I come thousands of miles to find him, *and I don't give up!*"

The next morning, Sheriff's Detective Bill Mulholland and Lieutenant Mel Fuller of the E.M.U. campus police found surprises in their assignment slots at the crime center. They were to report to the Inn America, the motel on Washtenaw Avenue where Peter Hurkos was encamped, and "cover" the mystic until further ordered. The two veteran officers reacted with indignation and disgust.

Mulholland and Fuller had been among those at the crime center just the night before enjoying a good laugh over this Hurkos business, having heard that Walter Krasny at the last minute had assigned one of his own men to *chaperone* this turkey—a young dick from the Ann Arbor *Juvenile* Division, for Christ's sake. Now *them?* complained Mulholland and Fuller.

Mulholland and Fuller's consternation deepened when they got to the Inn America. Contrasting with the relative nonactivity at the official crime center, the place was crawling with reporters and photographers.

Already in attendance in Hurkos' main-floor suite were Chief Krasny, impeccable and composed as always, and his assigned watchdog, a well-built, pleasant young officer named Bob Scofield, who looked just a bit sheepish at the appearance of the two dour new-comers. Hurkos appeared preoccupied. More affable was his traveling companion, Ed Silver, a cheerfully brisk, well-groomed man in his thirties. He was the husband of Hurkos' personal manager, Barbara Silver, and the psychic's spokesman. He himself was not involved professionally with Hurkos, Silver hastened to inform the detectives; he was president of a Los Angeles linen supply company and was just along as a friend and admirer of Peter's.

The day's agenda included visits to the respective sites where the victims' bodies had been found and also as far as possible to places they had been known to frequent. Mulholland and Fuller groaned inwardly; what a waste of time!

Hurkos seemed to sense their antagonism. He asked: "Who bring pictures of dead girls?"

Krasny produced a stack of large manila envelopes. Each had a victim's name printed across the front.

"Mix up on floor," Hurkos directed. "Don't show names."

They were spread out, face down, and the psychic hunched foward, studying them. After a few moments he reached down and picked up one envelope. Holding the name side away from him, he spoke. "This is picture of how you find girl's body, *ja?*"

"That's right."

Hurkos frowned. "I see only one shoe. One shoe is missing?"

Mulholland glanced at Fuller, eyes twinkling. He could see that it was Jill Hersch's envelope—and Jill Hersch, they knew, had been wearing *both* her shoes when found.

The Dutchman caught the detectives' silent amuse-ment. "I show you how she look in this picture," he said with a trace of irritation. Lowering himself from the couch, he stretched out on the carpet on his right side, legs spread, one arm extended, the other along his trunk. As an afterthought, he pulled up his shirt until it was bunched around his neck. "Like this," he growled up at them, adding, "small branch of tree nearby, also large stone. Look now."

Fuller was smug as he opened the envelope and withdrew an eight-by-ten glossy photograph. But as he looked at it his eyes widened. "I'll be a sonofabitch!" he exclaimed and passed the print to Mulholland.

Not only had Hurkos depicted the sprawl of the seminude body almost exactly—even to the broken tree limb and the rock alongside—but he was right about the "missing" shoe! The lower half of one of the girl's legs could not be seen in this particular shot, thus only one foot (and a single shoe) was evident!

Walt Krasny left for his office wearing a small, ironic smile. Hurkos and Silver got into Scofield's car and started off on their tour, Mulholland and Fuller— still muttering bewilderment—tagging behind in their own. First they went up north of Ann Arbor to the spot where Mary Grace Clemson's battered remains had been uncovered four months earlier. After tramping about the wooded area awhile, Hurkos breathed: "This one hit many times in head. Bad. Big, heavy thing . . . crush skull. Terrible!"

Next they drove a few miles east to the dirt road where Dale Harum had been dumped. Before the actual location could be pointed out, Hurkos scrambled from the car and limped purposefully along the roadside. Stopping, he peered down at his feet. "Little girl lay right here." It was the exact spot, give or take a few feet.

Back in Ypsilanti, they cruised the Eastern campus. At the McKenny Student Union, Hurkos got out and went inside. He looked into the cafeteria, wandered through the lobby, finally paused by a public telephone. "I think killer use this phone," he said. This interested the detectives. On the night of Jill Hersch's disappearance a year earlier, three male trespassers had been chased from McKenny Hall by the custodian, who'd come upon them in the lobby using one of the pay phones. Investigators had come to assume that these were the same three who a little later had driven off with the girl. But the telephone angle had not been publicized!

As though not perplexed enough, the detectives were treated to an extra helping of wonderment at lunch. Abruptly turning to Scofield, Hurkos warned his young escort that gas was escaping from the propane fuel cylinder in his camper truck at home. Scofield was dumbfounded: He knew he'd not mentioned owning a camper to Hurkos; this stranger knew nothing yet about how or even where he lived! Hurkos urged him: "You better check. Bad leak, maybe dangerous."

As much to disprove the man as anything, Scofield telephoned his wife. She laughed, but he insisted she go out back and look at the camper, just for the heck of it. When she came back on the line, she was gasping. "Bob, I just don't believe this! There *was* a leak —the stove tank valve! We could have had an explosion!"

Mulholland and Fuller were not unimpressed by all this, but they tried doggedly to maintain healthy skepticism. Some of these "revelations" of Hurkos' could not be readily explained, true; but others could—by no more than the clever perceptions of one who'd done his homework. It thus gratified them when Hurkos indicated especial interest in the Harum case. That was the one to which Mulholland in particular had devoted the longest hours, Dale having been so close to his own family; he and Fuller, who was his frequent investigating partner, together knew every detail and angle . . . including some confidential stuff just received that still needed following up. This could be a real test of just how psychic Hurkos was.

They all drove out to the abandoned farm on LeForge Road where Dale Harum had been murdered. Hurkos made straight for the fire-blackened ruins of the old barn (where the unused coil of black electrical wire had been discovered). After poking about, he halted. "*Ja,* here you find the . . ." He hesitated, groping for the right word, then put his hand to his throat and made a guttural choking sound.

Without waiting for corroboration, he turned and went toward the crumbling farmhouse. Picking his way through the litter inside, with what seemed unerring instinct he found the basement stairs and lowered himself below, the others following. He was getting worked up now. *"Ja, ja,"* he exclaimed, "he come here, spend much time here. He kill *her* down here—the little one. And others, too, maybe . . ."

Mulholland and Fuller communicated silently with narrowed eyes. Okay. Next?

Hurkos wanted to be taken to the vicinity where Dale Harum had been last seen. They drove slowly along Railroad Street and back. Hurkos peered about intently but did not comment. Back on LeForge, they were about to return toward Ypsilanti when Hurkos cried out: "Turn in here, quick!" He was feverishly indicating a complex of brick garden apartments set back from the road. The two cars pulled into the parking area in front and waited.

Hurkos was tense, as though listening: Perspiration dampened his face. "She come here," he blurted in a strained voice, "—the girl. A man . . . young man . . . student, I think. Yes, here—before she die!"

Mulholland and Fuller could not have been more astonished. Early in the investigation of Dale Harum's murder, a number of young men had been questioned or checked out. But it had been only the past weekend that Mulholland had received information hinting that Dale Harum might have had a secret boyfriend who lived in or frequented one of these apartments near her own house. There seemed no way Hurkos could have got wind of this.

Mulholland found his voice. "Do you get any name?" It sounded silly.

Hurkos stared off somewhere, his lips working soundlessly. Then he stammered: "This guy . . . hair . . . much hair, all over him, look like ape almost. I see scar, front of head"—his fingers moved across his forehead—"above eye. . . . Name, Mart . . . no . . . Marsh? Yes, Marsh . . . Marshall. Marsh or Marshall."

It was incredible. Marshall *was* the name Mulholland had got from his source! He turned questioningly to his partner. Fuller, too, had been gaping at Hurkos. He managed to clear his throat. "We'll check it out," he said.

Hurkos had slumped, appearing suddenly exhausted. "I go back to hotel now, I think. Take a rest."

Ed Silver, beaming with satisfaction, spoke up: "This is the way he works. He'll really bear down for a half hour or an hour, and then he's just knocked out —it takes everything out of him. He has to recharge, you know? He'll be fine again in a few hours."

Alone in their car, Mulholland and Fuller looked at one another with what-do-*you*-think expressions. "I don't know about you," reflected Mulholland at last, "but the guy *has* got me wondering."

"I'll deny it if you tell anyone I said so," drawled Fuller, "but right now I feel kind of spooked myself."

"Well," sighed Mulholland, "let's go see about this Marshall."

The building manager at the apartment project had no record of a recent tenant by that name. But a canvass of current tenants turned up an Eastern summer student who thought he recalled someone by that description—swarthy, thick-muscled, almost menacing looking (yet in fact pleasant enough)—who used to be around now and again. He lived somewhere in Ypsi, was a local resident not a transient, and was not a student at the university but some kind of employee.

At E.M.U., they found that there had been a Marshall on the campus maintenance crew until a few months previous. Zack Marshall; age twenty-two; last listed residence, River Street in Ypsilanti. At that address, however, the landlady told them that Marshall had moved out the past spring. He'd not left a forwarding address.

Mulholland and Fuller checked back with some of Dale Harum's former friends. Arthur Childs, the

seventeen-year-old who'd walked part of the way
home with the girl the evening she disappeared (and
who had been closely scrutinized by the police for
some time afterward), said he did know an "older
guy," about twenty-one or twenty-two, named Zack
Marshall—or "Marsh," as all the kids called him—
who hung around Depot Town sometimes.

Come to think of it, Childs suddenly recollected,
Marsh had been around *that* evening when—

Did he know where Marsh lived now?

Yes. Over on Prospect.

The house was in a residential area on the east side
of Ypsilanti. The disheveled individual who opened
the door to the detectives was so literally the image of
Hurkos' vision that the sight of him had the odd effect
of being both startling and familiar at the same time:
standing there in undershorts and a T-shirt, half awake
and sour, the husky Marshall could in fact be said to
resemble a gorilla—dark, thick hair matted every exposed part of his body except his face, and that was
shadowed with stubble. And he did have a jagged
whitish scar over his right eye!

His ferocious appearance, however, belied a surprisingly unassuming, soft-spoken manner. They told
him they wanted to talk with him about Dale Harum,
and he said, Oh, sure, and asked them to sit down
for a minute while he got some clothes on. He worked
nights at a local factory, and it was time for him to get
up anyway.

In questioning, Marshall readily acknowledged having known the thirteen-year-old girl. She was cute and
bright, he said, and she seemed to have taken a shine to
him. He did have some friends, or used to, in the
apartments over on LeForge—most of them had
moved out since school was over—and yes, he'd been
there on a number of occasions, to parties and such,
and had slept over at one pad or another from time to
time.

"Did you ever see Dale Harum around there?"
asked Fuller.

"I might have. I can't say offhand. She lived right nearby."

"Do you recall ever taking her there?"

"Never," he said. "I didn't *date* her. I'd see her around, is all—mostly down around Depot Town. She was just a kid!"

"When did you see her last?"

Marshall swallowed. "That night she . . . after supper, at Depot Town. She was with her crowd. I came by, and we said hello. I didn't see her again. . . ."

"You didn't spend *any* time with her that evening?" Mulholland inquired sharply.

"No. I was on my way to a date. We had to meet another couple. We were going bowling."

The detectives looked at one another. They took down the names of the others and the location of the bowling lanes. If they checked out, Zack Marshall would appear to have a solid alibi.

Before they left, the detectives asked if they could borrow an article or two of his clothing—perhaps even, if he could remember that far back, something he might have worn that last night he had seen Dale Harum. They explained, not without some sheepishness, about this fellow Hurkos who was in town sort of, well, helping the police.

Marshall stared at them, then said simply, "Okay, if you say so." He went to his bedroom and returned with a blue nylon windbreaker and a pair of brown moccasins. "Am I a suspect all of a sudden?" he asked directly.

The question was put without either belligerence or defensiveness; he was confused. Neither Mulholland nor Fuller could answer as directly; they were confused themselves now. They'd responded to Peter Hurkos' telepathic vibrations about Zack Marshall, but, close up, *they* had felt none. Like two old bird dogs, they'd poised, absorbing him, alert for any telltale slip—an inflection, a posture, *any* hint of deception or fear of guilt—and had detected nothing. "We'll be talking to you," was all Mel Fuller could think to say.

Back at the Inn America, without comment they turned over Marshall's jacket and moccasins to Hurkos. His face lit up in anticipation. Clutching the articles, he worked himself into his now familiar routine of intense concentration. They watched in silence as his facial muscles knotted into a severe grimace, as though he was withstanding some unbearable force. Perspiration ran from his pores. Then he slumped, suddenly a damp, empty sack of flesh.

"No," he muttered, shaking his head dully. "I don't feel nothing now. *Nothing*. This *not* the man. . . ."

This time Hurkos was right. Zack Marshall was not their man. A check on his whereabouts the night of the Dale Harum murder confirmed his alibi and cleared him of any possible suspicion.

On Wednesday the twenty-third, Peter Hurkos took a telephone call from a man who warned him to get out of Ann Arbor before he should be responsible for another murder. Hurkos got no vibrations from the voice on the phone. But to some of the police, it would soon seem like a premonition.

CHAPTER 13

THAT VERY NIGHT, at about 11:15 P.M., the resident
faculty adviser of Downing Hall, a women's dormitory
of Eastern Michigan University, telephoned the office
of the campus police. One of the student residents, an
eighteen-year-old freshman named Carol Ann Gebhardt, was missing from her room past curfew. She
had not appeared at dinner earlier, either, and in fact
had not been seen or heard from since midday. Her
roommates and friends were growing concerned.

The night security officer took down the details, told
the woman, a Miss Karen Parkins, not to worry, then
broadcast a routine alert to radio cars patrolling the
campus. He typed up a brief report, making one copy
for the Sheriff's Department, and with a yawn returned
to the paperback novel he had been reading.

Shortly after midnight, Miss Parkins took it upon
herself to call the girl's parents in Grand Rapids, to
see if Carol Ann might possibly have gone home.
Awakened from a sound sleep, the father said groggily
that his daughter was not there, they were not expect-

ing her. A little while later, Mr. Gebhardt, fully awake after having considered the disturbing call, telephoned the local State Police post. An inquiry was transmitted back to the State Police post at Ypsilanti, and from there, it was relayed to the Ypsi city police.

Sergeant Herb Smith found it, stapled together with a copy of the original university police report, when he reported for duty at eight Thursday morning. He downed a container of scorched coffee, then drove over to E.M.U. The girl's roommates, Catherine Hill and Sue Potter, seemed to be the last ones to have seen Carol Ann. That had been a little after noon on Wednesday, when she'd left them to go downtown to a wig shop on Washington Street to pick up a hairpiece she'd ordered. She had not shown up in the commons for dinner, and when the freshman 11:00 P.M. curfew came and went without any sign of her, they'd become concerned and gone to Miss Parkins.

Sergeant Smith asked them to describe Carol Ann, what she'd been wearing and so forth.

She was petite, just over five feet, probably not a hundred pounds. A nice build, especially for a small girl; cute face; short dark-brown hair. She'd had on a sleeveless turtleneck pullover, Orlon, blue-and-white-striped; old bleach-faded blue-jean cutoffs, cut above the knees (the monogram *CAG* sewn on the left rear pocket, one of them noted); and she was barefoot, they thought.

At the wig shop—Wigs by Joan—Smith introduced his partner, Sergeant Don Howell, to the proprietress, a statuesque twenty-seven-year-old blonde named Joan Enright. Her assistant, a heavy-set young woman with dark hair, was just finishing with a customer. When the customer had gone, Joan introduced them. "This is Helga Marks, my stylist."

After apologizing for the intrusion, Smith produced a small snapshot which he'd got from the Gebhardt girl's roommates and handed it to Joan. "Does this girl look familiar to you?"

She peered at it with knit brows. Too much sunlight

from the wrong angle distorted the subject's smiling face. "It's hard to tell," Joan said. "Who is she?"

Smith told her.

"Oh, sure," she said. "She was in yesterday. Nice kid. We'd done up a wiglet for her—you know"—demonstrating with her hands—"a piece you attach to the back of your own hair."

"What time was she in?"

"Oh, maybe twelve thirty, around that. Just about fifteen minutes or so, then she left. Seemed a real little lady. Except—"

"So she would have left here about a quarter to one," Smith calculated. "She didn't mention where she was going?"

"No. She said she was at Eastern, and I kind of had the feeling she was on her way back there. But—"

"Do you recall what she was wearing?"

"Oh, gee . . . a light turtleneck blouse, I think . . . no sleeves . . . stripes crosswise. Yes, I remember it showed off her figure real good."

"What else?" Howell asked briskly.

"Oh, a dark sort of skirt, short . . . or it could have been culottes . . . kind of airy and feminine, anyway."

"Not blue jeans, cutoffs?"

"No, I don't think so. And leather sandals."

"Sandals?" Smith considered. "Tell me, how come you remember her so well? I mean, you must have customers in and out all day. . . ."

"Well, I've been *trying* to tell you," Joan said with mock impatience. "Because of the guy on the motorcycle. I tried to talk her out of it, but—"

"What guy? *What* motorcycle?" Smith and Howell both had stiffened like hunting dogs.

"She rode off with this guy on his motorcycle. He was waiting for her outside."

"Why'd you try to talk her out of it?" resumed Smith.

"Well, because she told us she didn't *know* him. She said: 'This is quite a day for me.' And I asked why, and she said: 'I've done two things I never thought I'd do—buy a wig, and let a stranger give me a ride on his motorcycle.' He'd just picked her up apparently, around the campus somewhere, and I guess was expecting to give her a ride back. She didn't know if she should, and I told her she ought to think twice about taking lifts from strangers these days, you know? She was such a nice innocent kid. . . ."

"But she did go off with him?"

"Yes. Helga and I both watched to see what she'd do, and they—"

"So you got a look at this guy?" Smith could feel a small tingling of excitement.

"Yes. We both did. He didn't look bad. In fact, I thought he was kind of nice looking—neat, clean-cut, short dark hair. Early twenties, I'd say. Nice build. Maybe six feet."

"How was he dressed?" asked Howell.

"All I remember is he had a striped shirt, too—like the girl, you know?—short-sleeved . . . a polo shirt with colored stripes around. Green and yellow, I think. I'm not sure now."

"What about his bike?"

"Well, it was big, and loud, and shiny. It was dark blue, I think, and it had chrome all over it—even on the exhaust pipe—really shiny, like just polished."

"Could you identify the make?"

"I've ridden some. Looked to me like a Honda. She got on behind him, and they drove off that way"—indicating south, toward Michigan Avenue—"and at the corner they turned right on Michigan, and . . . well, that's all."

"That's not bad." The detective pocketed his notebook. "You've been a big help."

"What's this all about, anyway?" asked Joan. "Has anything—happened?"

"Don't know yet. The girl was gone all night. Might be nothing, but . . ."

"I *told* her. With these murders going on and all, I said—"

"Yeah," grunted Smith, eyeing Howell and edging toward the door.

At 10:45 A.M. Thursday, in the lobby of Downing Hall, a stocky young man with horn-rimmed eyeglasses and a mop of dark hair telephoned upstairs to Room 307.

"This is Joe Reidy," he identified himself to the girl who answered. "Carol Ann was supposed to meet me downstairs at ten thirty. What's keeping her?"

Sue Potter held her breath a moment. Joe Reidy. Carol Ann's boyfriend! She let out a little "Oh!" and said she would be right down.

Reidy reacted more with incredulity than alarm when Sue Potter haltingly told him that nobody knew where Carol Ann was. "I can't believe it," he said. "Carol Ann would *never* just go off without telling *someone*." He went to look for the resident, Miss Parkins, who directed him to the campus police.

John Hayes, chief of security at E.M.U., had been trying with difficulty to locate Reidy at his residence in Center Line, near Detroit, where he worked as a student counselor at St. Clement's High School. The officer was glad to see him.

Joe Reidy looked more like a college senior than a high-school teacher. He wore sneakers, jeans, and an open-neck shirt, and the mat of hair over his forehead and shaggy pork-chop sideburns and thick Zapata mustache managed to convey the deceptive appearance of both studiousness and diffidence.

Reidy said he'd left Center Line around 9:30. He and Carol Ann had a date to meet for coffee at 10:30 this morning. It just was not like her to stand him up, whatever might have come up, without getting in touch or at least leaving a message.

Hayes, who had just been in touch with Herb Smith, briefed Reidy on the little they knew so far.

The business about the motorcycle seemed to stir him. "I don't know if Carol Ann's ever *been* on a motorcycle," Reidy said. "I think she's scared of them.

But the other thing is, I just can't see her accepting *any* ride from someone she didn't know. She's always been dead set against hitchhiking. She's very down-to-earth."

Reidy said that he and Carol Ann had been dating for more than a year, and he loved her very much. They weren't actually engaged yet, but he had given her a pearl ring after her high school graduation in June, and he had no doubt they would eventually marry.

"When were you with her last?" Chief Hayes asked.

"Monday. We'd been together all weekend, and I drove out here again Monday evening. We bowled and had some pizza. She was the way she always is, easy, kind of bubbly. I remember we kidded about that wig she was getting—a 'fall,' she called it."

"Where'd you spend last weekend?" asked Hayes.

"With her folks at their summer place. Big Star Lake, up north of Grand Rapids. Then Sunday evening we came back and I dropped Carol Ann off here and went on to Center Line."

"And she gave no indication at any time recently that anything, or anyone, might be troubling her? She was getting along all right in the school?"

"Like I said, she was real loose, as usual. She seemed happy with Eastern so far, liked her roommates—everything was upbeat."

"Do you know if she ever . . . used, ah, stimulants?" Hayes inquired carefully.

"Drugs? Never!" Reidy bridled. "I never saw her take a drink, either. Not even beer. She was the cleanest girl I—"

Reidy stopped, gaping at Hayes but seeing beyond him, eyes suddenly filmy. "Oh, my God!" he choked. "Why do I keep saying *was*?"

While Joe Reidy's account of his own whereabouts Wednesday and Wednesday night was being verified (he had spent much of the day at St. Clement's High School preparing schedules for the ensuing fall term, and then in the evening had gone bowling with friends in Warren, outside Center Line), word was being passed quietly among the investigators manning the crime center about the missing coed.

Officially it was still only a local case involving the E.M.U. campus police and the Ypsi P.D., with no evidence as yet of foul play. But the haggard men and women of the homicide detail, their instincts stretched taut by so many months of repeated perplexity, sensed at once the demoralizing challenge of a new outrage.

The first step was to get out an all-points bulletin on the missing girl over state and regional police wires. Next, crime center detectives were sent to question the women at the wig shop again and to canvass the immediate area for possible corroboration from other observers. An Ypsi P.D. sergeant, Bill Stenning, who also functioned as a composite artist for the department, joined one detachment of investigators at Joan's. As Joan Enright and Helga Marks excitedly repeated their description of the motorcyclist, Stenning, hunched over a frilly vanity table, sketched out a pencil rough of a Caucasian male's face and head.

The key characteristics seemed to be that the young man was "good-looking," "clean-cut," with dark hair trimmed unusually short by current youthful standards; even his sideburns were unfashionably neat. The front of his hair, however, fell down over his forehead, "sort of casual." The only point of some disagreement about the youth's appearance was whether his hair was straight or curly. They settled on "wavy."

When Stenning finished, the women examined the sketch severely. "Well, it's not *exactly* how he looked," Joan Enright said.

"The eyes don't seem right," Helga Marks offered.

Stenning made the suggested alterations. Still they did not show enthusiasm. Finally, however, Joan said: "It's close. I think I'd recognize him from this. Don't you think so, Helga?"

Her associate shrugged. "I guess."

With a sigh—he was used to critics—the sergeant

thanked them, collected his sketching materials, and returned to headquarters, where he would set to work inking out a clean drawing for reproduction and distribution.

The women next were asked to accompany detectives to a Honda showroom on Michigan Avenue to single out, if they could, a model of the bike that most closely resembled the one they'd seen outside their shop. Helga could not seem to make up her mind, but after a few minutes of browsing Joan pointed to a motorcycle with a square mirror on its left handlebar. "It was like that one—I remember now, it even had that kind of mirror," she declared. The bike she'd indicated was a Honda 450. The sales manager said that, from her account, what they were looking for probably was a comparatively late model, 1965 to 1967.

This information was relayed back to the crime center, and a computer printout was ordered from Lansing of all motorcycle registrations in the Ypsilanti area. From among these not only could locally owned Hondas be isolated but, by cross-reference with required university vehicle registrations, many of the bikes operated by E.M.U. students could also be pinpointed. This was not foolproof—for one thing, not every student bothered to register his vehicle with the school, and for another, the police knew the difficulties of accurately tracing motorcycles, due to the frequent incidence of ownership transfers by bike freaks —but it was the most promising avenue yet.

Meanwhile, investigators visiting other establishments in the Washington Street block between Michigan and Pearl, the area of the wig shop, seemed to have got the corroboration they'd sought, if not much more helpful detail.

A young woman who on Wednesday had been tending the fountain in The Chocolate Shop, next door to Joan's, about midday had also noticed a young man wearing a striped shirt sitting on a motorcycle outside the shop. Noelle Crenna said he was there for about ten minutes, and then a young woman, also wearing a striped top, came over to him, climbed on behind the boy ("she had trouble getting on, like bikes were new to her"), and the two roared off in the direction of Michigan Avenue. Noelle remembered the cyclist as being dark, nice looking, fairly tall, trim of build, with "shortish" hair. But the real reason she'd paid particular attention was the fellow's bike. She was interested in motorcycles, had a number of friends who owned them, and this one looked pretty special—a Triumph, "loaded with gingerbread, and a good sound, like it was juiced up."

A *Triumph?* Was she certain?

Ninety-nine percent. She knew bikes, and she was almost sure that this one was a Triumph.

It couldn't have been, say, a Honda?

No way.

This did not sit well with the detectives. They had been eager to accept Joan Enright's positive ID of the bike as a Honda, such tidy elimination and pigeon-holing having given them the flush of comfort that things might have started breaking their way. Now this contrary identification, almost equally as "positive," dampened the outlook once again. Was it a Honda or a Triumph? Or *either,* for Christ's sake—?

They found one other person, a twenty-two-year-old Eastern coed named Josephine Marsh who worked part-time in an office supply store two doors from The Chocolate Shop, who also had a clear recollection of a young motorcyclist with a striped shirt. She hadn't seen him on Washington Street, however, nor riding off with a girl.

A little before noon on Wednesday, as she was walking to work from the Eastern campus, she herself had been accosted by just such a person. He had cruised alongside and stayed with her for half a block or so, revving his engine provocatively in short bursts, trying to talk her into taking a ride with him. He'd been pleasant enough, said nothing arrogant or obscene or threatening.

She had just kept walking, and after a minute or

two he'd laughed good naturedly and ridden off. She remembered his striped T-shirt, wide stripes of green or blue and a contrasting lighter color—a lighter green or yellow. Her impression had been of a handsome, serious face. And his hair wasn't long like most of the guys around the university wore it. The bike? Very shiny, well-kept looking, like it could have been a custom job. But she didn't really know anything about motorcycles; she had no idea what kind it was.

When there was still no trace of Carol Ann Gebhardt by Thursday afternoon, it was decided at the crime center to notify her parents officially. Her father said he would leave for Ann Arbor at once. He arrived by car that evening.

Kenneth Gebhardt was a slight, pale man in his fifties. He appeared to be fighting to repress mounting strain, and slowly giving ground. He smiled nervously, but his attempt to exhibit a reasoned confidence was betrayed by frightened eyes and trembling fingers.

He had brought a recent studio photograph of Carol Ann, which he gave to the detectives who greeted him and brought him into a quiet inner cubicle. "It really doesn't do her justice," he apologized. "She's much prettier."

The detectives asked him as casually as possible to tell them about his daughter. The picture that emerged of Carol Ann was an enlargement of the sketch the police had already got from her schoolmates and boyfriend. A clean, wholesome girl, openly interested in people and well liked by almost all who knew her. A good student, in the top third of her graduating class at Creston High School, she had won a full scholarship to E.M.U., where she was planning to major in special education.

The Gebhardts had been somewhat uneasy about her choice of school, in light of the terrible things that had been taking place in Ypsilanti and Ann Arbor. But there had been no talking her out of it, and she had even persuaded them to let her come down to the

university early for the summer session. She seemed
very content. Only last weekend when she and her
boyfriend had visited them at the lake she'd been in
high spirits, frequently reassuring them that everything
was peaceful and they had no cause to be concerned
about her. But she was not unaware of the dangers.

Kenneth Gebhardt paused and withdrew an envelope from the inside pocket of his jacket. "Here's the
last letter we got from Carol Ann."

It was a brief note, telling her parents how pleased
she was with her progress at the school: "I'm working
awfully hard, but I love it. It's so good to be doing
everything for myself at last. I realize now how much
you darlings have done *for* me. I love you. . . ." Enclosed was the front page of a recent issue of the student newspaper, *The Eastern Echo,* featuring a
summary of the area slayings with a new warning to
coeds, particularly new arrivals, to let all prudence
guide them in where they went and when and with
whom. Across the top of the page Carol Ann had
scrawled, "Don't worry, folks. *I am being careful."*

The letter was dated Wednesday, July 23. The detectives looked at Mr. Gebhardt, and one said: "Then
you must have only received this—"

"Just today." He forced a tight smile. "It gave us
hope, you see. . . ."

Since transmittal of the "missing" bulletin on Thursday,
reports had come in from various places—from Grand
Rapids to Windsor, Ontario, and points between—that
a young woman and man of the given descriptions had
been spotted here or there. Each of these quickly
proved meaningless.

Locally, inquiries by policemen sweeping through
Ypsilanti brought no new clues to the couple's whereabouts, nor did troopers and deputies scouring country
roads by car and fields and woods on horseback and
foot find any trace of them. Citizens' tips beginning to
flood the crime center had, typically, so far produced

no usable leads, and some of those followed up led to special aggravation.

One urgent telephone call on Friday evening directed police to Washtenaw Park in Ann Arbor, where the anonymous caller said they would find "a missing girl" tied to a tree. A squad of six officers raced there. They found no girl but, prowling the brush, did flush out a pair of furtive-looking teen-agers. The youths said that they, too, were looking for the missing coed. Why them, and why there? the policemen demanded to know. The boys finally admitted it was they who had phoned in the report. Why? *Had* they seen a girl in trouble there? What in hell were they up to? Squirming, they admitted that they hadn't actually *seen* a girl there . . . but they were into psychic phenomena, and, see, they'd felt these "vibrations."

The furious officers threw up their hands. Mother of mercy! Just what they needed: a couple more amateur goddamn *psychics!*

The tentative police flirtation with the powers and credibility of Peter Hurkos had definitely cooled; as the days had passed without his having contributed anything of real value, even many of the reporters who had flocked after him began to grow bored, and now, with a new mystery suddenly claiming priority attention, Hurkos no longer held the spotlight.

For Bill Mulholland and Mel Fuller, particularly, it had again become insufferable to have no more part in the investigations than to stick with Hurkos. By having to tag along on the Dutchman's erratic wanderings, compiling generally useless notes of his "findings," they were going nowhere.

The low point came Friday night, after an interminable, fruitless tour of the coffee houses and bistros of Ann Arbor's teeming youthful subculture. Upon their return to the Inn America Hurkos was handed a note at the front desk. The clerk said it had been left during the evening by a tall young man who said only that it was important and then had ducked out. The brief message, unsigned, cryptically hinted that there was "something interesting" to be found in a burned-out cabin up on Weed Road, a rural byway eight or nine miles north of Ypsilanti.

Hurkos fingered the piece of paper in one of his forced concentrations. After a moment, he turned sharply to the detectives: "Feel something strong here. Maybe the girl! We better go see!"

With misgivings, Mulholland notified the crime center. A squad was rounded up, and after midnight, in a heavy downpour, they slogged out into the countryside. Searching the length of Weed Road, they found no cabin, nor any remains of one. After a miserable hour, they straggled back, drenched and sorely dispirited.

Such, indeed, was the mood pervading the crime center by Saturday morning, July 26—sodden frustration and weariness and gloom. There seemed no relief from the insistent climate of defeat.

CHAPTER 14

BUT, ALTHOUGH THE crime center would not become aware of it until some twenty-four hours later, a chain of inquiry had begun that was destined to break the case wide open.

It developed inauspiciously enough. On Friday morning, newly assigned officers to the homicide investigations had been given an official briefing on the latest missing coed situation, including the most complete descriptions available of both the girl and the mysterious cyclist. Among the newcomers was a bespectacled young patrolman of the E.M.U. campus force, Larry Mathewson, twenty-two, who had been recommended by his chief, John Hayes, both because he was bright and had a good record and because he was young and student-oriented, having just graduated from the university in June. Mathewson had been a part-time patrolman while a student.

The young officer drove back to the campus, following the briefing, in a thoughtful mood. Something elusive had picked at his memory as he'd jotted down the descriptions of the pair being sought. And then it came to him. He'd been on car patrol Wednesday about noon, and remembered having seen a young man on a motorcycle, wearing a horizontal-striped shirt, stop on a campus street to talk with a good-looking blond coed. Though he didn't know his name, Larry recognized him as a student he'd seen around campus for a few years, a member of Theta Chi. They'd competed several times in interfraternity sports, touch football among other things, and he'd impressed him as a good athlete, from all indications a regular guy.

The blonde he had seen him with wasn't the one whose photograph Mathewson had just been shown, but it occurred to him that his fraternity rival might himself have noticed another guy on a bike, dressed similarly, cruising the vicinity at about the same time. What could it cost to ask?

He went to the Theta Chi house on Cross Street, a weatherbeaten gray frame structure with a dilapidated front porch sagging almost to ground level. A few young men lounged on the porch whom Mathewson knew to say hello to. He described the motorcyclist he was looking for.

"It sounds like James Armstrong," one of them said.

"Is he around?"

"He doesn't live at the house anymore. He took a room over on Emmet."

As Mathewson approached the rooming house at the corner of College Place and Emmet Street, he was struck by an interesting coincidence: directly across College Place, on the corner, was 703 Emmet, where Jill Hersch had been rooming when she was murdered the summer before. He wondered if James Armstrong might have known her.

Mathewson was informed by the landlady, a spry little woman of about eighty, that Armstrong was not in his room but that he might be around back in the garage. "He spends more time out there, working on them motorbikes of his, than he does upstairs," she said, just a hint of disapproval in her tone.

The ramshackle outbuilding behind the house was barely large enough to shelter a standard-size automobile. Outside, parked in the narrow driveway, was a late-model Oldsmobile, metallic silver in color, a Cutlass, while inside the garage were four motorcycles of varying sizes. Bent over one of them was a sinewy fellow in dungarees and soiled T-shirt, while another young man stood by watching. Mathewson knew the second one by name, Chuck Harris, who had been in some of his classes at Eastern.

"Hey, look who's here!" called out Harris, an affable, no-sweat type. The other straightened and turned, wiping smudged hands on a grimy rag.

"Hi, Chuck." Larry smiled.

"Official business? Larry's one of the campus fuzz." Harris grinned to his friend.

"I know, I've seen him around," said James Armstrong pleasantly. He was about six feet, trim and lithely muscular. His face was interesting; above a square athlete's chin, the features were surprisingly soft, rather sensual in a boyish way, but his eyes were set deep under heavy brows.

"Have an accident?" Mathewson asked, indicating the motorcycle Armstrong had been working on.

"No. Just tooling up. Doing some riding over the weekend. What's happening?"

Mathewson was surprised to hear a slight lisp in Armstrong's voice. "I hate to bother you fellows," he said, "but they've got us checking on that missing girl." He took out a small photo reproduction of Carol Ann Gebhardt. "I don't suppose either of you know her, or have seen her?"

Armstrong and Harris glanced at the picture, which had already appeared in the morning papers. They shook their heads. "I know *I've* never seen her," drawled Armstrong.

"Do you think it's the killer again?" asked Harris.

"Who knows?" Mathewson gestured.

"Maybe she just took off," offered Armstrong quietly.

"Well, she *was* last seen riding off on a bike with some guy. That's really why—"

"I got your plate, James. It's—" The soft voice had come from behind Mathewson.

"Hi, Donald," Harris said. "Do you know Larry Mathewson? Donald Baker." Harris added, as the two nodded: "Larry's investigating the missing girl."

Baker's eyebrows lifted, but he only nodded again in acknowledgment. In his hand he held an official-looking oblong manila envelope. A license plate, Larry wondered?

"I was just saying," he continued, "the reason I stopped by here is that I happened to see James on his bike the other day about the same time and in the area that we figure the girl was picked up, and"— directing himself to Armstrong—"I thought maybe you might have—"

Armstrong's eyes had narrowed so that they almost appeared to recede deeper behind the dark brows. "Saw me where, when?" he cut in, his tone somewhere between defensive and challenging.

"It was down by Sill Hall, oh, a little after noon the day before yesterday—Wednesday. You stopped and talked with a neat-looking blond chick. Not this girl," Larry added quickly, indicating the photo he still had in his hand.

"A blonde . . . by Sill Hall, that would be Lowell Street. . . ." Armstrong pondered aloud. "Oh, Ginny Lipton. Yeah, I remember. What about it?"

"Well, nothing about *that*. But you *were* riding around in the neighborhood, and I just thought you might have noticed something, maybe another guy cruising around."

"There are lots of guys driving bikes around there all the time," Armstrong said evenly.

"Sure, I know. Like I say, it's just a wild shot." Larry chuckled self-consciously. "What made me think of it, actually, was that the guy this girl went off with was described as wearing a striped pullover shirt, and—" *Striped shirt . . . tall, lean, handsome, short dark hair with medium-long sideburns.* He hesitated, appraising James Armstrong. His brown hair, though uncombed now, was barbered neatly, with trimmed moderate-length sideburns.

"And what?" Armstrong urged warily.

"Well, just that I remember *you* had on a striped shirt that day, and—" Larry moistened his lips, feeling awkward. "I thought possibly you could have noticed somebody else on a bike dressed the same."

Armstrong glanced across at his two friends before shrugging back to Mathewson. "Not that I remember. Sorry."

"Sure. That's the way it goes. Besides"—Larry grinned, hoping to lighten the tension he sensed among them—"if I'd had that blonde in my eye I don't think I'd have seen much myself. What's her name again— Ginny?"

Armstrong smiled, seeming to relax. "Ginny Lipton. Yeah, she's all right." The others smiled with him.

"Is she yours?"

"Not really. I've taken her out."

"Say, I wonder if *she* might have noticed anybody?" it occurred to Larry. "You know where she lives?"

"Down at Lowell and Jarvis. Garden apartments— the Americana-something, they're called."

"Thanks." As he was about to leave, his eyes fell across the big blue motorcycle Armstrong had been repairing. "Oh, wait a minute." He pulled out his notebook and pen and jotted down the tag number—F88-25—then moved over toward the three other bikes propped against the garage wall.

He caught a glimpse of Armstrong's expression and was startled by his thin-lipped anger. "What the hell are you doing that for?" he demanded.

"Hey, it's nothing personal," Mathewson hastened to reassure him. "We just have orders to take down every bike we see around. I guess they figure by process of elimination—"

"See, what did I tell you, Chuck!" snarled Armstrong. "They'll be hassling everybody who drives

a bike now. We're all freak-outs, right?" The soft face
had hardened with surprising venom.

"Take it easy, James," Harris tried to reason. "He's
only doing his job."

"Well, he can bug off and play policeman someplace
else," Armstrong snapped, turning his back on them
and stooping over his neglected motorcycle.

"Sorry," said Mathewson lamely. "See you around."

Mathewson hurried away from 619 Emmet Street
disturbed. He couldn't quite pinpoint why. Was it an
odor of disagreeableness, even hostility? Was it, specifically, the harshness of James Armstrong's abrupt, violent shift of temper?

It was not until Saturday morning that Mathewson reported again to the crime center. There he was given a
collection of mug shots of known sex offenders in the
area whose features bore a resemblance to the
description of the mysterious motorcyclist, and told to
check them out with the women on Washington Street.
Mathewson was glad to get out. The atmosphere in the
old seminary was depressing.

Joan Enright and Helga Marks at the wig shop
flipped through the plasticized photographs shaking
their heads, without comment or hesitating as much
as a beat. Larry then took the pictures next door to
The Chocolate Shop, but Noelle Crenna was not working.

He was about to return to the crime center when
James Armstrong crossed his mind again. Or rather,
Armstrong's blond friend, Ginny Lipton. As long as he
was downtown, he might as well look her up.

The garden apartments in which she lived—grandly
called "Bellmont Americana"—were less than a block
from Sill Hall. Ginny Lipton's apartment was on the
second floor. She answered Mathewson's third ring
looking, although by now it was after noon, as if she'd
only just awakened.

Identifying himself, he asked: "Do you know James
Armstrong?"

"Yes, I know him," she replied guardedly. "Why? Is he in any trouble?"

"No, no, not at all." He quickly explained his purpose, asking if she had seen anyone other than James cruising the area on a motorcycle last Wednesday.

She thought. "No, I'd just finished a class and was on my way here to grab a nap when James came along. We talked about fifteen minutes, and then he drove off and I came straight home."

"I take it you two—know each other pretty well?" Larry asked carefully.

"Oh, we dated quite a bit last winter. Not so much anymore, though. Sometimes he comes to the motel where I work and we go out. . . . Say, would you like a cup of coffee?"

"Sure," Larry accepted, pleased.

Ginny Lipton was bright and pert and easy to talk to. She was trying to earn her way through college and worked nights and weekends as a waitress in the Camelot Room, the restaurant-lounge of the Inn America. Larry asked wryly what kind of scene it had been the past few days with Peter Hurkos on the premises, and she rolled her eyes and said a *mad*house.

"Just *everyone* comes crowding around out there, trying to get close to him," she said, "—everyone waiting for the big 'revelation.' Even James has been out a couple of times, come to think of it. One night this week, he and a couple of his friends managed to get a table in the lounge right next to Hurkos and a group of reporters. James said he was hoping to catch some 'inside stuff' about the murders. But apparently all Hurkos did the whole time was his parlor tricks—you know, telling people personal things about themselves. He's pretty good at it, too. But not once did they talk about the murders. James thought he was just a big clown."

Larry was enjoying the girl, but he knew he ought to justify the extended visit. He showed her the mug shots, not mentioning that they were sex offenders, but she did not recognize any of them. Nor had she ever seen. she said, the missing Carol Ann Gebhardt.

It was time to go. As she escorted him to the door, Ginny said: "Sorry I'm no help."

Mathewson had his hand on the doorknob when he surrendered to impulse. "The shirt James was wearing that day. Do you remember it—what type it was, the colors?"

She stared at him. "Why, I don't know, it was sort of . . . a knit, short sleeves, high neck—not a turtleneck, a boatneck style. The stripes were . . . I'm not sure. Blue and yellow, I think. . . ."

"How about the motorcycle?"

"The motorcycle? I don't know. . . ." She was groping, trying to catch up to his unexpected turn of thought. "James always has different bikes. . . . There was nothing special about that one. Maybe it was especially shiny."

His heartbeat had picked up. "Ginny, do you happen to have any pictures of James? Any recent ones?"

"I think so." She went into the bedroom and after a few minutes came back with two three-by-five snapshots. Both were of James Armstrong, wearing a sweater. standing alone by a decorated Christmas tree. One was sharper than the other.

"When were these taken?" he asked.

"Last Christmas, during the holidays sometime, back home."

"Okay. If you don't mind," Larry said, "I'd like to borrow them for a little while. I'll return them this afternoon."

He drove back to Washington Street. Both women were still in the wig shop. He showed them the snaps without any comment. They looked at them hard. Then Joan Enright said: "I'll tell you. There's something wrong with the hair . . . but otherwise, this is pretty close. What do you think, Helga?"

Helga was frowning. "I don't know. It could be. But . . . I just don't know. The perspective is so different, the lighting. . . ."

Larry's pulse had accelerated. *Pretty close. . . . Could be.* But it still wasn't good enough. It wasn't an ID. "Can't you be any more definite?" he pushed.

"What do you want me to say?" Joan retorted. "This *might* be the same guy. It might *not*. You *want* us to—?"

"No, of course not," he cut her off. "Thanks, anyway. I may be back."

He walked out of the wig shop into the brilliant sunshine feeling unfulfilled. If only there were someone else to show these pictures to. The woman from The Chocolate Shop probably wouldn't be back until Monday. Then he remembered the girl who worked in the office supply store up the block, the one who'd said she had been approached earlier Wednesday by a motorcyclist whose description seemed to match the mystery rider's. What was her name again? He riffled through his notebook. Josephine Marsh.

The clerk on the main floor directed Mathewson downstairs to a supply room where Josephine was on her lunch break. He found her huddled over a metal desk, intent on a magazine as she absently munched a sandwich. When he said, "Miss Marsh?" she started and gulped down a mouthful of sandwich.

"Yes?"

"Excuse the interruption. Officer Mathewson of the E.M.U. police."

"I already made a statement," she said brusquely.

"I know. I just want to show you a couple of pictures." He paused to extract the snaps from his breast pocket. "Do you know this man?" He laid them in front of her on the desk top.

She leaned forward to peer at them. Almost at once her sandwich dropped from her fingers into her lap, smearing the skirt with mustard, and she squawked: "Shit, that's *him!*"

By midafternoon, Mathewson was back at the crime center painstakingly typing up a report. His nerve ends still tingled but he had willed deliberateness upon his thought processes. He wanted to be very careful and reasoned. After all, what did he actually have?

He had what appeared to be a definite "make" of James Armstrong as the striped-shirted young man on a shiny motorcycle who had accosted Josephine Marsh on a street near the Eastern campus shortly before Carol Ann Gebhardt disappeared with a cyclist of similar description.

He had a *possible* ID of the same subject as the one seen driving the missing girl away from the wig shop.

He had *tentative* corroboration from a female acquaintance (to which significant weight could be added from the officer's own observation) that the subject had worn a shirt that day similar to the one described by the witnesses on Washington Street; also from that female acquaintance, assertions that the subject had been cruising the area at about the critical time that day (again supported by the officer's personal observation).

Maybe the makings of something. Yet Larry realized he had to proceed with caution. For what he *didn't* yet have on James Armstrong—or anybody else— was *positive* identification as the man last seen with Carol Ann Gebhardt.

Moreover, there was one other essential they still had to have before sense could be made of any of this: a corpus delicti. Without that there was no crime—it was all smoke.

It was past four in the afternoon before Mathewson was satisfied enough with his report to sign it and turn it in to the investigations coordinator. The pros would know the right way to handle it.

At almost that very moment, in Sheriff's Department headquarters one hundred yards from the crime center, a uniformed deputy rushed into Doug Harvey's office with an urgent message. Corporal Ron Ritter had just taken a telephone call from a Dr. Daryl Stoneman. He and his wife, on an afternoon stroll in a residential section scarcely a mile and a quarter away, had just come upon a naked body lying in some brush. It appeared to be a young woman. She was unquestionably dead.

CHAPTER 15

LESS THAN TEN minutes after the doctor's telephone call, Sheriff Harvey arrived alone in an unmarked car. He had instructed Corporal Ritter to put out no bulletin, say nothing to anyone, until he had personally verified the report and phoned in. Harvey was working on an idea.

The Stonemans, recovering from their initial shock, were waiting for him at the site. It was a hilly, wooded hermitage of secluded custom-built homes, just off Huron River Drive. The Stonemans' house, a few hundred feet up an unpaved access lane called Riverside Drive, overlooked a thickly overgrown gully. The couple, halfway up Riverside, motioned the sheriff toward the gully. From the side of the road, Harvey peered over the edge and grimaced. The lifeless form lay about twenty feet down the embankment, sprawled on its belly in shrubbery. Harvey asked the Stonemans if he could use their telephone.

The first person Harvey contacted was Dr. Craig Barlow, the deputy county medical examiner. Next,

210

Booker Williams at the prosecutor's office, to whom he spoke in lowered, urgent tones. Finally, Harvey rang his own headquarters and got Lieutenant Stan Bordine.

"Stan," he said after filling him in, "we're going with Operation Stakeout. We need just a few people—ours, preferably. If we need more, see if John Hayes can give us some campus guys. Now look: I want the lid on this thing. No radio dispatches—nothing. Tell only those you have to, and tell them this is top secret. When everything's in the works, get out here yourself—I want you in charge. Get somebody solid to fill in for you. How about Mulholland—is he off the goddamned mind reader yet? . . . Okay, as soon as he's clear, have him and Fuller stand by at the crime center. It could be a long night. . . ."

Harvey sat back when he'd finished and regarded the Stonemans, who fidgeted across the living room trying hard to appear not to have overheard anything. He got up and walked over to them.

"Folks," he began with a tight smile, "we're going to need your cooperation. For the time being, we're not going to publicize finding that poor girl. We're going to try something. . . ."

The first to respond to Sheriff Harvey's summons was the deputy medical examiner. Clambering down into the gully, black bag in hand, Dr. Barlow went over the corpse as thoroughly as possible without moving it, that grisly task being reserved to the forensic experts from the police lab. The chief responsibility of the medical examiner in such a circumstance was to verify death, place a probable time, ascribe the likely cause, and note any attendant or contributory factors that might be evident.

From the victim's physical appearance—the body was completely nude except for brown leather-strapped sandals still on the feet—Barlow put the young woman's age in the late teens, twenty at the most. He estimated that she'd been dead three days or more:

decomposition had begun, with discoloration and some putrefaction of skin and tissues, but rigor mortis was no longer present. She had not been killed where she lay; the body's condition—including the relative buildup of insect ova through the hair and in exposed orifices— suggested that it had been in this place only twenty- four to thirty-six hours, or since already dead a day or two. Evidently it then had been rolled down the em- bankment from Riverside Drive, no doubt in dark- ness—which pointed, by Barlow's reckoning, to some time between nightfall Thursday and dawn Friday.

She had been both strangled and severely beaten— the side of her face that was visible, the left side, was a pulpy mass of bruises—but there was no way yet of specifying the precise cause of death. Superficial lacera- tions and swelling in the genital area indicated that the girl had been forcibly violated at the approximate time she expired, either before or immediately after.

The sheriff, meanwhile, had been joined at his im- promptu command post, the Stonemans' enclosed porch, by Lieutenant Bordine and then Assistant Prose- cutor Williams. A handful of deputies had already been positioned to seal off the tiny hillside community, from the foot of Riverside Drive to both ends of Chalmers Drive into which it merged. The security measures were effected as inconspicuously as possible—patrol cars parked out of the way, no flashing of dome lights, a minimum show of uniformed strength.

After the crime lab boys came and did their job, the stakeout would begin—waiting for the killer to re- turn to the corpse.

Why should the girl's slayer return? Neither Harvey nor any other policeman could give a reasonable an- swer as to why murderers were so often compelled to revisit the scene of their deeds. But it was so, more common in real life even than readers of mystery novels might expect. In the current string of murders, moreover, not only Harvey but other investigators had suspected for some time that the killer had returned

to several of his victims—in each case where a body
had gone undiscovered for a period of time.

Therein lay the possible key, they theorized: Where
there was an appreciable time lapse between a victim's
disappearance and her discovery, the chances seemed
stronger that her killer might be drawn back to where
he had left her. Why? To reassure himself, to gloat, to
weep?—it didn't really matter. The slightest chance of
that was worth going to almost any length for.

The idea of such a stakeout had appealed to Harvey
twice before, only to blow up each time before it could
be effected. Now was a chance to try it again. The
conditions seemed ideal. Only the perpetrator would
know where to look for the body. And while that in
itself would hardly be enough to convict anyone, it
certainly would supply them with a material suspect.

The time element was precarious, however. They
would have only one shot at pulling it off: this one
night. It could not go longer before, in the name of compassion—to say nothing of due process—the victim's
family would have to be informed. Earlier Saturday
afternoon, before the girl was found, Kenneth Gebhardt finally had been persuaded to return home—
chances were he was still en route. That was excuse
enough for Harvey.

Four detectives of the State Police crime lab arrived
from Plymouth at about 6:30 P.M. On their heels came
Prosecutor Delhey himself, having just returned from
a state prosecutors' convention at Mackinac Island,
where he'd been tied up since Wednesday. As the
scientific experts went to work, Harvey escorted
Delhey and Williams down into the gully to view the
victim close up. When the corpse was turned over onto
its back, the men had to wince. The girl had been cruelly assaulted, the forehead and face battered into an
indistinguishable grayish-brown lump; the right eye was
almost hidden behind swollen flesh, and blood stained
the puffed lips. At least one front tooth had been

knocked out. The throat and neck muscles had been crushed, evidently by a pair of powerful hands. Her naked body was also discolored with bruises in a number of places; the breasts were partially disfigured by what looked like burns of some kind. Deep impressions encircling both wrists and ankles indicated that she had been securely bound prior to death.

Her fingerprints were taken and dispatched to the crime center to be compared with those of Carol Ann Gebhardt previously lifted from her dormitory quarters. Meanwhile, the lab men scoured the area for anything they could find: a fragment of fabric, a cigarette butt, a detectable footprint or tireprint, anything that might provide a clue to the recent presence of another in that vicinity. By 7:30 dusk was crowding in, and they'd uncovered nothing.

The only item of consequence recorded finally was identification of the victim. Word came from the crime center that her prints compared positively with those of Carol Ann Gebhardt.

Back in the house—where the doctor and his wife kept the men supplied with sandwiches and coffee— the night's strategy was laid out by Sheriff Harvey. It was, really, not a very complicated operation: A half-dozen officers were deployed out of sight around a perimeter—two on a slope just below the Stoneman house, overlooking the gully; another pair across Riverside on a wooded knoll, some seventy-five yards off but from where all accesses to the location could be watched; two more in a car stationed in the Stonemans' driveway, poised to move out at the first alert of contact. All the men had walkie-talkies. The minute anybody was spotted approaching the site, he was to be picked up immediately. There was some discussion about leaving the body there to lure the killer, but Delhey promptly vetoed that. "Out of the question!" he snapped. "Good Lord, elementary respect . . ." He paused and squared his shoulders. "I want the body removed. At once."

Then Assistant Prosecutor Booker Williams came up with an idea. "What would you think of substituting something that could be taken for a human figure—a dummy, say like a store mannequin?"

Delhey considered, his expression a mixture of doubt and hope. Then he said: "We could try J. C. Penney's over at Arborland. They're open tonight."

Leaving Harvey with the admonition to have the body removed to the morgue by the time they got back, Delhey and Williams drove the mile and a half to the shopping center. At Penney's they persuaded a befuddled store manager, without explanation, to let them borrow a female window mannequin. Returning within a half-hour, they saw an ambulance from St. Joseph Mercy Hospital pulling out of Riverside Drive with the corpse of Carol Ann Gebhardt.

Delhey and Williams personally carried the undressed model form down into the gully and carefully placed it as the actual body had lain, partially covering it over with brush. Back on the roadside, looking down at it with Sheriff Harvey, in the gloom it appeared real enough. Delhey shook his head thoughtfully. "Well, I hope something comes of it."

The prosecutor and his assistant started to leave for the crime center . . . when Delhey had a final thought. "You *have* sent word to the girl's family?" he posed to the sheriff.

"I, uh, not just yet," replied Harvey hesitantly. "I figured if we could just buy a little time . . ."

"Oh, for God's sake, Doug!" sputtered Delhey. "It's been *four hours* since she was found! We've *got* to let them know!"

"Bill, please! We will—just give us one chance to pull this off! What difference can a few more hours make? We had to wait for positive ID, okay? So it's taken us a little longer."

Delhey opened his mouth to reply, then clamped it shut. What difference a few hours? He wasn't sure he could say anymore. Suddenly very weary, he turned and went to his car.

At about 11:30 P.M., the deluge that had been threatening most of the day broke loose. To the forlorn police officers rimming the black gully off Riverside Drive, it was the culmination of an evening of torment. Crouched silent and almost motionless for hours in dank foliage, stewing in their oozing sweat, they had become targets of lust for maddening swarms of mosquitoes, gnats, and biting flies. They had begged, over their walkie-talkies, for some kind of protection—netting, bug repellent, anything—but no way could the risk be run of bringing something out to them where they were.

Then came the cloudburst, soaking the hapless officers and reducing visibility. If anyone *should* come now, the chance was greater that he might slip by them—almost literally screened by the dimming sheets of rain. Nor did it appear, after close to an hour of unabating downpour, that it would soon let up. The whole idea was looking lousier by the minute.

It was about 12:15 A.M., Sunday, when John Markwell, an E.M.U. officer huddled miserably in shrubbery on the knoll across from the gully, spotted a runner: a figure darting across the bottom of Riverside, sprinting east on Huron River Drive—a white male was Markwell's fleeting impression, wearing a light-colored jacket or loose shirt that flapped behind —and disappearing a second later behind tall brush at the foot of the knoll.

"Did you see that?" Markwell cried hoarsely to the man on his right, a young sheriff's deputy named Basil Baysinger.

Baysinger had already half risen. "I thought I saw *something*. What was it?"

"It was a guy, running!" Markwell was excited. "Why don't we yell for him to stop—that we're police?"

"Maybe we ought to alert the others first?" Baysinger suggested. "The radio—?"

"Right, right, the radio." Markwell fumbled with the walkie-talkie. He blurted his sighting into the mouthpiece. . . . "Do you read?"

He pressed the switch, but only static came back. "Goddamn it!" He repeated the message.

This time, deep within the static a faraway voice could be heard, but they couldn't make it out.

Markwell spat in disgust at the unit. "Where do they get these things, in the goddamn five-and-dime? . . . Come on. We better get down to the road."

Thrashing and stumbling through the heavy, sopping brush, they fought their way off the knoll and onto Riverside Drive, about halfway between Huron River Drive and the command post up the hill. Markwell tried the walkie-talkie again. "Check out a man running along Huron—east from Riverside! Does *anybody* read—?"

"What man?" a clear voice jumped out of the receiver.

"Oh, for Christ's sake!" Markwell swore.

Precious minutes must have passed already. He again repeated the sighting.

"Roger. Stay put. Ten-four," the voice commanded.

Markwell and Baysinger could hear a car engine turn over up the hill and saw a sweep of headlights, going away from them, farther up into the woods.

The car bearing deputies Gene Alli and Bert Ardagast squealed out of the Stonemans' driveway and right on Riverside Drive. They followed Riverside up and around and down the other side of the hill, where it came together with Chalmers Drive just before Huron River Drive. Occasional lights from a few scattered houses were the only signs of life as their car followed the bumpy road through the driving rain, across the thickly wooded hillside and down. They came out onto Huron River Drive without having seen a single person.

Alli turned right and sped east. But Huron was clear all the way to the next cutoff, a quarter-mile off, a quiet lane that curled to a dead end against the concrete abutment of the US 23 freeway overhead. Pulling around, they cruised back alongside the river, scanning both sides of the road carefully now. Again, they passed no one before again reaching the turn-in to Riverside Drive, where a couple of the stakeout team appeared to have come down from their positions and were lurking in shrubbery near the corner.

Making a sharp U-turn, Alli stopped the car astraddle the intersection. Ardagast leaned out his window and stage whispered: "Anybody make contact?"

A bedraggled, dripping figure stepped out from behind a tree. It was Deputy Baysinger. "We haven't seen a thing since he first ran by here," he wheezed into the car. "He didn't come back this way, we're pretty sure. You guys miss him?"

"Looks like it," growled Ardagast. "We'll double back for another go-round. You fellows stick close by here. Try to keep the others informed." He rolled up the window, and the car spun gravel, leaping away east again on Huron.

By now the others on the hill had become aware that something was going on, and singly and in pairs they were making their way down, staying cautious about maintaining cover but irresistibly drawn to whatever was happening on the road below. And when Alli and Ardagast returned ten minutes or so later —still empty-handed—half a dozen confused and rainsodden policemen were milling about at the foot of Riverside Drive. (They'd just had a grim laugh at themselves. One, having excitedly "discovered" a fresh shoeprint in the mud of the roadside overlooking the gully, was in the process of removing his windbreaker to lay over the spot in order to preserve it from being washed away, when another, curious, bent to study the impression, then looked the first up and down with pity and drawled: "Keep your jacket on. It's your own footprint—dummy.")

They all could see that this was not the way this thing was supposed to have been handled. Somehow perspective, if not resolve, had got out of hand. By now, several passenger automobiles had driven past on Huron River Drive, and the occupants could hardly have failed to notice a band of men in the rain gathered around a car parked across the entrance to Riverside Drive. The operation seemed on the verge of coming apart. The man, or boy—there had been no way to gauge his age—glimpsed fleeing the scene seemed to have vanished.

Back at the Stoneman house, Lieutenant Bordine, who had waited with increasing anxiety for some word, exploded when he learned what had taken place.

A man out alone on such a night, in an area so secluded that a pedestrian might be a novelty in broad daylight, and they'd let the sonofabitch *get away?*

And as long as they'd blown their cover, had *any* thought been given to stopping civilian cars proceeding along Huron Drive immediately after the subject had been "lost"? He *might* have been picked up. He could be halfway to Detroit by now!

It was nearly 1:00 A.M. Bordine gritted his teeth and telephoned his chief, who had returned to the crime center. The reaction at the other end was predictable. As his blood pressure settled, Sheriff Harvey's mind started clicking forward again. He had to assume that they'd burned the surveillance, but that didn't mean they had to shut it down. His instinct persuaded him that it *was* the killer who had eluded their trap —why else would anyone be roaming around out there on such a night?—and that meant he had to send in more help to try tracking him down. More *experienced* men. And how about dogs? The guy evidently had been on foot. In that terrain, bloodhounds might save a lot of time picking up the trail.

This killer had to be such a maniac, and an *ego-*

maniac, that he might even come back—take another
risk to give the finger to the stupid police. And if, by
chance, the one who'd got away was *not* their man,
then the actual killer might show up yet.

The sheriff had some fast telephoning to do now. . . .

Booker Williams had dropped off into fitful sleep
on his living room sofa, feet up on the coffee table.
The children long since tucked in, he and his wife
had talked quietly awhile, watched the eleven o'clock
news together, then she had gone off to bed, leaving
him to sit and ponder the consequences should Doug
Harvey indeed pull a rabbit out of the hat this night
. . . and should he not.

Their situation was beyond doubt critical. The
police *and* the prosecutor's office had come under harsh
scrutiny. It was becoming a statewide issue: Was the
traditional machinery outmoded, so fraught with
worn-out procedures and counterproductive loyalties
and conceits that only a complete overhaul could save
it from neutralizing itself?

He felt most sympathy for his boss. Bill Delhey was
among the finest prosecutors in Michigan, perhaps in
the country, one of the most highly motivated public
servants and human beings Williams had ever known
. . . yet he could go down the drain with this if
failure persisted much longer.

For Delhey was, after all, an elected official. He'd
been in the county prosecutor's office since 1956, only
one year after his admission to the Michigan bar; he
had done an outstanding job, become chief prosecutor
in 1963, been reelected twice since. Yet, though the
next elections were three years off, it was doubtful
that even then could he survive such a debacle as
this unforgettable situation could well be recorded.

As for his own future, Williams felt less concerned.
He had a legal practice to return to. After graduation
from the U. of M. Law School in 1955, Williams had
hung out his private shingle in Ypsilanti to a built-in
and virtually exclusive clientele: There was a sizable

black community in the Ypsi area, and black lawyers were few and far between here.

It was Bill Delhey, in 1964 the newly elected county prosecutor, who had persuaded him to come over to the other arm of the law. He didn't expect Booker to give up private practice indefinitely, only so long as it would take to organize a reliable branch of the prosecutor's office in Ypsilanti. Delhey had made a moving personal appeal: He wanted to expand the full services of his Ann Arbor-based office, to make the apparatus of justice more accessible and responsive to *all* the people, and he needed a man of Booker's integrity to help him make that goal a reality. In the five years since, many of Delhey's aims had been realized, in no small measure due to the contributions of Assistant Prosecutor Booker Williams. But Williams himself had been growing restless of late; his personal responsibilities had multiplied—he and his wife now had seven youngsters to provide for, the eldest only thirteen, plus his aged, invalided mother. He had to start thinking again of the future.

There was no way, of course, that he would quit Delhey before the present unholy affair was settled. Never, until this killer was caught and put away, no matter *how* long that took. . . .

Lost in such thought, Williams had just dozed off, when he was awakened by Sheriff Harvey's telephone call. Harvey sounded urgent but undiscouraged; he had already sent for more men and tracking dogs, and they were going to beat the bushes until dawn if necessary. The sheriff seemed to have talked himself into a belief that they could still nab the killer before the night was over.

Williams saw it as a busted play, but he was too tired to argue the point any further. He said only: "Doug, I hope the girl's family has been informed by now?"

"Well, it's been pretty hectic, you know? I guess

we should, huh? I just—Look, could you get the State
Police—?"

"All right." Williams sighed. "I'll see you in a while."

First, he thought, bring Bill Delhey up to date. One
twenty-five Sunday morning. Lord, what a life . . .

By 2:00 A.M., at Delhey's orders the mud-splattered
mannequin was removed to the crime lab to test for
fingerprints. Had the mysterious intruder got close
enough to the "body" to touch it? None of the stakeout
team could say—they'd only seen him running. The
prosecutor felt that their only hope, as forlorn as it
was, to salvage anything out of this fiasco was the
possibility of prints.

Sheriff Harvey had not given up, however. Though
he'd been able to lay hands on only one bloodhound
and handler, when the rain began to let up the dog
was started sniffing around the gully embankment on
Riverside. Slowly, tentatively, it crept east along Huron,
deputies and troopers in tow. Meandering without much
positive sense of objective, dawdling at points on the
dirt shoulder, detouring occasionally off the road up
into the woods, in a half hour it led them only about
half a mile east, into a little side road called Thorn
Oaks Drive. There were a couple of isolated houses,
the first dark but the next still brightly lit, with several
cars parked outside . . . and the dog stopped before
this one. His handler looked uncertainly at the policemen. Two of them knocked at the front door. It
was opened by a young man, whose face dropped at
the sight of the armed officers.

It was a party of a half dozen or more couples,
all around twenty. After scanning the group and
taking names and addresses, the officers asked politely
if any of them had been out at any time in the past
few hours. None had. Shoes and clothing were examined. None were wet or muddy.

Feeling awkward, the hunters retreated.

And so through the waning hours of darkness their

miserable luck continued. At 4:00 A.M., the crime lab reported that the only prints found on the mannequin were those of Prosecutors Delhey and Williams. Operation Stakeout: another washout.

CHAPTER 16

AT 8:00 A.M. Sunday, a drawn Sheriff Harvey and the rest of an abashed crime-center leadership had to face a news conference and try to explain what had been going on since late Saturday afternoon. The reporters had begun to pick up bits and pieces of it during the night and had been incredulous. What they heard now provoked outcries ranging from shock to outright scorn. They left little doubt, as they scrambled to phone in their reports, that coverage of *this* catastrophe and its farcical handling would be merciless.

One figure prominent the past week already had stalked off. Peter Hurkos had never been officially informed of developments; he had learned of them only some twelve hours after the fact when awakened by a telephone inquiry from a newsman who suspected something was up and wondered—Hurkos being "so close to the investigation"—if he could shed any light. . . .

Hurkos' man Ed Silver then called Walter Krasny demanding that Hurkos be taken to the site. As it happened, at that hour the Ann Arbor chief himself had not yet been informed either of the girl's discovery or of the stakeout! A furious Krasny confronted Doug Harvey, who sullenly, and lamely, tried to explain that he'd just wanted to assure maximum security. Krasny said that he was going out to the scene at once and, furthermore, he was going to bring Peter Hurkos with him. Harvey snapped, "Like shit! It's my case, and I don't want him around!" Krasny turned on his heel and went to pick up Hurkos.

Harvey was there when Krasny, with Hurkos and Silver, drove up Riverside Drive at about 7:00 A.M. The sheriff glowered and seemed about to protest, but Krasny glared him down and led the limping psychic down into the gully. Men in jeans and fatigues were already ferreting through the underbrush.

The Dutchman poked about unenthusiastically for a few minutes. Then he turned to Krasny with a frown: "I come too late here. I don't get much. . . ."

"What *do* you get, Peter?"

He drew a weary breath. "I see a young man . . . and *not* American! He got some kind of foreign money. And I see . . . I don't know what it means, but I see a ladder, a short ladder. . . ."

"Yes—?" Krasny prompted.

"This is all I get now. Too late," he muttered. He glanced accusingly about at the sheriff and the other policemen looking on. "Hostile. No good for me. Everybody want Hurkos go home. Okay"—he reached for Ed Silver's arm—"we go, Ed."

That afternoon, the forlorn pair boarded a jet to California.

The official postmortem examination of Carol Ann Gebhardt's corpse was begun at one minute past noon on Sunday at the University Medical Center, under direction, again, of Dr. Robert C. Hendrix (the forensic specialist), assisted by Dr. John G. Patsakis and oral pathologist Dr. J. Phillip Sapp.

Dr. Sapp examined the girl's mouth; her identity

would be formally certified if the dentition and condition of her teeth matched the charts of Carol Ann's dentist in Grand Rapids, obtained by the State Police that morning and rushed to Ann Arbor. The broken tooth was a right central incisor, from the crown of which a fragment approximately two millimeters long was missing. It was a clean fracture, as from a sharp blow, which the dentist concluded had occurred quite recently—no doubt during the fatal assault.

Before Dr. Sapp could complete his own chart, however, he found something else: jammed back into the throat was a small, balled piece of coarse fabric; it was gold in color, measuring about four inches square, with a rough texture of burlap. Nobody could figure out what it might have come from. Obviously used to gag an outcry, whether or not it had contributed to the girl's strangulation was not determinable.

Dr. Sapp's dental comparisons did confirm the victim to be Carol Ann Gebhardt.

Then another startling discovery was made of a foreign object within the girl's body: stuffed deep into the vagina was a pair of female underpanties. Removed and carefully laid out on a specimen board, they were of delicate netlike construction, peach colored with a pastel floral design. (They were identified shortly as Carol Ann's.) The crotch area was torn or slashed, as was one side seam. Vaginal smears indicated the presence of male seminal secretions. Free blood found in the uterus, plus the thinned state of the endometrium, suggested that when penetrated she had been in the menstrual phase.

In addition to the countless bruises over the entire body, some so vicious that whole layers of skin had been stripped away and subcutaneous tissues exposed, there was a peculiar pattern of destruction of the chest and breasts: composition of the flesh, and particularly the nipples, had been altered—burned—by what appeared to have been the flow of some kind of corrosive liquid from her neck and shoulders down over her breasts. Had the attacker also tried to disfigure her with lye or acid?

Analysis of the victim's stomach contents produced partially digested bits of food distinguishable as frankfurter, vegetable carbohydrate such as found in corn or potato chips, pickle, salad greens, fruit—which fit what Carol Ann was known to have eaten for lunch on Wednesday, the last day she'd been seen alive. From these findings, Dr. Hendrix could deduce that she had died, or been in mortal fear of her life, shortly after that final meal. Normally it takes two to three hours after eating for a person's stomach to empty. Dr. Hendrix surmised that this girl's digestive processes had ceased anywhere from a minimum of less than one hour to a maximum of three hours after lunch. Since she was alive at least thirty-five minutes after leaving the E.M.U. dining commons that day—from 12:15 to about 12:50 P.M., the time she was said to have ridden off from the wig shop with the motorcyclist —it followed that the murder had been committed between approximately 1:00 and 3:00 P.M. Wednesday.

Interestingly, the wiglet that Carol Ann Gebhardt had had fitted that critical day, the item for which, as fate had worked out, she'd paid with her life, was nowhere in evidence. The women at Joan's had said she was wearing it when she left their shop. But it was absent from her remains at the morgue, and there had been no sign of it where her body was found. Either it had been lost en route, possibly during her struggles with her assailant—in which case, it could yet be at the place of attack—or, for some reason, the killer had kept it as a morbid souvenir. There was reason to believe that personal items of previous victims had similarly been collected.

One other detail of uncertain note came out of the autopsy: closer examination of the girl's panties revealed, clinging to the left inner surface, a concentration of tiny hair particles, which did not appear to be from her own pubic or other body growths. Under a microscope, they showed up as various shades of blond—her own hair was dark brown—and, more mystifying, possibly as *clippings*. Was there some connection with barbering?

Dr. Hendrix had the panties sealed in a glass jar to be delivered to the Michigan Department of Health in Lansing for more minute analysis.

Late Sunday afternoon, the corpse was released to the family.

Surveillance of 619 Emmet Street, where James Armstrong resided, had been initiated Saturday night, after Booker Williams returned to the crime center from the stakeout and read E.M.U. Patrolman Larry Mathewson's report of the afternoon. Armstrong seemed to be the only solid suspect thus far, and Williams had dispatched detectives Mulholland and Fuller to watch the boardinghouse. If the subject went anywhere, he was to be tailed but not intercepted. A lot more about this individual had to be found out before any action might be taken.

But so far the coverage on Emmet Street had turned up nothing. There still had been no contact with the subject when Larry Mathewson took over the watch on Sunday morning.

Mathewson sat in his car across from the house most of the day, breaking the monotony every so often by driving around the block and returning to a different parking place.

It must have been about 5:00 P.M.—Mathewson had lost close relationship with time—when the front door of the house opened for the first time and a young man emerged. He was slim, dark-haired, neatly dressed in sport shirt and slacks. Mathewson peered through his misted windshield and recognized the gentle-faced friend of Armstrong's who had come into the garage on Friday with a "plate" for James.

He skipped down the porch steps and, ignoring the light rain, crossed the street and made straight for the car. He tapped on the window, and Mathewson rolled it down.

"Hi," the young man said pleasantly, bending to eye level. "Larry Mathewson, isn't it? Donald Baker."

"Yeah, sure. How you doing?" Larry acknowledged, forcing a tentative smile.

"Are you waiting for somebody?"

Larry searched the other's face for a hint either of antagonism or facetiousness. "Maybe. Why?"

Baker hesitated a second, then asked almost shyly: "Is it anybody at our house?"

The policeman decided not to beat around the bush. "Yes, James Armstrong. Is he here?"

"I'm afraid not. He's away for the weekend—gone biking upstate."

"When's he due back?"

"Gee, I can't say for sure. Any time. By tonight, anyway. Is there anything I can do?"

"No. Thanks. It can wait."

They looked at one another in uncertain silence for a moment, before Baker said: "Well, okay then. Nice to see you." He walked off, back toward the house.

Mathewson watched him go inside, then contacted the crime center to advise that he had been "made," as well as that the subject evidently was away from the premises and might not return until sometime later. Should he break off the surveillance?

Definitely not! The reply was firm. Not before they could rush fresh hands down there to pick it up. There had been some new developments. Just hang tight until relieved.

On Sunday afternoon additional identifications had been made of Armstrong that had bolstered suspicion of him. Though tentative, and not damning of themselves, they were deemed by the higher-ups as sufficient to put Armstrong into a special category that required more careful handling.

A nineteen-year-old E.M.U. coed had come to the university police office to say that the composite sketch of the mystery cyclist bore a strong resemblance to a young man who had tried to pick her up the previous weekend. She and two girl friends were on their way to a party, when two young men had approached them in a gray or silver late-model car and offered them a lift. (Both were "nice looking"; each had short brown hair.) The girls declined, but they did stop for a while and converse with the pair. The driver—the one the drawing resembled—did most of the talking. He seemed personable and engaging, but there were two things in the conversation that struck her as "strange": One was his comment that he could not stand girls who had their ears pierced "because they left holes that defile their bodies." Then he told of once having strangled a cat with a length of clothesline . . . and to demonstrate, he put his hands to her throat. They were large, powerful hands, and she became frightened, but he laughed and asked her to go bike riding with him the following day. She said she would consider it—to put him off—and he said he would look for her then. As it turned out, it rained the next day anyway, and she did not see him again. She never did learn his name.

The snapshot that E.M.U. Patrolman Mathewson had brought in—James Armstrong standing by a Christmas tree—was shown the coed. She said yes, that was the man.

Another woman had contacted the Sheriff's Department at almost the same time Sunday afternoon, also in connection with the published police sketch. She reported that a few days earlier, as she had come out of a beauty shop in downtown Ypsilanti, she had been approached by a striking-looking young man who gave her a line about her having a model's figure and how he had a couple of friends, professional photographers, who would pay her fifty dollars if she would go with him to pose for them. The woman, in her mid-twenties and married, had turned him down flat.

She'd put the incident out of her mind until the sketch appeared in the Ypsilanti *Press;* then she told her husband that it looked like the man who had propositioned her, and he urged her to report it. A sheriff's deputy brought the snapshot of James Armstrong to the couple's home, and the woman said it was the same individual.

So it seemed this Armstrong was in the habit of accosting females, three such attempts, at least, now having been verified. And he did possess some odd characteristics: a revulsion for pierced ears and his sadistic taunts about strangling. (Someone at the crime center thought to look back through the medical reports on all the victims to date and found that five of the seven had had pierced ears—including Carol Ann Gebhardt.)

It was the crime center's decision, then, that while James Armstrong certainly now warranted priority attention, extreme caution was all the more urgently dictated. Should they move on him too soon, and he were the guilty one, they could lose him—at least put him on his guard, perhaps scare him off. They must be extra patient, watchful, diligent.

It was 11:00 P.M. before Armstrong showed up. Baker, reading in his room, heard the screen door below squeak open and clap shut, and he went out and met him at the landing.

"Hi. How was the weekend?" Donald asked.

James, looking a bit disheveled and soiled, grinned in weary contentment: "Not bad. But my tail is dragging. We rode hell out of those things."

He moved toward his own rooms at the head of the stairs.

"Before you get settled," Donald said, "there's been a cop, maybe more than one, waiting for you outside all day."

Armstrong's expression remained unmoved. Only the steely, brooding eyes, staring back at his friend, might have become smaller and a shade darker. Without a word, he turned and went back down the stairs.

He had his hand on the screen door when the figures of two men materialized on the other side.

"Can I help you gentlemen?"

"Uh . . . are you James Armstrong?" one of them asked.

"Yes. Are you policemen?" asked James guilelessly.

There was a strained clearing of a throat. "Yes, actually." They produced gold shields. "Ann Arbor Police Department. We'd like to talk to you. You mind?"

"No."

It was a mistake.

The two young Ann Arbor detectives were among a number of new recruits whose normal range of duties did not include homicide. And the briefing they were given when hastily pressed into service on Sunday evening was, unhappily, less than adequate to the situation. All they knew was that they'd been hurriedly enlisted to pick up a stakeout on the residence of a missing homicide suspect. And so, by eleven o'clock Sunday night, after almost five hours of anxious waiting and speculating, when a young man answering the suspect's description finally appeared, their spontaneous reaction was to make sure that he did not elude them.

There being no task force "regulars" at the crime center at the hour Armstrong was brought in, there was little notice as detectives Ben Peterson and Les Rodman led their suspect—one of dozens interrogated there that night—to a quiet corner and proceeded to take down his "pedigree."

His full name was James Nolan Armstrong. He was twenty-two, a senior at E.M.U. expecting to be graduated in January 1970. He was from Center Line, just outside Detroit. He had resided at 619 Emmet Street since early in 1968. Before that, he'd roomed at the Theta Chi fraternity house on Cross Street. He was no longer a member of that fraternity.

"Where'd you spend the weekend?" asked Rodman.

"Up at Ortonville with friends."

"What friends?"

"Chuck Harris, a friend from school and the frat,

and Chuck's brother Jim and his wife. Jim and his wife have a place up there."

"What's the attraction at Ortonville?"

"It's good for 'scrambling'—dirt riding."

"What type of motorcycle do you own?" Peterson picked up.

"I've got a few."

"Is one a Honda four-fifty?"

"No. I don't have a Honda."

"A Triumph?"

Armstrong hesitated. "I've got two Triumphs. And two Bultacos."

"Two what?"

"Bultaco—a Spanish make. Dirt bikes. Triumphs are street bikes, for just riding around, transportation," the young man explained patiently.

"What colors are the Triumphs?"

"One's green, the other's blue."

"What about mirrors?"

"They have mirrors."

"Any square ones?" asked Rodman.

"I've *used* a square one. . . ."

"Now," resumed Peterson, "where were you—tell us what you did—last Wednesday, the twenty-third?"

"Wednesday . . ." Armstrong thought. "Nothing special, I don't think. I guess I was around."

"Say around noon?"

"Noon . . . I don't remember right offhand."

"Isn't it a fact," Peterson insisted, "that you were cruising the campus area on your motorcycle . . . that shortly *before* noon you tried to pick up a female walking along the street . . . that a little *after* noon you stopped to talk with another young woman, named Ginny Lipton, on Lowell Street . . . that you were out to get *some* girl to go riding with you on that motorcycle—?"

"Oh, that was what Officer Mathewson was asking me about the other day," Armstrong replied evenly. "I wasn't out to 'pick up' anybody. I was just riding around. I didn't bother anybody."

"What about approaching strange females on the street?"

"Well, sometimes I'll do that, sure—strike up a conversation with a pretty girl. It doesn't mean anything. It's a kind of game everybody plays."

"How often do *you* play that 'game'?"

"I don't know. I don't keep score. Now and then." His mouth tightened.

"Well, how do you make out?" Rodman pressed. "It must be tough lately to get girls to hold still, what with all the murders putting everybody uptight."

"Sometimes I get lucky, sometimes not. It all depends." Armstrong made a what-can-I-tell you gesture.

"For instance," Rodman bore in, "what approach did you use on that little girl last Wednesday, when you persuaded her to let you ride her downtown to that wig shop?"

Armstrong stared at them. "Wig shop? *What* girl?"

"Come off it!" Peterson snapped. "Don't you read the papers, watch TV? You know damn well who we're talking about. Carol Ann Gebhardt, the murdered girl. You were *seen* with her!"

"Who said so?" Armstrong had flushed, but his tone remained steady.

"Witnesses."

"It's not true."

"They saw you. And later they identified you from a picture."

"I don't believe that. . . . What picture?"

"Oh, just a snapshot we got—" Peterson stopped. He shouldn't get too deep into what they had and where they'd got it.

"I don't care what you think you have," Armstrong said. "It's wrong."

The kid had been ruffled, but he was still pretty cool. They decided to attack from another angle.

"Do you have a striped T-shirt or polo shirt, green or blue and yellow, horizontally striped?" Rodman asked.

He thought. "Yes, I think I do."

"Did you wear it that day—last Wednesday?"

"I might have. But thousands of guys must have shirts like that."

"Which of your bikes were you riding that day?" put in Peterson.

"It would have been one of the Triumphs. . . . I don't remember which now."

"Where were you between twelve thirty and, say, one P.M. Wednesday?"

"Who can remember exact—? No, wait! One o'clock? That was the day I went to J and J's to pay a bill. I got there just about one o'clock."

"J and J's?"

"A cycle shop out on Ecorse Road. I do a lot of business with them. Everybody knows me there. They'll tell you. I came in about one, and the guys were just sitting around having their lunch. I was there an hour or more. . . ."

The detectives grudgingly took down the address and telephone number of J & J Cycle Sales and the names of those Armstrong remembered having seen there that afternoon. If these people backed up his story, especially the time element, it could knock the legs out from under any case that might be building against him. The murdered girl had left the wig shop and driven off with the motorcyclist just before 1:00 P.M. According to the autopsy, she had to have been fatally attacked by three or three fifteen at the outside, possibly quite a bit sooner.

"How is it," Peterson demanded, "that all of a sudden you're so clear about that particular day?"

"Because I also remember now," he said with renewed confidence, "where I went *after* J and J's. I stopped for a bite at a drive-in not far from there, over on Michigan Avenue—Roy's Squeeze Inn. Had a couple of hamburgers and a juice, till about two thirty. It comes back to me, I was talking with a guy I know who works the counter there, and we listened for a while to the All-Star game."

"What did you do when you left there?" asked Rodman disconsolately.

"Went back to Emmet Street and met a couple of the guys at the house—"

"What guys?"

"Tony Monte and Donald Baker. I'd promised Donald to teach him how to ride a bike, so we spent most of that afternoon riding—mostly over at Eastern's north campus parking field. Afterwards, he and I and Tony went out to supper—at Grants—and then we all came back about nine and watched TV."

"So you're saying you were with people who can vouch for you practically all that day and night?"

"I guess . . . oh, except there *was* one stretch that night, maybe a half hour or an hour at most, when I went alone over to my uncle's house. My uncle and aunt and their kids are away on vacation, and I was looking after the house and their dog. I'd forgotten to feed the dog, so I drove over—about nine thirty, I think. Then I came back and watched TV with Donald and Tony."

"Who's this uncle?"

"His name's Dana Loucks. He's a state policeman— here at the Ypsi post. Lives over on Roosevelt Boulevard."

The young detectives studied James Armstrong, their spirits foundering. Could they have been so far off the mark? Here was this clean-cut, straight-looking jock type, showing no strain of guilt pressure, in fact countering with what seemed to be a solid alibi for the critical day and time . . . and, as a topper, dropping that he's the nephew of a local *trooper!* Where the hell did this leave them? Rodman and Peterson stepped off to one side to confer a few moments. When they came back Rodman asked:

"Would you agree to take a polygraph test?"

"A lie detector?" Armstrong appeared uncertain. "I guess so," he said at last.

Rodman looked at his wristwatch: it was past 1:00 A.M. "Too late to set up anything now—the State

Police polygraph center is near Detroit—but we'll make arrangements first thing in the morning. You'll be notified, and somebody will come by to take you in. Meantime, stick close to your house."

Armstrong was silent most of the way back to Emmet Street. Just before they dropped him, he said:

"You really did suspect me of killing that girl?"

They squinted at him and at one another but said nothing.

James Armstrong shook his head and muttered almost to himself: "Wait till Uncle Dan hears about *this*."

It was almost one thirty and Donald Baker was beginning to doze in his chair when there was a tap at his door and Armstrong came into the room. He looked more disheveled than before, and paler.

"What happened?" asked Baker with a yawn, though he had come wide awake.

James sank heavily onto the bed, elbows on knees, staring at the floor. When he lifted his head, there were shadows around his eyes. "It was horrible," he said melodramatically. "You won't believe this. They accused me of being the murderer!"

His friend gaped at him as if unsure whether he was serious. "But *why*, James?"

"Well . . . they say there are witnesses who saw the guy, and I'm supposed to look like him. They had me down as some kind of damn sex fiend. . . ."

The other thought about it. "Look, if they did think you were such a hot prospect, how come they let you go?"

"Because"—Armstrong sighed with evident satisfaction—"I finally sold them my story."

"Your story?"

"About where I was that day—the day the girl got hit. I got an alibi, man!"

Baker didn't know why he suddenly felt a twinge of uneasiness. "You told them the truth, didn't you?"

"Sure I did." James's expression was sober, but

there was a flicker deep inside the icy blue eyes. "You're it."

"*I* am?"

"Sure. Don't you remember, that was the afternoon, Wednesday, when we took the bike over to the parking field? I *couldn't* have been off mugging anybody then, could I?"

"No, that's right." Baker brightened. "Then you *are* clear."

"I hope. . . . They asked me to take a lie-detector test."

"Really? And?"

"I don't know." James stood and slowly paced the room, thinking. "Maybe I'd better call my mother." He sounded as though he wished there were some other option left to him.

At the door he turned. "Donald, in case you're ever asked, don't forget the time we went riding that day. *Early* in the afternoon. Like around two thirty. Right?"

"Sure, James. I—" Baker hesitated. His gaze went vacant, and when he focused on the other again he was frowning.

"What's the matter?" prodded Armstrong.

"I'd thought it was later than that . . ."

"A few minutes maybe. *Around* two thirty, okay?" Armstrong's eyes riveted him. "Don't you fuck me up."

"No, James, I'll . . . remember."

Booker Williams and the other strategists at the crime center were furious Monday morning when they learned that James Armstrong, whom they'd taken such pains to handle with delicacy, had been crudely grilled the night before. The first contact with a hard suspect, and two dumb cops come along and risk blowing it. *Sonofabitch!*

There was nothing to do but play it out now. Arrangements were made with the State Police polygraph section at Redford, and in midmorning the call was made to Armstrong. There was no answer at his room.

Nettled with the beginnings of foreboding, two detectives drove to 619 Emmet Street. Armstrong had left a message with the landlady. He could be located at a lawyer's office in Ann Arbor.

They found him there with young attorney Robert Francis, a principal in the modest firm of Toomey and Francis. Not yet thirty, he had been a member of the bar less than a year and in private practice only a month. He had worked for the Washtenaw County Legal Aid Clinic before coming in with John Toomey, who was some seven years his senior. Toomey was away on a delayed vacation, leaving his new partner in charge of the office, and James Armstrong was the first piece of new business to have presented himself. . . .

James's mother, in Center Line, had been outraged when they'd spoken by telephone. She'd told him to sit tight while she contacted an attorney friend. A little later she'd called back, given him the name of one of the top law firms in Ann Arbor, Crippen, Dever & Urquhart, and instructed him to go there first thing in the morning before he spoke to *anyone* else. But the firm was too tied up to handle the young man's problem. Partner Charles Dever had recommended Toomey and Francis as a pair of bright, up-and-coming chaps. . . .

Now, facing the two detectives, with James sitting by impassive and collected, Francis was brisk and positive. The police had been incorrect, first of all— if not, indeed, beyond lawful procedure—in having interrogated his client without counsel present. His client was not obligated, therefore, to honor any supposed commitments made under duress. Meaning that they would *not* consent or submit to polygraph examination. Nor would his client now or in the future go anywhere or answer any further questions without benefit of counsel, and then only should a specific charge be lodged against him.

Was there such a charge?

The detectives glowered from Francis to Armstrong. "No," one grumbled, "not at this time."

"Then," Francis said, not moving from behind his desk, "that would seem to be that. Thank you, gentlemen, and good day."

CHAPTER 17

THE HOMICIDE TASK force was in a distressing state of disarray. There was open squabbling within the crime center, recriminations flying from agency to agency, man to man. The prosecuting attorney's staff was appalled. The Sheriff's Department ranted at the Ann Arbor Police Department for its incompetence. Ann Arbor shouted in return that if the county force kept others better informed there wouldn't be such foul ups. The Ypsilanti Police Department smarted because a suspect had been arbitrarily investigated in *its* jurisdiction by outside departments. Perhaps the most confounded and dismayed of all were the representatives of the State Police. The murder suspect at the center of all this tumult was related to one of their own troopers, and they'd only now become aware of it!

By noon that day, the State Police Director himself, Colonel Fred Davids, and his hard-eyed chief of detectives, Captain Dan Myre, had sped from Lansing to join the task force.

Dan Myre in particular was not one to abide chaos

any longer than it took to straighten it out. A large, rawboned native of Michigan's rugged Upper Peninsula, he was a crisp, direct man of few words but unquestioned presence. Myre had climbed methodically up through the ranks over two decades to earn a reputation as a bulldog, both as an investigator and a commander, and he was held in a kind of devoted awe by those under him and sincere respect by his peers in and out of the State Police.

Now Myre took it upon himself to direct some of his stern authority toward restoring a semblance of organization.

They had to get back to basics: You do this, you do that, and you do something else. For this there had to be a single central desk with the sole responsibility of handing out assignments and collating the playback the same way. And the "boss" of this operation should not be an *attorney*—such as Assistant Prosecutor Williams—no matter how smart legally, but a *policeman* trained in the nitty-gritty of detective work and in administration as well. Myre's suggestion was State Police Lieutenant Hap Morrison, one of his best division commanders who knew the district and most of the local dicks.

What it came down to, Myre told them, was that they still had a lot of hard digging ahead, on many fronts—and the only way they were ever going to close out this mess was by working together, not as a cooperative but as a *team*.

His logic, of course, was sound. By and large, the assembled lawmen, their competitive rancor quelled, agreed. (Even Sheriff Harvey, though still grumbling some over virtual usurpation of his authority as the county's top police officer, had to go along.) They had to let someone call the shots.

Main attention remained focused on James Armstrong. Detectives checking out Armstrong's stated whereabouts the previous Wednesday afternoon found, at first, that his account did seem to stand up. The proprietor and employees of J & J Cycle Sales confirmed that Armstrong had come in early that afternoon to pay for minor repair on one of his Triumphs. They produced a dated copy of the receipted bill, which he'd paid in cash. He'd hung around awhile, jawing with them while they took their lunch break.

The time was important. One mechanic said he thought Armstrong had come in around 1:00 P.M. or just after. This was disheartening to the detectives; but they kept asking. Somebody else said no, it was more like one thirty that *he* remembered Armstrong being there. A third person put his arrival closer to two o'clock. So there had emerged a possible variance of up to one hour between the time Armstrong claimed to have arrived there and when he actually might have.

At Roy's Squeeze Inn on Michigan Avenue, where Armstrong had said he'd gone next, his friend—a fifteen-year-old high-school student who worked there part-time—was positive that James had been in that day, because he remembered that they'd listened to part of the All-Star baseball broadcast while James ate. James had come in a little past 2:00 P.M. and left after maybe half an hour, the youth said.

This seemed another setback, in light of the relative-time theory gleaned from J & J Cycle Sales. There, everybody interviewed was agreed that Armstrong had been around the shop for at least an hour. If that were so, and if he *had* arrived at the nearby drive-in only minutes past two, then he had to have been at J & J's from about one as he'd stated.

But was the Squeeze Inn youngster's recollection entirely accurate? (Or could he already have been set up by Armstrong for an alibi?) The timing seemed to hinge to some degree on the baseball broadcast. Why be so definite about its being around 2:00 P.M. that Armstrong came in? Why could it not have been two thirty, or later? The game should still have been in progress as late as 3:00 P.M.—in which case Armstrong would have been in the cycle shop no sooner than one thirty.

Next, task force detectives got a reading of Armstrong's record in his home town of Center Line. It was spotless. He was remembered as the archetypal all-American boy: popular, a leader, one of the greatest athletes ever at St. Clement's High School (two-way football player—offensive end and defensive safety —and team co-captain; outstanding pitcher in baseball; three years' varsity basketball), and an honor student as well.

Armstrong had gone from St. Clement's to Central Michigan University at Mt. Pleasant. After one year, however, he'd switched back closer to home, entering E.M.U. as a sophomore in the 1966 fall term. In his first semester at Eastern, Armstrong showed himself a better-than-average student; teachers found him intelligent, alert, a quick study. But then, in the second half of that sophomore year, he began to slide. Although he should have been in the graduating class of 1969, by the end of this past school year he still was twenty-four class-hours shy of the minimum required for graduation. Yet, this summer, he'd not bothered to sign up for additional make-up classes.

Then a darker view of him turned up. In his junior year, he'd abruptly moved from the Theta Chi fraternity house to the rooms at 619 Emmet Street. His former frat brothers at first had been reluctant to offer any significant reason for that, citing only certain "differences of opinion." But it finally leaked out that Armstrong had been *forced* to leave Theta Chi under powerful suspicion, though unable to be proved, of his having lifted $40 from the house entertainment fund. And from there, bit by bit, evolved further hints that that may not have been *all* Armstrong had stolen.

The most fascinating of these came from a quite unexpected quarter—a several-week-old possible grand theft in Ypsilanti involving an unreturned rental vehicle. On June 21, two men in their twenties had leased the seventeen-foot yellow camper, outfitted with three bunks and kitchen facilities, from Hendrickson's Rent-a-Trailer on East Michigan Avenue. One of the men had been described as large, heavy, with a Latin appearance. His companion—remembered by a youthful female employee at Hendrickson's as being about six feet tall, with a solid athletic build, good-looking, with a "nice" boyish smile and neatly trimmed dark hair—signed the rental agreement and paid the deposit of $25. Producing a Michigan driver's license and an E.M.U. student ID card identifying him as John Katoski, he then made out a check for the balance of $80. As the two were leaving, having hitched the trailer to a silvery colored late-model Oldsmobile, the clerk reminded them that the vehicle was to be returned by June 28. Neither they nor the trailer had been seen since.

The check had come back from the bank stamped STOP PAYMENT. Police found John Katoski, an Eastern student from Redford, who a week earlier had reported his wallet, containing his driver's license and other ID, stolen from his locker in the phys. ed. building. The wallet had not been recovered. When Katoski was brought to the rental agency, the clerk said he was *not* the same man with whom she'd dealt.

There had been no progress since early July in tracing the trailer or its presumed absconders until the composite sketch of the motorcyclist was recently circulated. Then, trooper Bob Brandt of the Ypsi post, assigned by his immediate superior (who happened to be Corporal Dana Loucks) to work exclusively on the case, thought he noticed a similarity between that sketch and the description of the bogus Katoski. He went to ask the clerk at Hendrickson's if the two could possibly be one and the same.

The woman was startled: By God, she exclaimed, it *could* be him! She couldn't say with absolute certainty—the sketch wasn't an *exact* likeness—but yes, it could be!

Reviewing the data being compiled on Armstrong, it was noted that he'd told several people about a recent trip to California. And his landlady at 619 Emmet Street, Mrs. Baker, confirmed that he and Tony Monte had gone away together toward the end of June for about three weeks.

The question was then: If the trailer thief *was* James Armstrong—and his buddy companion Monte —where, if anywhere, might this escapade fit in with the murders?

For that matter, what part in all this belonged to the shadowy Tony Monte, who now, for some reason, seemed to have dropped from sight?

Not much was known about Monte. He and Armstrong apparently had met while both had worked the night shift at the Ypsilanti plant of Motor Wheel Corporation, a Goodyear subsidiary manufacturing auto brake drums.

Armstrong had started there in August of 1968 as a press operator, and in ten months' time he'd advanced to assembly line inspector. Monte, hired not long after Armstrong as a machinist, had quit the past May, and shortly thereafter had taken a room at 619 Emmet Street. Armstrong had quit the middle of June.

Employees at Motor Wheel Corporation described Monte as difficult to get to know—closed-mouth, suspicious, even brutish; most regarded him as an ox mentally as well as physically.

The last that the police knew Monte himself to have been in Ypsi—and in James Armstrong's company—was, according to his landlady, Friday, July 25, a day before the latest corpse was turned up. But from that point on, nobody seemed to have any idea of his whereabouts.

A quick check showed no local police record on Monte, and a request was filed with the FBI for a more thorough printout.

The investigators logged other insights of Armstrong from some of the girls he was known to have dated.

One, named Vera Bradley, said she and James were

supposed to have gone swimming the past Wednesday, the twenty-third, but he had stood her up.

The day Carol Ann Gebhardt had disappeared! Had he offered her any explanation later?

No. She'd not heard from him since.

Miss Bradley said she had met Armstrong around March at a local carwash. She had driven her car in, and he was there washing his motorcycle. They got to talking, and when she mentioned having just bought a Suzuki herself, he enthusiastically suggested they ought to go out riding together. After that they went out quite regularly, until about the middle of June.

What kind of bike did Armstrong have?

When they were going out he always drove a green Triumph, with high handlebars and a square mirror. Last time she saw him, though—a week ago Sunday— he was driving a different bike, a big blue Triumph.

What kind of mirror?

She didn't think that one had a mirror.

Had she ever noticed anything . . . *strange* about James? Any sharp, unaccountable changes of mood? Any indications of a violent temperament?

Miss Bradley thought hard. No, she could not say that she'd had any personal unpleasant experiences with Armstrong; he was usually considerate and attentive, generally a pleasure to be with.

Another of James's girl friends, Francine Jervis, an E.M.U. junior, called being alone with James an adventure. He was fun, but oversexed. She could recall one occasion, however, when they'd had a little unpleasantness—he'd turned surprisingly nasty, in fact. They had run into each other one evening as she was coming out of the E.M.U. library and he walked her home. Everything was fine until they stopped outside her house, and he began fondling her. Suddenly, in the middle of it, he held her away and glared at her: Are you having your *period?* he demanded, like an accusation.

She almost apologized: yes.

And he stepped back from her and spat out in a

choked voice: That is really *disgusting!* And he turned and strode off without another word.

She didn't know what to make of it. They hadn't gone out or been alone together since.

Another Eastern coed, Adele Judson, who had gone riding with Armstrong on several occasions, said he was always perfectly normal, although there *was* one time he'd startled her somewhat. They were riding past a wooded area, when, as they stopped to rest under some trees, James asked: Would she be scared if she knew he was the coed killer? She screeched in mock fright, but he wasn't smiling. She could be the next victim, he said, being alone with him as she was. She looked for the expected twinkle in his eyes, but he was regarding her very soberly, and she began to feel uneasy. But a moment later the spell was broken when he said, Let's get moving, and they resumed riding . . . and there was nothing more to it.

A fourth girl, Lorraine Gentry, also an Eastern undergraduate, repeated the pattern of the others: She'd never had any trouble with James Armstrong, liked him, indeed felt him uncommonly attractive. But, she did recollect an odd conversation they'd once had, when he expressed some ideas which seemed quite out of character for him. It was at a fraternity hop. They were dancing together, a slow dance, close . . . and he looked down at her curiously and asked if she were religious. She said more or less, which seemed to disturb him, and he asked how then could she dance with a man in such a way? Thinking he was teasing, she drew him closer and said it depended on the man. He drew back from her, his face angry, and snarled: Hadn't she ever heard of the Sixth Commandment? And he spun away, leaving her alone on the dance floor. . . . Later, though, he came back and apologized. As they stood talking, he said that the Commandments really didn't mean anything to him. They were just stupid empty words. He didn't believe in the Fifth Commandment at all. *Thou shalt not kill.* If a man had to kill, he killed. Whatever someone decided was right for

them to do, he said, they had to do it. She pondered
this, trying to grasp some deep meaning. He said: Did
she know what the perfect crime was? It was when
there was no guilt. Without guilt, there was no crime;
and without guilt, there was no way a person could
get caught. . . .

This last incident bore a remarkable affinity, the
investigators realized, with part of an English paper
of Armstrong's that one of them had come upon at
Eastern:

> If a person wants something, he alone is the de-
> ciding factor of whether or not to take it—re-
> gardless of what society thinks may be right or
> wrong. For example, if a person sees a piece of
> jewelry or something that he likes in a store win-
> dow, it is up to him to smash the store window or
> not, to take it or not, and up to his own intellect
> if he is to get away with it or not. It's the same
> if a person holds a gun on somebody—it's up to
> him to decide whether to take the other's life or
> not. The point is: It's not society's judgment
> that's important, but the individual's own choice
> of will and intellect.

The investigators also reviewed some of the other
homicides for any possible connection with Armstrong.
It came to light that in the summer of 1967 Armstrong had worked part-time in the university administration building—in an office just across the hall
from Marilyn Pindar's! Further, it had been established
that Armstrong and his friends often swam at Silver
and Half Moon lakes, as Marilyn and her crowd had.

Jill Hersch, the second victim, had boarded in the
rooming house directly across the street from Armstrong's. She too had worked at the university, and
she had been the visible type, cute, pert, gregarious.
He could hardly *not* have noticed her one time or
another. Moreover, in the file on the Hersch case
were the statements by two persons who knew Arm-

strong and had "thought" they'd actually seen him with the girl on the street earlier on the night she disappeared.

Somebody dusted off the year-old description by Jill Hersch's roommate of the young man who'd got out of the red and black car that picked her up in front of McKenny Union, the night she disappeared— *tall, muscular-lean, clean-cut, trimmed dark hair, green E.M.U. T-shirt*—against that given by the women on Washington Street of the motorcyclist who'd driven off with Carol Ann Gebhardt. A pretty damn close match.

A more remote coincidence, but intriguing nonetheless, was the discovery that Armstrong was an habitué of George's Huron Inn, a tavern in the vicinity of where Dale Harum was thought to have been abducted.

Pindar . . . Hersch . . . Harum . . . Gebhardt. To one extent or another, in each instance the probability was established that Armstrong could have known them. Four of the seven.

And then something else turned up. A janitor at the Woodland Hills apartment village (where the delinquent Mary Grace Clemson had often stayed over and turned on with friends) came to the Ann Arbor police headquarters to say that the sketch in the newspapers resembled a young fellow who'd also been a frequent visitor there—not to the same apartment as that girl and the others used, but one right close by. They showed him the snapshot of Armstrong. He said that could be the one . . . but he wouldn't swear on it.

Were the tenants of that apartment still there? No, he said, they were college students—three or four young college fellows sharing the apartment—and they'd all vacated in June.

So, possibly a fifth connection.

One detective, moved by the one girl's account of Armstrong's revulsion over her menstrual period, took to poring back through the official medical reports on each of the seven victims. At least three of the slain

females were known to have been having their periods
when killed, and while this had not been certifiable
in the other four cases, in each it was listed as possible.
Could their menstrual conditions have been the
salient common factor, inopportune discovery of which
in each instance had set the killer off? It could, if
they were dealing with someone who had a paroxysmal
fetish about this "disgusting" feminine impairment!

While the score of detectives had been scurrying about
backgrounding James Armstrong, the more prosaic task
of keeping the subject himself in close surveillance had
been picked up.

Three days of it had revealed practically nothing.

Monday afternoon, Armstrong rode one of his motorcycles (the green Triumph) around Ypsilanti and
the Eastern campus, pausing now and again to chat
with acquaintances, including several young women.
That evening he and Donald Baker went out in Armstrong's Olds, had sandwiches at the Ponderosa steak
house on Washtenaw, then went to a drive-in movie
in Ann Arbor.

On the way back into Ypsi, a little past ten, Armstrong detoured on Cornell Road and pulled into the
driveway of his uncle's place, State Trooper Dana
Loucks, who was vacationing with his family on Lake
Michigan. While Baker waited in the car, Armstrong
entered the darkened house, using a key that he
evidently carried with him, and stayed inside fifteen
to twenty minutes. He came out once and went to the
detached garage in the rear, where a dog's throaty
barking could be heard, then returned inside. After
a few minutes, the house went dark again and he
emerged, relocking the side door, and the Olds proceeded to 619 Emmet Street, arriving there about
eleven. Neither Armstrong nor Baker was seen again
that night.

Tuesday, Armstrong did not show until after noon.
He strolled up College Place to Cross Street, stopped in
a coffee shop for breakfast, dawdled about opposite

the campus with some fellows, then made his way back to the boardinghouse. In a little while, he backed the Cutlass out of the driveway, drove over to Interstate 94 and headed east toward Detroit.

By midafternoon he was at his home in Center Line, an incorporated village within the city limits of Warren, just north of Detroit. The compact red brick house was set in a row of similarly modest but neat dwellings on a quiet street just off heavily trafficked Route 53. In the driveway, wearing T-shirt and jeans, he leisurely washed his car, attended by an affectionate little blond boy (his sister's child, the detectives would learn, who lived there with Mrs. Armstrong). The two went in for dinner, and Armstrong did not reappear all evening.

Wednesday morning, the only one out of the house early was a well-put-together woman with luxurious black hair who, for one probably in her forties, was quite attractive, if perhaps a shade too made-up—Armstrong's mother. She drove into Detroit to the restaurant in which she worked. James himself was inside until early afternoon. Then he did some grocery shopping and meandered back. Later, he mowed the square of front lawn, puttered about in the garage until his mother got home.

In the evening, after dinner, he went across the street to a neighbor's and stayed there awhile (it turned out to be the home of a pretty girl, now twenty and a student nurse, with whom he'd been close for years). It was dark when he came out and drove off in his car, stopping off briefly at a couple of places —a pizza parlor, a tavern—and he was home before ten thirty.

Despite Armstrong's seemingly innocent behavior the past several days, however, from all else they'd learned about him, many of the local investigators—especially those around Sheriff Doug Harvey—were confident by Wednesday, July 30, that they were zeroing in on the right man. A number were already impatient to take him without further delay. Maybe they didn't yet have the hard evidence to put him away, but they felt that under pressure it could be squeezed out of him. Even the prosecutor and his staff were tempted. Yet, this was one pinch that just had to be loophole-proof. There was too much at stake. They would follow it through a little longer.

And then that very Wednesday—the day Carol Ann Gebhardt was buried in Grand Rapids—they got a shock. Up in Lansing, Governor Milliken invoked an obscure thirty-five-year-old Michigan statute which empowered the state's director of public safety to assume full authority, at the governor's discretion, over any local law-enforcement action. Henceforth, the State Police were to be in direct charge of the murder investigations. Director Davids and his aides would make the official announcement at a news conference on Thursday morning.

The Washtenaw County authorities were stunned. Sheriff Harvey, his jurisdictional prerogatives abruptly usurped, was livid: "Those back-stabbing, grandstanding sonsofbitches!" he exploded. "We do all the ballbreaking work, take all the shit, then just as we're set to make the score *they* move out front—!" Prosecutor Delhey was no less outraged, if more restrained. He would not comment publicly, but he felt he knew what had prompted the governor's sudden step: *his* police had become seriously concerned over the growing likelihood that *locals* would make the arrest of James Armstrong—to the embarrassment of the state organization when it came out that the prime murder suspect was a trooper's nephew! The State Police were covering themselves. Delhey fumed to himself. He could understand their motives, but it was unworthy. Cheap politics.

The news media got wind of the grumbling around Ann Arbor, and well before the official announcement Thursday the dramatic transference of authority was known. To the further dismay of the Washtenaw lawmen, editorial opinion was not sympathetic to them.

The Detroit *Free Press,* for one, which had grown progressively outspoken in criticizing the fruitless efforts of local law enforcement, immediately went to press with a scathing editorial:

THE KEYSTONE KOPS GET HELP

Gov. Milliken acted not a moment too soon in taking charge of the Washtenaw manhunt. He has put Col. Frederick Davids, state police director, in command of all the police forces and asked the FBI to join the search.

Despite the fact that seven young women have been murdered in the Ann Arbor-Ypsilanti area in slightly more than two years—the last five at the rate of one a month—the governor had to give local police forces every chance to find the murderer or murderers. But the Keystone Kops atmosphere of the past few weeks, especially since the seventh slaying a week ago, was too much.

Sheriff Douglas Harvey, Ann Arbor Police Chief Walter Krasny, and Washtenaw Prosecutor William Delhey have apparently been barely on speaking terms. Though Delhey was officially in charge, he was not told what Harvey's department was doing. Chief Krasny was frequently left in the cold. The sheriff's stakeout Saturday night, using a department store mannequin in place of the body of the seventh victim, flopped although a suspect came within touching distance of the "body."

The problem seems to be one that could not be solved without state intervention. Prosecutor Delhey cannot afford to anger Sheriff Harvey simply because he must work with him. Sheriff Harvey, despite his limited police experience, is considered one of the most powerful political figures in the county. Both are subject to mandates from the electorate.

What was required was a co-ordinated search by experienced experts who are not involved in local politics, not running for office, and not looking for glory. This the search will get under the direction of Col. Davids. . . .

Gov. Milliken's action certainly is no guarantee of an early solution to the cases, or even a solution at all. But at least the people of Washtenaw County can now know that they have the best possible help, and the people in charge are looking for killers, not glory.

Of all the slings and arrows suffered during the long, frustrating siege, none would leave so searing a wound in the gut of every law officer in Washtenaw County as this single contemptuous write-off.

It would gall all the more because it had been inflicted—though none yet fully realized it—so close to the end. . . .

CHAPTER 18

THE BREAK STARTED to develop innocently enough
Wednesday morning, when one of the Ypsilanti
troopers' own wives went down to her basement with
a load of clothes for the washer.

She was Fran Loucks, James Armstrong's pretty
thirty-two-year-old aunt.

The Louckses had returned late Tuesday night from
their twelve-day holiday, and early the next morning
Fran got up to do the laundry Dana and the three
boys would need after two weeks of carefree neglect.
As she placed the laundry basket on top of the washer,
she noticed splotches of what appeared to be dried
black paint across the floor, almost like a trail, extending ten or twelve feet between the entry from the
recreation room and the corner where the dryer was
situated. Alongside the dryer, lengthwise against the
foundation wall, lay her husband's much-used step-
ladder, with black spatters on it, too. She knew these
spots were not there the last time she'd been in the
basement. The evening before they'd gone away, she

had brought the boys down and, as was her practice, given each a haircut under the ceiling light next to the dryer. When finished, she'd been sure to sweep the floor clean, as always.

That Dana! thought Fran Loucks. *You'd think he'd have taken the time at least to clean up his mess before going off on vacation!* She remembered how that night, as she'd bustled about packing, getting them organized, Dana had insisted on painting the upstairs hallway—of all times! She put the wash in, then went upstairs to the kitchen, and he was there at the table, scanning the morning paper over a glass of orange juice. "Hi," he greeted her without looking up from the paper. "Looks like there's nothing new on the murders."

Fran shivered. "Please, I don't want to hear about it. God, I wish you didn't have to go back to that so soon!"

"Yeah." He glanced back to the newspaper. "I wonder if they'll assign me to the crime center? I'd better look in at the post sometime today and see what I can expect for tomorrow."

Fran was silent for a moment. "That reminds me," she said, simulating the stern attitude she might take with one of their rambunctious sons. "I can tell you what to expect around here before you go *any*place."

"Which is—?"

"Clean up the paint you dribbled all over my nice clean floor downstairs."

He frowned. "I don't remember spilling any paint. Where?"

She took his hand and led him down into the laundry room. *"That's* where."

Dana looked at the floor in puzzlement. "That's black. I was using white. I never saw that before." Dana knelt to examine a couple of the larger stains. They were dry and not glossy—no telling how long there, but there was scarcely a trace of dust on them —and they looked sprayed rather than dabbed or splattered. Flat black spray paint. Dana thought he had an old aerosol of that, half-used, in the storage rack at the other end of the furnace room. He rose and went over to look. But the spray can was not among his other paints and tools. He knew he hadn't used it in a while. He wandered back to the laundry area, studying again the trail of black spots across the floor. "On my ladder, too. I know *that* wasn't like that when we left." He glanced up at Fran, who seemed to be searching for something between the electric washer and the oil tank where she kept an old utility table.

"You didn't throw out an empty Bold box I had here?"

"I'd never be so bold," he said lightly.

"I did a big wash that last day and used the last of it. I'm certain the box was still on this table when I cut the boys' hair that evening." She looked around, perplexed. "And my ammonia's gone. It was right there on the shelf. Did you use that for anything?"

"Not lately." Dana's face had clouded, and Fran recognized the almost imperceptible tightening of his muscles that meant he was becoming concerned about something. She watched him as he strode around the perimeter of the basement, examining the small ground-level windows. Each was locked and appeared undisturbed. "I want to check something upstairs," Dana said and bounded up the steps.

He was back in ten minutes, looking more thoughtful now than concerned. "Everything's secure," he reported, "—windows, both doors."

"Then do we have ghosts?"

"No." Dana smiled. "I think what we have—or had—is James."

"James!" Fran brightened. "For heaven's sake, of course! He's the only one *could* have been in while we were gone." Then her smile faded. "That scamp! What was he *doing* down here? Look." She reached into one of the laundry tubs and extracted a balled, discolored rag, once a man's cotton undershirt; it was still damp, and there were tiny bits of hairlike fuzz clinging to it.

"Maybe he tried to wipe up the paint," offered Dana.

"Well, he thought of it too late then," said Fran, unfurling the soiled material. "There's no sign of any paint on this thing." She sniffed it. "He didn't use the ammonia on it. Probably just water. Dummy kid."

Dana shook his head: "What I just don't understand is what he could have been doing with *paint* down here."

James Armstrong had long been, in the most important respects, very much a part of the Loucks family. He cherished his Aunt Fran, who'd been close to him all his life, and he looked up to her husband, often going out of his way to bring friends to meet his "favorite uncle." (Often, too, James would pop into the Ypsi post while Dana was on duty, hanging about to savor, wide-eyed and a little breathless, the flow of ceaseless activity in which his uncle was absorbed. Within the past year James even had seriously brought up the advisability of his joining the State Police himself. Dana thought that would be fine—after he finished college.)

For her part, Fran thought the world of the spirited, engaging young buck, was even maternal in ways— though she was only ten years older than he. And Dana, who was thirty-five, regarded him with the protective fondness of an approving senior brother. The three Loucks boys—Dana, Jr., nine; Donnie, seven; Daryl, five—idolized their "Uncle James," always ready to toss a ball or dive into any of their games and participate as one of them . . . never condescendingly.

As glad as all the Louckses were, though, that James seemed to have "adopted" them as his substitute family, this also was a source of particular sorrow to Fran. For it meant that James had drifted even farther from his own mother, just as had his brother and sister before him. Their mother was Fran's sister Louella, to whom she had been very close. Her sister had had more than her share of heartaches.

Louella (called "Peg" in their family) was the

eldest and Fran the baby of three sisters and a brother reared in Ontario of French-Canadian stock. All had migrated to Michigan in the 1950's; the other sister, Caroline, and the brother, Maurice, separated to distant parts of the state, while Peg and, lastly, Fran stayed in the environs of Detroit. Peg, having fled Canada at thirty, already twice-divorced and saddled with three young children—desperately seeking a fresh start in the anonymity of the metropolis—had got herself embroiled in a third disastrous marriage. Fran, still in her late teens, bright-eyed and hopeful, was just embarking on her own life, enrolled at the University of Detroit.

Mutual need for companionship and solace had drawn the two naturally together, despite their thirteen-year difference in maturity as well as age, and a stronger bond of affection grew between them in those circumstances than might ever have been likely back home. One catalyst was Peg's children, whom Fran adored—Thomas and Dawn and little James, all so young and lost—and who themselves found welcome delight in so youthful and spirited an aunt to come and brighten the gloom of their bewildering lives.

This was a great comfort to their mother, struggling to patch together a shattered family; and Peg, too, was revitalized by Fran's infectious verve and optimism, qualities she'd begun to despair of ever retrieving. Fran in turn absorbed and learned to respect the older woman's earthy pragmatism and gritty perseverance.

The sad irony, Fran had been moved to think many times since, was that so little had turned out well, or unregrettable, for Peg in her own life. The worst, from Peg's children's standpoint above all, was that none of them had ever in a real sense known a father.

Peg was a teen-ager when she'd married Warren Anderson during World War II and had borne him a son while he was off with the Canadian army. After his return they'd quickly had a daughter and another son. Then, barely a year after James's birth, Anderson had run off with another woman. They had never seen him again.

Peg had rebounded precipitously into a second marriage. It lasted a year. (Her children scarcely remembered *that* "father's" name years later.) It was then that Peg had taken the kids—aged eight, seven, and five—across to Michigan, determined both to sink permanent roots for them and not to allow herself to wither, for she was still a youthful and uncommonly handsome woman.

Her third husband had been Philip Armstrong, who was some ten years her senior. He had a good-paying job as an auto mechanic and seemed equal to the burdens of built-in fatherhood. When he talked of formal adoption of the children, Peg had their surnames changed legally from Anderson to Armstrong and each naturalized an American citizen. The couple had scraped together a $9,000 down payment and moved into a modest but secure home in Center Line.

But stability was to last little more than two years this time. Peg would discover to her horror and disgust that she'd married a boozer who, after getting tanked up, as often as not would vent his degradation viciously upon her and the children. The relationship soon devolved into an ugly repetition of blood-curdling rows —recriminations and denunciations and angry blows, furnishings upended and dashed, utensils flying—and terrified children screaming, tugging at the battling pair, or fleeing them in panic.

It ended in another divorce in 1956. And that was the last memory Peg's children had of any sort of "settled" home life.

Left with little more than a house scarred with bitter memories, Peg had set out on her own to salvage a family out of the disorder. And (her sister Fran would marvel) for quite a time it appeared that she had managed admirably. She'd gone out to work—mostly at the long and odd hours of a waitress in Detroit restaurants—unstinting in her determination to provide for the children's material needs. Though excom-

municated from the Church herself, she'd insisted on
their remaining Roman Catholics and getting parochial
educations, which she considered superior. She'd
scrimped to pay off the house mortgage, so that they
would always feel they had a *home*.

And if she found too little time during those, their
most formative, years to share much of herself with
them; if they themselves hungered for lack of the
essential childhood nourishments of ready parental guid-
ance and instruction, of the warming reassurances of
cohesion, of closeness, such deprivations were not
evident as they grew into adolescence. Each emerged
appearing as brightly groomed and well adjusted as
any youngsters privileged to have bloomed in more
stable environments—Tom sturdy and level-headed,
Dawn a flowering blond beauty, James vibrantly alive.

During the first few years of Fran's marriage, she
and Dana had seen quite a lot of Peg's kids. Like their
mother, they had taken right away to the strong, gentle-
humored young policeman; and after the newlyweds
rented an apartment not far from Center Line, Tom
and Dawn and James spent about as much time there
as they did at home. Peg, so often absent, had been
grateful for so happy and safe a refuge to occupy them.
And Fran and Dana had loved having them around,
getting as much enjoyment from them as they soon
would from children of their own.

When Dana was transferred to Flint and they had
to move there in 1961—bringing with them their own
first-born son—they left with an image of three
sprightly teen-agers who, collectively, seemed to em-
body a loving tribute to the faith and will of an
indomitable mother.

The Louckses weren't long gone, however, before
that image had begun to tarnish and crack, revealing
more shadow than substance behind it. They heard that
Dawn, at sixteen, had turned "wild"—delinquent from
school, away from home days at a stretch, reckless
and unmanageable. At eighteen she became pregnant,
and, under pressure from her mother, married the boy.

Not long after Dawn's baby was born, chilling word filtered through the family that James had beaten his sister badly enough to send her to a hospital! The story, pieced together, was that James had come upon Dawn one night with a strange man. In sudden fury, the youth—almost eighteen then and powerfully built —pounced on the pair; he beat the man nearly unconscious, then turned on the girl and, cursing her as a tramp, cuffed and kicked her bloody. It was the first time anyone had known James to behave violently. It seemed to bespeak a rage long simmering—and perhaps not just against his sister alone.

James soon thereafter began to visit the Louckses more frequently—almost with insistent regularity, it appeared—driving his first car, a 1956 DeSoto, the sixty-odd miles to Flint almost every weekend. Generally, he seemed his normal ebullient self, delighting in roughhousing with Dana, Jr., who was five, and Donnie, three, or untiringly playing with the baby, Daryl, who fascinated him. Sometimes he brought a girl he'd begun dating, a pretty youngster named Jeannie, and his aunt and uncle were pleased by the gentle fondness James showed her. Looking at him at such times, they could not picture him ever lashing out at anyone.

Fran and Dana began to notice, however, that James would become reticent, even somber, whenever discussion got around to his own family. And at any mention of his sister, he turned stony. Only once in all the months was he moved to speak any word of Dawn, and then it was uttered with a venom that was startling. Fran had expressed sympathy and concern over the unpleasant turns the girl's life seemed to have taken, when James, whose expression had grown darker, suddenly burst out: "That *bitch!*" Then he rushed outside and sat alone in his car until he was composed.

It was his feelings about his mother that troubled Fran Loucks the most. James never brought Peg into their conversations. When asked about her, his response would be flat—polite, correct, but without any feeling whatever, rather as though they were speaking of some distant acquaintance. Fran had to wonder how much James knew—and how affected he'd been—about his mother's ongoing relationship with the man from Lake St. Clair who, she knew, was quietly helping to support Peg and her children. Was that what had created the void among them all—especially James, always before so clear-eyed and trusting? Somehow it was more barren than common teen-age alienation from parents and authority. What consanguinity they may have shared seemed to have turned to dust. It was as though Peg's struggles for their survival and preservation had left her short of blood with which not only to infuse life into them but to keep them whole. And as her supply had dried up, they'd had to turn to other sources.

Fran grieved for her sister; as a mother she could appreciate the hurt Peg must feel. About all Fran could do was to leave their own door open to James and the other children, who might keep coming to them seeking the nourishment they so passionately needed. Maybe, in time, they could be turned back around. . . .

It was after the Louckses moved back down to Ypsilanti in August 1967, Dana having then been reassigned to the post there, that James became a virtual member of the family. By then the Armstrong family situation had grown more distant. The oldest, Tom, having completed college, had taken his own apartment and reportedly planned to marry; Peg and the others saw little of him. Dawn had been divorced and returned to her mother's house with her child; she constantly complained about the arrangement, nonetheless, and evidently still pursued her own selfish pleasures, often leaving Peg to care for the baby.

As for James, he seemed to have hardened. He'd since learned that his mother's devoted patron was contributing materially to his own schooling. Yet he no longer displayed, as he once might, any resentment or even self-consciousness over this, instead accepted it with the same cold detachment that Fran had per-

ceived in him for Peg herself—a cynical new side of
the youth, in his aunt's eyes, that was most disturbing.
James seldom troubled to go home anymore, even from
E.M.U., and then only to bring a load of laundry, or to
get his car serviced at a particular shop in Center Line,
or to see the girl Jeannie . . . only rarely for his mother's
sake, when Peg might almost have to beg him to come
with excuses about manual chores needing doing
around the house. His responses at such times revealed
no more than the barest spark of filial responsibility still
flickering within him.

To James, the Louckses had become—as he often
put it to them brightly—his "main folks." He would
drop in at any hour, any day, to pitch in with household chores—play with the kids, or pop a bowl of corn
and kick off his shoes and sprawl on the living-room
floor in front of the TV, feed or walk the dog (James
was the only one outside the immediate family that the
big shepherd, Dutch, would allow near without attack-
ing), or take Fran shopping. Since the local murder
scare had turned critical, when Dana was away James
would not let his aunt go any distance from home without him as her escort.

Thus they'd had no compunctions about asking
James if he would mind keeping an eye on their house
and feeding the dog while they were on their vacation.
He said he'd be happy to, but that he'd misplaced his
duplicate key to their front door. Dana promised to
leave a key to the side door under the mat, and James
said fine, he would look after everything. . . .

Now, back from vacation, the Louckses had the
vague feeling that something was out of synchroniza-
tion—little unexplained things: the sprays of black
paint in the basement; the missing Bold box and ammonia container; the damp rag in the washtub. And
there were other small peculiarities. Fran had left a
note in the kitchen for James, about half a watermelon
in the fridge, but the melon had been untouched—almost unthinkable, knowing him. And Dana's note,
reminding James that if he wanted to use the air-

conditioning he had only to replace a blown fuse, was still propped on the fuse box downstairs, the particular socket still empty—odd, because James could be expected to have attended to a detail like that for his uncle.

And then one other small puzzler noticed by Fran that afternoon as she was finishing her last batch of wash: Just before going away, she'd hung a good shirt of one of the boys to drip-dry from a water pipe in the laundry room, and now the shirt had some kind of brownish splotches on one of its sleeves which definitely weren't there before.

It wasn't until after supper, with the boys fed and permitted to leave the table, that the couple had a chance to talk again alone.

"I'm really not trying to make anything *big* of it," she said, having described several new inconsistencies in the house. "But it all does seem a little peculiar. . . ."

"There's probably a simple explanation for everything," said Dana. "Have you talked to James?"

"I called again a little while ago, but he still doesn't answer." She glanced at the wall clock. "He's probably out eating at this hour—I'll try him again later. I was hoping he might look in here. He knew we were due home."

Just then the telephone rang. "Maybe that's him now," said Fran, rising to answer it.

She held out the receiver to her husband. "It's the post."

Dana recognized the voice as Sergeant Browne's. "Dan, I know you go back on days tomorrow, but is there any chance of your dropping over here tonight? Sergeant Walters wants to talk to you."

"Anything special?"

"Yes . . . but it'll keep till you get here. We'll be looking for you." Browne hung up.

Dana drove over to the post on Michigan Avenue about eight o'clock. He exchanged greetings with some of the men, then found Sergeant Chris Walters, who was assistant post commander. The two went into a vacant cubicle.

Walters, a burly open-faced man with sad eyes, did not bandy words. "Dan, you know about the latest murder we had while you were away, the little girl from Eastern—?"

"I saw it in the papers. Anything going on that?"

The other nodded solemnly. "I guess you *don't* know about your nephew. The homicide guys have him down as a suspect."

Dana stared at him. "My nephew—?"

"James Armstrong. The fact is, the way things are shaping up he seems to be a *prime* suspect."

"James?" Dana's head swam. "I can't— How? What—?"

Walters filled him in on the major points of suspicion —motorcyclist with striped shirt, cruising, girl hunting on the fateful day, partial ID by witnesses, his backing down from a polygraph test. . . .

"It doesn't sound like all that much," Dana protested "—not for *murder*."

"I'm just giving you some of the highlights as I know them," said Walters. "There's more, some not directly connected with this homicide." He ran down the developing evidence that James might also be a thief, perhaps an inveterate one. "They've got him under twenty-four-hour surveillance. I thought you should know. It could get a little sticky for you . . . with your wife and all."

"Well, yes! I mean, I'm glad you let me know. But Holy Mother! It's awful hard to believe. He's always been a good kid. Fran is crazy about him." Dana paused. "This will kill her."

"Have you heard from the boy since you're back?" asked Walters.

"No. We've tried all day to get in touch with him. He was sort of looking after the house and the dog for us, but we found a few odd things around the place, and—"

Walters' eyes had narrowed. "What kind of things?"

Dana quickly related the string of little mysteries. "It doesn't amount to much," he concluded. "But the thing is, if James can't explain them, then it looks like somebody else must have got into the house while we were gone. I just can't figure out how."

"No signs of b-and-e?"

"No. That's it. The place was tight as a drum."

"And James—?"

"He was the only one with a key."

"Did you check all your valuables?"

Dana caught the inference and shook his head firmly. "Nothing's missing, except the junk I told you. Even so, though, if James doesn't have the answers I'm going to report it in the morning." He had a sudden thought. "Say, you don't suppose they've already picked him up?"

"Not that I know of. I can call over to the seminary and ask."

"Do that, will you, Chris? I'd like to know. Looks as though there are a lot of things I'd better find out about."

While Sergeant Walters put in his inquiry to the crime center, Dana wandered about the half-empty headquarters, mind abuzz, unconscious of the familiar surroundings and faces. James and a *murder?* If he hadn't heard these things tonight, in this place and in this manner, he would have rejected it without hesitation . . . but was he being completely honest? Was he trying to bury the unworthy memory of the thought that had caused him more than a moment's recoil just the past weekend back at Beaver Island? He'd sat in the tent browsing through the previous day's Detroit *Free Press,* its front page emblazoned with the blown-up composite sketch of the hunted motorcyclist who could be the coed's killer and the eyewitnesses' descriptions in bold type alongside, when that unexpected dart had pricked him and made him stiffen: *James?*

He couldn't imagine then why such a notion should have come to him, and he'd searched himself for any conceivable genesis for it in the past, but in vain. He'd told himself finally that it had been just one of those uncontrollable flashes that people sometimes found it impossible to understand, and he'd put it out of his mind. Until now again. Was *that* the pesky something that was bothering him?

"What's the matter—your mother-in-law spend the vacation with you?"

He looked up to find Stu Lucky smiling over him. Only then did Dana realize he'd sat himself at his friend's unoccupied desk. His jaws hurt, and he realized he must have been grinding his teeth.

"Hey, Stu," he said, rising. "I was a million miles away, I guess. How've you been?"

"Pretty fair." Lucky studied him soberly now. "I take it you've heard about your nephew?"

"Just did. How long have you known?"

"It only developed the last day or so, at least from what I can tell. I still don't have the scoop on it. I wanted to call you today, but I figured"—he gestured apologetically—"what the hell, it might turn out to be nothing, why spread a false alarm?"

Sergeant Walters came up to them. "Dan, nothing's gone down. They've still got him staked out."

Dana nodded. "Did they say where right now?"

Walters looked at him warily. "I don't know if they—?"

"Chris, I'm a cop," Dana said with feeling, "I'm not about to burn anything like this, relative or no relative. But he *is* my nephew, and I have to ask him a few things about my house. That's all, believe me."

The sergeant hesitated, then said: "They say he's been at his mother's, in Center Line."

"Thanks."

Driving back to Roosevelt Boulevard, Dana made one firm decision: He would still not tell Fran any of this. As Stu had said, and he himself passionately wanted to believe, it could turn out to be a mistake after all. Then, later, they could *all* have a laugh about it.

Trying to sound casual, he asked Fran: "Any word from James?"

"I tried him again a little while ago," she said, "and this time I got that friend of his, Donald Baker. He said he thought James might be home with Peg."

"Did you get him there?"

"I thought I'd wait till you got back, then we could both talk to him."

Fran called her sister in Center Line, but James was out and she wasn't sure what time he might be back. She said she'd have him call if it wasn't too late.

At ten thirty the telephone rang. Dana heard Fran's exclamation from the kitchen: "James! How are you, love? . . . Listen, you devil, what have you been up to—?"

Dana, flushing at the unknowing implications of his wife's remark, strode into the bedroom to pick up the extension.

"—yesterday, so I just decided I ought to pay a visit home," James was telling his aunt. "Why? Is everything okay?"

"James," Dana cut in.

"Uncle Dan! Hi!" The youthful voice sounded glad.

"Hi. Look, a couple of things. What did you paint down in the basement? There are black spatters all over the floor of the laundry room."

There was a pause on the line, then James said: "I didn't paint anything."

"Did you *notice* any on the floor down there?" urged Dana.

"Well . . . no, I don't think so."

"Were you in the basement at all? I see the fuse for the air conditioner is still out, and my note still there on the box."

"Oh, gosh, I *meant* to do that, Uncle Dan. I'm sorry. I only went down to the basement about one time, is all —to check the windows and the water heater."

"Come to think of it," added Fran, "were you around my washer or tubs at all? There were a couple of things there *I* can't find now, either. You didn't throw any of my stuff out?"

"Wow, you all must think I ran amok around there

while you were away!" James exclaimed. "Aunt Fran, I didn't touch anything, I swear. I didn't see anything out of place at all. . . ."

After they hung up Dana felt restless, and decided to take a spin over to the post again and pick up Stu Lucky, and maybe have a few beers after he got off.

On the way to the post he thought about the telephone conversation. And some things that had bothered him began to crystallize: Either James had lied about the paint—in which case, *why?*—or, if he'd told the truth, some other person or persons had been in the house. But if the house had not been broken into —and he felt sure it had not been—then whoever it was either had been there with James, been admitted by him, or gained access by means of James's key. But then, by neglecting to mention that he had let anybody else in, he'd not told the *whole* truth. And, again, why?

He waited for Lucky, not saying much to anybody else, and at midnight they went to a nearby tavern and drank beer. Then Dana started telling Stu some of these puzzling things, and it soon became obvious that the paint on his basement floor really haunted him. Lucky decided to be blunt: "Have you scraped up any of this paint to see if there's anything underneath it? Maybe it's to hide something else."

Dana looked dumbly at his friend, shaking his head. "Like what?"

"How do I know?" He shrugged. "But if this business is driving you so ape, the least you can do is investigate."

Dana stared into his beer, then downed it. "Come on," he said.

The two men went back to Dana's. Under the glaring overhead bulb in the laundry room, Dana showed Stu the mottled trail of black. As the other crouched for a closer look, Dana got a heavy screwdriver from his tool box.

He knelt alongside Stu and, his breathing becoming rapid, dug the tip of the screwdriver under the edge of one of the larger splotches. A black fragment, still a little pasty underneath, was loosened and dislodged. They bent low to examine the uncovered spot of floor. Their eyes met, somber and questioning. Dana moved quickly to another of the stains . . . and another . . . Stu at his shoulder. After a few minutes they stood and looked at one another in heavy silence. Dana's forehead was damp with perspiration.

Stu inhaled deep and let it out slowly. "It looks like blood, Dan," he said.

CHAPTER 19

DANA LOUCKS SAID nothing to his wife. He got up at 6:30 Thursday morning, made himself coffee, and was out of the house before 7:30. He fidgeted at his dispatcher's desk, avoiding chatter with the other men, until the post commander, Sergeant Carl Freedborn, came in. He followed Freedborn into his office, closed the door behind them, and reported tersely, without equivocation, the odd and now possibly grim discoveries at his house.

The telling points did not escape Freedborn: that blood seemed to have been spilled in the Louckses' basement sometime within the previous twelve days; that James Armstrong was the only one who could have had and/or provided access to the house during that time; and that Armstrong had lied, or withheld information, about what had happened there.

Freedborn grew agitated. "We'd better tell somebody about this. Let's run out to the seminary."

At the crime center the two men were greeted by Captain Walter Stevens, a stocky, twenty-nine-year

273

veteran who was C.O. of the 2d State Police District. His normally pleasant features turned serious as he listened to Dana's account, and then he said: "Let's go."

The Loucks house was quiet when the men entered —Fran and the boys were still in bed—and they went straight to the basement. The captain examined the floor, looked closely at the reddish-brown stain on the sleeve of the boy's shirt, and decided. "I'd like to call in the crime lab. Take me back to the seminary."

Colonel Davids was talking with Captain Myre and Bill Delhey. Stevens briefed the three on the find. There was instant and unanimous agreement to send in the crime lab technicians.

"Make it as quiet as possible," cautioned Davids. "We don't want any premature whistle blowing."

Dana returned home to await the lab detectives. When he walked in, Fran was on the phone in the kitchen. Covering the mouthpiece with her hand, she said to Dana: "It's James. He wants to know if you found out any more about that paint."

"Not sure yet," he said, trying to sound casual. "The lab guys are coming over."

Fran, her eyes wide on him, told this to James.

Hanging up the phone, she said: "James is anxious to know how it comes out." She looked at him curiously. "The *lab?* What *is* it?"

"Frannie," he said gently, "last night, downstairs, Stu and I believe we found traces . . . of blood."

"Blood . . ." she repeated mechanically, not quite comprehending.

He clasped her hand. It had turned cold. He had to lay it all out. "Frannie, there's something else. I don't know if it has any connection . . . but it could be tough." And, drawing a deep breath and smothering her hands in his, he told her about James.

She sat there looking at him, her face ashen, as stricken with horror as if he had just told her for the first time that he himself had only months to live. "Oh, Dana," she said first, so gently that it startled him.

Then her eyes started to swim. "Oh, Dana! Not James. Oh, God, not *James!* Oh . . . my . . . *God!*" she wailed and slumped forward upon the kitchen table, buried head between outstretched arms. She lay there in uncontrollable misery, retching sobs wracking her body, Dana clumsily stroking her jerking neck and shoulders with his huge hands, until finally he persuaded her to her feet and helped her, sagging, into the bedroom and onto the bed. Her face to the pillow, she continued to weep steadily. Donnie and little Daryl crept just inside the door, expressions fearful, and Donnie whispered: "What's the matter with Mommy, Dad?"

"She'll be all right, boys," he assured them softly. "Mommy just had some bad news about—someone she cares a lot about. You go on outside and play. We'll see you later."

Dana sat with his wife until the crime lab team came.

Detective Staff Sergeant Ken Christensen and Detective Gene Weiler from the Plymouth crime lab arrived at about 11:00 A.M. Dana led them down to the basement where they set right to work testing the bloodlike stains. It was engrossing to watch: They were almost surgical in their step-by-step procedures, carefully laying out their instruments and paraphernalia around a section marked for incision, taking pains to set up and strategically focus high-intensity floodlamps, then hovering over the exposed area.

One of the men knelt low, a scalpel in one hand and in the other a slip of white paper held close to the patch of stain, and gently scraped tiny fragments of the brownish-red material onto the paper. With great care he passed that to his partner. Then, while the first moved on to another spot, the other delicately poured the residue into a vial containing a colorless liquid.

After several tests, Ken Christensen came over to Dana. Christensen was a tall, quite youthful-appearing man in his mid-forties who was always handsomely groomed and carried himself with the assurance of a successful executive. "We're not getting anything, Dan." He frowned.

"What do you mean?"

"The basic procedural test for blood is to place the sample into an amphetamine solution—the Benzedrine test, it's called. There should be a color reaction: If it *is* blood, the solution turns a bright blue-green. Here, nothing is happening."

Dana was startled. "You mean it's *not* blood?"

"It doesn't seem so."

"What is it, then?"

"We're trying to determine that—"

Gene Weiler interrupted. "It looks like varnish stain, the kind used on split-rail fences and picnic tables."

"Varnish—!" Dana exclaimed, his face flushing. "Oh, for Pete's sake . . . now I remember! When we first moved in I stained some window shutters down here." He seemed relieved and embarrassed at the same time. "I'm sorry. I wouldn't have dragged you fellows out but, I was just so sure—"

"Forget it." Christensen squeezed his shoulder. "I'm glad it wasn't, not here anyway."

As Christensen helped Weiler pack their gear, Dana thought of his wife upstairs, struggling with her grief. *She* would be relieved, thank God. The other problems James had could be sorted out later. He started for the stairs . . . then halted, as his attention was drawn again to Ken Christensen across the basement. Something on the floor had caught the lab man's eye; first he bent low, motionless, then he went to his hands and knees. Lowering his head until his line of vision now was only inches above the floor, he crouched there poised like a hunting dog, his gaze fixed on the space between washtubs and dryer illuminated by the flood-lamps.

After several hushed moments, he called out sharply: "Gene! Take a look at this!"

Weiler knelt beside him, studying the floor from the same angle. He turned to Christensen questioningly: "Are you thinking what I think you're thinking?"

"That's it."

"Holy Christ! *Here?*"

It was hair. Tiny barbered hair clippings. An accumulation of bits of hair had been discovered on the underpants of Carol Ann Gebhardt, and nobody could figure that out. At her autopsy, on Sunday, the soiled panties had been sealed in a glass jar and delivered to the Michigan Department of Public Health in Lansing for analysis. The next day there had been a report from Curtis Fluker of the Health Department's crime detection lab.

More than three hundred small hairs had been removed from the girl's panties, varying from one to twenty-one millimeters (approximately one-twenty-fifth to seven-eights of an inch) in length. They were definitely human hairs, but not the victim's. In all probability they were hairs from the head; and since they showed every characteristic of having been clipped—not cut by scissors but by *clipper*—they were most likely male. The only place anybody could think of where the girl, no doubt in mortal crisis, might have lain stripped to her underthings and got hair clippings on her panties was a barbershop. But nobody had felt comfortable with that deduction.

Christensen turned to Dana Loucks. Dana explained that his wife regularly trimmed both the boys' and his own hair here in the basement—using a barber's clipper because they all wore their hair short—and in fact had last done the boys' the evening before they'd left on vacation.

All right. The possibility could not be ignored: It had to be determined if the two batches of hairs matched. That would have to be done in Lansing. Hair was just too difficult for the limited facilities of the Plymouth crime lab. They could process prints and ballistics and narcotics and most basic tests there, even blood identification to a degree, but precise analyses and comparisons of such exotic elements as hair demanded the sophisticated equipment and expertise of full-time forensic scientists.

So, recharged with purpose, Ken Christensen and Gene Weiler got back down on their knees and, with hand vacuums, set about meticulously collecting and packaging every bit of debris—hair, lint, dust, everything—that could be sucked off the Louckses' basement floor.

Poor Dan Loucks, Christensen thought, he probably doesn't know which end is up anymore. He'd called them for blood; they were leaving with hair.

They'd about finished vacuuming, when Weiler, still crouched low, making one last inspection of their handiwork, snorted: "Uh-oh!"

Christensen turned and bent to look. The tip of Weiler's forefinger traced a crusty reddish-brown spot on the swept-clean concrete in front of the washtubs. "More redwood varnish?" asked Christensen.

"I don't think so. I think this *is* blood."

Christensen quickly retrieved the blood-testing equipment. Weiler lifted a speck of the stain with the scalpel and slid it into the vial of clear solution. The liquid turned blue-green.

They looked at one another, then removed their jackets again and proceeded to go back over the entire basement, inch by inch.

Within an hour they were able to isolate at least two other traces of dried blood: a dot on the floor in the corner where the dryer was, and a drop on the foundation wall by the washing machine; there was a possible third, the stain on the sleeve of the boy's shirt hanging over the tubs, but this would have to be verified by a laboratory fabric test. Only in the lab, too, would they find out if any of it was human blood and its type—and if it could have come from the body of Carol Ann Gebhardt.

Christensen went upstairs to find Dana Loucks, who had gone to sit with his wife. Alone in the kitchen, Christensen quietly told him of the latest findings and said he had to inform the crime center. Loucks took it with stony composure. "I suppose they'll pick up James now," he said.

Christensen nodded. "If he hasn't run."

Dana smiled ruefully. "He's in town at least. Fran told me she was looking out the bedroom window just a while ago and saw him riding past on one of his bikes— sort of checking out the house. He's probably guessed something's up."

Loucks returned to the bedroom, and Christensen got on the kitchen telephone. First he called Plymouth and instructed another of his own men, Detective Tom Nasser, to hustle over with his Leica and plenty of film. Then he dialed the crime center for Captain Dan Myre and was told that the chief of detectives was at a luncheon at Weber's Inn with the other bosses.

Christensen had Myre paged at Weber's. Captain Walt Stevens got on the line.

"What've you got, Chris?" asked Stevens. "We're pretty tight."

"It's hot, captain. Maybe a blockbuster. Should I come out there?"

"That big? You bet. And don't talk to anyone else. When you get here, Captain Myre and I will see you in private first."

Fifteen minutes later, Christensen was animatedly detailing for the two superior officers everything uncovered at the Loucks house. Myre and Stevens were impressed.

"First thing to do is contact Lansing and get some more technical people down here," Myre said. "And the house should be sealed off as soon as possible."

"What about Armstrong?" asked Stevens.

"That's a little tricky. As I see it, what we've got to do is make sure Armstrong's in the net without hauling him in too soon. If we could latch onto him some way, just for a few hours, until the lab boys have done their job. Any ideas?"

"I think we could get some help from his uncle," Stevens put in. "The boy has been very close to the Loucks family, so there's strong attachment there. If we sent Loucks, with back-up of course, to have a long talk with his nephew . . ."

"That's good," said Myre. "But we mustn't do it at the crime center. Too many reporters and other cops around. We'd blow it right off the bat, and still not be in a strong enough position to make a firm arrest. When we take this guy, I want him sewed up *tight!*"

"How about our place, in Plymouth?" suggested Christensen. "It's not far, and there are no press hanging around, only our own people."

"I like it," Myre said at once. Turning to Stevens: "Okay. Walt, you set it up. Have Corporal Loucks contact the suspect. You be the back-up—then we'll be sure everything goes right. Get him out to Plymouth somehow, hang onto him as long as you can . . . and we'll play it by ear from there."

By 1:30 P.M., the neat home on Roosevelt Boulevard was beginning to swarm with activity—inside, anyway. Outside, all seemed normally placid: Arriving detectives parked their vehicles on adjacent streets and walked unhurriedly to the house, and unmarked radio cars posted to the area stayed discreet distances away.

Fran Loucks was getting ready to leave with her three sons. Dana had suggested that she and the boys get away for the rest of the day, and she'd arranged to visit her sister Caroline up in Flint. Dana excused himself from a conference with Captain Stevens and went out with them to the car. He lifted the two smallest boys, one in each arm, and nuzzled them. Then he shook hands with nine-year-old Dana and bade him look after their mother. "Why aren't you coming too, Daddy?" complained five-year-old Daryl, who was most eager to start the outing.

"Don't you know anything?" Donnie, seven, reproved his little brother. "He's going after a bad guy!"

Dana and Fran looked at one another sorrowfully. The hardest part, later, would be telling the boys about "Uncle James." Fran's eyes appeared about to well again, and he took her gently into his arms. "Stay as long as you want, babe," he murmured.

She nodded against his cheek but said: "Probably be back tonight."

"If you want. It should be over by then."

She looked up at him fervently. "Don't let them hurt him. See that he's treated okay, will you?"

"I will."

"Tell him I'm praying for him. ... ."

With Captain Stevens at his side, Dana telephoned his nephew at Emmet Street (where the surveillance team had just reported him) and said he wanted to have a talk with him.

"Sure, any time, Uncle Dan," replied James. "You sound kind of serious."

"I think it is, James."

There was a pause. "You want me to run over there?"

"No, we'll come to your place."

There was a pause. "Somebody else will be along?"

"Yes."

"Another—policeman?"

"Yes."

Dana could hear him draw a long breath. "But *you* are coming, aren't you, Uncle Dan?" James asked, his voice quavery.

"Yes, James, of course.

"All right, then . . ."

James's rooms at the head of the stairs were small and sparsely furnished. The bedroom had only an open daybed and a small chest of drawers; the parlor featured a black simulated-leather couch, faded white wicker easy chair, scarred, red-enameled wooden table with a heavy brass lamp, and a newish twelve-inch portable TV on a metal stand with casters. On the wall behind the couch was a black velvet tapestry, which James said was from Mexico. The other walls were decorated with a variety of cut-out magazine photos of motorcycles. There was a small, frayed scatter rug in the center of the floor, with patterning of no longer determinable origin.

They sat, the policemen on the couch—Captain Stevens sitting back, observing the suspect, Dana leaning forward, elbows on knees—James upright in the wicker chair. Dana glanced uncertainly at the captain, then cleared his throat.

"James, I must tell you," he began stiffly, "as you yourself may even now be aware, you have come to the attention of some of our people investigating the death of that young female student last week. I still don't have all the details, not being a detective or normally getting involved in homicides. But when your name came up, well, naturally, I did feel very much involved."

He took a breath and explored James's face. It was solemn but otherwise lifeless. He seemed to be returning his uncle's gaze, until Dana perceived that the blue eyes were not meeting his own but fixed somewhere short of him, as though lacking either the will or strength to complete the connection. Dana swallowed a sudden lump in his throat.

They talked to him and questioned him for an hour, and James did not look directly at either his imploring uncle or the terse Stevens the whole time. His responses were remote, unanimated, often monosyllabic, as the two policemen went back over the old ground: his whereabouts and actions on Wednesday, July 23 . . . the girls he'd allegedly tried to pick up . . . how he was dressed that day . . . what motorcycle he'd ridden. He acknowledged that he owned and could have worn a striped polo shirt and, at their request, produced it from the bedroom closet: The inch-wide horizontal stripes were green and yellow (which proved little, since witnesses were so divided in their color descriptions). He said he had not known or ever met any girl named Carol Ann Gebhardt, that he had not even recognized the victim from her picture in the newspapers.

Next they went into the matter of the Loucks residence. He said again—his gaze withdrawing a little

farther from his uncle's—that he'd not done any painting or spraying in the basement while the family was
away. He had not brought anyone else into the house,
nor had he loaned his key to anyone.

"Then you concede," put in Stevens, "that you are
the only one who could have been inside your uncle's
house during the past two weeks."

James frowned. "Unless somebody got in some other
way—a burglar maybe."

"No," said Dana. "There was no forced entry."

"Well, then, I just can't explain it," James said, looking blank. He seemed to brace himself to bring up a
touchy point: "I don't understand why there's so much
concern about the paint anyway."

Dana glanced at his superior. Stevens decided to
carry it from there.

"It looks as though paint was sprayed in certain
places to cover up something. Bloodstains."

James clasped his hands tight in his lap. His un-
focused eyes brimmed again. But he did not speak.

"That is, what someone must have *thought* was
blood," Stevens continued. "Which only makes it more
mysterious. Because it turned out not to be blood at all.
Just varnish—redwood varnish stain—that had been
on the floor all the time."

James drew a sharp breath that caught in his throat,
and then, as though a plug had been dislodged, the
tears spilled out and ran down his cheeks.

"But the point is," the captain plowed on, "why
would this someone *think* it was blood, and what was
so frightening about that to make him try to cover it
up?"

James wept aloud now, restraint failing him. He'd
sagged, and his wiry frame was shaken by tremors.
Finally, with evident effort, he raised his bowed head
and, shaking it violently, managed to blubber: "I
don't know, I don't *know!*"

"James!" Dana cried pityingly.

"There's a way to settle this quickly," Stevens cut in,
exploiting the breach. "Agree to a polygraph test."

James did not respond at once, just slumping miserably.

"Will you do that?" prodded Stevens. "Come with us voluntarily to take such a test? It could establish your innocence once and for all."

The youthful head nodded slowly behind the hands.

"Good! I'll call right away and set it up." The captain went into the other room to telephone.

Dana and James did not speak in the several minutes they were alone, and the boy's eyes, moist and raw, remained cast down.

Stevens returned, looking satisfied. "It's all arranged. We can get going any time."

"I think," James said, clearing the rasp from his voice, "Mr. Francis ought to know."

"Mr. Francis? Your lawyer? Well, of course, that's your right." Stevens swallowed annoyance. "I'll call him right now and he can join us in Plymouth. We'll send a car for him, if he wants."

James dully said okay, then asked if he could have a minute to clean up before they went. As they watched him go down the corridor, Dana said to the captain, "I didn't know Plymouth had a polygraph section."

"It doesn't. But it's a way to get him there as we'd planned."

They got to the State Police scientific laboratory in Plymouth shortly past 4:00 P.M. Armstrong was deposited in one of the offices and Stevens went straight to a telephone and called the crime center in Ann Arbor. Dan Myre told him that the lab people were still working but that they shouldn't be much longer. Sit tight, Myre said, keep the suspect occupied.

Stevens went into the office with Armstrong and asked if he wanted anything—cigarettes, coffee, a Coke. James said no.

"Look, son," Stevens, said, adopting a fatherly manner, "it would save us all some time here if you wouldn't mind cooperating. We'd like to get some pictures of you, and as long as you're here, fingerprints too."

James looked uncertain. "I don't know if I'm supposed to do anything. . . . That is," he said haltingly, "unless Mr. Francis says it's okay. I mean, aren't there those rights and all?"

Stevens walked around the desk, thinking furiously. The kid was right, of course. He would have to be more careful. Nobody must do anything that, by jeopardizing the suspect's defined rights, could nullify evidence. He opened the office door and called to Dana Loucks:

"Come here for a minute, Dan. I'm going to read him his rights."

Attorney Robert Francis appeared shortly before five and consulted a few minutes alone with James. When he emerged he was bristling. "What's this talk of polygraphs and picture taking and fingerprinting?" he demanded. "Has my client been booked?"

"No, counselor," Captain Stevens volunteered. "Not yet."

"Well, what are you holding him on?"

Stevens threw a glance toward the others. "He's not in custody. He came here voluntarily . . . for questioning."

"In what connection?"

"Homicide."

"Which homicide?"

"Carol Ann Gebhardt."

"Fine. Question him—in my presence, of course. But remember, there's a limit on how long you may detain him in that status. After a reasonable time, if you have not formally charged him, booked him, I will take him out of here. I want no misunderstanding about that."

"We're aware of the law, counselor," Stevens acknowledged curtly and turned away.

Other officers had been arriving—Lieutenants Bill Mulholland and Mel Fuller, E.M.U. Patrolman Larry Mathewson, Sheriff's Corporal Gene Alli, the two Ann Arbor detectives, Ben Peterson and Les Rodman, who had interviewed Armstrong Sunday night—and with

Captain Stevens they began interrogating James in
shifts of twos and threes. Dana Loucks stayed outside
in the main room, pacing, sitting, standing at the glass
partition, watching fretfully.

Much of the same grounds were covered by each
combination of interrogators—each careful not to touch
upon certain aspects of the investigation that Armstrong was not yet aware of—and, although the whole
process was designed mainly to borrow time, the results were disappointing. James was unresponsive, his
answers seldom going beyond *yes* or *no* or *I don't know*
—when he answered at all, which Francis frequently
advised him not to do. James seemed totally calm
through it all, as though now drained either of feeling
or of caring.

It went on like that for more than two and a half
hours, and Captain Stevens, for one, grew increasingly
anxious. Twice during that time he telephoned Ann
Arbor, only to be advised that the lab results were nowhere near reportable yet, that he would have to hang
on a while longer.

It was going on twenty minutes before eight when,
the spent detectives having broken for coffee and cigarettes, Robert Francis left James in the office and
came out to Stevens, who was standing with a dejected
Bill Mulholland.

"I think the interview is about over, gentlemen,"
the attorney said bluntly. "You people are asking the
same things over and over. My client has told you all
he has to tell, and evidently you have run out of questions. Therefore, I'm taking James out of here. Unless—do you have anything else?"

Stevens and Mulholland looked from the lawyer to
one another. "You go make the call, Bill," said the
captain, "while I try to talk to—"

"Wait," interjected Francis. "What call?"

"To Ann Arbor," Stevens replied. "To see if they
want us to make an arrest."

Francis regarded him coldly. "Five more minutes,
captain—then we're gone."

Mulholland found a vacant office and got Dan Myre at the crime center. Outlining the precarious situation, Mulholland asked what they should do. "Have we got enough yet for the pinch?"

The usually firm chief of detectives hesitated. "Now we're getting into the legal areas," he worried. "I think maybe it's a decision for the prosecutor. Hold on." There was a long pause. Then Booker Williams came on. Mulholland quickly summarized the predicament for him.

"We *could* order an arrest now," the assistant prosecutor pondered. "The question is, Would it stand up to examination? If we could have just a *little* more time. If the hair and blood samples do match up with the victim—"

"Where does that stand?"

"I'm sitting by the phone now, waiting to hear from Lansing. I can't say when that might be."

"Well, all I can tell you is," Mulholland repeated sourly, "our butts are up against the wall here. If we have to let them walk now, Armstrong could take off and keep going all the way to South America."

"I'll have to speak to Delhey," Williams said. "I'll try to get right back to you. Keep stalling as long as you can."

Mulholland returned to find Stevens and Francis still debating, somewhat more heatedly now. It seemed that one of the officers of the crime lab cadre had snapped a few Polaroid shots of Armstrong while his lawyer's attention was distracted.

It was the last straw for Francis. He strode inside and took James by the arm and led him out—past the gathered officers, all now sharing the same stricken look.

"Good evening, gentlemen," the gritty young attorney tossed at them as he and Armstrong headed for the exit. "My client has a prior engagement."

Just then a female civilian employee called out across the bullpen: "I have a call for either Lieutenant Mulholland or Captain Stevens."

Mulholland picked up the nearest extension: "Mulholland!"

"Bill, Williams here. The boss says *go*."

"Go?"

"Book him!"

CHAPTER 20

PROSECUTORS DELHEY AND Williams had gone out on a long, spindly limb when they'd ordered Armstrong's arrest.

At the time, around 8:00 P.M., they'd still had no definitive report from the scientific people. Examination of the Loucks house had finally been completed about 7:30, and Walter Holz's preliminary opinions were that the hair samples, at least, did appear similar to those deposited on Carol Ann Gebhardt's panties. But verification would have to wait until Holz got back to his full testing facilities in Lansing. Regarding the traces of blood, no reliable evaluation of type could be given short of the lab, although Holz was willing to guess that it was human blood.

But the prosecutors felt they had to gamble. Now, however, as the hours ground by without encouraging word from Lansing, they were beginning to agonize —trying to concentrate on drafting the intricate affidavits necessary to explain the charge and to persuade a judge to issue warrants. The particulars were meaningless, however, without the vital ingredients from the lab.

It was past 11:30 before the call came. Walter Holz had concluded his initial analyses. They indicated strongly that the hairs did match and that the blood samples, definitely human, were Type A, the same as Carol Ann Gebhardt's.

At 4:24 A.M. Friday, August 1, District Court Judge Edward D. Deake—having been roused, grumbling, out of bed by the assistant prosecutor—signed the first authorization for search warrants. These covered the vehicles of James Armstrong: a 1968 Oldsmobile Cutlass and two of his motorcycles, both Triumphs. There was ample reason to consider these possessions as possible sources of evidence against the accused: His alleged victim was believed to have been abducted on a motorcycle that could have been a Triumph; and later her dead body was believed to have been transported in some sort of closed vehicle, presumably an automobile, from the murder scene to the place where it was subsequently found.

The prosecutor's plea to search Armstrong's living quarters took longer to consider. Beyond the possibility, as yet undetermined, that at some time between the victim's abduction and the disposal of her corpse, the accused could have had her in his rooms, the proposed justification for searching the premises struck the judge as ambiguous. Among the specified items that police wanted to look for were "a purse" . . . "earrings" . . . "women's shoes" . . . "a silver necklace-chain" . . . "female undergarments" . . . "a woman's gloves" . . . and "a .22-caliber firearm." Taking the last first, nowhere in the bill of particulars of the crime in question was any mention made of the use of such a weapon in its commission. Nor had it been otherwise particularized that so many of the stated victim's personal belongings were believed missing.

To the chagrin of the prosecutor's office, Judge Deake held off issuing these critical warrants while he pondered. It was not until 10:00 A.M. Friday that, moved perhaps by the urgent pleas of Booker Williams, he overcame his misgivings and signed them. And then, four carloads of policemen, including a contingent from the crime lab, swept into 619 Emmet Street.

In the three hours it took them to strip James Armstrong's rooms, they found little of what they were looking for: articles specifically tying Armstrong to any of the murder victims. They did come up with an aerosol spray can, partly used, of quick-drying black paint, and a box of 175 usable rounds of .22-caliber shells. In addition they found one large bread knife, a Camp-King pocketknife, a multi-bladed linoleum cutter, and several other fine-honed cutting instruments (in a glass dish also containing a variety of innocuous trinkets and numerous keys). But that was it. No evident "souvenirs" of the other slayings. To the feverish men at the crime center, who had worked themselves out of long depression into an exhilarated state of optimism, it was a cruel reversal.

Their frustration deepened to a torment during questioning of Donald Baker, one of a number of Armstrong's known intimates hustled to the crime center that day. In the course of eliciting what knowledge he had of Armstrong's recent movements, the interrogators were rocked by his halting but explicit account of an incident that had taken place the past Monday night:

That evening, he said, the two had gone out to eat together, then to a drive-in movie. They'd returned to Emmet Street about eleven. On the way up to their rooms James remembered he'd forgotten to close the windows of his car and went back down, Baker trailing after him. After rolling up the windows, James opened the car's trunk and lifted out a square corrugated cardboard box over which was thrown a dark green woolen blanket, which he then carried up to his room saying nothing.

The two sat watching television there for a while, James silent and apparently deep in thought. Abruptly he rose and went into his bedroom and came out with the box in his arms, saying he was going out for a while. Baker got up to open the door for him, and it was then that he got a glimpse into the contents of the box, an edge of the covering blanket having been tossed back: There was a woman's shoe, leather, kind of maroon in color; what looked like a purse made of burlap-like material; some rolled-up blue-jeans-type fabric. That was all he could make out. James was gone about half an hour. When he returned, he had nothing with him. Baker asked what had happened to the stuff he'd left with. James said he'd just decided to get rid of it.

As the full implications of this episode sank in, the policemen's hopes were dashed. If Baker's account was reliable, their suspect had disposed of what could have been Audrey Sakol's missing shoe, Jill Hersch's handbag, Mary Grace Clemson's jeans, and Lord knew what else—just the things they'd hoped to find in his possession. Monday night. One night after Armstrong had been forewarned by being grilled prematurely!

Recovering with difficulty, they asked themselves what Armstrong would have done with that box. The surveillance report for that night had him in the rooming house by eleven and did not mention his leaving again. Then, unless he'd eluded notice, which was regarded as unlikely, he must have disposed of the box and its contents on the premises. Where? How? Buried in the back yard? Hidden somewhere in the garage or basement? Burned . . . the *furnace?*

A squad was rushed back to 619 Emmet Street. While one group scoured the grounds and garage, another rummaged frantically through the basement. Neither unearthed anything such as Baker had described. In the furnace were only cold powdery ashes.

A search of the prisoner's silver-gray Olds by Ken Christensen and his technicians proved almost as disappointing at first. They were seeking any bits of "trace evidence" to indicate whether Carol Ann Gebhardt, or any other of the homicide victims, had ever been in that car. The automobile was almost immaculate, as though recently vacuumed and scrubbed—which of course, they realized, was exactly what Armstrong had done just a couple of days earlier at his home in Center Line (as a surveillance team had watched him do it!). In two and a half hours all they were able to pick out were some fingerprint smudges, a few unidentifiable strands of hair and bits of fiber lint in the passenger compartment, and one rusty bobby pin dug out of the trunk's right rear fender well.

They were about ready to give it up, when one of them cried out that he thought he had a speck of dried blood! It was down behind the front seat, in one of the crevices for the center seat belts. Dislodging the seat, they reexamined the fabric and all the seat-belt channels. Several more traces were found down in there. Triumphantly, they removed the front seat entirely and had it trucked at once to the Michigan Public Health Department lab in Lansing.

Late that Friday afternoon, August 1, the accused killer of Carol Ann Gebhardt was presented in a lineup staged at the county jail. The procedure was simple: Five men, all wearing identical gray work uniforms, were led out under a battery of overhead lights. Observing them through windows were the witnesses, Mrs. Joan Enright and her associate at the Ypsilanti wig shop, Mrs. Helga Marks, accompanied by a representative of the prosecutor and a sheriff's deputy. Behind them, anxiously watching, were attorney Robert Francis and Sheriff Doug Harvey.

As the five prisoners took their places facing the windows, standing or shuffling awkwardly in the spotlights, the tall, muscular white youth who'd come out second from the end was ordered to switch places with the one in the center of the lineup.

After a moment, behind the glass, Joan Enright said to Helga Marks: "That's him! Isn't that him?"

"Looks just like him. I'm sure it's him!"

The man from the prosecutor's office said: "You both are stating that the man now in the middle is the one you saw ride away from your shop with the girl?"

They looked at each other, then chorused: "Yes, he's the one."

A disembodied voice echoed over a loudspeaker: *"Man in the center: Turn sideways."*

The two women nodded. "That's him, all right!"

"Okay," the loudspeaker intoned, *"that's all. Take 'em back in."*

It was a moment of deep satisfaction for every lawman present. Only one of them felt any unease. Sheriff Harvey himself. He was thinking about—and now regretting—something he had done that morning that he could only pray would not come back to haunt him. . . .

There had been a lot of edginess after the initial searches of the accused's property. And as Friday had dawned, the operation seemed to be dragging. It was aggravating: They just weren't coming up with the *clinchers* against this guy. And then Harvey had got his first look at the Polaroid shots of Armstrong that someone had brought in from Plymouth—the first recent likenesses of him other than the now well-worn "Christmas tree pictures." The witnesses had been unable to make a positive ID of Armstrong from the old snapshots, but maybe they could from these new ones. And so, without telling anyone, he had taken three of the prints and slipped off from the crime center at eight o'clock in the morning.

He'd awakened Joan Enright and her husband at their Ypsilanti apartment and laid the pictures out on their kitchen table. The wig shop proprietress, less than pleased by the intrusion, had stared at them: "It looks something like the man, but I still couldn't say for sure."

Harvey had grown agitated: "He's just been arrested! His name is James Armstrong. . . ."

But Joan had just shaken her head again, saying she was sorry, and Harvey had said testily that they'd be notifying her to come to a lineup, and he hoped then she would be able to identify the guy.

From there, he'd gone to Helga Marks's apartment and shown her the pictures, but Helga also refused to say that the young man in these pictures was definitely the one she'd seen outside the shop. Harvey had stormed back to the crime center, furious. But they *had* identified the right man in the lineup and Armstrong was locked up tight now. He could only hope his impetuous act would not blow the critical identification.

Meanwhile, the reporters and TV cameras were waiting; it would be national news by suppertime. Whatever else might happen, now was the big moment all had been waiting for.

Some 2,400 miles west in Salinas, California, a man named Robert Taylor was settled in a favorite easy chair watching the seven o'clock network news. Taylor's interest perked up partway through when the anchorman reported that a long manhunt in Michigan had been climaxed that day with the arrest of a twenty-two-year-old college senior. Film clips were flashed on the screen showing a handsome clean-cut young man being led, manacled, by grim-faced lawmen into the courthouse at Ann Arbor, Michigan.

The accused James Nolan Armstrong of Center Line, Michigan, is an education major at Eastern Michigan University in Ypsilanti. Three of the murder victims had been students at the same school—including the last, eighteen-year-old Carol Ann Gebhardt, a newly enrolled freshman from Grand Rapids. . . . The rumors here are that Armstrong has been under scrutiny since shortly after he returned from a trip to California about mid-July . . .

Robert Taylor was sitting bolt upright, his mind racing. Taylor, thirty-six, was an investigator for the Monterey County district attorney. For more than a month he and the local police had been stymied by a brutal homicide case of their own—a pretty seventeen-year-old girl visiting Salinas, found strangled in a ravine near Carmel.

There had been nothing that really could be termed a clue. The only lead at all was a young man from out of state whose car was thought to have been seen cruising the vicinity at the time the girl was last seen, on June 30. A friend of the slain girl told of having met a man of similar description in the same area just the day before. According to the girl friend, the young man, who'd called himself only "James," drove a late-model Oldsmobile Cutlass with Michigan plates. He said that he and a friend were there on vacation, having brought their own camper-trailer, that he was a senior at some college in Michigan and hoped to become a teacher.

The girl had described him as early twentyish, about six feet, wiry athletic build, very good-looking, dark hair trimmed short but sideburns longish.

The TV news had moved onto another topic. Robert Taylor was out of the chair and dialing his telephone. "Operator," he said crisply, "I want the district attorney in Ann Arbor, Michigan."

To the homicide investigators in Ann Arbor, the telephone call from California came as a surprise dividend. Their accused killer and the man sought in Monterey County did sound as though they might be the same individual—physical description, approximate age, stated name and place of origin and occupation, type and appearance of his automobile—and, all important, timing: The California slaying had taken place about June 30; and that, by all accounts, was when James Armstrong was thought to have been in California.

Not that, should it prove that James Armstrong had also killed in California, it necessarily promised Michigan direct help in prosecuting its case against him. But it could add impressive weight to the probability

they hoped to cultivate—even if it could never be substantiated in court—that the murderer of Carol Ann
Gebhardt was in fact a multiple killer.

One item in the California rundown did strike a
note possibly relevant to the Ann Arbor slayings: the
camper-trailer brought out from Michigan. No one yet
had any clear idea what significance the missing trailer
might have in the murders. The only hope was that the
trailer might yield evidence *relating* to any of the
crimes—perhaps as a storage place for the grisly me-
mentoes that the investigators were sure existed. The
California police were asked to try to trace it there.

On Saturday, August 2, the Monterey County Sheriff's Department reported back to the Michigan State
Police that they had the trailer. It had been found,
where evidently it had been for some weeks, in an
alley at the rear of a house in a ramshackle section of
Salinas.

The following morning, Ken Christensen and Tom
Nasser of the Plymouth scientific laboratory were on
a jet to the Monterey peninsula.

The Salinas police escorted Christensen and Nasser to
a wrecking lot where the yellow trailer had been removed and secured. It was the one from Hendrickson's in Ypsilanti, all right. The Michigan officers,
aided by a Monterey sheriff's detective and another
from the Salinas Police Department, went over the
vehicle inch by inch. They found nothing, not even a
legible fingerprint—surprising after a cross-country
trip. It must have been cleaned out, deliberately wiped
spick and span inside and out.

The owner of the rundown clapboard house behind
which the trailer had been discovered was a leathery-
skinned man in his eighties named Argentino Monte,
who turned out to be the grandfather of Tony Monte.
He said the trailer had been brought there toward the
end of June by his grandson, whom he had not seen
for several years, and a friend—a tall, nice-looking
young gringo. They had slept in the trailer at night,

each day going off somewhere in their car, a shiny gray Oldsmobile. Then one day they'd driven off and not come back. The trailer stayed in the alley undisturbed.

Whether or not the trailer would ever tell the police anything about the crimes, one thing it did establish was where Armstrong and Monte had been during a specific important period. They had taken the trailer from Ypsilanti on June 21. According to the old man's recollections, the two were in Salinas from sometime before the end of June through about the first week of July. By mid-July they were known to have been back in Ypsi.

Thus they would have had up to two weeks in the Salinas-Monterey area—just about the time-span between the disappearance of the victim there and the discovery of her corpse, brutally battered and strangled with a piece of her own belt.

The slain girl was Ginger Lee Neary, seventeen, a tall, well-formed, pretty blonde from Milwaukie, Oregon, who had been visiting with a young family in Salinas, Adele and Ken Barkas, formerly neighbors back home.

Ginger, going into senior year of high school, was on her first unescorted summer vacation trip. It had been carefully planned. First, she had stopped off a few days in Sacramento with relatives of her divorced mother. After a couple of weeks in Salinas, she was to bus down the coast to Lompoc and stay with her father's brother and his family. Her father and stepmother, driving from Oregon, were planning to pick her up there and continue on south to the Los Angeles area, where they would visit other relatives and see the sights, including Disneyland, before returning home.

Ginger had been in Salinas a week, and—she wrote in her final letter to a friend in Milwaukie—she was just getting over the strangeness and starting to enjoy herself. The chief reason was another seventeen-year-old she'd become friendly with, Allison Bertold from Fort Worth, Texas, visiting for the summer with her married sister and her husband, Marj and Fred Gault, who were friends of the Barkases. Together the girls had begun to meet a few interesting boys, and— Ginger wrote—she was beginning to wish that her own stay might be extended.

Before 1:00 P.M. on Monday, June 30, Ginger had left the Barkas home on East Acacia Street to mail that letter and then go on to meet Allison, whose sister's house was six blocks away. She told Adele that she would be back later in the afternoon, by four or five at the latest, as she was to babysit for the children that evening.

She did not return. At suppertime, Adele telephoned the Gaults. Allison said she had not seen Ginger all day. Worried, because Ginger was always so reliable, Adele waited only until seven. Then she put through long-distance calls to Oregon, to the girl's mother, first, then her father. Neither had heard from their daughter. At 7:19, Adele called the Salinas police.

Inquiries produced only one person who had seen the girl at all that afternoon. A neighbor of the Barkases, an Ann Rey, said she was walking past the Barkas house, on her way to shopping, when Ginger had come out about one o'clock. They said hello, stopped to chat briefly and after a few moments parted. The last Miss Rey saw of Ginger she was crossing to the north side of East Acacia and walking east toward Pajaro, the next cross street.

The girl seemed to have vanished without a trace. Still, as there was no indication of either abduction or violence, she was listed by police as another probable teen-age runaway—a conclusion easily reached by police in California, where young people dropping out was so commonplace as to have become part of the life style.

When four more days went by, however, without word of Ginger—and after a round of anxious telephone calls to relations along her planned itinerary, none of whom had heard from the girl—her parents were apprehensive enough to begin searching for her themselves. Ginger's mother and fifteen-year-old brother flew to Monterey. Her father, arranging leave from his shop superintendent's job in Portland, set out alone to drive the nearly eight hundred miles, intending en route to look for himself around such drop-out havens as Sausalito and Berkeley and Santa Cruz, for whatever unlikely good that might do.

From Salinas, the former Mrs. Neary, a controlled, organized woman, methodically conducted a self-styled publicity campaign, canvassing the media from the Monterey peninsula up to San Francisco and Sacramento and down as far as Los Angeles, soliciting appeals for her missing daughter. At her own expense, she had printed thousands of circulars—on pink stock, featuring a black-and-white head shot of Ginger along with her vital statistics (five feet six, 130 pounds, hazel eyes, fair skin, shoulder-length coppery blond hair); a description of her last-known appearance (wearing a short red pants dress with small white floral design, matching fabric belt, full sleeves with white cuffs, white collar, white sandals, carrying a large straw tote bag); and offering a "generous" reward (NO QUESTIONS ASKED) for any information leading to the girl's "location and return." She and her son, her ex-husband, local friends, even a number of sympathetic policemen in the area, posted these in store windows, bars, gas stations, and depots from Big Sur to San Jose.

None of this brought any response.

On Sunday, July 13, in midafternoon, a pair of teen-aged youths from Carmel, a small, quaint seaside community on the Monterey peninsula some twenty miles southwest of Salinas, were rummaging in a deep, heavily thicketed ravine called Pescadero Canyon just north of the city limits. They were continuing their hunt, begun the day before, for fossil remains as part of a vacation project for Carmel High School. On

Saturday, they'd been bothered by a putrid odor near one of their digging spots—as from a dead animal's rotting, somewhere hidden in the dense foliage—but had been unable to pin it down. It was still there, even more foul-smelling.

Picking through the brush, they uncovered what at first revolting sight looked to be a slab of festering meat. But when they pulled away more branches, they saw to their horror what it was—or had been: a person. A female, apparently naked. Blackened flesh oozing. Matted blond hair crawling . . .

An emergency crew was at the canyon inside ten minutes. The remains were nude except for two places: White sandals were still on her feet, and around her neck—wound and knotted tight, like a garrote— was a cloth belt, red with a small white floral design.

Death by strangulation was confirmed by County Coroner Christopher Hill, Jr., who reported the throttling was so vicious that the larynx was ruptured. The victim, about seventeen, had been dead approximately two weeks, the doctors estimated—probably having lain where she was found most of that time, although it was impossible to say if she had been killed there.

Where she lay, in the deep shadows of giant Pacific pine, was a tangle of wild plant life—including a hardy overgrowth of poison oak shrubs (as one luckless detective would shortly appreciate to his great discomfort). The body was not in a place where it could have been rolled down a slope from the top of the ravine but had to have been carried in—so deep into the thicket that in another week or two it might have been swallowed up and never found.

The dead girl was formally identified the next day as Ginger Lee Neary. Salinas dentist Dr. Gerald Dannemiller compared a chart of her teeth by telephone with the girl's dentist in Milwaukie, Oregon, Dr. Robert Wu, whose records of her matched. And Adele Barkas was able to confirm that the red cloth belt used to strangle the girl came from the pants dress Ginger had been wearing when she'd left the house for the last time.

On July 15, her body was escorted back to Oregon for burial by her parents—reunited temporarily in tragedy.

Salinas detectives returned to the neighborhood where the Barkases lived and inquired, house by house, shop by shop, for anybody who might remember having seen her. Sheriff's investigators, led by chief of detectives Captain Derol Smith, did the same in Carmel and surroundings. Other officers, by car and on foot, combed the length of Route 68, the main road between Salinas and the peninsula.

They came up with a few things. Two sheriff's deputies patrolling Route 68 found a partially unused bus ticket, still in its jacket, near a bridge crossing Toro Creek, a few miles west of Salinas. The unused portion was one-way from Salinas to Lompoc, California. The original ticket had been Portland, Ore.–Sacramento, Calif.–Salinas.

Then two eighteen-year-old youths walked into a California Highway Patrol station off Route 68 with the large straw tote bag. They said they'd found it under the Toro Creek bridge about July 1; its few contents had been just some paper hankies and a few hard candies—no purse.

Next, a Salinas resident produced a wallet-sized plastic picture folder, filled with snapshots of smiling teen-age-looking girls, which he said he'd also found about July 1. This had been two or three miles farther west of Salinas, just off Route 68, near the bottom of a road called Laureles Grade (a scenic drive up through the Hidden Hills and down the other side into the Carmel Valley). A check with friends confirmed that the folder had been Ginger's.

These findings, put together, suggested that whoever had picked up the girl on June 30 (and it had to be assumed that she'd gone off that day, voluntarily or not, in *some* car or other vehicle), had driven her out on Route 68 and taken the mountain road to

Carmel—or else, at least, had returned that way, alone. Her belongings must have been disposed of along the roads sometime after she was dead, whether going or coming.

Then a Salinas housewife came forward with the recollection of an incident she'd observed on June 30 in the neighborhood where Ginger Neary was last seen. Late that afternoon, Mrs. Lucille Henderson had been driving on East Acacia Street and pulled up at a stop sign at the corner of Pajaro. She noticed, approaching from the opposite direction, a silver-colored car also slow as it approached the intersection; but suddenly, not stopping, with a screech of rubber it accelerated, made a sharp left in front of her and sped north on Pajaro. The driver she'd glimpsed as a clean-cut young man with dark hair, and next to him was a girl with what appeared to be "sandy" hair who was wearing "something bright red." The car's plates were dark, definitely out-of-state; and she thought the rear bumper carried a trailer hitch.

Monterey D.A.'s investigator Robert Taylor and sheriff's detective Tom Shepherd, teamed on the case, went to ask Ken and Adele Barkas if that sketchy description sounded like anyone Ginger might have gotten to know during her stay. Not that they knew of, they said.

But when the detectives next asked the same of Ginger's friend Allison Bertold, they were luckier. The winsome little brunette reacted with surprise. *She* knew—had encountered once, at least—a fellow such as the one described, but to her knowledge Ginger had not. She did not know how Ginger *could* have. Allison herself had met him only the day before Ginger disappeared. . . .

It was on Sunday, June 29, after Allison had visited Ginger at the Barkas house on East Acacia. At about 2:00 P.M. she'd left and was walking up Pajaro Street to her sister's home on Harvest, six blocks north, when a gleaming silver-gray car, coming south, pulled alongside and the driver called to her.

A square-jawed, good-looking young man with a warm, boyish smile, he politely asked if she could tell him how to get to some place or other—she couldn't remember now where—but she said she was sorry, she was pretty much a stranger in town. He said brightly that he was too, and they got to chatting about how each happened to be in California. He didn't try to get her into the car; instead he got out and stood at the curb talking with her.

He was tall, maybe six feet, slim but muscular in a clean white T-shirt and faded tight-fitting dungarees. He wore his sideburns longish, to the bottom of the ears, but otherwise his dark brown hair was neatly trimmed and combed, except for one lock falling casually across his forehead. His pale, deep-set eyes were direct and penetrating. Allison guessed he was four or five years older than she—which was about right because soon he told her he was a senior in college back in Michigan. His name was James, he said.

She liked him. They talked easily, and Allison was beginning to think it was a lucky day for her; he seemed genuinely interested in her. He asked where she was living, and he offered to drive her the rest of the way. At the Gaults', Allison invited James in for a soda. She introduced him to her sister Marj, a pert, outgoing woman of twenty-nine, and when he heard that she taught at the high school he told them with evident enthusiasm of his own plans to teach. He had only a few more credit hours to make up in the fall before he would graduate and be eligible for a teaching certificate.

The three chatted pleasantly for about a half hour. James said that he and a friend had towed a trailer out from Michigan and were living out of it, parked at another friend's house in Salinas. He said he was enjoying his visit, except that he missed his motorcycles—some of the local roads, especially up through those hills toward Monterey and Carmel, would be sensational on a bike.

Saying that he and his friend would probably be

around another week or two, he suggested, as he was leaving, the hope that he might see Allison again. Allison and Marj watched him pull away in the sleek silver Olds, which had black leather or vinyl upholstery. The rear plate was deep red with white lettering—Michigan—and above it, a trailer hitch was clamped to the bumper. When he was gone, Marj smiled at her younger sister and said she thought he was very nice.

That Sunday evening, when she and Ginger Neary were together, Allison had spiritedly described her encounter with the dreamy college man from Michigan. She was sure she would see him again. Ginger had shared her anticipation almost as eagerly as she herself.

But Allison never did see "James" again—nor her friend Ginger, either. Until now, it had never occurred to her to connect the two.

Nor could the police readily presume such connection. There was, after all, no evidence that the young man from Michigan *had* ever met the murdered girl; all they had was the apparent coincidence of her girl friend having met someone of similar description one day, and the unconfirmed possibility that the same individual might have been in the vicinity the next day —*perhaps* with the victim in his car, but still alive.

Still, it was all they did have, and certainly they should try to find that young man and ask him some questions. A bulletin, therefore, was put out locally describing the car and its driver.

Days went by without results. Finally, an inquiry was dispatched to the authorities in Michigan for help in locating the subject.

In Lansing, the matter did not stir immediate interest. They were being asked to dig through enrollments at the hundred-or-so colleges and universities across the state, and/or the countless thousands of Oldsmobile registrations in Michigan over a several-year period—not knowing either the model or year of the car in question or its registration number—to try to pick out a male identified only as "James" (his given name or surname?), assuming that that *was* his name and, if it was, that the vehicle was in fact registered in such a name.

Considering that the subject was not even formally listed as a fugitive, was sought only for questioning in a crime two-thirds of a continent away, it seemed a fairly routine request to be handled when there was time and more manpower available. The Michigan police were up to their ears just then with plenty of trouble of their own.

For the day the California inquiry was processed was July 24, and another coed had just been reported missing in Washtenaw County.

It was August 5 before Ken Christensen, still in California, got a chance to telephone Lansing to learn the results of the tests on the front seat of James Armstrong's car. Now he was also curious to know whether the car had yielded anything in connection with the Neary case.

Analyst Curtis Fluker of the Health Department gave Christensen this report:

The blood samples unquestionably were of human origin—and not James Armstrong's. They were thought to be Type O, though this had yet to be verified by more extensive tests. The one Michigan victim whose blood had been Type O was Audrey Sakol. What was the California victim's blood type? asked Fluker.

Christensen said he would find out. Anything else?

Just one other thing, Fluker said. A tiny piece of fabric, found wedged down inside the center hinge between the folding seatbacks—a red cotton material with a white dot on it, perhaps part of some design pattern. Did that mean anything?

Ginger Neary's pants suit!

Excited, the Michigan detective hastened to inform his California colleagues. He would take a piece off the cloth belt used to strangle the girl back to Michigan for lab comparison with the fragment from Armstrong's car. If they matched—! He would also like to take with him samples of the girl's blood to compare with that found in the car.

The Monterey County lawmen were embarrassed. They couldn't supply him with any of the vital samples he wanted. A sample of Ginger Neary's blood *had* been taken, but by then she'd been dead and decomposing so long that it was too putrid to do anything with . . . and so it had been thrown out. Christensen, a thoroughgoing professional, could not believe his ears.

On August 7, at the Public Health lab in Lansing, Curtis Fluker analyzed the two pieces of red fabric. They matched in every respect: each 100% cotton; each filler-printed with similar red dyestuffs (the white dot design on each of like size and shape); each woven in the same plain weave, with double threads in one direction and a single thread in the other, the diameters of each of the threads identical. The fragment retrieved from Armstrong's car was of the same material used to strangle Ginger Lee Neary.

It seemed irrefutable, then—even without matching blood samples—that the girl murdered in California had been in that car just before her death. Or just after.

CHAPTER 21

ON AUGUST 6, the day before James Armstrong's first
scheduled court appearance in Ypsilanti, his elusive
friend Tony Monte was run down by the FBI in Phoenix, Arizona. Michigan had two charges against
Monte: larceny "by conversion," as an accessory in
the fraudulent rental of a vehicle (the trailer found in
California) removed from the state without intention
of returning it; and now, possession and concealment
of stolen property (a diamond ring—one of the seventeen stolen, along with a blank checkbook, from an
Ypsilanti apartment back in March). But of course,
what they really wanted from Monte was the story of
his association with James Armstrong.

How much did he know about the murder of Carol
Ann Gebhardt—or any of the others?

Flown back to Michigan, Monte was arraigned on
the two felony charges. Represented by court-appointed
counsel, he stood mute on both counts. Judge Henry
D. Arkison scheduled separate preliminary examina-
tions, one, on the stolen-property charge, for August
27, and the second, on the larceny by conversion, for
September 3. Bail was set at $7,500 for each.

Tony Monte was a native Californian; his mother was dead, his father remarried and divorced, the rest of his family scattered along the Pacific coast. Tony had been in and out of trouble since adolescence and had dropped out of school at age sixteen. Arrested a number of times for petty offenses, he'd had only one conviction recorded against him—in Riverside in 1963, when he was nineteen, for burglary and possession of marijuana. He'd served eighteen months.

About 1966, Monte had made his way east—to Detroit, where he worked at various factory jobs. Having picked up a knowledge of machine tooling, in 1968 he got a machinist's job with the Motor Wheel Corporation in Ypsilanti and moved there. Every indication was that Monte and Armstrong, having been thrown together at Motor Wheel, had started their burglarizing team in the late winter or early spring of 1969. Monte admitted to most of this. But he emphatically denied any knowledge of the area's killings. He himself had not known any of the victims and was not aware that James had; he couldn't even remember ever discussing the murders with James. In no instance had any actions of James's excited the faintest suspicion in Monte—not about *them*.

Pressed about the last homicide, Monte recalled that on Wednesday, July 23, he had not seen James until late in the afternoon. Tony and Donald Baker had been together a few hours earlier, and James showed up at the house around four or four thirty and took Baker out for a bike lesson. Later, the same evening, the three of them went out together to eat, then watched TV in James's room the rest of the night.

Monte said he didn't notice anything "different" about Armstrong the next few days—not uptight at all, just the usual puttering with his bikes. He was looking forward to scrambling that weekend.

Then why had *he* suddenly taken off and disappeared about that time?

It was after James had told him about that cop nosing around the garage on Friday, Monte said. That got him worried, plenty. He was afraid that things might be getting hot, and it might be a good time for him to get lost. He rode a bus from Ann Arbor all the way back to California. After about a week, he hopped down to Phoenix to a friend's—and that's where the FBI picked him up.

And that was all he knew.

They put him through several polygraph tests. All the results indicated that he was telling the truth with respect to James Armstrong.

Tony Monte thus proved a major disappointment to the Washtenaw County prosecutors. Sure of a conviction on the felony charges against him—what with having recovered much of the stolen loot he'd fenced —they had held out a recommendation of leniency if (a) he would "cop a plea," thus saving the county the time and expense of a court trial, and most particularly if (b) he "cooperated" fully in telling them all he knew about James Armstrong.

Monte, understandably, had gone along with their deal. He had nothing to lose. And he had given them plenty on Armstrong's own burglary activities—though none of that would have much value as evidence in a homicide trial.

But about the murders he'd been able to add nothing.*

If the investigators were frustrated in having extracted too little helpful information from Monte, they were in a state of befuddlement over how much they'd been getting from Donald Baker.

Baker had been questioned constantly since the day after Armstrong's arrest. He was fascinating. Usually, friends of an accused could be expected to clam up; but

* And in the end, Tony Monte seemed to have gotten all the best of the prosecutor's office. On November 17, pleading guilty to both felony counts, he was sentenced to five years' probation; on each count, a fine of $50 and payment of $300 court costs; and a separate order of restitution in the amount of $1,500 to be made to Hendrickson's Rent-a-Trailer of Ypsilanti. Monte was back out on the streets for Christmas 1969.

Baker just talked and talked answering *everything*. If he stumbled, or said he couldn't remember, with enough prompting he would remember.

Such as with the business of Armstrong's alibi. It was Armstrong's story that he could account for his time between one and 2:30, the critical afternoon of July 23, and that by a little past 2:30 he was back at 619 Emmet Street and with Baker and Tony Monte the rest of that afternoon and evening. If this alibi could not be disproved, the whole case against Armstrong could be neutralized.

The first crack had come with the disclosure by Monte that it was not 2:30 but more like 4:00 or 4:30 that Armstrong had first joined Donald Baker and himself. Put to Baker, at first he disputed Monte's statement—sticking to "about two thirty."

But as the insistent detectives prodded him, he admitted that maybe it *had* been later . . . closer to four.

Then why had he said 2:30?

Well, James had put that in his head. Baker remembered, now, that he'd made rather a point of it after he'd been taken in for questioning by those two detectives.

And he went on. The night of the twenty-third, when they were all watching TV, about 9:30 James left him and Monte for a while, saying he wanted to work on one of his bikes—and was gone until about 11:30. And no sooner had he come back than he said he'd forgotten to feed his uncle's dog and left again—this time returning around 1:00 A.M.

As to whether he'd ever seen Armstrong bring anything "unusual" into the house—say, any articles of female apparel—Baker first said not to his recollection . . . but then, with scarcely a change of gear, he proceeded to reel off the incredible account of James and the cardboard box full of women's things!

And the knife. A four-inch hunting knife had been found in Baker's own dresser drawer, wrapped in a T-shirt. He explained blandly that Armstrong had given him that the night of the box incident! He'd seen

James remove it from beneath the seat of one of his
bikes, and then James had asked him to keep it for
him . . . so the police wouldn't find it, Armstrong had
said. (The knife, subsequently examined in the crime
lab, had been found clean even of fingerprint
smudges.)

From there Baker went on to tell them—to their
astonishment—all about his friend's campaign of thievery. James had started by swiping parts for his motorcycles—from ornaments to handlebars, fenders, then
to wheels, whole engines, stripped-down chassis. He
always seemed to have "new" bikes—some no doubt
pieced together from various stolen parts, others probably stolen in toto. Baker said he knew of at least one
that James had simply taken from a parking space
somewhere around the university and calmly walked
the several blocks to Emmet Street as though it were
out of commission. He was especially clever at repaint-
ing, switching identifiable parts, disposing of what
could not be disguised; and by the time he'd finished
working it over, the real owner wouldn't have recognized it if James had ridden up and offered him a ride.
Just a week or so earlier, he had shown up on this latest
one, a heavily chromed blue Triumph. (And he'd
talked Baker into going over to the state offices to re-
register it for him and pick up the new plate. Donald
was just returning with that stuff the day Officer
Mathewson was nosing around.)

But the motorcycle thefts weren't all. James had
lately begun branching out, burgling homes with his
friend Tony Monte. What had disturbed Baker most
about this was that he could see James wasn't doing it
for the money—he didn't *need* money. He was always
working at odd jobs around Ypsi, and he also regularly
got an allowance from home; and he wasn't a big party
guy or drinker, nor did he need to spend a lot on chicks.
It was just for the kicks, the satisfaction—stealing for
its own sake.

Baker's interrogators registered all this, blinking in
wonderment, then brought him back to Armstrong's

motorcycles, specifically to his memory of the afternoon they'd gone riding. He said the one James had taken him out on was the green Triumph. He recalled that before they started out James switched the license plate and a small round mirror from the blue to the green bike. Baker noticed that the blue bike was warm at the time, as though driven lately, while the green one was cool.

They pressed him about that mirror: Wasn't it a big *square* mirror? But this was one point he would not bend on. They kept at him, but he kept answering back, almost apologetically, no, he was sorry but he did not recall a square mirror.

How did such a couple of unalike guys—the *macho* "easy rider" and the studious music-lover—ever join up, they wanted to know?

They'd met, Baker said, late in junior year—1968 —when each had found himself staying over alone in Ypsilanti during the spring school break. It was just one of those things, a mutual need for companionship. Their different natures seemed to complement one another. It was an easy, undemanding relationship. Yet they never really became confidants or buddies; neither was that type.

Among the wide disparity of their mutual interests was girls—types of girls. James never went for the cool or cerebral; he liked *physical* ones, well-equipped and adventurous. And he found plenty, usually around the McKenny Student Union. Often he would bring them back to his room, sometimes two and three in a night. But as awed as Baker was by James's insatiable appetite, he was impressed by his friend's apparent finesse. He always treated his conquests gently, like ladies—which may have been part of his charm. There was only one time Baker remembered James getting rough, and that had been funny. . . .

It was a night just a couple of months ago. From across the hall, Baker noticed James hustle this well-stacked chick into his room, as usual. But in a little while she came busting out and down the stairs, James chasing her, swearing—it was like a Marx Brothers' scene. When James came back later, he was still muttering: One thing he couldn't *stand* was a damn cockteaser!

The interrogators' interest stirred. *When* had this taken place?

"Oh, early in the summer," he said.

"A Saturday night, maybe?"

"Possibly. James always made out best on weekends."

"Could this girl have been wearing a white mini, a purple top?"

"I didn't get that close a look," he said. "I guess she could."

They showed him a photo of a young woman. "Does this look like the one?"

Baker pinched up his face. "It's hard to say. It *might* be. . . ."

The detectives exchanged bright glances. The photograph was of Audrey Sakol!

They brought out photos of other of the victims: Did he recognize any of *them?*

He riffled through them. No.

A detective tossed one of the pictures back in front of him. "Not even this one?" It was Jill Hersch.

Had Armstrong ever mentioned, or had Baker any personal knowledge of, his having given a lift to a girl who looked like this outside the Student Union about a year ago?

Baker's eyes widened and he looked around at them uncertainly, as though trying to grasp how much they knew. "Well, that's a really odd thing," he said at last. "I remember how James and I commented later on the coincidence. One night last summer, *we* stopped and picked up a girl there—"

They'd *what?* When? What girl?

Catching his breath, Donald Baker told them, falteringly at first, then with successive embellishments, three versions of a story which—when finally boiled

down under their relentless pressure—sent the blood
pounding into their heads:

It was a Sunday night. Three of them were cruising
around Ypsi—he and James and another fellow driving whom Baker hardly knew, a friend of James's; it
was the other fellow's car. (He couldn't recall the make
or color. It *could* have been red and black.) They
found a door open in the Union, and James tried to
telephone a girl he knew, but the custodian chased
them out. They drove around the block and, coming
back, saw two girls at the bus stop, and James called
out to them. One came up to the car and said she
needed to get to Ann Arbor, and James put her up
front between himself and the driver. Right away he
turned on the charm, and Baker, in the back seat alone,
stretched out in anticipation of a long night.

But instead of going toward Ann Arbor, they drove
back to Emmet Street. There, James said he would
take the girl in his own car, and Baker got out and went
up to his room, and the other fellow drove off. It must
have been after 1:00 A.M. before Baker saw Armstrong
next. James came into his room, and Baker asked him
if he'd scored. James told him he'd parked with the girl
in the big K-Mart lot out on Washtenaw and thought
he was starting to make it with her pretty good, when
she got scared and wanted to get out of the car. He
tried to talk her into staying, and they had struggled a
little, so finally he opened the door and threw her out,
and he drove off, leaving her there.

The only reason the episode had stuck in his mind at
all, Baker told the officers, was that after the news of
the Hersch girl's murder had come out a short time
later, and he'd noticed the similarity of circumstances,
James had made a strong point about neither of them
mentioning the "coincidence" to anyone.

They kept at Baker about the identity of the third
male in the car that night. But he kept insisting that he
couldn't remember. . . .

To the wondering detectives, this guy was a unique
piece of work. There was no immediate way to evaluate

how much of his disclosure was fact and how much
adroit accommodation to their own suggestion, prompting, and obvious intent. They took Baker in to the Redford State Police post for polygraph testing.

The examiners' conclusions, in summary, were that
Donald Baker personally had had no part in that or
any other murder.

But he had given them quite a lot to chew on, digest,
and follow up—indeed, the makings of at least one
good back-up case.

Following the wedge provided by Donald Baker, the
investigators gave renewed attention to the two E.M.U.
students who a year earlier had claimed to have seen
Armstrong and Jill Hersch together prior to her disappearance that night of June 30.

Ted Shaefer and Eileen Gaffney were interviewed
separately and together, and eventually they seemed
to agree on the following points: Both were *positive*
now that it was Armstrong and Hersch they'd seen that
night. And they narrowed the probable time gap to
"between eleven and eleven thirty." Considering the
new information the police were working on, that was
close enough.

They also kept seeking links between Armstrong and
each of the other victims. But what few leads they had
were remote:

Marilyn Pindar. Among items confiscated from
Armstrong's room was a souvenir coin from Expo '67.
Marilyn Pindar had brought home such a memento
from Montreal in June 1967, and her mother had noted
it missing from the dead girl's effects. . . . She and Armstrong had worked in the same building at E.M.U.
during the 1967 summer. And both had frequented
the beaches at Silver and Half Moon lakes. However,
there was as yet no proof that the two were acquainted.

Jeanne Holder. No apparent ties at all—except that
there *was* evidence that Armstrong had owned a .22
pistol, the caliber of weapon used to kill Holder.

An E.M.U. student who knew Armstrong had told

police that he'd seen Armstrong firing a small revolver once the past spring out in a field outside Ypsi. Donald Baker confirmed that he'd seen such a pistol in Armstrong's room, although he could not say what caliber. And Tony Monte said that he'd financed his bus flight in late July by hocking a number of stolen items, including a handgun swiped from Armstrong's room! He couldn't readily dispose of the pistol, however, and had "ditched it somewhere" en route to California. It was definitely a .22, he said.

There was little hope of ever recovering such a gun. And Armstrong refused to acknowledge he'd ever owned one. So there seemed almost no chance of tying him to the Holder slaying.

Mary Grace Clemson. The only possible connection here was that both she and Armstrong were known to have been frequent visitors to the Woodland Hills apartment complex between Ypsi and Ann Arbor. But their respective friends there had lived in different buildings, and none had been located so far who could say that Armstrong and the girl might ever have encountered one another.

Dale Harum. No connection here . . . only the most tenuous conjecture based on knowledge that Armstrong had regularly driven his motorcycles over the back roads outlying the E.M.U. campus, including the area in which the Harums lived, and that he'd occasionally dated a girl who had a garden apartment on LeForge Road, in one of the projects not far from the girl's home. Very thin.

Audrey Sakol. More promising—possibly even a second back-up case against him.

First, the trace of Type O blood found in Armstrong's car. Sakol was the only local victim having that blood type (although it would be reassuring had they been able to confirm that the girl slain in California had *not* been Type O).

Then, in sequence: An interview with Armstrong's girl friend, Jeannie, in which she stated that on the first Saturday night in June (a date she recalled from a

particular family event that weekend) she and James
had had their first serious quarrel, and he'd broken
their planned date and stormed off. It was June 7, the
night Sakol was last seen. . . . A statement by a fellow
Eastern student of Armstrong's that he'd seen him
around ten that night in downtown Ann Arbor, walking
on Liberty Street near State—just a stone's throw from
Sakol's residence on Thompson. . . . A tip that Armstrong used to drop in sometimes at the Rubaiyat Cafe
in Ann Arbor, a place on Main street where Sakol was
also known to go on occasion. (But neither employees
nor regular patrons could place the two together there.
Nor did any of her friends recollect her having known
or ever mentioned knowing anyone named James
Armstrong.) Finally, Donald Baker's account of Armstrong, in a rage, having chased a "stacked" young
woman fleeing from his room one night—quite possibly
Saturday night, June 7.

This case needed a lot more work, but the investigators felt it was shaping up.

Still, as things stood, at optimum they might be able
to lay only three of seven murders on James Armstrong
—and that, to most of the lawmen who'd suffered the
tormenting hunt these past two years, would be deeply
unsatisfying. Most were personally convinced that they
had finally locked up *the* killer, but few could know
real peace of mind until every conceivable doubt was
dispelled that all seven murders in fact had been
solved. And it was beginning to appear that the only
way they might ever get that satisfaction would be if
James Armstrong confessed.

But their prisoner was not about to make it so easy for
them.

They'd thought he might be on the verge of cracking
once soon after his arrest, in a reaction to his horror of
having been thrust suddenly into a cramped, dank
cage in the basement of the county jail. It was what
jailers and inmates called "the hole"—a windowless
concrete cubicle screened by heavy steel mesh, con-

taining only a wooden bunk and a small hole in the cold
floor for personal urgencies; unlit except for the gloomy
reflection cast by a dim ceiling lamp out of sight down
a corridor, the only way to guess at time was by the
whoosh every quarter hour of a deodorizer mechanism
somewhere. Alone there, curled up miserably in the
eerie silence, Armstrong wept and sniveled through
much of the first dark night.

Then, on the second night, August 2, he called out
for a guard. Tearfully he said he had to talk . . . to
somebody.

At about 10:30 P.M., Lieutenant Ken Schultz located Sheriff Harvey at an Ypsilanti bar. The new
prisoner, he exclaimed, was making noises like he
wanted to spill his guts! Harvey gulped down his drink
and raced to the jail.

Outside Armstrong's cage, the sheriff, controlling his
own excitement with difficulty, asked evenly: "All
right, son, I understand you want to make a statement?"

The youth looked pitiful. Every muscle in his lean
frame seemed to have turned to jelly. His eyes were
puffy and his cheeks streaked with tears. He nodded,
whimpering.

"I think it's a good idea," Harvey said gently. He
nodded to Schultz. "The lieutenant here will bring you
up to my office—it's more comfortable there. I'll go up
now and get everything set."

Harvey took the stairs two at a time, his heart pounding more from anticipation than exertion. In his small
private office, he pounced on the telephone and dialed
Prosecutor Delhey at home.

"Bill, you'd better get over here," he urged. "It's
Armstrong. I think he's about to give me a confession."

"Oh, God!" Delhey gasped. "I'll contact his attorneys—they *must* be there for this! Don't even ask
the boy how he *feels* until his counsel is present."

"I've got you." As he hung up Lieutenant Schultz
brought Armstrong in. In the light Harvey thought
he looked even more bedraggled. "Sit down, James.

We'll have to hold off just a bit. We're calling your lawyers so you'll be fully protected. Is there anything we can get you, a Coke, or—?"

"Could I . . . talk to my mother?"

"Sure, I guess so. You mean bring her here?"

Armstrong nodded and looked down at his hands.

Harvey located Mrs. Armstrong at the Louckses' in Ypsilanti, where she and her other son and daughter had been staying. Waiting for her to arrive, the sheriff tried to occupy James with small talk, but the dismal youth was unresponsive.

Louella Armstrong swept into the jail, Tom and Dawn behind. The elder son was a bit taller than James, with gentler features. The daughter resembled neither; she was fleshy, with a hard look, the sheriff thought, from too much makeup and an overdone orange bouffant. The mother's appearance was a little top-heavy, too, but she was attractively dressed and carried herself with visible presence.

"Have you called James's counsel?" Mrs. Armstrong demanded at once.

"Yes, ma'am. On the way," replied the sheriff.

"I would like to talk with James first, please," she said. "In private."

Harvey closed them in his office and waited, fidgeting, outside. In a little while William Delhey strode in accompanied by his chief investigator, Roy Tanner. Then attorneys John Toomey and Robert Francis arrived.

After almost an hour, Mrs. Armstrong emerged, her expression impenetrable. "Thank you," she said quietly. "I think James is ready now."

Sheriff Harvey started for his office—

"Just a minute please, sheriff," Francis intercepted him. "We'd like a moment with our client." He and Toomey edged past the disgruntled Harvey and closed the door behind them.

The attorneys were in with Armstrong another twenty-five minutes. When they came out, Francis said:

"You can talk with him now, gentlemen."

Delhey asked: "You'll join us, of course?"

"No," said Francis, glancing at his partner, "that won't be necessary."

The three startled lawmen looked around bleakly at one another. They went into the office. "Okay, James," Harvey said in a friendly tone, "here's the prosecutor, Mr. Delhey. What did you want to tell him?"

Armstrong's eyes were dry again, his face blank. He sat easily erect in the same chair, one leg crossed over the other. "Well . . ." he began, looking up directly at the tall Delhey and considering his words, "I want to confess that I did help steal that trailer."

The men stared down at him. "And—?" prodded Delhey.

"And . . . a few other things, maybe. But *nothing* that big." The corners of his mouth hooked in a trace of a smile.

There was a pause before Delhey repeated hoarsely, "Nothing that big . . ."

"No."

The prosecutor squared his shoulders. "All right. Mr. Tanner here will take any statement you want to make on that. Good night." And he turned and marched out.

Sheriff Harvey glared at Armstrong a moment, then he too walked away.

CHAPTER 22

JAMES ARMSTRONG'S PRELIMINARY examination * for the murder of Carol Ann Gebhardt had been set for August 7.

It was exactly two years to the day since the discovery of Marilyn Pindar's corpse and the beginning of the terror that everyone now called The Murders.

A large crowd turned out at the antique district courthouse in Ypsilanti that morning. Among them were Charles and Margaret Pindar, who had come up from Willis to try to get a look at Armstrong—not out of vindictiveness, but in the simple hope that if, by seeing him, they might gain some perception that his *was* the last face their daughter had seen in life, they could go home satisfied that, for them at least, the long uncertainty was over.

---

* In Michigan law, "preliminary examination" in a felony case is tantamount to a grand jury hearing, in which the prosecution must establish both that there has been a crime committed and that there is some evidence that an accused was the perpetrator. The difference is that in Michigan generally such evidence is presented not to a panel but to a judge, who then alone decides whether or not it is sufficient to bind the defendant over for trial.

But the Pindars, who could not get into the tiny courtroom, never saw the prisoner—nor did anyone among the hundreds of curious gathered outside. Formidable security arrangements had been made for this, the accused killer's first public appearance. There had been whispers all week that Armstrong might never make it to court. It was Sheriff Harvey's concern to see that he did, and he had taken all precautions: The night before, he'd had his charge whisked from the jail to a hotel in Ypsilanti and locked up in a room under guard by two deputies; then shortly after dawn this morning, Armstrong had been hustled out through the hotel's rear and was safely inside the courthouse before 7:00 A.M. Harvey also had positioned more than two dozen heavily armed men at all entrances and approaches to the courthouse, and riflemen were conspicuous on rooftops on all sides.

But nothing happened . . . not only outside but inside the courtroom itself.

The much-anticipated hearing was both surprisingly brief and inconclusive. Defense Attorney John Toomey began by advising District Judge Edward Deake that he and his young partner, Robert Francis, were withdrawing from the case at the request of the accused.

Actually, it was James's mother's idea. Shortly before the hearing, the two attorneys had been summoned to the judge's chambers. There they'd found James with his mother's attorney friend Stafford Hardy III, who told them that Mrs. Armstrong's wishes were that they withdraw in favor of counsel to be appointed by the court. Francis had turned to James himself for support, but the youth was red-eyed and seemed befuddled. He could only murmur distractedly that he supposed they had ought to do as his mother wanted.

So now, in open court, Toomey and Francis formally resigned the defense.

Judge Deake swore James in and asked him if this was in accordance with his own wishes. The defendant, standing tall and straight now, neat in a pale blue sport jacket, white shirt with dark blue tie and slacks, said it was.

What was his financial situation? His voice surprisingly firm, James said that he was a student at the university, unemployed, without a bank account or other ready funds.

Did he own any property of value? At the present time, James said flatly, he possessed one operable motorcycle.

The judge therefore postponed preliminary examination one week, pending selection by the court of new defense counsel.

As Armstrong was led from the courtroom, he passed his mother standing anxiously in the first row of benches. For a moment their eyes met, hers glistening wet, his dry and guarded. Her features contorted with emotion, she mouthed *Don't worry, baby, don't worry.*

He read her face without a flicker of expression crossing his own, then he was by her. She reached out after him, trying to touch him, but her hand only brushed a deputy. Another deputy cautioned her to hold her place.

That was it. Less than thirty minutes in all.

The court appointed Richard W. Ryan to represent James Armstrong. Ryan asked for Robert Francis and John Toomey to assist him through the preliminary examination.

At that postponed hearing, on August 14, William Delhey, for the People, introduced nine witnesses, and after five hours Judge Deake ruled that there was "reasonable cause" to believe that James Nolan Armstrong had committed a felony. The accused—now a defendant—was bound over to the circuit court for trial.

Richard Winfield Ryan, fifty-four, tall, gray-haired, distinguished, was a partner in what was then perhaps Ann Arbor's most prestigious law firm, Burke, Burke, Ryan, and Rennell. He probably had as much trial experience as any attorney in the area, considerably more, in fact, than his friend and now adversary Prosecutor William Delhey. Although the bulk of Ryan's experience lay in civil suits—torts, liability—he had made his mark in criminal cases as well. His selection by the court as James Armstrong's new counsel was regarded locally as a distinct plus for the defense.

Boning up with the two younger lawyers, Ryan absorbed from them a passionate feeling that they had a good chance of beating the indictment. Francis and Toomey felt there were a number of solid grounds: improper procedures by the police, both before and after Armstrong's arrest; rather tenuous identification of the accused by alleged eyewitnesses; questionable scientific evidence that would be the real crux of the prosecution's case; and the improbability that the defendant could expect an impartial trial in this emotion-charged community—a circumstance obviously calling for a change of venue.

There was one other thing. From their contact to this point with James Armstrong, Francis and Toomey genuinely believed him to be innocent.

All sound points. The only conclusion Ryan had to make for himself was a personal judgment of the accused. He went to the jail to introduce himself to his client. Armstrong impressed him. The youth was bright, direct, personable. Of his appearance and manner, thought Ryan, looking ahead, James would make an attractive witness in his own behalf.

The lawyer asked him if he had killed Carol Ann Gebhardt. James looked him square in the eye and said he hadn't. Ryan believed him.

On September 5, in circuit court in Ann Arbor's modern county building, Armstrong stood mute to the charge of murder in the first degree and Judge John W. Conlin entered for him a plea of not guilty. Defense counsel then moved to suppress certain evidence and testimony offered by the prosecution in the preliminary examination and also to direct the prosecution to provide full disclosure of all physical and scientific evidence in its possession.

Judge Conlin, however, noting that transcripts of the

earlier proceeding had not yet been filed, declined to rule on the motions before having studied those transcripts. He thus adjourned the hearing until October 3.

When court resumed, the defense waded into the significant issue of suppression. They moved to declare Armstrong's arrest illegal, and thus all primary evidence resulting therefrom inadmissible, because (a) it had been effected under false pretenses and without sufficient warrantable evidence against the accused at the time; (b) search warrants were obtained by misrepresentation and improperly executed; (c) there were improprieties connected with the identification of the defendant by alleged witnesses, which invalidated their testimony as well. Cited specifically was Sheriff Harvey's indefensible effort to influence witnesses Joan Enright and Helga Marks by showing them pictures of the arrested Armstrong prior to identification of him in the lineup (plus the subsequent clumsy maneuver of shifting the accused from one place to another in the lineup so as, obviously, to make him stand out).

As for the search warrants, there were misrepresentations by the police as to what they would be looking for. Viz: They'd asked for a warrant to impound and examine defendant's automobile. But to date there had been no prior indication, stated or implied, that any vehicle other than a motorcycle had figured in the crime in question.

More specifically, included in these warrants were at least three glaring items that the prosecution knew bore no relation to the charge against Armstrong: (1) A .22-caliber firearm. No firearm was involved in the instant case! (2) Fingerprints of Marilyn Pindar in both his car and his apartment. She had been slain in July of 1967. Defendant's car was a 1968 Oldsmobile, which he did not acquire until the fall of 1968. And he did not move into his present address until February of that year. (3) Prints of Jill Hersch, also in his car. She was killed in July of 1968—again, months before he acquired the Oldsmobile.

What it all amounted to, defense held, was that the

police and prosecution simply had had suspicion that James Armstrong was involved with *some* crimes, but that lacking real proof, had arrested him first, *then* asked for the court's blanket permission to turn the key on his life. The defense, therefore, moved for dismissal.

Judge Conlin declared the arrest legal. As for the other matters, they would be considered and ruled upon at a subsequent hearing, which he set for October 14.

On that date, Conlin ruled against defense motions both for dismissal and arbitrary suppression. Ryan then raised the issue of change of venue. Conlin agreed to hear arguments on that on October 29. But by then, Judge Conlin had been caught up in protracted pretrial hearings in the Edgar Hatton, Jr., homicide case, and he had again to postpone the Armstrong hearing to December 17.

Armstrong had long since been moved from his solitary cage in the basement to a cell upstairs, in the jail's so-called maximum security wing. In the improved conditions, able to circulate among other inmates, his state of mind had gradually settled to stoic acceptance of his position.

His mother wrote nearly every day and visited him each Sunday afternoon, and her theme was consistent: Chin up, they would get through this, she was going to get him out. He was still her "baby."

James wondered why his Aunt Fran never came anymore. She wrote every so often, and she'd sent him some packages of fruit and homemade cookies, books and magazines; but since a couple of visits right at the beginning, she'd never come back.

His mother didn't know and didn't care. He should forget about the Louckses. They could not help him. . . .

These months had been an unreal time for Dana and Fran Loucks and their boys, all feeling so desperately in the middle, agonizing over somehow having "betrayed" ones they so loved. But it probably was most telling on Fran, not only for James but for Peg.

Because of all this, she feared she'd lost her dearest sister.

She hadn't been able to tell Peg right away of the awful, unwanted role she and Dana had been compelled to play. That frantic midnight call from Peg: *James has been arrested! For MURDER! Oh, Fran, how? What can we do? Can't DANA do something? They've put James in a CAGE—like an animal. My baby! . . . Oh, Fran—!* Fran could only reach out to her then, try to be her strength.

She'd gone with Peg to the jail the next afternoon. When James was finally brought into the prisoners' cage, Fran could have died for the two of them. Peg rushed to him, flinging herself against the steel-mesh partition, trying to touch him, crying out consolation to her son. James's eyes were red-streaked, his hair tousled, but he seemed devoid of emotion, not responding to his mother in any way that Fran could see, just stolidly waiting out her anguish: *It's all right, Mother. Take it easy. . . .*

Then James had noticed Fran, standing off to the side. And for the first time his eyes showed life and his face softened: *Aunt Fran!* She moved to the cage alongside Peg, and James placed his hands on the screen and pushed his fingers through to touch hers. Suddenly he was a scared boy again, and his fears spilled over pleading lips: *For God's sake, Aunt Fran, HELP me!* Choked herself, she promised to try, they all would be trying . . . and she turned to Peg. Her sister had stepped away, and her face was a frigid mask then, shafts of hurt and resentment boring at Fran from slit eyes.

The door between them closed firmly later, when they were alone, as Fran at last brought herself to tell Peg all that had happened. Withdrawing from her, Peg gathered Tom and Dawn and returned that day to Center Line. None of them ever returned to the Loucks house, or ever called. . . .

Richard Ryan had begun to have second thoughts

about his client. The optimistic defense he had assessed
was showing signs of fragility. James's alibi witnesses
for the time of the Gebhardt slaying were inconsistent;
there were possible gaps that could prove inconclusive.
The prosecution's witnesses might be more convincing
in their identification of him as the motorcyclist than
Ryan had at first thought. The scientific trace evidence
in the Louckses' basement was, of itself, potentially the
weakest and yet at the same time strongest indictment
of Armstrong—technically, open to impressive attack,
but from a jury's unscientific, curiously human view-
point, raising the unavoidable question: Just how did
those damaging materials happen to get there if not
through the defendant?

And Ryan had also discovered some of the unpleas-
ant things about Armstrong that the police had learned.
It was becoming plain that the boy was not the All-
American Boy he looked to be. Could he even use
James as his *own* character witness?

And then Bill Delhey came to him with a report that
James, in an emotional moment, was again indicating
that he might want to "tell everything!"

Sheriff Harvey, despite all proscriptions to the contrary, had never stopped trying to soften up his prize
prisoner. He'd only gone from heavy-handed intimida-
tion to the buddy approach—infiltrating the youth's
defenses with talks about shared interests, like sports or
motorcycles (the sheriff admitted to being a bike
freak!). And he'd succeeded in weaning a few cautious
flickers of response.

Then had come a day in early November when
James's emotional state seemed just right. He'd had to
undergo another unnerving lineup, standing with four
others under hot lights for an hour while unseen witnesses observed them—for purposes unspecified—
from behind a see-through mirrored wall. James was
despondent when it was over and, Harvey felt, vulnerable. The sheriff brought him to his office. There, he
let James know that the lineup had been for *him,* that
it had to do with the Audrey Sakol murder . . . and im-

plied that the results decidedly had gone against him. It was beginning to appear, Harvey chirped, that even if James *could* somehow wriggle out of Gebhardt, they would only nail him on another. The sheriff shook his head sympathetically. Life in prison was all James could look forward to, no matter what. . . .

Unless . . . nobody really wanted the tragic waste of one who might yet become a useful member of society were he able to be rehabilitated. Even if such a person had killed seven people, if he was *sick* he couldn't really be accountable; there couldn't be *guilt* if he said, yes, I killed those people, but I never knew what I was doing, *please help me!* . . . Then it would not be a matter of punishment but *treatment*. And when he was well, he could walk away a free man and make amends in his own way, between himself and his God. It would take courage, but if he were to confess . . .

Damn that Doug Harvey! thought Richard Ryan. He told the prosecutor to call the sheriff off. Of course he would not permit his client to "confess"! Then Ryan hurried to the jail and had a long private talk with James.

It was a dismaying interview. The boy no longer was denying so firmly as he had that he was guilty. He was even wondering about a possible plea of insanity!

Where had he got *that* notion?

From Sheriff Harvey, James conceded. He wasn't saying that he was guilty, but the possibility of life in prison—!

Had he lost all confidence in his own defense, that his innocence, once established, would prevail?

He just didn't know anymore. . . .

Ryan was left greatly disturbed. He decided upon a bold course. Had James ever been given a polygraph examination? He was not thinking now of submitting him to a police testing but to a private one. It might be the only way they could intelligently plan which course to follow next—as to either the most effective defense strategy or, if it seemed to be the only other viable option, "insanity."

Whatever Mr. Ryan thought best, James said.

Back at his office, Ryan made the arrangements. He informed Prosecutor Delhey that the examination was to be unconditionally confidential and the results inaccessible to later use by the prosecution until, or if, authorized by defendant or his counsel. Delhey understood; he was intrigued.

The next night, Ryan and Sheriff Harvey, flanked by armed deputies, took Armstrong from the jail in a whipping rain across Main Street to the county building. On the second floor, Judge Conlin's chamber had been set up for the testing, and the polygraph operator was there, a marshal standing by.

Armstrong was seated and rigged up to the machine. Then all but the operator left the room, and the door was closed.

Ryan and Harvey, with the two deputies and the marshal, waited tensely in the adjoining office.

Forty-five minutes dragged by . . . close to an hour. Then the door opened and the operator appeared in the doorway. His face was grim. Behind him, they could hear sniffling, rhythmic sobbing. "Mr. Ryan," the man said, "I think you'd better come in."

They stood together in the doorway a minute or two, whispering. Then Ryan went into the other office, shutting the door behind him. After another half hour, Ryan emerged. Armstrong came out behind him, head bowed, shoulders drooping; a sob escaped him, sending a tremor through his frame.

Ryan said very quietly, but positively: "All right, gentlemen, the experiment is over. You may take my client back now."

Sheriff Harvey stared at him. "Did you get what you wanted?"

The lawyer returned a steady gaze. "What we 'got' is nobody's business but ours. As far as you or anybody else is concerned, it never happened. And," he added pointedly, "there'll be *no statements.*"

Tight-lipped, the sheriff wheeled and, taking hold of Armstrong's limp arm, led him roughly back to jail.

James's mother was shocked and bitterly indignant to learn of the secret polygraph test of her son. Whose side was Ryan on? What *right* did he have—? He summarized the tentative conclusions the distressed analyst had drawn from the incomplete examination . . . and said it might be wise in the circumstances to consider a change in James's planned defense. If they could show that he had *not* been in full control of his senses . . .

Plead *insanity?* Mrs. Armstrong rose up in a rage. *Never!*

Three weeks later, Richard Ryan was off the case. He wasn't surprised. He *was* relieved.

If defense attorney Richard Ryan had not been surprised when he was fired by Louella Armstrong, he was to be astounded—along with everyone else—by the caliber of his replacement. Somehow the woman had managed to retain one of the premier law firms in Detroit, Louisell & Barris.

Senior partner Joseph Louisell was acknowledged as among the canniest and most successful trial lawyers anywhere. His fees came almost exclusively high —prohibitive, surely, to a young defendant claiming indigence and a divorced mother whose only visible means of support was as a restaurant waitress!

The rumor mills churned out all manner of fascinating speculation as to what *really* lay behind this improbable new development—the two most extreme, and therefore most popular, theories being that either (a) "Mafia money" had, for some mysterious reason, found its way into the Armstrong case, or, on quite another level, that (b) some big New York publisher or major Hollywood film studio (or a combination of the two) had committed enormous sums in return for the sole rights to James Armstrong's "true story."

The truth, however, was much less exotic or arcane than people wanted to believe. Louella Armstrong, determined to spare nothing for her embattled son, had managed it almost singlehanded—with a little help from her monied friend—primarily by remortgaging her home.

She had started shopping for a change of counsel from the moment she'd learned of the polygraph test that Richard Ryan had permitted without her knowledge or consent. Good God, what kind of defense was *that?* Louella often encountered lawyers at the restaurant she worked at in downtown Detroit, which was close by the criminal courts. She knew some of them by name. To say hello to, even.

Ivan Barris, partner of the great Louisell, came into the restaurant many mornings for late breakfast. Louella stopped at his table one day and asked him if he could recommend a good attorney. Barris was not encouraging. It *was* an interesting case, of course, but she had to understand the costs of such an undertaking. However, if she did wish to pursue it, she might have a talk with one of their junior associates, an extremely bright, vigorous young lawyer named Neil Fink.

Fink saw her and was personally enthralled by her predicament. He didn't care all that much about the money. He saw it frankly as a tremendous opportunity: the biggest murder case in the area in ages, the defendant possibly being railroaded. There was everything to gain, hardly anything to lose.

Neither Louisell nor Barris liked it. It was too iffy. There was too much public feeling about it. (The people *wanted* their murderer!) Nor was there even much prospect, evidently, of being compensated adequately.

But Neil Fink was forceful as well as ambitious. He argued that it would be in the best tradition of the law, the truest intent of justice. It would be *courageous*. And Mrs. Armstrong thought she could raise about $20,000 ($15,000 of that by taking out a new mortgage on her house in Center Line, with her patron as cosigner).

Twenty thousand would barely cover a couple of months' *expenses!* Ivan Barris protested. Louisell also was doubtful, but he continued to hear Fink out.

The intense young man could be a hell of a trial lawyer one day, the wily courtroom veteran considered.

Finally, Louisell sat back, characteristically loosening his rumpled tie, and said it was really against his better judgment . . . but they might as well look into it anyway.

Joseph W. Louisell and Neil H. Fink presented themselves at the rescheduled hearing on December 17 and requested a further continuance of at least another month to allow adequate time to assimilate themselves into the case. Judge Conlin set January 21 for the pretrial hearing at which a trial date might finally be decided upon.

The defense next filed a new motion petitioning for a change of venue, previously submitted by Richard Ryan.

Personally Judge Conlin felt that there was really no place else in Michigan where Armstrong would receive any more impartial a trial; the so-called publicity about both the long series of murders and the final apprehension of the accused hardly had been confined to Washtenaw County—it had been followed anxiously, breathlessly, everywhere in the state, across the Midwest, doubtless in many parts of the nation at large. Nonetheless, Conlin agreed to put it to the state court of appeals for an opinion.

The determination came back that a change of venue from Ann Arbor was not deemed appropriate unless and until all efforts to seat a "fair" jury had failed there. The motion thus was denied a second time.

All this back-and-forth caused still further postponements in the pretrial hearing—past January 21 into February.

Then, on February 11, the court was informed that Joseph Louisell had been stricken by a heart attack and was in intensive care at a Detroit hospital. The hearing was adjourned once again, to April 20.

On April 15, in Salinas, California, a Monterey County grand jury finally sat to deliberate an indictment against James Nolan Armstrong in the murder of seventeen-year-old Ginger Lee Neary nine and one-half months before. . . .

This action had become rather an erratic football. By the fall of 1969, the Monterey police, their investigation buttressed by some invaluable help from Michigan criminalistic laboratories, had been convinced they had a solid case against Armstrong. District Attorney Bertram A. Young, however, was unenthusiastic about pursuing a formal indictment. If Armstrong was convicted and sentenced in Michigan —which, from all Young knew of the circumstances, seemed a good probability—why should California bother? By the time they might ever get their hands on him, there would hardly still be a public mandate for his recall to Monterey County . . . nor, to be practical, was it by then likely to serve any useful political purpose locally.

Young also resented what he regarded as unconscionable pressure put on him by Michigan to follow up with an indictment. The prosecutor's office and State Police there were working on the principle that if Armstrong were charged in California—where he could face the death penalty, as against mandatory life in his home state—he might be persuaded to "cooperate" in helping Michigan to close the books on the Washtenaw murders.

Still . . . it *was* tempting. Monterey did have a compelling case against Armstrong. Several witnesses had positively identified him (from photographs) and also his car, in which his victim was believed to have been last seen. (The make on the car had been bolstered by records at Tolan Cadillac-Oldsmobile in Salinas, where it had been serviced three days after the girl's disappearance: work order #24061 there showed minor repairs to a 1968 Olds Cutlass, Michigan license number RV-0101, registered to L. M. Armstrong— James's mother—of Center Line, Michigan.)

Then there had been the tip from Armstrong's friend, Tony Monte. In September, following Monte's return to Ann Arbor from Phoenix, Monterey Assistant District Attorney Ed Barnes had accompanied Investigator Bob Taylor and Detective Tom Shepherd east to interrogate him and, if they could, Armstrong himself. The accused killer would not talk to them, but Monte had proved communicative. Among other things, he mentioned the case of poison oak that James had picked up and sought treatment for while in the Monterey area.

This had excited the California investigators. The particular spot in the dense Carmel ravine where Ginger Neary's body had been lugged and abandoned was clustered with poison oak—at least one detective who'd searched the brush there had come down with a painful infection from it. Taylor and Shepherd had scouted all the physicians in Salinas and environs and found one who, in the first week of July, had treated a young man fitting Armstrong's description!

They also, of course, had the piece of red fabric discovered behind the front seat of Armstrong's car by the Michigan crime lab, which matched the cloth belt used to strangle Ginger Neary—making it virtually certain that she had been in that car during the last hours of her life.

Thus, California did appear to have a tryable case, and Young had found himself unable to resist indefinitely the tide of pressure, not only from Michigan but within his own constituency.

When, early on April 15, word reached Neil Fink in Detroit of the Salinas hearing, he immediately telephoned Judge John Conlin in Ann Arbor. Fink asked him to intercede with the California authorities to vouchsafe that should an indictment result there it be sealed, lest the news have a disastrously prejudicial effect upon prospective jurors in Washtenaw County and perhaps destroy the last possibility of Armstrong's getting a fair trial anywhere in Michigan. The judge agreed and relayed such an official request to the Monterey County district attorney.

The Monterey panel deliberated that entire day, hearing testimony from fourteen state's witnesses. At 6:30 P.M., an indictment of murder in the first degree was returned against the accused.

At the precise time of this verdict, back in Detroit Neil Fink was at the theater watching *Hello, Dolly!* with his wife. At intermission, he was summoned by a call from an associate, who informed him of the California indictment. Racing to his office, he spent an hour on the long-distance telephone tracking down a former colleague from Detroit who now practiced in Berkeley, Dave Rosenthal. Fink talked Rosenthal into getting to Salinas by the fastest means possible to initiate legal steps to *insure* a ban on disclosure of the indictment.

It being too late that evening to fly to Monterey, Rosenthal drove the 115 miles from Berkeley. About 10:00 P.M., P.S.T., he reached Superior Court Judge Gordon Campbell, who agreed to issue an oral injunction that night sealing the grand jury minutes.

But it was already too late. Whether by misdirection or perversity, barely minutes before Judge Campbell's order was handed down, word of Armstrong's indictment got out and was being transmitted over the national news wires. No one ever acknowledged the leak —the Monterey district attorney's office claiming that it had abided by the first request from Michigan.

It hit like a bombshell in the Ann Arbor area, just as Neil Fink had feared. He was bitter; he felt it had been a setup, that the Michigan State Police had engineered it to guarantee the worst damaging effect on his helpless client.

There was nothing he could do about it but enter another petition for a change of venue for defendant's trial. Judge Conlin was sympathetic . . . but he again ruled against the motion.

CHAPTER 23

THE OPENING DATE for the Michigan trial of James Armstrong was finally set for June 2.

Joseph Louisell was back, gray and depleted alongside the brisk Fink; yet the sage authority of his presence, the very bulk of the old campaigner, lent a challenging air of confrontation to the proceedings. Nonetheless, it was plain that Neil Fink was carrying the ball in this case, Louisell preferring, for the moment, to coach from the sidelines. Limited in resources, Fink had taken on but one investigator, a beautiful twenty-year-old coed at E.M.U. named Margo Doble, who, as editor of the student newspaper, *The Eastern Echo,* had been covering the murders from the beginning.

Fink saw the prosecution's case in a four-part sequence: one, establishing that the accused had in fact been cruising through Ypsilanti on his motorcycle around midday of July 23, 1969; two, that he had been positively identified by the two women in Wigs by Joan as the motorcyclist who'd driven off with Carol

Ann Gebhardt between 12:30 and 1:00 P.M. that day; three, that pathology had determined the time of her death to have been no later than 3:00 P.M. the same afternoon; and four, that trace evidence had confirmed the victim's presence in the basement of the vacant Loucks home, to which only the accused had access at the time . . . *ergo,* James Armstrong was the only person who could have killed her.

There was little rebuttal that could be made to James's cruising that day—the prosecution would present a bagful of testimony affirming that. Nor could the time of death be disputed—pathology was pathology.

The defense did have three areas on which to focus its rebuttal: one, on the alleged "positive" eyewitness identification of the defendant as the motorcyclist who had driven off with the victim—a key prosecution point which had several questionable aspects to it; two, on defendant's *actual* whereabouts between approximately 12:50 P.M. that day, when the victim was last seen, and 3:00 P.M.—to which at least three alibi witnesses would testify; three, on the highly technical and, it was felt, debatable methods by which the state claimed to have confirmed the victim's presence in the Loucks house.

Fink and Louisell believed the identification by the wig shop women most vulnerable and repetitioned the court—as Ryan had done without success—that their testimony be held inadmissible at trial.

Judge Conlin returned a ruling that, while there surely had been irregularities in the identification procedure, the relevant point in the end was that the witnesses had *not* identified the accused from the pictures shown them—indeed, had refused to be persuaded or intimidated into doing so—but *had* identified him at the lineup (and in the presence of counsel). The women's identification of Armstrong would stand, to be believed or not by the trial jury.

On the morning of Tuesday, June 2, Courtroom No. 2 on the second floor of the Washtenaw County Build-

ing in Ann Arbor was jammed to capacity minutes
after the doors were opened. A long line of disappointed spectators had to be turned away.

At least two-thirds of the courtroom's sixty seats
were allotted to the news media. More than forty
newspapers, magazines, television and radio outlets
from around the nation, plus local press and wire-
service representatives, had sought credentials. Many
out-of-town newsmen had to be denied unless they
would agree to share facilities.

Security precautions surrounding the defendant were
exceptional. Although the county building was only
across North Main Street from the jail, the prisoner
was to be transported back and forth daily in an ar-
mored police van, surrounded by sheriff's deputies
under the personal command of Sheriff Doug Harvey.
All traffic was to be halted on Main and the inter-
secting streets each time the van took Armstrong between the jail and the underground parking facility of
the courthouse. He would enter the county building
through a heavily guarded private entrance in the
basement and be taken upstairs directly to a sealed de-
tention room just off the trial courtroom.

The trial began with *voir dire,* selection of a jury. An
initial panel of fifty prospects had been called from the
county's eligible June list of 350, and two additional
panels numbering sixty and fifty respectively had also
been notified to be ready. The court was prepared to
exhaust the entire list to seat fourteen final trial jurors
(including two alternates) agreeable to both sides.

Judge Conlin patiently explained the procedure to
be followed: The first fourteen prospective jurors would
be called up at random, and each would be examined by the judge to find possible cause why he or she
should be excused. Any excused would be replaced by
another from the empaneled list, who would be similarly examined. It would continue this way—as long as
might be necessary—until the judge had passed, i.e.,
had found no cause to excuse, fourteen of them.
Then each of that fourteen would be subject to exami-

THE MICHIGAN MURDERS 341

nation by both prosecution and defense attorneys.
Either side could dismiss any "for cause"; in addition,
the prosecution was permitted up to fifteen "peremptory challenges"—i.e., the right to excuse any juror
with or without expressed cause—and the defense,
twenty. Any so excused would have to be replaced by
new jurors. Then of course the process of initial examination by the judge would have to be repeated until
there were again fourteen "passed" jurors, and then
the examination of each by opposing counsel would
resume.

Joseph Louisell and Neil Fink sat side by side at the
defense table with a poker-faced James Armstrong. On
the other side, however, Prosecutor William Delhey
was alone. His chief assistant, Booker Williams, who
had worked so hard both on the murder investigations and then in spearheading the intricate prepara-
tion of the case, was absent, occupied with a stunning
personal tragedy. The previous week, his thirty-seven-
year-old wife, Arletta, had suffered a cerebral hemor-
rhage. She had not yet regained consciousness, and
Booker refused to leave her side at the hospital.

Judge Conlin asked each prospective juror a series
of questions about his or her background, education,
occupation, etc. Then he read to each the entire list
of sixty-six principals who were to take part in the
trial—fifty-eight announced witnesses (forty-six for the
prosecution, twelve for the defense), plus opposing
counsel and their aides, the defendant, and the judge
himself—asking if the juror knew or had prejudice, one
way or the other, toward any. Finally he asked how
much each was acquainted with the facts surrounding
the case—had read, heard, or discussed—and whether
he or she had formulated any opinions or conclusions
as to the innocence or guilt of the accused.

One of the first examined was a middle-aged housewife, a thirty-year resident of the community. The
judge gently elicited from her that she probably did
already have an opinion about the defendant.

Based on what? inquired Conlin.

On that there haven't been any more murders since—

Then the defendant would have to *prove* his innocence in order to change her opinion?

She knew *she* certainly would want to clear herself if she were innocent—that was just the way she felt about it, the woman added.

Now, now . . . The judge smiled at her benignly. She had every right to her own opinion, there could be nothing wrong in that. Excused. . . .

John Conlin, sixty-five, was a full-blooded sculpture of what everyone wants or hopes a judge to be. Spencer Tracy come down from the screen to real life. White-haired, ruddy-complexioned; responsive features that could be transformed in a flash from grave concern to twinkling humor . . . a sagacious Irish countenance mirroring in one view the solidity of Holy Name Society communion breakfasts and years of fish every Friday, and in another the heartiness of Saturday night beef and bourbon. Perceptive, wise, imperturbable, warm, he was always in command and commanded respectful confidence.

After forty years in the law, the last thirteen as a jurist, no objection ever caught John Conlin by surprise, no approach to the bench ever was received with other than courteous solicitude, recesses were always cheerfully granted (partly, at least, because the judge welcomed any chance to light up a cigarette; he was a two-to-three-pack-a-day Camel smoker). Trial participants all were addressed by name. Ignorance or misunderstandings of law—by jurors *or* counsel—were acknowledged with patient explanations. Deception was never presumed.

Conlin had not particularly wanted this difficult case. He had been chosen by lot from among the other available circuit judges, drawn by the court clerk. But once assigned, he had done all his homework. And no one, the defense included, could have hoped for a better man to sit here. . . .

It took the judge three court days, through Thursday, June 4, to pass a panel of fourteen jurors. Eight women and six men were sworn and tentatively seated. Examination by opposing counsel would begin on Monday the eighth.

On Sunday, Arletta Williams died at St. Joseph Mercy Hospital without ever having regained consciousness. She left her husband with seven children, the oldest fourteen, the youngest a year and a half.

Her funeral service was set for Wednesday afternoon, the tenth, at the Metropolitan Memorial Baptist Church, burial at Sheldon Cemetery in Wayne County, a few miles east of Ypsilanti.

Court was recessed that day.

Prosecutor Delhey exercised the first peremptory challenge of a juror (the civil libertarian-type wife of a University of Michigan sociology professor). Joseph Louisell followed with one for the defense (a stern-faced factory worker, formerly from Tennessee and an ex-marine).

It was only the beginning. Sharply conscious of the change-of-venue issue, both prosecution and defense were determined to be meticulous, ultrascrupulous in working to pick not merely the most "favorable" jury in either view but the most absolutely impartial. The maneuverings would continue for a full month. . . .

The engaging Louisell dominated these early proceedings. He was an old master at it, lingering over his selections with all the unhurried, loving calculation of a chess player.

Louisell bore no resemblance to the so-called Detroit "mouthpiece" of the headlines. Fifty-four, portly, rumpled, hair casually tousled, with soft eyes that saw and understood much behind rimless spectacles that often slipped down his nose, wearing a round sad Dickensian face that suggested a subdued jollity, he could have been anyone's family doctor, the kind who still made house calls.

A native of Duluth, Minnesota, son of a lawyer, from the University of Minnesota Louisell had gone on to University of Detroit Law and, upon admission to the bar there in 1941, had stayed. For three years he was an assistant prosecuting attorney for Wayne County. Then he'd gone out on his own, and he'd done well. His first headlined trial had been in 1950 when, as a thirty-four-year-old court-appointed counsel, he'd successfully defended a former United Auto Workers officer and convicted felon, Carl E. Bolton, in a shotgun-murder attempt (in 1948) on the life of U.A.W. President Walter Reuther. (After a twenty-two-day trial, the jury needed only an hour and a half to acquit Bolton—whereupon he was returned to the state prison to serve out a previous ten-to-fifteen-year sentence for armed robbery.)

After that, Louisell had been tabbed a "star" criminal lawyer, a label given permanence as, over the next two decades, he had taken on as clients such reputed organized-crime figures in Detroit as Pete Licavoli, Tony and Vito Giacalone, Mike Rubino—all cited by a United States Senate rackets committee in 1963 as "syndicate" bigshots. Few outsiders realized that the bulk of Louisell's practice—as much as two-thirds—actually resided on the dry, "respectable" civil and corporate side of the law, where the wealth and security were.

But Louisell's courtroom manner was neither aggressive nor stuffed-shirt. He was just folks, Clarence Darrow underplayed: flourishing a crumpled handkerchief to mop his brow, perspiring in the summer's heat, an occasional luxurious stretching of his arms and neck, and the friendly wink at a juror fascinated watching his girth unfold. In questioning, he was almost unfailingly courtly, understanding, smiling and nodding at responses. But when, every so often, he bore in on someone with a salvo of abrupt, pointed questions, a tense hush seized the courtroom, as though an immense undercurrent of power, long and patiently contained, was about to be unleashed.

Louisell thus held center stage throughout the long *voir dire*. For every one of the prospective jurors he repeated the same performance, asked the same moving question: Lumbering around behind the handsome, sober young defendant, placing his great fatherly paw on the seated Armstrong's shoulder, in a voice liquid with compassion: "Now look into your heart, Mrs.———, and tell us if you feel that you could consider all the testimony in this case in good conscience, and by a vote of Not Guilty return James here to a place in the community?"

Not "the defendant" or "the accused." Just "James here." Big, protective Joe Louisell's adopted "son." It was a hard moment of truth for each of them.

On June 29, a jury still not empaneled, the defense again petitioned for a change of venue. This time the motion was based on a survey conducted throughout Washtenaw County, at counsel's request, by James McConnell, a Ph.D. in psychology at the University of Michigan. Dr. McConnell, employing U. of M. students as volunteer interviewers, since mid-April had canvassed a random sampling of former jury members. His results showed that 95 percent of those responding knew of James Armstrong and recalled at least some pretrial publicity about his case; and more than 85 percent identified him specifically with "the murders."

Judge Conlin took the offering under advisement—then again denied the venue motion. The judge had already decided privately that if the entire panel of 350 eligible jurors was finally exhausted before a jury was formed, then *he* would recommend change of venue, probably to Lansing. But the thought that kept troubling him was, if they couldn't put together an intelligent, fair-minded jury in a progressive city like Ann Arbor, where *could* they?

By July 9, 294 eligible jurors having been examined, thirteen had been seated, although any of those still could be subject to peremptory challenge by opposing counsel—three challenges then remaining to the defense and four to the prosecution. That morning, a possible fourteenth juror was examined and passed by Judge Conlin . . . Conlin, and at noon, the court recessed for lunch.

Resuming at 1:30 P.M., the prosecution said that it had no objection to the last juror tentatively seated. All looked toward Louisell and Fink, almost sure to challenge *somebody*. There was a pause, and then Louisell rose and said:

"Your Honor, I believe we have a jury."

William Delhey and Booker Williams (back in the fight now) almost fell off their chairs. Then they embraced.

The decisive panel had six men and six women. Of the twelve, seven were university or college graduates, two had some college, two were high-school graduates, one had been educated up to the eleventh grade. Four of the men were engineers (one of them also a retired high-school principal), one an automotive systems analyst, another a factory worker. Of the women, aside from Mrs. Vining, two others were married to U. of M. professors, one was an elementary-school teacher, two listed themselves as "housewives" (although one of these also had a fulltime outside job). The jury ranged in age from twenty-eight to seventy-one.

Judge Conlin ordered the actual trial to begin on Monday, July 20.

James Armstrong had been waiting almost one full year.

The first morning was given largely to opening statements by opposing counsel.

"The People will show that on July Twenty-third, Nineteen Hundred and Sixty-nine, James Nolan Armstrong deliberately and maliciously took the life of Carol Ann Gebhardt. . . ." Prosecutor Delhey detailed the points of the prosecution's case briskly, without histrionics or other florid show of outrage. Cool, precise, authoritative, Delhey was the reassuring symbol of public guardianship, a figure of integrity all the more impressive for his appearance—tall, silver-haired, icy blue eyes, firm jawline.

Neil Fink spoke for the defense. Only three years out of Detroit College of Law, Fink's presence contrasted sharply with Louisell's. Short but solidly built, dapper in expensive suit and colorful tie, Fink gave the impression of urgent aggressiveness—the fast-talking lawyer of impatient mind and sharp tongue.

Fink charged that the prosecution's whole case was built on misinformation, falsehood, and insupportable conclusions as to so-called scientific "evidence" . . . and, he added, on vindictiveness. He turned and addressed the jury: "I am convinced that after you have listened to all the testimony in this case, you will go into the jury deliberation room with total fidelity to your oaths. You will have a doubt—a reasonable doubt, a serious doubt, not a capricious doubt—and with the fidelity to your oath, you will return a verdict of Not Guilty."

The first three days of the trial set the stage for drama.

First, witnesses recalled the details of Carol Ann Gebhardt's disappearance. And the medical examiner's and pathologist's autopsy reports established that her death had come approximately between 1:00 and 3:00 P.M. on the day of her disappearance.

Then the prosecution began to weave the defendant into the scenario. E.M.U. Campus Patrolman Larry Mathewson described having noticed James Armstrong riding a big, heavily chromed blue motorcycle shortly after noon on July 23, wearing a horizontally striped T-shirt. Seven additional witnesses then testified as having also encountered Armstrong cruising the vicinity that Wednesday; all young females, each had been approached by Armstrong on his motorcycle. All these encounters had taken place between approximately 11:30 A.M. and 12:30 P.M. within a ten-square-block area on the university's perimeter, the last on Ballard Street, between Forest Avenue and Cross Street.

Looking at an exhibit map of Ypsilanti, it was easy to see what the prosecution was building up to. Ballard Street was probably the most direct walking route from the campus to the downtown shopping area. If Carol Ann Gebhardt set out walking from her dormitory to the wig shop, the probabilities were strong that she would have taken Ballard Street. The walk would have taken her about fifteen minutes. Since she'd left at approximately 12:25, Carol Ann might well have been walking along Ballard Street at about the time James Armstrong was on the same route "cruising."

The fourth day of the trial, the focus turned specifically to the defendant's motorcycles.

First to be called on Thursday, July 23 (the anniversary of Carol Ann Gebhardt's death), was the young woman with whom Armstrong had made a date to go swimming on that day one year before, but who'd been stood up.

Vera Bradley, herself a motorcycle buff, said that he'd usually driven a green Triumph with high handlebars, a square rear-view mirror on the left bar. But on Sunday, July 20, 1969, Armstrong had showed up on a big blue heavily chromed Triumph, a 650, which Miss Bradley had not seen before—with standard handlebars, no mirror. He told her he'd got it while in California recently.

Prosecutor Delhey asked Miss Bradley if she had ever seen the blue Triumph again.

She said she had. The day James was arrested, there was so much talk about *the* motorcycle that she went to his boardinghouse on Emmet Street to see for herself if it could be true. In the garage she saw four bikes, chained together: two smaller machines, Bultacos, and the two Triumphs. The Triumphs each looked a little different. The blue one now had high handlebars, like the ones that used to be on the green bike, and the green bike had standard bars.

Then how could she tell with certainty that the blue Triumph was the same vehicle that defendant had driven with her that Sunday, the twentieth of July?

Because, puzzled by the different handlebars, she took a close look at both bikes. And she knew enough about motorcycles to tell that, aside from the bars, they *were* the same. The blue Triumph even had a dent in the front fender, which she'd particularly noticed.

The only mirror on either Triumph then was a round, kind of beat-up one on the green bike. She saw no sign of the square mirror James used to have. She remembered how he used to switch that from one to another of his bikes, whichever one he wanted to ride. . . .

Delhey then requested permission to bring into court Armstrong's two Triumph motorcycles. As deputies wheeled in the pair of glistening machines, positioning them, upright on their kick stands, in front of the jury box, the courtroom stirred, every neck craning for a look.

Then Joseph Louisell cross-examined Vera Bradley. The young woman would not change her statement that the high handlebars now on the blue Triumph formerly had been on the green—that, in substance, they must have been switched.

"Miss Bradley," Louisell boomed, "were I to represent to you now that these high handlebars—which you claim to have been on the green Triumph in the spring of nineteen sixty-nine—were in fact purchased only in *July* of that year, would *that* change your testimony?"

"No, sir. Because I don't believe it's true."

"No further questions."

No further questions? The courtroom buzzed. Why would Louisell quit so easily?

The reality was not so puzzling. Louisell and Fink knew very well that James Armstrong had stolen the blue Triumph—at the least. They had gone as far as they safely could go with specifics about his motor-

cycles, without risking opening a can of worms that the
hungry prosecution might find especially savory.

Joan Enright was called. Under William Delhey's careful questioning, the blond wig-shop proprietress told
her story evenly enough. Carol Ann Gebhardt had
come into Joan's at 12:30 Wednesday, or a little after.
She was in the shop fifteen or twenty minutes. While
Helga Marks worked on Carol Ann's hair, Mrs. Enright happened to glance out of the shop window and
noticed a young man sitting on a motorcycle just outside on Washington Street, apparently waiting for
someone. She went to the open doorway to get a better
look at him: He had on a striped kind of T-shirt and
Levi's; dark-haired, trimmed short but with longish
sideburns; nice looking. His bike had a lot of chrome
on it, with a dark blue tank. The handlebars (re-
plying to Delhey's direct question) were standard,
and there was a square mirror on the left bar.

Carol Ann left the shop, and Mrs. Enright and Mrs.
Marks both saw her climb onto the back of the young
man's bike. They watched as the two drove away,
south toward Michigan Avenue.

"That would have been," Delhey asked, "about a
quarter to one, ten of at the latest?"

"About that."

"Did you ever see Carol Ann Gebhardt again?"

"No."

"Or the motorcyclist?"

"Yes."

"On what occasion?"

"In a police lineup at the county jail on August
first, nineteen sixty-nine."

"Do you recognize him now in this courtroom?"

"Yes. The defendant," she said, pointing to James
Armstrong.

Armstrong's face darkened as he stared back at her,
his eyes narrowing and lips tightening.

Neil Fink took the cross-examination.

He had planned a two-pronged attack: Doubt to

be laid not only to her alleged identification of James Armstrong as the motorcyclist, but also the critical time factor.

Could the deceased, he began, have entered her shop any earlier than 12:30 that day?

"I don't think so. I suppose it's *possible,* but—"

"Could it have been *later?*"

"It could have been, some."

"Say, twelve forty-five?"

"I really don't think it was that late. But I wouldn't want to swear. . . ."

"So if she'd come in a little before twelve thirty, say twelve twenty-five, she would have been out of there by around twelve forty. And if she'd come in after twelve thirty, say any time up to twelve forty-five, it would have been close to one o'clock before she left. Correct?"

"Yes, but as I say—"

"Let's go on. You testified that you noticed a man on a motorcycle outside, and you stepped into the doorway to observe him. How far would you say he was from where you stood?"

"I don't know. Twenty feet, maybe."

"Would you say *thirty* feet?"

"I guess it could be. . . . I don't know."

"It is just thirty feet, as a matter of fact. Mrs. Enright, do you have twenty-twenty vision?"

"No."

"Do you wear eyeglasses?"

"Sometimes."

"For what reason?"

"For . . . distance."

"Were you wearing your glasses this day, as you viewed the man on the motorcycle?"

"No . . . but I didn't have to. I could see him pretty clearly."

"You could. Mrs. Enright, the next day following the incident, when the police came to your shop, did you describe the man you'd seen to a sketch artist of the Ypsilanti Police Department?"

"Yes."

"And, in your opinion at that time, did the sketch produced resemble the man you'd described?"

"Well, not exactly. . . . There were things he just couldn't seem to get right."

"Isn't it a fact that you and your assistant—having 'observed' the motorcyclist side by side—could not even then agree on a number of his features?"

"Yes, some, but—"

"Didn't you, for example, insist that his hair was curly, and she that it was straight? Wasn't there disagreement about the length of his sideburns? And his eyes? His chin?"

"Maybe. I don't recall. . . ."

"Now subsequently, on at least two occasions did not police officers come to you with photographs, snapshots, of James Armstrong?"

"Yes."

"And were you on either occasion able to recognize him, identify *him* as the man you'd seen on the motorcycle outside your shop?"

"No."

"And yet—having been shown these pictures—soon afterwards you *were* able to pick him out of a police lineup?"

"Yes. But then—"

"How far would you say you were from the defendant at that lineup?"

Joan Enright hesitated.

"Twenty feet? Thirty?"

"I suppose . . ."

"One more thing, Mrs. Enright. You say you're rather familiar with motorcycles?"

"I know something about them."

"When the police first interviewed you, what make motorcycle did you tell them you'd seen Carol Ann Gebhardt ride away on?"

"Well, I'd *thought* it was a Honda. . . ."

"A Honda. That's all."

The woman from The Chocolate Shop testified that she also had seen a young man in a striped shirt waiting outside on a motorcycle for ten or fifteen minutes around 12:30 P.M. on the day in question. Being a motorcycle enthusiast herself, she was more interested in the vehicle than its rider, and she positively identified it as a big Triumph with a dark blue tank and chrome all over. After a while, a girl also wearing a striped shirt or blouse approached and drove off behind the young man.

But in cross-examination by Louisell, Miss Crenna said that while she agreed, more or less, with the general description of the cyclist—about six feet, trim, solid build, clean-cut, short dark hair with longish but neat sideburns—*none* of the published composite sketches had looked like the fellow to her.

Even now, having seen the defendant, she could not state with certainty that *he* was the one.

The sparring thus ended over what obviously was a critical issue, identification and placement of the defendant as the last person to have been with the victim. To many of the spectators, it appeared to be a standoff.

CHAPTER 24

DONALD BAKER WAS called to testify on Monday afternoon, July 27. Trimly tailored, soft-spoken, at times seeming quite shy, Baker, deftly coached by Prosecutor Delhey, told of the close relationship that had developed between James Armstrong and himself, starting in about the spring of 1968 on through July 28, 1969 —the last time he had seen James until this moment. . . .

Baker said, of Wednesday, July 23, that he did not see James Armstrong that day until well after four in the afternoon, when James came back to the house on Emmet Street. He then took Baker out for a couple of hours to teach him how to ride. Before they left, James switched the license plate and mirror from his blue Triumph to the green. Baker noticed that the blue Triumph felt warm, while the green bike, which they were going to use, was cool.

That evening, Baker and Armstrong and Tony Monte went out for dinner and returned to the house a little after nine. About 9:30, James said he was going down to the garage to work on a bike. He came back about 11:30. The three of them started watching TV. But after a few minutes James left to feed his uncle's dog, returning after 1:00 A.M.

Before turning Baker over to cross-examination Delhey thought of another question.

"About the motorcycle lesson the defendant gave you on the afternoon of July twenty-third: Did that ever come up in subsequent conversation?"

"Yes, one other time," Baker said.

"What was that occasion?"

"It was the following Sunday night . . . or early Monday morning . . . after James came back from questioning by the police. He told me to be sure to remember what time we'd gone riding that Wednesday—that it had been *early* in the afternoon."

"How early did he suggest it had been?"

"About two thirty."

"And what time *had* it been, actually?"

"After four thirty."

James Armstrong's expression had grown steadily blacker during the last part of Baker's testimony— glaring up at the witness box, shaking his head in protest, lips finally twisting in a silent, clenched-teeth *No!* as though having forcibly to restrain himself from rushing forward and throttling his once close friend. Neil Fink put a steadying hand on the young man's arm as Joe Louisell stood to cross-examine.

"Mr. Baker, did you yourself at first tell the police that you and James had gone riding about two thirty or three o'clock that day?"

"Yes, but—"

"Then what caused, or persuaded, you to testify to the later time?"

"I just decided to tell the truth."

"Very good. Now I shall ask you if you had known, ever met or seen, Miss Carol Ann Gebhardt, the deceased?"

"Not that I can ever recall."

"And as James's close friend, are you aware if *he* knew her?"

"Not to *my* knowledge."

"All right. Now, that night when James was hustled off by the police—later, when he informed you that they seemed to regard *him* as a suspect, how did you react?"

"I couldn't believe it. I thought he was joking. I mean, they could have suspected *anybody* who rode a motorcycle."

"And when James told you they'd asked him to submit to a 'lie-detector' test, what did he say his response had been?"

"He said he'd told them he would."

"Very well. You've stated that you did not see or speak with James again after the night of July twenty-eighth. Tell us now what happened on August first, after you found out he'd been taken into custody."

"I was at the Student Union in the morning, and the word got around. I went back to the house . . . and then some policeman came and took me in for questioning."

"Took you where?"

"Over to that seminary by the sheriff's headquarters —what they called the crime center."

"And what happened there?"

Baker swallowed, suddenly appearing ill at ease. "They . . . questioned me."

"For how long?"

There was a thick pause. Baker cleared his throat and then related—drawn out from time to time by Louisell—his long ordeal of police interrogation and pressure.

After that first interminable weekend, when he had been kept in virtual custody almost sixty hours, for months they'd continued to badger him, picking him up practically every other day and bringing him back to the crime center for more questioning—the same questions, over and over. . . .

"Was there," prompted Louisell, "one point in particular that seemed to absorb these officers?"

"The mirror . . . on James's motorcycle." Baker's voice was a hoarse murmur. "I kept telling them that the only mirror of his that I'd ever seen was an old round one. They insisted it was square. . . ."

"They insisted," repeated Louisell.

Baker went on to say that he'd never asked for legal counsel during this period because he was scared. Any time he mentioned a lawyer, he said, the policemen warned him: If he was innocent, he didn't need a lawyer. They *could* have arrested *him,* but hadn't. They still could. . . .

Even after Baker had been graduated from Eastern, early in 1970, and had moved to New York City, they didn't let up. There were constant calls from Michigan, needling him, reminding him that he'd better "cooperate." One policeman even telephoned his new employer, he related, informing him about the murder case Baker was involved in! Finally, in the spring, Baker warned the Michigan police that if they didn't stop harassing him he *was* going to take legal action; he just couldn't stand anymore. . . .

"Harassing . . ." mused Louisell with pointed clarity that echoed through the hushed courtroom. Then he turned back to Baker. "Were you offered any sort of deal to testify for the prosecution against your friend?"

For the first time in his unhappy recitation, Baker looked up sharply: *"No, sir!"*

"But then I suppose none was necessary," muttered Louisell in a perfectly audible stage whisper. "No further questions."

James Armstrong's other former companion, Tony Monte, was next to take the stand. Delhey's examination was short and specific. It centered on the chronology of events on that Wednesday, July 23.

Monte met Donald Baker at the house on Emmet Street around 1:00 P.M., and the two of them went out together for about three hours. They returned sometime after 4:00, and about 4:30 James Armstrong came in. Armstrong and Baker went out for a while, then later all three went out to eat. Back a little past 9:00, they watched TV. Armstrong left them, returning about 11:30. In a few minutes he left again and came back this time around 1:00 A.M.

"Your witness," Prosecutor Delhey said.

Fink didn't even rise: "The defense has no questions of this witness, Your Honor," he said.

A bemused Judge Conlin peered down at the defense table. He supposed he could understand why they would be leery of delving too deeply into Tony Monte's former association with the defendant—if they stumbled into the larceny area, the prosecution would jump. Still, the judge was rather surprised that the clever Louisell, to say nothing of the impulsive Fink, had not *chanced* it. Monte might have been able to shed so much light. . . .

The prosecution called State Police Sergeant Dana Loucks,* who told his story without adornments. There wasn't much for the defense to challenge in Loucks's testimony. Why would he be untruthful? The boy was his own nephew, whom he had loved!

But Louisell felt they could at least fight a holding action. "Sergeant," he began, "regarding these abnormalities found in your home upon return from vacation —paint on the basement floor, articles disarranged or missing, and so forth. In your subsequent investigations, did you come upon any evidence that pointed specifically to your nephew as the one responsible . . . any clue that told you by its very presence or nature that *only* James could have done these things?"

"Well, no, nothing specific. But—"

"You had left a note on the fuse box in the basement, asking him to replace a defective fuse. Had the fuse been replaced, or, for that matter, the note itself apparently handled?"

"No."

"Was that characteristic of your nephew, as you knew him, to have neglected such a request?"

"No . . . I can't say it was."

---

* Loucks had been promoted to sergeant in August 1969.

"Your good wife had also left him a note, advising James of watermelon saved especially for him in the basement refrigerator. Had the melon been eaten, even touched?"

"No, but—"

"Was *that* like your nephew James?"

"No, not at all. . . ."

"Then aside from your natural assumption—which could not have been more reasonable—that James was the only one who *could* have been in the house during your absence, upon your return you found nothing explicitly affirming that he actually had been there? . . . In fact, there were some indications to the contrary, isn't that so?"

"Well, put that way— But when I asked him—"

"—he *told* you he had been. Sergeant, knowing youth as you surely must, can you not conceive of such a one as your nephew, with his great respect for you and your family and the great value he placed on your regard for him, bringing himself perhaps to 'cover up,' so that you should not be disappointed in him for having failed to do what you'd asked and expected?"

"I can *conceive* that, yes . . ."

"Did James tell you he'd lost a key to the house that you'd previously given him?"

"He said he'd mislaid it. I gave him another one before we left."

"And had he found the original key by the time you returned?"

"No—he said not."

"So he has never returned *that* key to you?"

"No."

"But he did return the second key?"

"Yes."

"Thank you, sergeant."

Mrs. Dana Loucks repeated much the same account as had her husband, detailing the series of puzzling surprises that had greeted them on their return from vacation. She distinctly remembered having swept the

basement laundry area, as always, after she'd trimmed
Dana's and each of the boys' hair there the night before
their trip.

Delhey had her bring out that the implement she always used was a Wahl professional hair clipper.

Finally, Delhey asked Mrs. Loucks how she personally had been affected upon learning that her
nephew might be involved in a terrible crime.

She said she'd come close to collapse. James had
been almost as dear to her as her own sons. . . .

For the defense, Joseph Louisell led Mrs. Loucks
gently back over some of her testimony, filling in a few
spots that he felt needed clarification. He was exceed-
ingly careful with her; she was a sympathetic figure,
who obviously was under considerable strain recalling
these tortured memories.

"Mrs. Loucks," he asked, "were you requested by
the police to supply them with a résumé, a list of everything you remembered in and about your home at that
time?"

"Yes. Which I did."

"That was sometime later, was it not—October, I
believe?"

"Yes, I believe so."

"Presumably by then you were more composed—?"

"Sir"—dark eyes flashed in her wan face—"I have
not been *composed* for the past year!"

"Of course. However, I do find something peculiar
about the list you did make up at that time." He showed
her a copy. "Here we have your recollections written
down some two months after the fact . . . after, one
might expect, due time for reflection . . . and nowhere
is there a mention of a bottle of ammonia missing, or a
box of detergent, Bold or otherwise, or of finding a
mysterious damp rag in your washtub—all of which
you have remembered today, almost a year later. Why
should we suppose this is?"

"I don't know. I suppose at that time I was still occupied, trying to understand— There seemed to be

more important considerations then. These things probably just never seemed important until later. . . ."

"Then you were reminded—or prompted—on some later occasion. . . ."

"Nobody reminded or prompted me. I *remembered* later."

"You did. That explains it then. Thank you."

The one missing piece of evidence that the prosecution felt would seal its case was somebody who had actually seen the defendant with the deceased at or near the Loucks house at Roosevelt Boulevard and Cornell Road in the early afternoon of July 23, 1969. But that never could be substantiated. The best they could come up with was a woman, a neighbor of the Louckses', who stated positively that she'd seen a young man of the defendant's description around the Loucks house and riding away from it on a powerful motorcycle.

Mrs. Loretta Farmer was called to testify. Her home was directly across from the Louckses', at the opposite corner of Cornell and Roosevelt; from the front of her house she had a clear view of the other's side door, driveway, and garage in the rear. During the period the Loucks family had been away, she had noticed a young man frequently around their house and garage, evidently caring for the Louckses' dog. Generally, however, she hadn't paid him much mind, and she couldn't say she'd seen a motorcycle in the vicinity . . . until this particular day.

It *wasn't* Wednesday the twenty-third, of that she' was sure, for she'd been away from home much of that day. But either the next day, or on Friday the twenty-fifth, late in the afternoon she had just driven into her own driveway when she looked across and noticed a big motorcycle, with a dark tank (deep blue or black) and a lot of chrome, parked in the Louckses' driveway near the sidewalk.

Then the side door of their house opened and a young man came out, secured the door behind him and strode down the driveway to the motorcycle. He appeared to be the same one Mrs. Farmer had been seeing from time to time: slim, medium height and build, dark hair, wearing jeans and a nondescript short-sleeved shirt. What caught her eye just then was what he was carrying: a large box of Bold. The young man started up the motorcycle and, the Bold box in one hand, sort of held out in front of him over the handle-bar, drove off north on Cornell.

She could not, however, state positively that the young man had been James Armstrong. . . .

Joseph Louisell had but one question for Mrs. Farmer:

"Is it true that in your original interview by the police, in August nineteen sixty-nine, you stated that you could not be certain just when this incident had taken place—that it *could* have been *before* the twenty-third of July?"

"Well, at the time—"

"Yes or no, please."

"Yes, I believe I said that."

"That's all."

CHAPTER 25

On the tenth day, Friday, July 31, the trial entered the vital technical and scientific phase by which the defendant's fate might well be decided.

If it could be proved beyond question that blood found in the Louckses' basement had been the deceased's, and that tiny hairs recovered from the victim's panties could only have come from the floor of that basement, there could be little doubt that Carol Ann Gebhardt had been there, at least in an injured condition, and probably attacked and killed there. And if the jury were persuaded that James Armstrong had been the only person with access to that place at that time, and that, further, there was reason to believe that it was he with whom the girl had been last seen alive, he had to be a goner.

If the defense could *dis*prove, or at worst cast reasonable doubt on, the absolute veracity and application of the prosecution's scientific conclusions alone, regardless of what else the jury believed about the defendant it was bound at least to consider acquittal.

The lead-off prosecution witness was Curtis Fluker of the Crime Detection Unit, Michigan Department of Public Health. At his laboratory in Lansing, Fluker had tested and typed blood samples both from the Louckses' basement and from the body of the deceased. Both showed up as Type A.

In cross-examination Louisell made much of why the blood samples had not been subtyped, it being possible to break down any blood typing into subgroups of 1, 2 and 3. Also, he wanted to know why other tests had not been made beyond the A, B or O typings—for an *Rh* (Rhesus) factor, or M or N factors, and so on?

Fluker said that his lab did not have adequate supplies of antisera on hand to go into more extensive tests.

"So," Louisell concluded, "you had two blood samples both indicated to be simply Type A. What, sir, would you say is the percentage of population in the United States having Type A blood?"

"Probably forty or forty-five percent," Fluker conceded.

The next witness was Walter Holz, chief of the Criminalistics Section of the Department of Health's Division of Crime Protection. A graduate chemist, Holz's responsibility was to collect, analyze, and compare "trace evidence" (bloodstains, seminal traces, hairs and fibers, arson debris) gathered by law enforcement agencies.

Assistant Prosecutor Booker Williams led Holz into the matter of the hairs found on the panties of the deceased. Holz said that a total of 509 hair particles were removed from the panties. Microscopic examination showed them to be human hairs—head hairs, not pubic—and they did *not* match the victim's own hair.

The particles ranged in length from one millimeter (one-twenty-fifth of an inch) to twenty-one millimeters (approximately seven-eighths of an inch). And from the "crenated" arrangement of the cuticles—the outside edges flattened and irregular—Holz was convinced they had been cut by clippers.

In color, the hair particles ranged from blond to light brown to dark brown, with intermediate tones within that spectrum. And microscopically, Holz said, marked similarities were observed in the internal characteristics of these hairs to the comparison hairs collected from the floor of the Louckses' basement—the clippings from the heads of Dana Loucks and his three sons.

These similarities—in addition to the crenated cuticles, which indicated that each had been clipped from the same source—were notable both in their medullary structures and the distribution of pigmentation in their cortexes. Both samples contained hairs completely absent of medullary material, others with sparse amounts, others in which it went from "fragmented" to "continuous." In both samples, too, pigment granules were seen to be arranged similarly in the cortexes— few granules more randomly placed in lighter hairs, progressively more granules bunched in closer distribution as the hairs got darker in color.

Williams asked: "Evaluating these several points of similarity, could you then come to a reasonable conclusion as to the origins of the respective hair samples?"

"Yes. It was my conclusion that they all came from the same source."

"Did you subsequently take any steps to confirm this conclusion?"

"Yes. In August and September of nineteen sixty-nine, and again in February of this year, I took the samples to the Gulf General Atomic research laboratories at San Diego, California, where they were further studied and compared under a highly sophisticated technical process known as 'neutron activation analysis.'"

"And—?"

"And my conclusion was supported."

Louisell took the cross-examination.

"Mr. Holz, correct me if I am in error"—his syrupy tone did not quite conceal a tart edge of incredulity— "but is this not the first time ever that a Michigan court has heard a scientist testify that two specimens of hair, one from a known source and the other unknown, have been determined from *microscopic comparison* to have had a common origin?"

"It could well be."

Louisell was silent for several beats, looking at Holz perplexed, as though struggling to grasp the full significance of a truth revealed which he, for all his open-mindedness and capacity for learning, had hardly thought conceivable. It was an effective performance. The jury watched him, then obediently turned to reappraise the witness, and Holz squirmed just a bit.

Louisell then had Holz relate how he had made his initial analyses, of the samples collected from the basement floor and those from the victim's panties, in a little over two hours the night of July 31, 1969—from about 9:15 P.M. to 11:30 or so—at which point he'd telephoned Assistant Prosecutor Williams from Lansing and informed him that he thought "he had something." After that, of course, Holz put in, more thorough microscopic examination continued.

"How many hair particles, actually, were examined —from the basement floor, and from the panties?"

"Sixty-one separate hairs from the panties, and fifty-nine from the floor," replied Holz.

"Sixty-one and fifty-nine! Doesn't it seem at all unreasonable to you, sir, that such apparently *definitive* comparisons could possibly be drawn from so inadequate a sampling?"

"It's possible. It's been done—"

"Has it? And what of the lengths of these hairs? How could you possibly hope to detect all the pertinent characteristics of such *tiny* specimens—especially of their medullary structure? Isn't it true that in such short lengths many hairs might not even have a medulla to detect?"

"Yes, but—"

"Then how on earth could the two sets of samples be definitively 'compared'?"

Louisell hammered away at Holz, getting the state's chemist to agree—citing a Dr. Paul L. Kirk of California, acknowledged by Holz as an outstanding scientist in the field of hair comparison—that, in general, the *least* satisfactory hair samples for comparison purposes were barbered clippings.

The defense attorney referred to FBI standards for scientific examination of hair:

"I assume we all would consider the Federal Bureau of Investigation an expert forensic source?"

"Yes, by and large."

"And has not the FBI concluded, from its well-documented experience and vast technical capabilities, that hairs that are either fragmentary or not fully developed are *not* suitable to adequate or reliable examination?"

"As a blanket theoretical statement, I would have to agree with that. *However,* in certain instances there are many individual characteristics even in such hair from which it *can* be positively determined that a sample of unknown origin did come from a particular person or animal, to the exclusion of all other persons or animals of the same family."

Louisell abruptly switched to another tack: "What about incidental debris? Included among the hair specimens collected from the basement floor, were not also found a number of other foreign elements—particles of wood, paper, minerals, textile fibers?"

"Yes."

"Mr. Holz, this past spring did you ask the highly regarded Fabric Research Laboratory of Taunton, Massachusetts, to do a comprehensive analysis of these hair samples?"

"Yes. I went there myself."

"In what form were the samples prepared?"

"In what we call dry mounts—like slides."

"And included amongst the hair thus mounted, were there also samples of the random debris collected along with the hair from the basement floor?"

"Well, no . . ."

"Were you encouraged by the analytical results at the Fabric Research Laboratory?"

"They . . . we had some areas of disagreement."

On Wednesday, August 5—the thirteenth day of trial
—the prosecution called Howard Lee Schlesinger of
the Gulf General Atomic Corporation, San Diego.
Schlesinger, with a master's degree in science from the
University of Chicago, was a specialist in forensic
chemistry. Previously he had been an analyst of meta-
bolic diseases for the National Institutes of Health at
Bethesda, Maryland, and later had worked five years
in the Alcohol and Tobacco Tax Division laboratories
of the U.S. Internal Revenue Service.

Booker Williams had him explain "neutron activation analysis." It was, he said, a process whereby, by
measuring applied radioactivity, the elements making
up a sample of trace material could be identified even
at very low concentrations, which other analytical processes might be unable to detect. (In a nuclear reactor,
a given sample was bombarded by high-intensity neu-
trons; a number of the material's chemical atoms became radioactive; and this irradiation then could be
measured to identify the various elements sought, both
qualitatively and quantitatively.) The process, Williams had Schlesinger bring out, was now a widely accepted scientific method of comparing hair samples to
determine whether or not they came from the same
source.*

Schlesinger said that Walter Holz had delivered to
him seven samples of hair: four represented as having
been cut on August 18, 1969, from the heads of
Trooper Loucks and each of his sons; two different
samples collected from the basement floor on July 31,
1969; and a seventh, identified as hairs from the vic-

* The acknowledged originator of neutron activation analysis was
Dr. Robert J. Jervis of the University of Toronto, who had devised
the process in the mid-1950's when requested by the Royal Canadian
Mounted Police to find some more scientifically accurate method of
determining common hair source than by mere microscopic examination.
Its first forensic application in North America had been in a 1958
Canadian homicide case, and in Michigan it had been used one other
time since in a criminal case.

tim's panties. All seven samples were subjected to different periods of irradiation: first one minute, then one hour. Lastly, samples No. 5, 6, and 7—the two from the floor and one from the panties—were irradiated for an additional period of fifty hours.

"And what was the result of your analysis?" Williams asked.

"Samples five, six and seven showed twelve elements in common. And the conclusion I reached was that the hairs from the girl's panties, with a distinct and high level of probability, came from the same source as the samples taken from the basement floor. . . ."

Louisell took on the witness.

"You testified that samples five, six and seven showed twelve elements in common. Then your comparisons—and subsequent conclusion—were based on that number of elements?"

"Not exactly. Some had to be eliminated for various reasons."

"You eliminated some. How many?"

"Well, four of the elements were found to be normal components of human perspiration. Three others were doubtful for one reason or another."

"Four and three—seven. That left five. You made your final comparison based on just *five* elements* that seemed in good agreement?"

"Essentially, yes."

"Mr. Schlesinger, what is a 'controlled study'?"

"That is when a certain number of samples is analyzed for the effects of one or more variables upon results obtained."

"And from a controlled study, one can derive a great deal of data?"

"Yes, certainly."

"So in using the technique of neutron activation analysis, as applied in this case, in order to reach a valid conclusion you would have to refer to data avail-

---

* Gold, mercury, antimony, zinc and selenium.

able in this area already compiled under controlled conditions?"

"Yes, one must use available data."

"I believe the data you used was that previously compiled by a number of experts in the field—Dr. Jervis, who originated the process, and Dr. Colman in England, Dr. Lanahan, Dr. Dyer, Dr. Bate . . . ?"

"Yes, I'm sure."

"Isn't there a great deal of literature by Dr. Jervis and others stating that one cannot really come to any valid conclusion in comparing hairs without a minimum of *ten* trace elements that show good agreement —'good agreement' being when elements of two samples vary little or not at all?"

"Dr. Jervis has said that . . . and some of his students . . . yes."

"And, according to Dr. Jervis—do correct me if I err—fifty hours is the *minimum* period of irradiation from which to draw an accurate reading of at least ten trace elements. Now, in your tests only the samples five, six and seven were put through fifty-hour irradiation. Samples one through four (the head hairs known to have come from the four Loucks males), to which the others were to be compared for confirmation purposes, were irradiated a maximum of *one* hour. Is that correct?"

"Yes."

"How many elements might one expect to detect in a one-hour irradiation period—three, four at the most?"

"Possibly, yes. . . ."

Louisell returned to the defense table and Neil Fink picked up with Schlesinger. In a lengthy series of terse, snappish questions enlarging on the element-by-element composition of hair in general and of the particular hairs tested, Fink took issue with the scientist's reasoning in having "arbitrarily" (as the lawyer put it) eliminated certain key elements—notably chromium, manganese, and cobalt—thus severely limiting the basis for a fair and reasonable comparison.

Schlesinger explained that the hairs from the basement had been on the floor some time—at least two weeks (from the night of July 17, 1969, when Mrs. Loucks cut the boys' hair before leaving on vacation, to July 31)—and thus had naturally accumulated some alien debris, among which doubtless were certain elements that might not have also shown up among the hairs from the victim's panties. As for the latter, Schlesinger said, those hairs had to have been on the panties for a period of time as well—probably three days at least (from July 23, the day she was attacked, to July 26–27, after her body had been discovered and examined)—and, the panties themselves having been in an unusual location, within an orifice (the vagina) of a dead person, there might well have resulted a transference of certain bodily elements to those hairs. . . .

"The trouble with crime samples," Schlesinger noted, "is that they are *not* laboratory samples. I have personally never seen two cases in which, given such physical evidence, the histories were exactly the same. So it is not really possible to report with complete accuracy, to chart or apply hard-and-fast standards, where there is no reliable factor of respectability."

"Of course not," Fink agreed. "The only reliable standards then are original data, isn't that so?"

"And one's own feelings—"

"And your own *feelings?*"

"It may be unfortunate, but in many cases you must also use subjective evaluations—based on the circumstances surrounding a particular set of samples, plus your knowledge of work in the field and your own prior experience."

"And awareness of the results you want to reach?"

Schlesinger bristled. "Are you saying that I forecast the results I was going to reach here, and then slanted everything toward that?"

"Well, you did come up with the desired result. When people bring a sample in, you *know* what the desired result is, do you not—?"

"I may know what *they* desire the result to be. . . ."

The next witness for the prosecution was Vincent P. Guinn, professor of chemistry at the University of California's Irvine campus near San Diego.

Guinn, who held bachelor's and master's degrees in chemistry from the University of Southern California and a doctorate in physical chemistry from Harvard, formerly had been with Gulf General Atomic for eight years, heading up its activation analysis group, and for twelve years before that in the research section of Shell Development Company. He had published some 120 papers in the area of radiochemistry, primarily in sub-branches such as neutron activation analysis, and had a long list of professional credentials (American Nuclear Society, American Chemical Society, American Physical Society, Academy of Forensic Science, among others). At the present time, he was a member of an advisory committee to the United States Atomic Energy Commission in its program on isotope radiology; and the previous year he had been one of four consultants to the International Atomic Energy Commission in Vienna, concentrating on the forensic application of neutron activation analysis.

"Dr. Guinn," Booker Williams began, "in nineteen sixty-nine did you confer with Howard Schlesinger of Gulf General Atomic prior to, during, and following Mr. Schlesinger's analysis of certain hair samples from Michigan, and did you subsequently have occasion to review the report of the values and concentration of elements found therein by Mr. Schlesinger?"

"I did."

"Based on the elements found, and their values, did you yourself come to any conclusion with reasonable scientific certainty respecting those samples?"

"Yes. At that time, I did not make my own detailed calculations; but simply by looking at the numbers and comparing them to what we know from our own and others' work . . . such as Dr. Jervis' . . . just looking at the degree of agreement, it seemed very definitely feasible to state a high probability that sample number seven [the hairs from the panties] had the same origin as samples five and six [hairs from the basement floor]. . . .

"Yet the more I studied it the more I realized it was a unique problem that required really careful thought: Here were two samples from the floor of a basement where four persons regularly had their hair cut, and presumably each sample contained a mixture of hair from all four of those people in some unknown proportion. Now to my knowledge, no one ever before had taken hair samples from two, three, or four persons and mixed them and analyzed them—all the data in our scientific literature on this subject are based on samples of hair from *individuals,* analyzed separately so as to obtain some idea of the range of composition in the head hair of different people.

"The question was then: What would mixing hairs from *four* different people do to the range of values that could be expected from analysis? There had to be some basis by which to interpret results. So, more recently, I went back and undertook more detailed calculations. . . ."

Dr. Guinn went on to describe at length his approach to this problem of multiple hair samples (an intricate series of calculations, relying heavily on neutron activation analysis research and thesis data compiled not only by Dr. Jervis but by Dr. Perkons, another Canadian scientist), trying, he said, to be "very conservative" in evaluating comparisons between the mixed samples and the hair from the panties. And in the end he'd come to the same conclusion: There was a high probability that these hairs all were from the same source.

Williams asked: "And will you tell us your conclusion as to the *extent* of this high probability—?"

Neil Fink objected: "We object to any opinion about statistical probabilities as prejudicial and misleading. The very data upon which the witness would base such an opinion, Your Honor, were compiled by experts who are in total disagreement with his conclusion! How can one cite for his source material another expert who doesn't support him?"

Williams: "Your Honor, Dr. Guinn *has* used certain figures from those other men's theses, but he has relied on his own expert knowledge and his own calculations in reaching his conclusions."

Judge Conlin thought a moment, then: "I am inclined to disagree with defense counsel. The witness may answer."

Williams repeated the question, and Guinn said: "I might point out that Dr. Jervis himself also believes in probability calculations. . . .

"If we took the entire population of the United States, about two hundred million, and arbitrarily broke it up into groups of four persons each, we would have fifty million groups. From this number, I would say there might be no more than thirty groups in the whole United States whose hair would appear similar to these particular samples—only about one hundred twenty people out of two hundred million. Were we to make the same type of calculation for a more restricted area, such as the State of Michigan: out of a *nine million* population, perhaps only one or two of these random groups of four persons—*four to eight people in all*—would be apt to have hair similar to our test samples."

These devastating statistics had a noticeable impact on the jury, and Williams and Delhey looked as pleased with themselves, in turning Dr. Guinn over to the defense, as Fink and Louisell were evidently dismayed.

But Judge Conlin then gave the defense something to chew on: Before adjourning, he wanted the record to show that the court had examined a copy of a letter from Dr. Guinn to Mr. Williams, dated July 24, 1970, referring to Dr. Guinn's recent return from Southeast Asia. In this letter, Dr. Guinn had written that he had begun making his calculations based on Mr. Schlesinger's report and would advise Mr. Williams of his conclusions as soon as they were completed. He also

stated that he would be glad to appear at the trial any
time, now that he'd returned. . . .

Neil Fink's eyes lit up. The letter indicated that
Guinn had only *begun* his "intricate" series of calculations as late as July 24—less than two weeks before
his astounding testimony of today!

Thursday morning, August 6, Fink eagerly cross-
examined Dr. Guinn. His first question was: When
had Dr. Guinn actually begun, and when had he completed, his highly complex calculations?

"It had been suggested to me back about June that I
might be asked to testify. I said that I was due to go out
of the country for a month or so but would be available,
if needed, when I returned. When I got back, around
the middle of July, I learned that the trial had not yet
progressed appreciably. So, although not yet advised
officially that I *would* be called, on about July twentieth
I began to think about these calculations. . . ."

"And where did you do your thinking, sir?"

"At first, partly at the university—California—
partly at home."

"And where lastly?"

"Here, in Ann Arbor, after my arrival last weekend.
I worked on them through the weekend and actually
finished about one o'clock Monday morning."

"When had you learned, finally, that you were to be
a witness in this trial?"

"Just late last week."

"So when you were called to testify, and even upon
your arrival in Ann Arbor, you still had not completed
these most difficult, as you say, *unprecedented* extra-
polations—?"

"Not quite . . ."

"—but rushed to finish them in time."

"I wouldn't say I *rushed* particularly."

"But you did *complete* them?"

"To *my* satisfaction, yes."

"Dr. Guinn, certain men, scientists, have great experience and knowledge in the field of activation an-

alysis of hair—yourself included, I'm sure. But if you had to pick one man as *the* outstanding expert in the field, whom would you choose?"

"Well, I don't think it's really fair to pick out just one individual—"

"If you *had* to choose, would you say it was Dr. Robert Jervis, the originator and pioneer of the process?"

"As I say, it's not fair to— But I suppose, yes, Dr. Jervis—"

"No more questions."

Booker Williams rose:

"Your Honor, the People rest."

CHAPTER 26

BEFORE CALLING THE first defense witness Neil Fink presented three motions:

One, to strike the testimony of Walter Holz as to his conclusion, stated with "scientific certainty," that the hair on the deceased's panties compared with and was of the same origin as the hair on the basement floor. Mr. Holz himself had admitted that nobody before had ever so testified in court, and that nobody before had even attempted to draw such a conclusion with *reasonable* scientific certainty. The fact was, Mr. Holz used the defendant as a "guinea pig"—which would seem, in a capital case, to be grossly unfair!

Conlin: Motion denied. Mr. Holz's qualifications were sufficient to state a conclusion of probability. Therefore, his testimony was more a matter of its credibility and weight in deliberations of the jury, rather than of its admissibility.

Fink next moved to strike the testimony of both Howard Schlesinger and Dr. Vincent Guinn—Dr. Guinn, especially. In making his calculations on so speculative a problem, which had never been attacked before, he admitted he approached it mathematically with pencil and paper instead of in the controlled conditions of a laboratory, as other experts do. Mathematical computation might be necessary in designing a new type of aircraft—how much runway it should need to take off, and all the various weight and speed factors that would have to be taken into consideration—but surely no one would want to send up a full load of passengers in an untried plane without first making test runs under controlled conditions! Fink moved, therefore, to strike Dr. Guinn's testimony with respect to statistical probabilities.

And the defense also moved to strike *all* testimony referring to "neutron activation analysis."

Conlin: Motions denied on the same grounds as earlier—the witnesses being qualified, their testimony came down to credibility and weight, not admissibility.

Fink's final motion was for a "directed verdict": "The prosecution's case is so riddled with inherent incredibility that even to commit it to a jury seems a manifest injustice! I simply cannot believe that if this case were tried in a vacuum—was not *the Armstrong case,* so-called—that it *would* ever go to jury. But this *is* 'the Armstrong case,' and it is being dealt with in that concept . . . and so, for the record, I make this motion for a directed verdict, so that the record is adequately protected."

The judge said: "I do feel that, of course, the prosecution's case is entirely circumstantial. However, sufficient evidence—circumstantial though it may be— *has* been produced so far . . . in several areas . . . which, if believed by a jury, could result in their finding defendant guilty as charged. The proof of the *corpus delicti* is adequate to go to the jury."

The defense opened its case by calling Joe Majors, owner of J & J Cycle Sales in Ypsilanti.

Majors said that on Wednesday, the twenty-third, Armstrong came into his shop between 1:00 and 1:30

P.M. Majors knew that to be the time because that was when he and his employees ate lunch every day—around one o'clock. He himself was at his desk, eating, when Armstrong entered through the back and came up front and told Majors he wanted to pay his bill. Majors said he would receipt the bill as soon as he finished eating, and Armstrong went back to the service department to wait. Majors couldn't say just how long Armstrong stayed in the shop ("He was always around, like part of the furniture")—maybe an hour. . . .

William Delhey took the cross-examination.

"Do you remember speaking, on August fifth, nineteen sixty-nine, with Sergeant William Canada of the Ann Arbor Police Department?"

"Yes. I don't recall the date. . . ."

"Didn't you tell Sergeant Canada at that time that James Armstrong was in your shop at *three* o'clock on the afternoon of July twenty-third?"

"No, sir."

"Did not Sergeant Canada sometime later return with a typewritten paper, which he asked you to read and sign?"

"Yes."

"Did you sign it—here [showing Majors the sheet of paper] at the bottom?"

"Yes."

"As you then read this paper, did you make any corrections in the statement?"

"Well, I remember telling Sergeant Canada *he* should make some corrections."

"Do you recall that, at your direction, Sergeant Canada changed the time from three to two P.M.?"

"No, sir, I don't recall him doing that."

"I call your attention to some handwritten notes at the top. That was put there before you signed the paper, was it not?"

"Sir, I really can't recall."

"It says— I will read just a portion of it, if counsel will permit."

Louisell spoke up: "Before any portion of this statement is read into evidence, I want to have a look at it."

Conlin directed the prosecutor to let defense counsel examine the paper. Louisell and Fink huddled over it, and their faces clouded with, first, befuddlement and then agitation.

What no doubt had once been a neatly typed, brief statement (*The undersigned states that on the afternoon of July 23, 1969* ...) now appeared as an almost indecipherable jumble, words crossed out or overwritten in hand, scrawls of inserts and addenda crowding every margin, along with unreadable chicken scratches that were supposed to pass for signatures.

Fink burst out: "This is a farce! *What* statement? *What* notes?"

"Your Honor," Delhey said, "the witness has said that *he* read it, and he recognizes his own signature—"

Judge Conlin rapped his gavel once. "Gentlemen, gentlemen! Please. Mr. Fink, may I see the statement?"

"Yes, sir. But please don't give it the dignity of calling it a 'statement.'"

Conlin ruled that the paper could *not* be admitted as a People's exhibit.

Delhey then began boring in on Joe Majors:

"Did you not tell Sergeant Canada that you were *not* sure what time James Armstrong had been in your shop on July twenty-third?"

"I don't think I gave anyone, the police or the defense, any specific time. ..."

"How *do* you fix the time that day?"

"Because I always eat around one o'clock."

"Never later?"

"It can be a little later. ..."

"A little later. As late as one thirty?"

"Not usually. But it can happen."

"Then it could have happened on July twenty-third? It *could* have been as late as one thirty that day, could it not?"

"I guess it's *possible*."

"Could it have been as late as *two* thirty?"

"I'm pretty sure not."

"Well, would it be fair to say that on a given day you are likely to have your lunch any time between, say, one and two P.M.?"

Majors considered. "Yes . . . I would say so."

The next defense witness was Paul Dano, a service employee at J & J Cycle Sales. He said that on July 23 the defendant had come into the shop at approximately 1:15 in the afternoon and stayed at least forty-five minutes, maybe an hour or even an hour and a half. He fixed the time by the fact that he also was still eating his lunch, and they ate there as a rule around 1:00 P.M. As to the length of time Armstrong spent there that day Dano remembered him talking for quite a while with Ray O'Connell, another mechanic, at his workbench in the service department. Armstrong frequently hung around like that.

Dano denied having told the police that Armstrong was there at 3:00 P.M., or even 2:00 P.M. (Fink showed him the disputed statement.) Dano said he had read that and signed it, but he'd noted that a change should be made in the time. He thought that whatever changes were made must have been done after he'd signed it. He said that Sergeant Canada had come around the shop at least half a dozen times, going over this question of the time again and again. Dano finally had signed the statement—upon being promised that corrections would be written in—to get the police off his back, he said.

Delhey picked up on that:

"Were not the changes you indicated made in your presence?"

"I . . . can't recall."

Delhey handed Dano the statement and asked him to read a particular section aloud:

"*Dano also puts the time of Armstrong being in the shop at around*—well, typed in here [Dano interrupted himself] is three P.M., corrected to two P.M. *He states that Armstrong hung around for about an hour before leaving."*

"Now think: Wasn't that correction, *two* P.M., inserted before you signed this paper?"

"I . . . yes, I guess it was at that."

"Didn't you also state in questioning at the time that it could have been anywhere between one and two P.M. that James Armstrong had *arrived* at the shop that day?"

"Well, I was asked to give, you know, a general time, and . . . I *may* have said it was somewhere between one and two."

Peter Hackman, a salesman for J & J, was sworn.

"What time do you recollect," Fink asked him, "James Armstrong being in your shop that day?"

"Between twelve thirty and one thirty P.M."

"Has your memory been tarnished, or have you been confused in any way, by anyone connected with any law-enforcement agency?"

"Objection!"

Conlin: "Overruled."

"Yes," Hackman answered, "by Sergeant Canada of the Ann Arbor police. I feel I was harassed by him and others. I was interviewed time after time at the shop. I finally gave them a taped statement while sitting in the squad car—at which point I would have gone along with just about anything they wanted me to say which seemed even remotely possible."

"All right," Fink resumed. "Now, going back, you said that James Armstrong was in your shop between twelve thirty and one thirty. Did you ever give Sergeant Canada a statement that it could have been between twelve forty-five and one thirty P.M.?"

"I may have, on some occasion. I may even have broadened the end time to two o'clock. After a while, I was getting so confused about what I actually did remember or didn't—"

"One more thing, Mr. Hackman. Do you consider

yourself thoroughly versed in the subject of motorcycles—not just their selling features, but in handling,
riding them, and so on?"

"I think so. I've been driving as well as selling all
kinds of bikes for about four years."

"What would you say the feasibility would be for
someone to start up and take off on a six-fifty Triumph,
driving with just one hand while holding some other
object in the other?"

"I would say very little. I doubt it can be done."

William Delhey had but one question in cross-
examination:

"Let me clarify something, Mr. Hackman. You did
state on the record, in front of witnesses, that it could
have been as late as *two* P.M. that the defendant came
into your shop that day?"

"Yes, but—"

"That's all."

The last "alibi" witness was Ray O'Connell, the J & J
shop mechanic, who affirmed that on July 23 he had
conversed at some length with James Armstrong in the
rear of the shop. O'Connell, who'd been tied down at
his workbench much of that day, could not specify a
time, but it seemed to him that Armstrong must have
been in between twelve noon and two o'clock . . .

Delhey was brief and incisive:

"Mr. O'Connell, so that I fully understand, you are
saying that the first time you *saw* the defendant on that
occasion was sometime between noon and two P.M.?"

"Yes, sir."

"So it could have been as early as twelve *or* as late
as two that he came in?"

"Yes, I suppose so."*

* The defense had planned to call a final alibi witness—the teen-aged
counterman at Roy's Squeeze Inn, where Armstrong claimed to have
been from about 2:00 to 2:30 P.M. on July 23. Defense investigator
Margo Doble, checking on the youth at Belleville High School, found
that he had a record of truancy. Neil Fink at last decided to cancel
him—instinct warning the lawyer that the boy could be unstable and
unreliable as a witness, especially perhaps in hard cross-examination.

On Friday, August 7—the fifteenth day—the defense introduced its first scientific rebuttal witness.

Auseklis Perkons, Ph.D., a Canadian, was a private consultant in the field of forensic science, with specialization in neutron activation analysis. With bachelor's and master's degrees in chemistry, he had gained his doctorate from the University of Toronto in nuclear chemistry (under Professor Robert Jervis) with a thesis on hair individualization study by activation analysis. From 1960 to 1969, Perkons had been employed by the Ontario Center of Forensic Science in Toronto; then for six months he'd gone to the Far East as a United Nations adviser to the government of Ceylon in the field of radiochemistry, with particular emphasis on forensic uses of activation analysis. He had published fifteen papers on hair analysis; lectured widely; and was a fellow of the American Academy of Forensic Sciences, a member of the Canadian Institute of Chemistry and the American Nuclear Society, among other groups.

Dr. Perkons also had been consulted—by the police —in Michigan's only other criminal case involving hair analysis.

Neil Fink began:

"You have examined the reports of Mr. Schlesinger and Dr. Guinn on their analyses of the key hair samples in this case—that is, samples five, six and seven?"

"Yes."

"Now, assuming that all their qualitative and quantitative analyses as to the elements represented are correct, can you state an opinion with reasonable scientific certainty as to whether sample number seven [hair from the panties] came from the same source as numbers five and six [from the basement floor]?"

"It is very hard to base scientifically certain opinion on such a small list of data. It seems to me, in looking at it, that the number of elements indicated in samples five and six are in fairly close agreement, with some exceptions—so these could possibly come from the same source. As opposed to that, sample seven shows significant differences, and I would be inclined to say that number seven has a different origin."

"Different from samples five and six, you mean?"

"Yes."

In cross-examination, Booker Williams questioned Dr. Perkons closely as to the extent and method of his analysis of the prosecution's test reports. Then he asked:

"Did you do any probability calculations on these figures?"

"No."

"But in many cases in your work you do calculate mathematical probabilities?"

"Yes—but never on hair *mixtures*."

"But you *have* calculated and reported mathematical probabilities in professional tests you have run on sample trace elements of *hair?*"

"Yes, but—"

"Nothing further."

In redirect, Fink asked Dr. Perkons to explain why he did not attempt to calculate probabilities in this instance.

"For the simple reason that conditions here *preclude* the use of probabilities, because there is a mixture of hairs of unknown proportion. It is not possible to apply any mathematical method to arrive at an 'average' before it is known precisely what proportion the mixture consists of."

The defense called Dr. Robert Jervis of Toronto. The "expert's expert" in neutron activation analysis, to whom all others seemed bound to refer or defer when discussing that field, was a balding redhead in his forties with a ruddy, genial look and a courteous manner. He held bachelor's degrees with honors in both physics and chemistry and a master's and a doctorate in physical chemistry. For the past twelve years he'd been professor of applied chemistry at the University of Toronto; for six years prior, he had worked in the research chemistry branch of Atomic Energy of Canada, his principal concentration having been radiochemistry. Dr. Jervis had published some sixty-five papers on activation analysis, thirty of them on the subject of hair. He was a much sought lecturer by forensic scientists the world over.

Fink: "Is neutron activation analysis of hair now a scientifically recognized method of making comparisons of hair?"

"I would have to give you a qualified answer. Under ideal circumstances, where a sufficient sample of hair exists; where circumstances lead one to believe that it could be hair from one person, and where a reference or comparison sample from one person can be obtained without too great a lapse of time; and using good procedures to determine as many as possible trace elements in the hair—then one *can* do a comparison and draw some conclusions. But the strength of such conclusions would depend on all these factors."

"Regarding these hair samples we're calling numbers five, six, and seven: Do you have an opinion, within reasonable scientific certainty, as to whether or not sample seven came from the same source as samples five and six?"

"I cannot support the conclusions that number seven came from the same source as numbers five and six. In fact, my own conclusion would have to be, looking at these numbers, that the only opinion justified is that sample number seven did *not* come from the same source as numbers five and six."

"When you render that opinion, sir, is that based on a gross analysis rather than a probability?"

"Yes, because I don't think there is a basis for computing probabilities here. We must have a sufficient number of points for comparison, and five trace elements is *not* a sufficient basis of comparison to try to establish a common source."

Booker Williams asked Dr. Jervis:

"Is it not true, sir, that you have reported in one of your journals a murder case in Canada in which the Royal Canadian Mounted Police used as evidence a hair comparison based on only *two* elements, which *was* admitted as testimony in trial?"

"Yes . . ."

"Thank you."

Fink jumped on this in redirect and had Dr. Jervis explain that *he* had not had any connection with the instance cited. A physicist he'd trained had attempted such a hair comparison because it seemed to link up with other evidence, and the police actually had expected it to be rejected by the court. In any case, Jervis said, he himself had not been consulted about whether it was appropriate or conclusive. Also, that case had taken place in 1958, when neutron activation analysis still was a quite new and uncertain process.

Williams returned with a final question:

"When have you *personally,* doctor, last actively examined trace elements in hair by neutron activation analysis?"

"About nineteen sixty-four . . ."

On Monday morning, August 10, Samuel J. Golub of Massachusetts took the stand. Golub was a director of the Fabric Research Laboratories in Taunton, Massachusetts, where Walter Holz had taken the victim's panties and various hair samples for analysis the past May. For twelve years Golub had headed its section on microscopy and fiber analysis. He had bachelor's and master's degrees in biology from the University of Massachusetts and his doctorate from Harvard. He was regularly called upon to train fiber analysts for the U.S. Federal Trade Commission, the Bureau of Customs, and various American and international companies. He'd done fiber and hair analyses for several law-enforcement agencies in Massachusetts and also had appeared for the defense in cases similar to the present one in New Hampshire and Connecticut.

In questioning by Louisell, Dr. Golub said that although human hair and some textile fibers made from animal hair—for example, wool, alpaca, mohair, cashmere, camel—are constructed in exactly the same way, human hair can be distinguished microscopically if one knows the essential identification characteristics. In fact, he said, with human hair, given an adequate number of fibers and good representative hair, including roots and good lengths and preferably tips as well, certain *groups* can even be distinguished—Oriental and Negroid, say, from Caucasian.

"Take a brown-haired Caucasian," Louisell asked. "Do you feel there are enough characteristics peculiar to this type of hair from which a scientist could conclude that two different samples of such hair came from a common source?"

"I've studied this quite extensively. And in no case of mixed samples—even when given complete fibers with roots and tips, full lengths of hair—have I ever been able to make such a distinction. The simple problem is that brown-haired people with roughly the same range of brownness have a very great variety of brown in their heads—from light to dark brown to almost black—so that the characteristics normally used for identification are so variable within *one* person's head, to try to compare *two* different sources is impossible."

"Do you know of anyone in this field who has ever drawn the conclusion that a given specimen of hair from an unknown source had a common origin with hair from a known source?"

"I know of no reputable fiber analyst who calls himself 'scientist' who has claimed to be able to do this. Indeed, I would say that with brown-haired people, considering the enormous number of them . . . if one has two samples that are not *known* to be from the same source, the odds are astronomically high—perhaps a million to one—that they are *not* from the same source!"

"Is body hair, again in a brown-haired Caucasian, usually distinguishable from head hair?"

"If you have an entire hair, it usually is. However, with short segments, in which all the key characteristics are not present, you often cannot make the distinction."

Louisell then led Dr. Golub into the visit to his laboratory the past May by Walter Holz of the Michigan Department of Public Health, who brought various hair samples and the panties of Carol Ann Gebhardt for comprehensive analysis.

Golub said he was surprised, first of all, that all of Holz's samples were "dry mounts" (hairs mounted simply between two relatively thick glass slides) and had been, according to Holz, examined that way only and not also by oil emulsion (suspended in mineral oil under strong light). Oil-emulsion mounts definitely gave a clearer microscopic view of an entire hair or fiber sample; with a dry mount, light tended to bend around the hair or fiber, obscuring the ends or scale edges.

With this, Louisell asked the court's permission to show several photographic slides illustrating the difference between oil-emulsion and dry mounts—three examples of each type.

The courtroom was darkened, and on a screen set up before them the jury viewed the six 35-mm. slides— of head hairs, magnified one hundred times, taken from three brown-haired employees of Golub's laboratory. As projected, the hairs mounted in an oil emulsion did show up much more distinctly than those dry-mounted.

Booker Williams cross-examined:

"Dr. Golub, it is your contention that dry mounts are inferior because under a microscope a head-on view of, say, a hair will show up fuzzy in some areas even while perfectly clear in others?"

"That's right."

"But cannot the microscope be focused by its operator to sharpen the image, clarify any given segment of the hair that he wants to look at?"

"Well, yes, this is true. . . ."

Following a recess, the defense recalled Dr. Golub.

The most surprising observation he had made—the analyst said in resuming his testimony—among the items that Walter Holz delivered to the research lab was that, in examining Carol Ann Gebhardt's panties under a stereomicroscope, he could detect virtually no trace of textile fibers on the fabric. Nylon stretch material in contact with a floor in a laundry area, such as that part of the Loucks basement where the panties were supposed to have been, almost certainly should have picked up *many* textile fibers—yet all Golub found was one tiny fragment of red rayon, a fraction of a millimeter in length. He said he'd asked Holz whether the panties had been laundered since their recovery, and Holz said he didn't believe so.

How had Holz explained it, then? Holz had said he didn't know.

Regarding the hair samples which Holz had categorized as "cut" or "clipped," Golub said that only a few of these could be verified as having been cut; the rest may or may not have been. In any case, he regarded the angle of cut as insignificant—and no proof that these hairs all had come from the same location—since, first, there were too few samples to compare, and second, the variation of cutting angles even among these was too wide to invite any reasonable conclusion.

"What were the lengths of these hairs?" asked Louisell.

"From one-sixteenth of an inch to three-eighths."

"Doctor, do you have an opinion as to whether any *meaningful* comparison study can be made between hair segments that short and other known quantities of hair, for the purpose of arriving at a conclusion that the two samples had a common source?"

"It's absolutely impossible. Hair varies along its entire length—by diameter, medullation, its scale-edge character and scale spacing, by just about every characteristic of hair—and if you take a segment as small as a quarter of an inch from one portion of a single hair it will be vastly different from another portion of the same hair! This is, I am sure, the opinion of all fiber analysts."

Golub went on to tell of one envelope brought him by Holz that contained hairs represented as having been removed from a box in which the Loucks family kept their hair clippers. These hairs, medium brown in color, ranged in length from an eighth of an inch to one inch—and he noted that none of the mounted samples of hair purported to be from the victim's panties were as long as the longer of these hairs from the clipper box.

He'd examined three other envelopes or packets also brought to him by Holz. One contained about a hundred hair segments said to have been taken from the basement floor and cleaned of "debris"; these hairs ranged in length from three-sixteenths to ten-sixteenths of an inch, their average color medium brown. A second packet contained several hundred similar hair segments as well as debris—traces of paint, wood, coarse plant fibers, and a great many textile fibers— also described as from the floor of the Loucks laundry area. (*Why, then, was there no such debris on the victim's panties?*) The third packet contained longer hair segments said to have been separated from the second packet—some ten hairs, a half-inch to four inches long, several with roots and tips present; under the microscope, Golub observed one of these to be damaged, its end crushed as though it had been stepped on, and several others with "gulches" (mechanical breaks) in them—again unlike the hairs from the panties, none of which were crushed or fractured in any way!

"What did you do next, doctor?" prompted Louisell.

"I decided I would like to examine hair shorn from women's thighs by electric shaver. I asked two of my female assistants, both Caucasians with brown hair, if they would be good enough to do this and bring me samples of their shavings."

"You then compared the characteristics of the hair particles thus obtained with the hair identified as being from the girl's panties?"

"I did."

Louisell was stretching it out, heightening the drama. "And what did you find?"

"These samples—which I photographed after examining—I found to be of the same general character and indistinguishable from the hair taken from either the panties *or* the basement floor. The simple reason being, as I've said, that no one can make such a distinction."

Louisell asked the court's leave to show another photographic slide. This was a mount displaying the hairs and debris (Holz's packet number two) collected from the basement floor. "What does this show us, doctor?" asked Louisell.

"It shows the ratio of textile fibers alone to hair is about ten to one. And it reinforces my opinion that any nylon panties in contact with such a floor area, especially under any sort of pressure, *should* have picked up a large number of these textile fibers along with hairs. Yet, as I've stated, all I found on the girl's panties when Dr. Holz brought them to me was *one* minute red fiber."

Tuesday morning, August 11, with Dr. Golub back in the witness box, Louisell led off with a further demonstration of 35-mm. slides—magnified laboratory mounts of hair and debris collected from the basement floor of the Loucks house only the past June 10.

At that time, Neil Fink had finally secured permission to inspect those obviously key premises—Sergeant Loucks, the defense had repeatedly complained, having until then refused them entry. With an aide, and escorted dourly by State Police Captain (formerly Lieutenant) Hap Morrison, Fink first pressed two strips of transparent tape onto the basement floor, one at a point eight to ten inches in front of the clothes dryer, the second ten inches farther away. Each of the two-to-three-foot lengths of tape then was lifted, packaged, and marked under Captain Morrison's watchful eye. Next, a new pair of women's white nylon-knit stretch panties were removed from an unopened plastic envelope and rubbed on the floor at various spots; these also were marked and placed in a jar. The package and jar were sealed and initialed by Fink's associate in Morrison's presence, locked in a briefcase, and flown to Massachusetts the next day for delivery to Dr. Golub.

Louisell had taken pains to have this process explained, so as to underscore the dramatic simplicity of the testimony to follow. Dr. Golub said he'd found on the recent strips of tape samples of the same type of debris as found on that floor a year earlier; and on the new panties—Louisell had him stress this—in addition to a few small hairs he'd found considerable fiber litter, as might be expected in a laundry area.

The point was well made: Once again, why had not the *victim's* panties shown comparable quantities of such debris if indeed she had lain on that floor?

Finally, Louisell closed in:

"Doctor, from all your studies, then, do you have an opinion, based on reasonable scientific certainty, as to whether or not the short hair segments found on the deceased's panties, brought to you by Mr. Holz, had a common origin with hair from the basement floor?"

"My opinion is that they did not."

"Would you state for us your reasons for that opinion?"

"First, the hairs on the panties were all, with only a couple of exceptions, one-quarter of an inch or less in length. This represents hair growth of about one week. If in fact this was indicative of the hair 'population' on that basement floor, it would mean that the residents of that home, four or more, had to have their hair cut *at least every week*. Further, it would mean that the operator of the hair clipper had to be so precise, with so steady a hand, that never was the angle of the clipper turned in such a way that hair longer than one-quarter of an inch was cut! This seems highly improbable to me.

"Secondly, we know that hairs longer than a quarter inch were also found on that floor—hairs one inch, an inch and a half, up to four inches long—and there is no reason why *they* shouldn't have attached themselves to the panties also. It is totally improbable.

"Lastly, it is inconceivable to me that a fabric of that

sort could have been pressed against *that* floor without picking up *some* textile fibers—a floor, as we've shown, on which textile fibers outnumber hairs by at least ten to one."

"If the panties," Louisell asked, "had contained such hairs before being laundered, would you expect that they might be laundered out?"

"Many would; some would remain. Of course, hair segments in wash water can be redeposited on that sort of fabric."

Louisell set himself up for the haymaker:

"If panties were to be laundered by hand in a wash-basin in a girls' dormitory—where some brown-haired girl had clipped her bangs, say—would it be possible in your opinion for the panties to pick up—"

"Objection!" snapped Booker Williams.

"Sustained."

"In your judgment, doctor," Louisell tried again, "could that many hairs—over five hundred—be explained by the presence of a young woman sitting in a wig shop having her hair cut?"

"I can only speculate—"

"Objection," interrupted Williams again. "We're not looking for any speculation here."

"Sustained."

"Your witness," said Louisell benevolently.

Williams cross-examined Dr. Golub through the afternoon. The assistant prosecutor's questions were rapier sharp. He induced Golub to concede that, for all his strong feelings that it was impossible to draw any definitive conclusions about the hair, he was not able to say with certainty that the hairs on the victim's panties were *not* the same as hairs on the Louckses' basement floor.

He got Golub to acknowledge that the reason why all the evidentiary hair samples delivered to him by Walter Holz were dry-mounted was that *only* dry slides could have been subjected to neutron activation analysis, which could not be used on "wet" or oil-emulsion mounts.

And, reshowing Golub's photographic slides of the panties, Williams got the analyst to agree that when the projector's focus was adjusted, moved this way and that, there *were* more man-made fibers evident on the panties than Golub had stated—a number of blue fibers in addition to the red one he'd said was all he'd seen. . . .

Despite his last acknowledgments in cross-examination, Samuel Golub had been a most impressive witness for the defense—perhaps even devastating. His testimony seemed to have, if not shattered, at least left severely damaged one of the prosecution's major supports. The prosecution would have to go all out to produce a convincing rebuttal.

CHAPTER 27

WHEN COURT RESUMED on August 12, Conlin asked: "Does the prosecution have any rebuttal?"

Booker Williams recalled Department of Health criminologist Walter Holz.

Anyone who knew Williams well might have perceived in him a certain intensity perhaps not so evident earlier. The always polished assistant prosecutor, impeccable in a fine-tailored vested blue suit, now gave off the barest impression of a cat stalking—as though he sensed prey and was gauging his opportunity to spring.

Williams referred Holz to People's Exhibit No. 42 —the dead girl's panties. "Is Exhibit forty-two one of the articles you took to Dr. Samuel Golub for examination?"

"Yes, sir."

"And Dr. Golub did examine it while you were there?"

"Yes."

"And he reported finding just *one* textile fiber on these panties, a small fragment of red rayon?"

"That's what he claimed."

"Now, Mr. Holz, do you know if there were actually *more* fibers contained in that exhibit?"

"Yes, there certainly were."

"Did you subsequently prepare an exhibit containing what *you* found on Exhibit number forty-two?"

"Yes, I did. I believe it is numbered Exhibit sixty-three."

"This [showing him a slide mount]?"

"Yes, sir."

"Tell us when and how you prepared Exhibit number sixty-three."

"It was after my visit to Dr. Golub this past spring —on July twenty-fifth. It was prepared from the *entire* panties, under a stereoscopic microscope employing magnification up to and including seventy-five diameters. First I examined one surface of the panties, then the other surface, completely. The debris I found was removed and dry-mounted."

"All right, then what did you do?"

"I made a number of photographic slides, thirty-five millimeter, of this mount, and also a couple of others showing additional debris taken from the panties, and finally one of an oil-emulsion mount, which comprised only hair from the panties—twenty slides in all."

Williams then, methodically, with the savor of a craftsman fashioning a matchless syllogism, had Holz identify, one by one, each of the twenty photographic slides.

Joseph Louisell stood and asked the court if he could put a procedural question to the witness. Judge Conlin said he could if Mr. Williams had no objection. Williams bowed to his adversary.

"Mr. Holz," the defense attorney asked, "were these slides available to you at the time you testified here a week or two ago?"

"Yes, sir."

"I see. . . ." Louisell sat down slowly, a look of consternation on his face. He huddled with Fink, who also appeared upset.

"I now move, Your Honor," Williams resumed, "to admit these twenty slides into evidence—as People's Exhibits eighty-one through one hundred."

"Any objection, Mr. Louisell?" inquired Conlin.

Louisell, frowning, only shrugged. "I see I overlooked something," he murmured aloud.

The exhibits were tagged and admitted, then Williams requested the courtroom be darkened. There was a rustle of anticipation. Williams waited until it was still:

"Those photographs are magnified how many times, Mr. Holz?"

"Twenty to one hundred times."

It was a stunning demonstration. Slide after slide showed accumulations of "debris," particularly of man-made fibrous materials not previously evident, which Holz had removed from the victim's panties. With each slide, Williams asked Holz to identify the various materials. All would have been expected to be found—indeed, had been soundly established by the defense as what *should* have been found but were curiously "missing" from the panties—on the floor of a typical home-laundry area.

The last slide, of the oil-emulsion mount of hairs taken from the panties, provided an exclamation point. Holz pointed out "wedges"—notches—part way into the magnified hair samples:

"It has been my testimony," he said, "that this is typical of clipper-cut hair—the clipper approaching hair segments from only one side, unlike scissors, and not quite cutting them off."

"Thank you," Williams said. "Lights, please. The defense may cross-examine."

Louisell drew himself up wearily.

"Surely you recall Dr. Golub's astonishment at having found scarcely *any* textile fibers on the panties.

Could it be that as a result you then became concerned about this relative absence and—?"

"Yes. As a scientist, his concern was my concern."

"When were these photographs taken?"

"The evening of July twenty-sixth and the early morning hours of July twenty-seventh."

"Your photographs of Exhibit number sixty-three —are any repetitive?"

"There are no duplicates, if that's what you mean."

"All originals. . . . Mr. Holz, how did you happen in the first place to wait until July of nineteen seventy to prepare slide mounts undertaking to show the presence of textile fibers on the original panties?"

"I waited specifically to make sure the panties were clean of all other material—that is, hairs—before making a final count. I realized this would be my final opportunity to remove any debris from them."

Louisell hesitated . . . seemed about to ask another question . . . then, with a small, helpless gesture, turned and moved back to the defense table and sat heavily.

Booker Williams rose and said crisply: "The People rest."

There was a stillness through the packed courtroom, a common suspension of breathing for just a moment, as if in a shared intuition of climactic resolution. With the testimony of Walter Holz, the prosecution had, many in the courtroom felt, pulled off what had seemed only remotely possible—a compelling rebuttal of the defense argument that Carol Ann Gebhardt might never have been in the basement of James Armstrong's uncle's home.

Now one question played across everyone's mind: Had the defense any final, saving trump?

Would James Armstrong himself at last be called to testify for himself?

The prosecution had prayed that he would; Delhey and Williams ached for a one-on-one crack at this defendant. If Armstrong dared get up there as his own character witness, they would show the jury what was really behind that choir-boy mask of his—another Dorian Gray!

They wouldn't be able, of course, to dig into any of the other murders. They might, if the cards fell right, bring out his shocking record of thievery—this all-American "boy," as Louisell characterized him so paternally. But they certainly should be able to get on record a few other trenchant items about his real "character":

The E.M.U. coed who swore that he'd lured her up to his room and tried to force himself on her, until she'd broken loose and fled. And the countless others shuttled to Emmet Street, as his neighboring roomer, Donald Baker, could be recalled to affirm. And the several young women who'd given the police detailed statements about his erratic sexual hangups and philosophies.

They could even produce a girl who'd told of Armstrong's having brought her to the Loucks house and made advances to her only the weekend before Carol Ann Gebhardt was murdered there.

And the photograph that he'd posed for in that male "nudie" magazine—*that* was already a collector's item in the community, having come out just at the time of Armstrong's arrest. It was in the September 1969 issue of *Tomorrow's Man,* a pocket-sized monthly picturing page after page of muscular young men posing in only breech cloths or bikini briefs. On page 34 was a full-length shot of a handsome, powerful-looking youth in a white brief, with the caption: *Bill Kenyon displays a fine arm in this pose. Here is a teen-age bodybuilder who is a future great.* "Bill Kenyon" . . . unmistakably James Armstrong.

They could do quite a job on this defendant, *if* he testified.

Even to this late hour, however, the defense had remained sorely undecided about having James take the stand. They knew, naturally, much of what the prosecution had on the accused's other illicit and questionable activities. And Joe Louisell felt strongly that their risk

THE MICHIGAN MURDERS 401

was too great of unlocking the door to that forbidden
territory. At the slightest crack, their opponents could
rush in and overwhelm them.

But Neil Fink was inclined to chance it. Determined,
as he'd put it, to go for broke in this case—he'd
already bluntly informed Judge Conlin that the defense considered only two verdicts possible: murder-
one, as charged, or acquittal!—Fink sensed that if
James did *not* finally rise and straightforwardly pro-
claim his innocence, if he *remained* silent, the jury
must wonder why . . . must consider an implication of
dark secrets, even a shadow of guilt.

Fink was aware of a significant body of opinion
among people in the community, especially among
the younger, that the wrong man was accused here
—either that James was being framed, or simply that
he was innocent. Some felt he must be taking the rap
—stoutly in one view, foolishly in another—for another, or others. Many who knew him honestly could
not believe that *he* could be a murderer, and they
would not believe the despicable things the prosecution was bound to say of him. Others, who did not
know him personally, found it difficult to accept that
this nice-looking boy from a decent background could
really have done such terrible things; there had to be
something wrong. . . .

That's what Fink was tempted to play on even with
the jury: that James's naturally clean, decent appearance, his polite, soft-spoken manner—even his slight
boyish lisp!—could influence them sympathetically.
There *were* character witnesses who would testify for
him as well—and not just similarly bright-faced local
youngsters, who would say they knew James only to
be carefree, fun-loving, unmalicious, but admiring
adults, respectable citizens who would enumerate the
young man's qualities of loving, unselfish goodness
(his own Aunt Fran, one of his accusers, could testify
for him about that—his gentleness with children, for
example!).

Several young married women in the Ypsilanti area

had come forward to tell how James had, at the peak
of the murder scare, firmly insisted on staying with
them, or escorting them shopping or home, on nights
when their husbands were unavailable. His favorite
teacher in high school, a nun who had written regularly
since his arrest with assurances of her faith in him; his
high-school football coach, who had publicly called
James a "fine youngster" . . .

As for the admitted risk of exposing James to incriminating cross-examination, if the questioning could
be controlled, restricted, to matters *only* connected
with *this* case, they just might get away with it. But
that was a big *if,* to be decided only by Judge Conlin.
Therefore, on Tuesday, the eleventh, Fink and Louisell,
Delhey and Williams had met with Conlin to explore
this crucial area.

Fink had begun by proposing that, if and when
the defendant were to be called, any questions that
would disclose or even suggest *other* crimes should be
inadmissible. Delhey's retort was that any cross-
examination that might bring out other offenses would
be proper so long as they were shown to be somehow
tied to this case.

Judge Conlin had pondered and then said:

"Any reference to a defendant's prior arrests or con-
victions of course *may* be asked for impeachment purposes. Also, any other crime brought out either in
evidence or by examination of Mr. Armstrong, showing a relation to his *blue* motorcycle, would be permitted. But any inference of crime pertaining to how
he *obtained* that or any of his motorcycles would *not*
be admissible—which, again, is not to preclude questions regarding his *use* of the motorcycles, only how
he obtained them. Obviously, there also can be no
reference to any other murders hereabouts.

"Are you going to put him on next?" Conlin asked,
looking from Louisell to Fink.

There was a pause, then Fink replied: "Well, Your
Honor, perhaps we really should give it some more
thought—until tomorrow, anyway."

Late Tuesday afternoon, after adjournment, Fink had decided to meet the problem head on. He and Margo Doble went to the jail to thrash it out with James. (At first, the guards would not let them in— Sheriff Harvey's orders! Angered, Fink telephoned Judge Conlin, who immediately called Harvey and ordered the two admitted to visit the prisoner.) James was brought to them in a tiny windowless room with cement walls and scarred linoleum on the floor; heavy mesh screening that cut the cubicle in half made it seem even smaller.

They talked to James through the partition. "Do you want to go on the stand?" asked Fink.

"Sure," James said easily. His eyes ran over Margo, and she blushed. She'd noticed him a number of times in court stealing long appreciative glances at her legs, which miniskirts showed off to good advantage. "Why?" James asked, returning attention to his lawyer. "Don't you want me to?"

"I'm not sure. There are still some things I've got to find out."

"I've told you everything, Neil."

"I don't mean that. I mean—well, like how you'd take cross-examination. It could be rough."

"I'm tough." James winked.

"We'll see. . . ."

Fink started asking questions that the prosecution could put to him, slipping in innuendo, inferential accusations, challenging denunciations, such as a Delhey or a Williams might. And he *got* rough—rougher even than his adversaries were apt to—boring in on the young man, pricking, riddling him for a full hour.

At first James responded evenly, earnestly, as he'd been coached. But Fink's intense, relentless pressure began to unsettle him. He was a thief. A cheat. A sadist. ("Aw, come on, Neil. Don't say things like that, even pretending!") He was a pervert, homosexual, *bi*sexual! ("Now stop it, Neil!") He'd tried to rape other girls. ("Shut up, damn you!") He was capable of trying to "make it" with his own aunt! He'd almost

killed his sister once because she was a tramp, a pig!
His *mother* was a kept woman, a *whore!*

James clawed at the screening—"You lousy sonofabitch! I'll break your mouth!"—his voice a hateful
squeal. Tears of rage and frustration streamed down
his cheeks.

Neil Fink sat back with a sigh and glanced sorrow-
fully at Margo, who sat rigid beside him, appalled.
"James, I'm sorry," he said finally. "I just had to see.
You had to see. That's the way it could be up there."
Fink shook his head. "I don't know, now."

At dinner that evening with Louisell, they had gone
over and over all the arguments, pro and con, about
calling James to testify the next morning. Louisell was
more than ever convinced that it could be a disastrous
mistake. But Fink, to whom the elder attorney had
deferred most of the decision making in this case,
continued to wrestle with it, almost like a desperate
gambler down to his last stake who still could not let
go of losing dice.

By Wednesday morning, Fink had come to one decision—that *he* would not decide alone. In judge's
chambers before trial resumed, he had outlined his
dilemma and asked if Conlin would permit James to
talk with his mother about it privately. She, clearly,
had a dominant influence on him. If she were to
come out and say, "Put my son on," then they would.

In the interest of assuring the defense fair opportunity to play out every possible card, Judge Conlin
had agreed to the unusual proposal. James and Louella Armstrong were brought together in Conlin's chambers—an emotional meeting for both; mother and son
touching, embracing for the first time in over a year
—and they were left alone.

They had been in there close to a half hour. When
the door opened, Louella Armstrong came out weeping openly. Her eyes were puffy, her makeup streaked
with running mascara. She wore the stunned look of a
woman who had been totally unprepared for a shocking, irreconcilable truth. Fink watched as she groped

her way out into the corridor and realized that she must never have even suspected that her son might really have done evil things.

James had emerged slowly then, forlorn, eyes also red and wet, his features drawn in pain. One look at him told Fink what he had to know. . . .

Now Judge Conlin looked to the defense table: "Do you wish to present any further witnesses . . . Mr. Louisell? . . . Mr. Fink?"

Louisell stirred. He cleared his throat. "No, Your Honor," he said tonelessly.

"Both sides rest, then?"

"Yes. . . ."

CHAPTER 28

OPPOSING COUNSEL GAVE their final arguments on Thursday, August 13, the nineteenth day of trial.

Prosecutor William Delhey took a little over an hour to tick off, with cold, matter-of-fact precision, the facts the state had laid one atop another against the defendant. "Common sense," he concluded, could dictate only a verdict of guilty.

Neil Fink was next. He was contemptuous of the state's "so-called facts." Most of them, he insisted, had *not* been proved but remained fuzzy allegations, growing largely out of the demands of mass hysteria for *somebody* to pay for unsolvable crimes. Common sense, indeed, had to recognize considerable doubt in this case. And doubt demanded acquittal.

Joseph Louisell, summoning all his compelling presence, waxed passionately eloquent for almost an hour and three-quarters. Striding back and forth, voice booming . . . gripping the rail of the jury box, addressing the jurors softly, intimately, every so often pausing dramatically to mop his glistening face with a huge handkerchief . . . hunching over the lawyer's podium, tapping his forefinger to emphasize points . . . solemnly reminding the jury of its awesome responsibility of deciding, on grounds that were questionable at best, the future of this young victim of circumstances before them.

He labored hard on the "crucial" issue: The prosecution's contention hinged essentially on the testimony of Mr. Holz that it was possible to determine through microscopic examination that hairs found on the girl's panties were the same as hairs found on that basement floor. Holz had admitted, Louisell recalled, that such testimony stated as fact was the first of its kind in any murder trial. "We travel with Mr. Holz in this case through waters never charted before!" Louisell proclaimed.

Louisell was especially scornful of the testimony of the wig shop women: All they could really claim, he said, was that "they saw Miss Gebhardt with James—" He flushed and corrected himself: "—with a man on a motorcycle."

Booker Williams spoke last. He was brief and sardonic:

"I don't know whether esteemed counsel's slip a moment ago was Freudian or not—but it was one of the few times in this trial that I have agreed with him."

Judge Conlin was late getting started Friday morning. As he left his chambers for the courtroom, to instruct the waiting jury, Neil Fink met him just outside the courtroom door. "Judge," the young lawyer said anxiously, "we'd like to make an unusual request. I know it's late . . . but can you charge the jury as to *four* possible verdicts?" (Earlier, Fink had rejected second-degree murder and manslaughter.)

Conlin eyed him. "It *is* late, Mr. Fink. I'm afraid the facts of this case, as they've been presented, no longer allow us any leeway for lesser offenses. I will have to charge the jury as you've wanted all along. . . ."

Conlin spoke to the jury without interruption for an hour and a half, summarizing both prosecution and defense cases and clarifying certain fine points of law involved. "Now, ladies and gentlemen," Conlin said gently but firmly, "in this case there can be only *two* verdicts that you can render: Guilty of murder in the first degree, as charged, or Not Guilty. . . ."

An hour later, Judge Conlin, prosecutors Delhey and Williams and defense attorneys Louisell and Fink sat together around a large luncheon table at the City Club, a smart gathering place for many of Ann Arbor's professional people. Unwinding over cocktails, they traded polite compliments on the conduct of the trial and guesses as to how long the jury might be out.

Speculation among the lawyers ran from hours to days. Judge Conlin, however, raised the gloomy prospect of a hung jury—which would mean mistrial and the necessity of going through it all again. If that should occur, it might also mean that the defense would then get the change of venue it had sought.

Joseph Louisell, mellowing on his third martini, shook his head. "I think we'll get a Guilty verdict. I won't hazard a guess as to how long it will take them, but . . ."

With a resigned smile, he clapped a paw on his young associate's shoulder. "You sweat it out, Neil. I'm going home to Grosse Pointe and put my feet up. I *don't* think there'll be any need for me to return."

As Fink and the others stared at him, Louisell set upon his lunch with gusto. When finished, he rose, bade them all a hearty good-by, and left.

The Armstrong jury was out all weekend (not sitting on Sunday), and all day Monday the seventeenth, and Tuesday. . . .

Twice on Tuesday, Judge Conlin summoned the panel from their deliberation room into Courtroom No. 2 and asked if they could foresee "reasonable probability of early agreement." Each time, the foreman explained uncomfortably that they had not yet reached unanimity, but he was sure there was every prospect. . . .

Throughout that afternoon and into the evening, rumors of how the jury was voting fled the courthouse corridors, as always, and out to the taverns and restaurants nearby where news reporters and attorneys and policemen waited fretfully. The most "authoritative" word—which usually meant a leak from some less-than-uncompromising marshal or court functionary who'd been slipped a few bills by some less-than-scrupulous newsman—had it that the jury's first vote on Saturday had gone 9–3 for conviction . . . on Monday, 10–2 . . . and on this, the fourth day, there was thought to be just one holdout.

But after dinner Tuesday evening, the jury retired, still undecided. That night a cloudburst thundered over Ann Arbor—to some, a grim reminder of the heavy rains that had preceded so many of the area murders the past several years. During the storm, talk spread of heated, increasingly bitter disagreement among the jurors.

The jury was back in the deliberation room at 8:30 A.M. on Wednesday, the nineteenth. Within minutes, the bailiff was summoned inside. In another minute, he emerged and hurried to Judge Conlin's chambers. "They have a verdict, Your Honor," the bailiff said.

"Advise counsel and have the defendant brought over from the jail," said Conlin.

A few minutes past 9:30, James Armstrong entered the courtroom, still with that sure, athletic stride. He wore a neat blue sports ensemble—pale jacket, navy slacks, blue shirt, rep tie. But his face was stony, immobile, as he took his place next to Neil Fink, alone now at the defense table.

His mother was there, rigid, scarcely breathing, in her front-row place, flanked by her daughter and the young woman, Jeannie, with whom James had developed so affectionate a relationship, and a young priest from St. Thomas Church. Two rows behind were Sergeant Dana Loucks and his wife, Fran. James's aunt had her hands clasped on a rosary. Near them, eyes intent on the young defendant, sat Pamela Gebhardt, eldest sister of the slain girl.

At 9:34, the jury filed in. When they were seated, the clerk called the roll. Then: "Members of the jury, have you agreed upon a verdict? Who speaks for the jury?"

Foreman William Billmeier rose: "I speak for the jury." His voice was scratchy and a little tremulous. "We have reached a verdict."

"Read it," the judge directed.

"We find the guilty—" He coughed, blushing. "Excuse me. We find the defendant guilty as charged of murder in the first degree."

There was a sharp gasp throughout the courtroom. James's sister, Dawn, moaned and, her features contorted, began to cry. Her mother did not move a muscle; only her face, which had gone ashen, betrayed any pain. There had not been a flicker across her son's face.

Conlin turned to the defense table. "Do you wish the jury polled, Mr. Fink?"

"If you will."

The clerk polled each juror, asking: "Was that and is that your verdict?"

Each replied: "Yes, that is my verdict." Several answered with heads bowed, eyes cast down. A couple of the women may have been weeping.

"Members of the jury," spoke Judge Conlin, "I thank you for your diligence, sincerity and obvious interest. You are now excused." The panel broke and milled out into their private corridor behind the courtroom, plainly relieved that the ordeal was over . . . anxious only to avoid the reporters and cameras sure now to pursue them.

Conlin then said: "The defendant will be remanded to the custody of the sheriff prior to sentencing. I will set sentencing for Friday, August twenty-eighth at eight-thirty in the morning." The judge rapped his gavel with a note of finality. "Court dismissed."

As the courtroom began slowly to clear, Louella Armstrong pounced forward and, with a piercing wail, threw herself on James, still motionless at the defense table. (Fink glanced imploringly at the bench, and Judge Conlin nodded his approval to the marshals converging on the woman.) Crying loudly, she clutched her son, hugging him, pulling his head to her bosom, patting him, caressing him . . . a pitiful tableau echoing centuries of tragedy and sorrow.

James did not embrace his mother. He looked up once, his face as lifeless as a statue's, and caught sight of his Aunt Fran, standing frozen at her seat, on the verge of tears herself. Only then did the deep blue eyes appear to cloud over, and his wide taut mouth quivered. Fran thought he was trying to say, *It's all right* . . . She had to turn away and grope for her husband's arm.

After a few minutes, James and his mother were gently disengaged by the marshals and he was led away to the prisoners' lockup. Louella watched him go . . . then, disheveled, still sobbing, she stumbled from the courtroom. She paused near the doorway at sight of Fran and Dana. They could not read the expression on her ghastly smeared face, but her staring eyes were on fire. Then, after a long moment, she passed them without a word.

Dana Loucks led his wife through clamoring reporters to Prosecutor Delhey's offices. There, in a small unoccupied room, Fran wept.

Booker Williams slipped away from the official celebration early. He found State Police Sergeant Earl James, the gentle, bookish student of criminology who had worked with him on the murder investigations as long and hard as anyone. "Earl," Williams said, "would you mind driving me somewhere?"

He had James drop him first at a florist, where he

picked up a bouquet of assorted roses. Then James drove him east, beyond Ypsilanti, to the small cemetery where his wife had been buried a little over two months before.

James stood apart as the slim, dapper assistant prosecutor, all at once looking very much older, placed the flowers at the headstone, then knelt quietly for several minutes. When he arose and approached the policeman, Williams' face was wet with private tears of his own.

He had promised his wife to resign the prosecutor's office and return to private practice when this case was over. Now he would . . . but with her gone, the promise, the future, somehow was empty.

Courtroom No. 2 was almost empty on Friday morning, August 28, as Judge John Conlin passed sentence on James Armstrong: "There is only one sentence I can pronounce on this kind of offense: That sentence is that you shall be punished by confinement and hard labor in the Southern Michigan State Prison at Jackson, for life."

Normally following sentencing, it should have been a week or so—what with winding up official paperwork and other red tape—before the convicted prisoner was shipped off to the prison where he was to serve his term. The paperwork on James Armstrong, however, had all been completed or dispensed with before he was sentenced. That very afternoon, he was on his way to Jackson under heavy guard.

Sheriff Harvey was taking no chances—there had been at least a dozen threats received that Armstrong would not get to prison alive. Armstrong was locked alone in the rear of a screen-meshed station wagon, a deputy with a 12-gauge shotgun watching him from the front passenger seat. Two detectives, armed with AR-15 automatic rifles, followed in an unmarked car. Ignoring traffic lights, the two vehicles sped from the jail onto the I-94 freeway, then barreled west at eighty miles an hour. They had their prisoner safely inside the state prison, almost forty miles away, in less than an hour.

There James Nolan Armstrong was given a new identity—No. 126833.

EPILOGUE

ALTHOUGH PROSECUTOR WILLIAM Delhey declared, following his conviction, that James Nolan Armstrong was also considered a prime suspect in the six other Washtenaw County murders, no charges of these other crimes were ever brought against him. Nor are any ever likely to be.

There having been no new evidence in any of the other murders the violent deaths of Marilyn Pindar, Jill Hersch, Jeanne Holder, Mary Grace Clemson, Dale Harum, and Audrey Sakol remain, officially, unsolved.

In the fall of 1970, California Governor Ronald Reagan filed for Armstrong's extradition to stand trial for homicide there as well. Michigan Governor William Milliken, in whose sole power it was to sanction such a request, decided in 1971, after a protracted exchange of formal messages between the states, not to implement it.

The indictment against Armstrong in Monterey County, therefore was "shelved" due to the obvious unavailability of the accused. (The Monterey district attorney's office, nonetheless, continued unofficially to claim that, should Armstrong somehow gain release in Michigan—by reversal through appeal, say—the California indictment could be reissued.)

The efforts of James Armstrong (still represented by Neil Fink*) to appeal his conviction have been unsuccessful:

In 1972, the Michigan Court of Appeals ruled that his trial had been conducted properly and affirmed the verdict.

In 1974, the Michigan Supreme Court denied application to appeal the appellate decision. Petition was then submitted to the U.S. Supreme Court for a writ of *certiorari* to review the Michigan Supreme Court order. It was rejected.

Early in 1975, the U.S. District Court in Detroit was petitioned, solely now on the change-of-venue issue, for a writ of *habeas corpus* (meaning, precisely, that a person restrained of liberty be delivered bodily before the court so that the lawfulness of his restraint may be investigated and truly determined). This, too, was denied.

Appeal of that decision was brought to the U.S. Court of Appeals in Cincinnati, where it was rebuffed. Finally, the U.S. Supreme Court was importuned once more on the habeas corpus issue. Late in 1976, the court declined to hear that plea.

Thus, in the end, it appeared that James Armstrong's only practical hope of release rested on the possibility —which would seem remote, at best—of eventual commutation of his sentence by order of the governor. By Michigan custom, the earliest that could happen would be in 1990.

Meanwhile, from the Jackson State Prison, Arm-

---

* Fink and Joseph Louisell parted company soon after the Armstrong trial, Fink moving on to become a senior partner in another Detroit law firm. Louisell died of a heart attack two years later at age fifty-seven, while campaigning for a Wayne County judgeship. Judge John Conlin, sixty-eight, died two months after Louisell.

strong at last has spoken out in his own defense. In his seven years there he has granted several interviews to news media . . . insisting ever more stoutly, and bitterly, that he is innocent of any of the coed murders.

Non-Fiction
Bestsellers
From
POCKET BOOKS